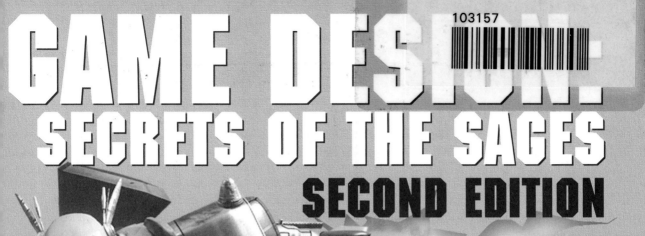

GAME DESIGN:
SECRETS OF THE SAGES
SECOND EDITION

verts[q->vertex_ref[j]].v[u] - new_point[u]:
verts[q->vertex_ref[j]].v[v] - new_point[v]:

crossing point is positive ((slope

EDITED BY MARC SALTZMAN

///||BRADYGAMES
TAKE YOUR GAME FURTHER™

GAME DESIGN: SECRETS OF THE SAGES, SECOND EDITION

LEGAL STUFF

Brady Publishing
An Imprint of
Macmillan Publishing USA
201 W. 103rd St.
Indianapolis, IN 46290

ISBN: 1-56686-987-0

Printing code: The rightmost double-digit number is the year of the book's printing; the rightmost single-digit number is the number of the book's printing. For example, 00-1 shows that the first printing of the book occurred in 2000.

03 02 01 00   4 3 2 1

BRADYGAMES STAFF

Editor-In-Chief
H. Leigh Davis

Title/Licensing Manager
David Waybright

Creative Director
Robin Lasek

Marketing Manager
Janet Eshenour

CREDITS

Production Editor
Robin Drake

Book Designer
Kurt Owens

Cover Designer
Tim Amrhein

Production Designer
Trina Wurst

Indexer
Johanna Van Hoose Dinse

OVERVIEW

DEDICATION

This book is dedicated to Kellie Sherman for her endless love and support.

ACKNOWLEDGMENTS

A very special thank you goes out to all of the members of the electronic gaming industry who have taken the time and effort to contribute to this book.

Thanks to Steve Schafer for his affability and professionalism in creating the first edition of this book, and for believing that people who play games might also want to know how to create them. Thanks to Leigh Davis for her cunning expertise and advice, and for helping orchestrate this second edition. Thanks to Robin Drake for her proficient editing and encouraging words. Finally, thanks to the production staff for their hard work on this book. We literally could not have done it without them! Particular thanks go to Kurt Owens for the spiffy new design and to Trina Wurst for her quick and efficient layout work. Thanks to all!

ABOUT THE AUTHORS

MARC SALTZMAN, COMPILATION EDITOR

Marc Saltzman is a freelance journalist for over 50 game-related and consumer publications, including *USA Today*, *Entertainment Weekly*, Entertainment Tonight Online, *Modern Maturity*, *Playboy* magazine, Playboy.com, *Yahoo! Internet Life*, Next Generation, *PC Gamer*, *PC Accelerator*, *Gamecenter*, Gamesmania.com, *Golf Digest*, *Stuff magazine*, and many more. He has also written three books and one CD-ROM for Macmillan Publishing and two in-game manuals: *Quake II* and *Sin*.

CONTRIBUTORS

The following game and level designers, programmers, musicians, producers, sound engineers—and many other titles and job functions could be added here—provided the core of this book: their insights into and experiences with the fascinating world of game design. (For biographical information on many of the contributors, see the Appendix at the end of this book.)

Peter Akemann	Sinjin Bain	Mark Bernal
Kurt Arnlund	Andrew Barnabas	Eric Biessman
Marc Aubanel	Bob Bates	Cliff Bleszinski
Ted Backman	Tom Bazzano	Dan Bray
Kelly Bailey	Liz Bell	George Broussard

Michael Büttner
David Cage
Tim Cain
Melanie Cambron
Carol Caracciolo
Louis Castle
Trevor Chan
Hubert Chardot
Jim Charne
Jason Chu
Kevin Cloud
Steven Coallier
Bryce Cochrane
Vance Cook
Nick Corea
Brad Crow
Matthew D'Andria
Stuart Denman
Mark Dickenson
Barry Dorf
Scott Easley
Sacha Fernandes
Toby Gard
Alex Garden
Richard "Lord British" Garriott
Ron Gilbert
Rick Goodman
Harry Gottlieb
Charles Gough
Rodney Greenblat
Mario Grimani
Orlando Guzman
Tom Hall
Evan Hirsch
Peter Hirschmann
Rodney Hodge
Bryan Horling
Sean House
Matt Householder
Jason Hughes
Paul Jaquays
Jane Jensen
Todd Johnson
Matthew Lee Johnston
Adam Kahn
Michael Kelly
Geoff Kirk
Dave "Zoid" Kirsch
Joe Koberstein

Maarten Kraaijvanger
Marc Laidlaw
Michael Land
Franz Lanzinger
Tim Larkin
Marc LeBlanc
The Levelord
   (Richard Bailey Gray)
Adam Levesque
Susan Lewis
Bill Linn
Mark Linn
Doug Lombardi
Al Lowe
Tony Lupidi
Jean-François Malouin
Michael McCart
Mitzi McGilvray
Michael D. McGrath
Seumas McNally
Brad McQuaid
Jordan Mechner
Sid Meier
Ellen Meijers-Gabriel
Michael Meyers
Shinji Mikami
Harry A. Miller
Shigeru Miyamoto
Richard Moe
Peter Molyneux
Steve Moraff
Ray Muzyka
Gabe Newell
Mike Nichols
Mike Nicholson
Tetsuya Nomura
Paul O'Connor
Marty O'Donnell
Scott Orr
Genevieve Ostergard
Alexey Pajitnov
Rob Pardo
Alan Patmore
David Perry
Kurt Pfeifer
Steve Polge
Bobby Prince
Matt Pritchard

Josh Resnick
Brian Reynolds
Chris Rippy
Seth Robinson
John Romero
Bill Roper
Jason Rubin
Michael Rubinelli
Hironobu Sakaguchi
Michael Saladino
George "The Fat Man" Sanger
Chris Sawyer
Kevin Schilder
Carl Schnurr
Joe Selinske
Bruce C. Shelley
Toby Simpson
Chris Sivertsen
Brandon Smith
Randy Smith
Warren Spector
Joshua Staub
Phil Steinmeyer
Timothy J. Stellmach
Jay Stelly
Jonas Stewart
Greg Street
Gonzo Suarez
Tim Sweeny
Tommy Tallarico
Chris Taylor
Chance Thomas
Greg Thomas
Joel Thomas
Daniel Thron
Emmanuel Valdez
Rick Vandervoorn
Jeff Vogel
David Walls
Robin Ward
Roberta Williams
Tim Willits
Jay Wilson
Mike Wilson
Jeane Wong
Will Wright
Greg Zeschuk
Jon Zuk

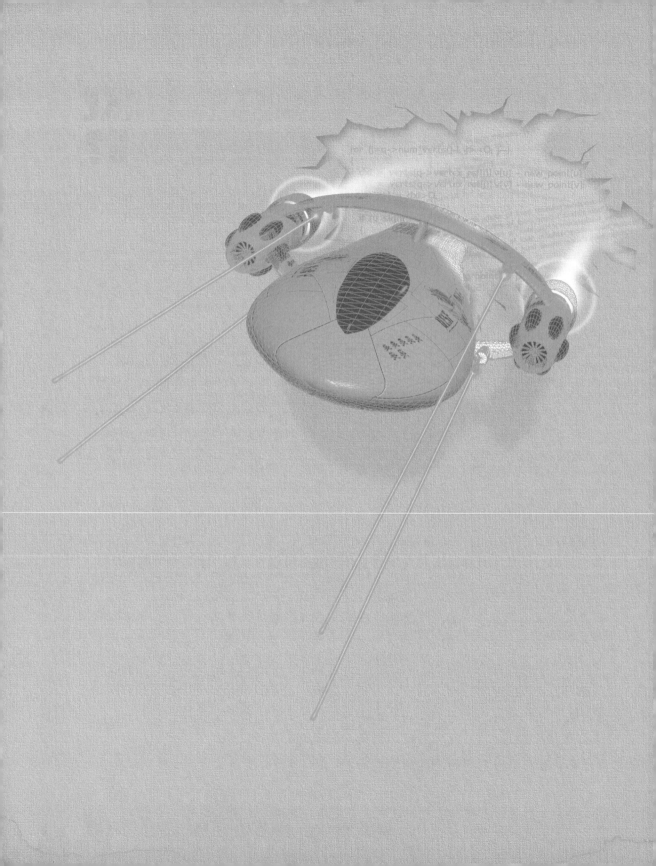

SO YOU WANT TO MAKE A GAME, HUH?

Quite simply, there has never been a better time to create your very own game. The tools have never been easier and better, the industry has never been more ripe, and the Internet, as a medium, is one of the most incredible technologies for gamers and game developers everywhere. And don't forget about console gaming— we're just about to witness an unprecedented four-way battle between Microsoft's X-Box, Nintendo's Dolphin, Sony's PlayStation2, and Sega's Dreamcast. Strike the iron while it's hot, as they say.

Creating games for a living may sound like only a dream job, but thousands of people are doing it as you read this, and many quite successfully. And you don't need millions of dollars to design a hit game, either. Take for instance Wizard Works' *Deer Hunter*. One of the cheapest retail games to develop was also one of the best-selling titles of 1998 and 1999, with over two million units sold in the United States alone. Why did it do so well? Because it was a great idea coupled with clever marketing and a relatively low price tag. And once you have a success like that, you can imagine the sequel and franchising opportunities. *Deer Hunter II* and *III*, for example, have already sold over a million units each. And you thought the *Blair Witch* movie was the only recent rags-to-riches story.

According to the NPD group, a marketing information provider, the reported retail sales for computer and console game software and hardware in 1999 exceeded a whopping $8.8 billion dollars in the U.S. alone (note: this includes kid's educational games, too, or *edutainment* software). Needless to say, this young and bustling industry is absolutely booming, so the big question remains—what do you want to be doing in the 21st century?

As you probably noticed by this book's title, you're holding the second edition of *Game Design: Secrets of the Sages*. The first book was released in the spring of 1999 and I'm pleased to report that it garnered quite a bit of critical praise and worldwide commercial success. In fact, it has been translated to other languages, and I've had the distinct pleasure of traveling the world to lecture budding game designers based on this book (as far as Hong Kong and Korea). So, we here at Macmillan were forced to sit down to think hard of a way to make this book bigger, better, and bolder than the last version. Here we go...

Let's first cover what this book *isn't*. This book will not require budding game programmers to be familiar with advanced concepts such as data structures, algorithm analysis, or anything like that. For the most part, the entire book is in easy-to-comprehend language; if acronyms, technical jargon, or industry slang are used, the word(s) are followed with a brief definition or clarification.

In addition, while the book is called *Game Design: Secrets of the Sages*, it covers much more than just game design. Sure, it explains how to write a solid design doc and how to decide what kind of game to create, but it also caters to all the members of a development team—programmers, artists and animators, sound engineers and musicians, plus the entire business side of gaming. This includes how to properly market your game, working with the press, the best ways to test your product, why a killer Web site for your game is essential, the do's and don'ts of technical support and customer service, and much, much more. Furthermore, a good chunk of the second half of the book is devoted to breaking into the exciting gaming industry, whether you want to be a solo shareware game designer, you want to start your own full-blown development company and need to pitch your idea to a publisher, or perhaps you prefer to squeeze in at an existing development studio or publishing company.

Because this book covers so much ground, you may or may not want to read it all the way through. Feel free to jump back and forth from chapter to chapter as dictated by your personal tastes.

Also, be sure to keep in mind that each chapter could really be expanded into a book itself—or even a series of books, for that matter. Therefore, in case further reading is desired, most chapters contain a handful of great Web links and Usenet newsgroups to surf to or books to pick up, plus there's a chapter toward the end of the book reserved for the best game design resources out there.

Finally, we listened to the feedback collected from those who read the first edition of *Game Design: Secrets of the Sages*, and we've tweaked this sequel considerably. You wanted more console game design? You got it—we've talked to Nintendo's Miyamoto, to Capcom's Shinji Mikami, to Square's Hironobu Sakaguchi, and Naughty Dog's Jason Rubin, to name just a few designers. You asked for more PC game gurus? We tracked down Will Wright, Warren Spector, Chris Sawyer, Tim Cain, Tim Sweeny, and Trevor Chan to add to the already stellar lineup. You demanded advice on how to create massively-multiplayer online RPGs? We've got Brad McQuaid, VP of Verant Interactive and Producer/Programmer on *EverQuest*...

Whether you're into action games or strategy, sims or sports, adventure or role-playing games, or puzzles/classics—or think you've got what it takes to create the next Pokémon phenomenon—we've got over 150 of the gaming industry's most savvy developers anxious to pour out advice on a myriad of topics, pooled from their many years of experience in the limelight.

So go ahead, dive right in and get in the game. With help from our sages over the next few hundred pages, the only thing between you and your hit game is your imagination...

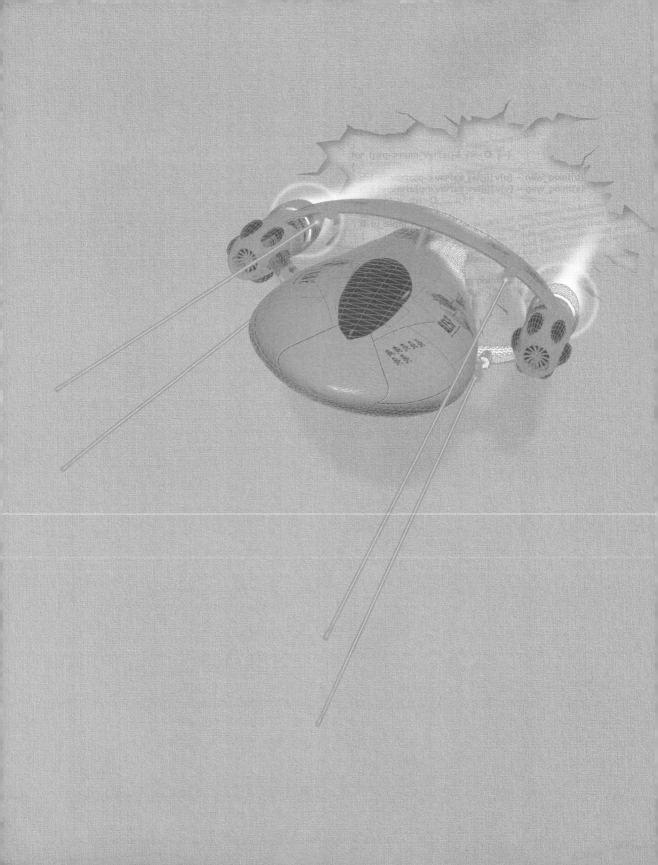

CHAPTER 1
GAME GENRES AND PLAYING PERSPECTIVES

Before diving into this book, we should cover a few of the basics. The first section of this chapter clarifies the differences between gaming *genres*. This is very important so that we're all on the same wavelength. Plus, before you sit down to design your game, you will ultimately need to choose a genre or a combination of genres to help solidify your vision.

There will be a number of terms thrown around over the next few hundred pages to explain how the game is played and/or the view the player has of the action. Words like *top-down*, *first-person perspective*, *third-person perspective*, and *isometric* will be explained and illustrated with an example.

So, as Duke Nukem says, "Come get some..."

GAME GENRES

ACTION

Action games (or "twitch" games) typically rely more on hand/eye coordination than on story or strategy. They're generally fast-paced and reflex-oriented. The most popular type of action game for the PC is the first-person perspective 3D shooter (more on this in a moment). id Software's *Quake* series and Epic Games' *Unreal Tournament* are recent examples. Fighting games, such as the *Soul Calibur* from Namco or Midway's *Mortal Kombat* series, fall into this category, as do "platform" side-scroller games (GT's *Oddworld: Abe's Exoddus* or Interplay's *Heart of Darkness*) and "over-the-shoulder" games such as the *Tomb Raider* series from Eidos Interactive.

Action games are arguably the most popular genre for both PC and console systems. But there are many different flavors of action games. Half-Life, for example, is a 3D shooter but adds a deep, involving story element. (Used with permission by Sierra Studios)

STRATEGY

Strategy games emphasize logical thinking and planning. They often stress resource and time management, which usually take precedence over fast action and character involvement. Tactical organization and execution are necessary, and the game creators usually place the decision-making skills and delivery of commands in the player's hands.

As opposed to turn-based games such as Microprose's *Civilization* or 3DO's *Heroes of Might and Magic*, real-time strategy (RTS) games add an active element and force the player to consider multiple events occurring at the same time. Examples of such games are Blizzard's *Starcraft* and Ensemble Studios' *Age of Empires*.

Blizzard's sci-fi epic Starcraft is one of the best selling real-time strategy games of all time, with over three million units sold—and counting. (Used with permission by Blizzard Entertainment, Inc.)

ADVENTURE

Adventure games involve the player in a journey of exploration and puzzle-solving. These games usually have a linear storyline in which you, the protagonist, set out to accomplish a main goal through character interaction and inventory manipulation. Some traces of the action genre may be found in these games. Good examples of adventure games are LucasArts' *Grim Fandango* and Brøderbund's *Myst* or *Riven*.

ROLE-PLAYING GAMES (RPGS)

Role-playing games (RPGs) are similar to adventure games, but rely more on character growth and development (usually involving player statistics), conversation, and strategic combat than on puzzle-solving. Huge, epic quests and fantasy worlds with *NPCs* (*non-player characters*) are common, and storylines are not always linear as in traditional adventure games. Side quests are also not uncommon to the genre.

Often computer role-playing games are referred to as *CRPGs*.

Action may play a significant role in an RPG, as in Blizzard's *Diablo* and Squaresoft's *Final Fantasy VII*, or more strategic elements may be necessary, as in Bullfrog's *Dungeon Keeper*. Older RPGs, referred to as *MUDs* (short for *multi-user domains* or *multi-user dungeons*), are exclusive to the Internet and are text-only. The majority of them are played via Telnet instead of over the World Wide Web. Most gamers, however, have shifted interest over to the more graphical proprietary online RPGs such as Origin's *Ultima Online* or Sony's *Everquest*.

Squaresoft's Final Fantasy VII, left, and Interplay's Baldur's Gate, right, are two popular RPGs of late, though their look and gameplay are quite different. (Used with permission by Sony Computer Entertainment America, Inc. and Interplay Productions, respectively)

SPORTS

Sports titles simulate a single-player or team game from an instructional or player perspective. Realism is important, as are fast action and tactical strategy. Examples of popular sports games include the *NHL* series from Electronic Arts, Acclaim's *WWF: Warzone*, Microsoft's *Links LS 2000*, and Midway's *NFL Blitz 2000* (though the "realism" gets blown right out of the water on this one).

SIMULATIONS OR SIMS

Sims realistically simulate a given animate or inanimate object or process. Most often, sims place the gamer in a 3D first-person perspective and re-create machinery such as planes, tanks, helicopters, and submarines. Examples include Interplay's *MiG Alley* and NovaLogic's *Armored Fist*.

Jane's Combat Simulations' F/A-18 is an example of the most popular kind of sim—aerial combat simulations. Realism is the number one objective when designing these kinds of games. (Used with permission by Electronic Arts, Inc.)

There are also sims that mimic the animal kingdom, such as Sanctuary Woods' *Wolf* or Maxis' *SimEarth*. "God-game" sims are those that require the (often megalomaniac!) gamer to build and manage cities, communities, and other resources on a grander scale; Maxis' *SimCity 3000* or *The Sims* and Bullfrog's *Populous: The Beginning* are good examples.

NOTE So where exactly do *racing/driving games* fit into the picture? Well, if you think about it, these kind of games can be their own category of game genre, or they may fall into action/arcade (EA's fantasy-esque *Need For Speed* series), the simulation genre (UbiSoft's *Monaco Grand Prix Racing Simulation 2*), or under the sports genre (Sierra Sports' *NASCAR Racing 3*).

PUZZLE OR "CLASSIC" GAMES

The *puzzle* or *classic games* include older, more historic games of leisure such as cards, tile games, trivia, word, or board games. Chess, checkers, backgammon, *Mahjongg*, and *Solitaire* are perfect examples. Recently, "classic" games have also included simpler and smaller-scale computer games, such as older arcade favorites and games that may lack a deep story or player commitment (*Tetris*, *Bust-A-Move*, and *Minesweeper* are great examples). Keep in mind that some of these games borrow elements from multiple genres (as illustrated in the RPG examples) or toy with different playing perspectives.

NOTE A "new" genre of games has evolved lately, in both arcades and on the home front, known as the *music* genre. Games such as 989 Studios' *Bust a Groove*, Sony's *Parappa the Rapper* or Konami's *Dance Dance Revolution* focus on music, singing, and dancing. This is an exciting new trend that's sure to continue well into the future.

PLAYING PERSPECTIVES

Here's a quick rundown of all of the varied playing perspectives.

FIRST-PERSON PERSPECTIVE

As touched on earlier, *first-person perspective* is an approved choice among the action game designers. In 3D shooters, the view of the gaming environment is as though the player is seeing it through the character's eyes, such as 3D Realms' *Duke Nukem 3D* or Acclaim's *Turok: Dinosaur Hunter*.

Genres other than action games take advantage of this popular perspective, too, including most simulations (for example, Microsoft's *Combat Flight Simulator*), adventure games (Mindscape's *John Saul's The Blackstone Chronicles*), strategy games (Activision's *Battlezone* or 3DO's *Uprising*), and role-playing games (Westwood Studios' *Lands of Lore III*).

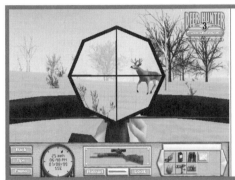

A first-person perspective view is often preferred since it adds to the believability of the world and overall immersion factor. Pictured here is a screen shot from Deer Hunter III. (Used with permission by GT Interactive Software Corp. and Wizard Works, Inc.)

THIRD-PERSON PERSPECTIVE

Also known as the "over-the-shoulder" view, the *third-person perspective* is another popular choice among game designers these days, especially since most games are in 3D. A third-person perspective is when the player can see onscreen the character he or she is playing. This has its advantages, too, since more of the environment can be seen while playing, plus you can see the moves your character can make—impossible in a first-person perspective view.

Many console and PC games use this view, including the *Tomb Raider* series, *Mario 64*, *Legend of Zelda: Ocarina of Time*, *Crash Bandicoot: Warped*, *Metal Gear Solid*, and *Resident Evil*.

Eidos Interactive's Tomb Raider was one of the first big hits to use a third-person perspective with an "intelligent" camera that followed heroine Lara Croft around. This is a screen shot from the latest game in the series, Tomb Raider: The Lost Artifact. (Used with permission by Eidos Interactive, Inc.)

This perspective is not limited to just action/arcade games: Sports games (almost all of them) honor this view, as well as RPGs (*Heretic II*, *Final Fantasy VIII*) and adventure games (*King's Quest: Mask of Eternity* and *Gabriel Knight III: Blood of the Sacred, Blood of the Damned*, to name two).

TOP-DOWN PERSPECTIVE

Top-down perspective is exactly as it sounds. The game is viewed looking down, as if the "camera" was hovering over the game itself. The genre that uses this perspective the most is the strategy game genre—both turn-based and real-time versions. This is because of all the minute micro-management details and tactical placement of troops on a landscape for battle. The player must be able to access the units and survey the situation with one glance. Good examples of top-down games are Blizzard's *Starcraft*, Microprose's *Civilization*, SSI's *Steel Panthers*, and even Pokémon *Red*, *Blue,* or *Yellow* for the Color Game Boy.

Non-strategy games that use this perspective include Monolith's retro RPG *Get Medieval*, older *Ultima* and *Zelda* games, and many classic 2D games of yesteryear, including arcade hits *Centipede* and *Frogger*.

Don't forget about pinball simulations. Most of these games utilize a top-down view as well. Pictured here is a table from the Balls of Steel expansion pack. (Used with permission by 3D Realms/Apogee, Inc.)

ISOMETRIC

Often confused with top-down is the *isometric* point of view. This is a slightly tilted "three quarter" view that hovers up and off to the side of the gameplay and gives the impression of 3D. Good examples of this kind of perspective are Blizzard's *Diablo*, Interplay's *Baldur's Gate*, and Activision's *Twinsen's Odyssey*.

Blizzard's Diablo II, left, is an isometric action/RPG; The Sims, right, is an isometric people simulation. Many game developers prefer this view because the characters and the environments can be seen by the player at the same time. (Used with permission by Blizzard Entertainment, Inc., and Maxis/Electronic Arts, Inc., respectively)

FLAT, SIDE-VIEW

The *flat, side-view* is the traditional two-dimensional "side view" of the action, a perspective that has become less and less popular over the years for its gameplay and aesthetic limitations. This view was popularized with the once-common "side-scroller" or "platform" games in the late 80s and early 90s, such as a few *Mario Bros.* and *Sonic the Hedgehog* games.

Some current games still use this perspective, and it may prove to be a refreshing change from all the first-person and third-person perspective games these days. Examples include Epic Games' *Jazz Jackrabbit 2*, Microprose's *Worms 2*, Monolith's *Claw*, and GT's *Oddworld: Abe's Exoddus* or *Oddworld: Abe's Oddysee*.

Monolith's Claw, left, and Mindscape's Creatures 2, right, use traditional 2D flat screens for the gameplay. (Used with permission by Monolith Productions, Inc. and Mindscape Entertainment, Inc., respectively)

TEXT-BASED GAMES

There are very few *text-based games* that don't use graphics at all, or very sparingly. Aside from the classic text adventures from the early 80s, such as the famous *Zork* series from Infocom or Douglas Adams' *Hitchhiker's Guide to the Galaxy*, today's *You Don't Know Jack* is a good example of this type of game.

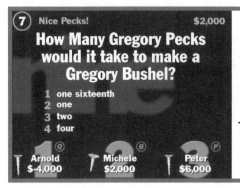

Berkeley Systems' *You Don't Know Jack* is an extremely popular trivia CD-ROM series and online game series. Most of what's seen on the screen is in text, coupled with audio narration from the game's host. (*You Don't Know Jack* is a registered trademark of Jellyvision, Inc., image used with permission of Jellyvision and Berkeley Systems, Inc.)

It should be noted that many games allow players to change the playing perspective, depending on what's going on in the game. Examples from different genres include Microprose's *European Air War*, Electronic Arts' *Need for Speed: Porsche Unleashed*, LucasArts' *Jedi Knight*, and Red Storm Entertainment's *Rainbow Six*.

There is also a lot of experimentation these days with both genre mixing and playing perspectives.

CHAPTER 2
GENERAL GAME DESIGN: ACTION AND STRATEGY GAMES

Considering that good game design is more of an art form than a science, it can often be difficult to ask someone to "teach" it to you. As an analogy, it's like asking Lennon or McCartney how they wrote a song like "Yesterday," or how Salvador Dali conceived a painting such as *Persistence of Memory*. In fact, it's often more difficult to analyze and tutor on game design, since it incorporates more senses than any other art form, not to mention that it's often a group effort *and* an interactive medium to boot.

Having said that, we are very fortunate to have some talented game designers who are able to put their avenues of inspiration into words and game design processes onto paper. Naturally, there are as many ideas on approaching game design as there are developers, but over the next two chapters, we've got some inspiring and enlightening advice from some of our young and bustling industry's finest.

 Before diving into these words of wisdom, remember one thing— all the glitz and glitter poured into games these days, such as expensive art, animation, real actors, or the best musicians, cannot cover up for poor gameplay.

This chapter features designers from the action/arcade and the strategy game genres.

ACTION/ARCADE GAMES

SHIGERU MIYAMOTO, NINTENDO

The honorable Shigeru Miyamoto is the general manager of entertainment analysis and development at Nintendo Co. Ltd. in Kyoto, Japan. He has created and designed some of our industry's most beloved series, including *Donkey Kong*, *Mario Bros.*, and *Zelda*. At the 1998 Electronic Entertainment Exposition (E3), Miyamoto was honored as the first inductee into the Academy of Interactive Arts and Sciences Hall of Fame.

During a conversation with Miyamoto, through his interpreter, he was asked for the most important pieces of advice to give new game designers. He responds as follows:

> What is important to understand is that those who are making games are completely devoting themselves to the games. Because of such devotion, they can make unique, independent games. On the other hand, because of too much involvement, they are unable to objectively comprehend how the actual players would feel when they play the game for the first time. It is important to note that devotion to game creation has these effects.
>
> Another important element is a belief that creators are artists. At the same time, however, it's necessary for us creators to be engineers, because of the skills required for the creations.

Miyamoto says making games "fun" is Nintendo's only objective, and they're always making an effort to accomplish this goal. (Used with permission by Nintendo of America, Inc.)

In Chapter 4, Miyamoto discusses how he creates such time-withstanding characters as Mario and Link; in Chapters 8 and 12, he discusses programming and the all-important user interface, respectively.

KURT ARNLUND, ACCOLADE

As a programmer on *Mechwarrior 2: NetMech*, the *Interstate '76* series, *Heavy Gear*, and most recently Accolade's *Slave Zero*, Arnlund has learned a thing or two about game design. He has two key pieces of advice to share:

IMMERSION

> Create a game environment that is so detailed that the player can get lost in it and forget he's even playing a game. This doesn't mean having the finest, most detailed texture maps of any game. This means creating the illusion that the game universe is bigger than it really is. Cracks in walls that hint at whole other areas of the world where life continues as usual. Cars and people on the streets going about their everyday business. If you can create the illusion that the game is a living puzzle and the player is but a small piece of the puzzle, then the player is likely to get drawn into this puzzle even more. I'm constantly sucked in by games that make me feel like I'm really there. Good examples would be *Half-Life*, *Duke Nukem*, *Jedi Knight*, *Monkey Island*.

HAVE FUN DOING IT

Second, Arnlund reminds designers that if the game isn't fun, it's not going to get attention.

> If it doesn't get people's attention, then they're not going to tell their friends about it. If they don't tell their friends about it, it probably is not going to sell well. You want to create a game that people are going to tell their friends about. The slightest bit of tedium and the player is most likely going to put it on the shelf and forget about it. There are few things I love more than calling up friends when I've discovered XYZ in a game, or I was completely amazed by how they executed feature B in a game. I love getting people riled up with the same excitement I have about a game.

Arnlund says he'd like to continue to work on creative projects that don't just push the technological limits of the available hardware, but also give the game players new experiences that are different from anything they have seen before.

TOBY GARD, CONFOUNDING FACTOR

You may not be familiar with the name Toby Gard, but chances are you're aware of his most beloved creation—Lara Croft. Toby Gard left Core Design as lead graphic artist and game designer on the revolutionary title *Tomb Raider*, to launch his own development studio alongside fellow Core Design lead programmer Paul Douglas.

Concerning general game design, Gard says your objectives should be contingent upon your resources. He explains:

> If you are forced into using a type of technology, e.g., a certain engine, or are limited in any other way by your platform or programming, then you have to come at your design from that direction first. For instance, at its most severe, if you're making a Game Boy game, then you already know you're limited to it being 2D and having pretty serious speed and memory restrictions. No *Quake* 12 for you then.

"Assuming that you'll be making a game for the PC or one of the newer 3D consoles, however, as is more often the case these days, your restrictions are pretty loose." That said, he offers the following:

> I prefer working from this direction, because you can take a pure idea and you know that in some form you will be able to make it happen, however hard that route is. So then you need an idea, right? Well, I think we all have about a million of them each—it's whatever gets you excited, like wanting to be in Star Wars or showing people how much fun snowboarding is. Then all you need to do is go down to the pub and talk endlessly about what would be cool about it with your mates, or preferably with whoever you're going to make the game with.
>
> During that time, you need to be constantly solving the "How the h--- can we do that?" technical questions. Even if you're just saying stuff like, "Well, we need shadows. *Quake* does shadows, so how are they doing that, and can we use a similar technique?" During this period you should be thinking an awful

lot about how your control system will work. I'm a believer in compressing your control system down to the minimum number of buttons to achieve your aims; that way you tend to get an elegant rather than a cumbersome control system. You're basically aiming to be in the position where you have such a clear idea of what the game will be like, that you can actually play it in your head. When you can do that, if you're visualizing it hard enough, you'll be able to see and address loads of the flaws in the idea before you've implemented a d--- thing!

Therefore, these are the three most important things for me: a) visualize the control system, including game mechanics; b) have technology ideas for how to implement all of the above; and c) write it all down!

Gard divulges how to create a successful lead character in Chapter 4.

Gard's next project will be the action/adventure epic Galleon. For more information, visit www.confounding-factor.com. (Used with permission by Confounding Factor, Inc.)

CARL SCHNURR, RED STORM ENTERTAINMENT

As producer on the award-winning *Rainbow Six* and *Rogue Spear* series, Carl Schnurr has plenty of enlightening words to share with budding designers, in a number of areas.

FEATURES

It's not hard coming up with scads of cool features to add to your game, but it's hard to narrow them down to the ones that truly make a difference. Every feature included in your game should be considered extremely carefully. What other features does it affect? Does it add enough to the experience to justify the cost in development time? Does it truly add to the fun factor without obscuring the overriding vision?

LEVELS

I've always enjoyed games that allowed me to approach them how I wanted to, rather than forcing me down a narrow path. The trick is to make a level that's rich with possibilities—give players a handful of balanced ways to beat the level rather than telling them, "This is how you must beat the level." We used this design philosophy with the levels in *Rainbow Six* with great success.

Urban Operations is the name of the first official mission pack for the best-selling Tom Clancy's Rogue Spear. Here's a "shot" taken from the nail-biting action. (© Red Storm Entertainment, Inc.)

VOICE TALENT

> Pay good money for good talent. It's worth every penny. Sure, you could get a friend to do the voices, but it will probably show—if not in the final quality, then in the time it takes for them to get it right. Get yourself a good casting person (preferably in L.A.) to get samples for you, and be willing to pay Screen Actor's Guild (SAG) rates for professional talent. You'll be glad you did.

CONTRACTORS/FREELANCERS

> Treat all of your contractors just like you would an employee. Interview them thoroughly before signing anything and always check references. Make sure that each of you clearly understands the deliverables verbally before committing signatures to the contract. Ensure that the contract contains specific references to reworks and redos. Monitor their progress closely and don't be afraid to fire them if they breach the contract.

GAME VISION

> If you can't get someone excited about the game with a five-minute talk and a one-page sell sheet, either rework the concept or trash it entirely. This is the time in the project when it's cheap to do that—before you've committed resources.

FOCUS

> Game before glitz. If the core game is flawed, who cares if you have beautiful cut-scenes or killer music? People may buy the game based on glitz, but they'll love it or hate it (and tell others their opinion) based on the game itself. Make sure you have a killer game first, then add the polish. Too many game companies do it the other way round.

GABE NEWELL, VALVE SOFTWARE

Half-Life was Valve Software's debut product, racking up a number of "best of" awards from around the world. Gabe Newell, managing director at Valve, shares some tips on creating successful games:

> The first thing you need to understand is, "Why is this an interesting game? What about the experience we're providing for a customer is unique or worth their time and money?" This is a very serious question, and most game designs fail at this point.
>
> Part of the reason that game designs are led astray is that some choices—such as rehashing an existing game design with a slightly modified gameplay or art direction—will work under certain circumstances and not others. People doing a sequel to a hit game can get away with a much less innovative game design. (As an aside, this kind of "looting the franchise" approach is likely a pretty bad idea in the long run, even though version 2 of something [popular] will still sell pretty well.) Other companies seem to think that they can do game designs that are sequels to other people's games, and that has a much lower likelihood of being successful, for a variety of reasons.

With *Half-Life*, Newell says they started from an experiential definition of what they wanted to build. "We knew how the player was supposed to feel playing *Half-Life*, and used that to make a whole bunch of decisions." What exactly did you want the player to feel, and how did you accomplish it?

> Prior to starting work on *Half-Life*, I had been reading a bunch of Stephen King. In particular, there was a novella he had written called "The Mist." The primary aspect of the story that really appealed to me was this sense of an ordinary world spinning out of control. Setting a tentacle monster in a grocery store, for instance. There were elements of science fiction crossed with horror, which I really liked. And in general the main character was struggling with realizing he had to be the main actor in the situation, that people who should be on his side were turned against him, and that even though bad things were happening, the shape of the catastrophe wasn't very clear for a long way into the story.
>
> Given how I had felt playing *Doom*, it seemed possible to put a player into that kind of intense, scary action experience. I wanted to get away from the notion of "shooter," where the player is the deadliest thing in the universe, who just jogs around killing everything.
>
> The character of Gordon Freeman [was left] as transparent as possible to the player. There's no voiceover, no third-person camera or mirrors. We tried never to pull the player out of the experience through cut-scenes, voiceovers, or even Easter eggs or other obviously authorial devices. We made the other characters in the game sympathetic and helpful, and then we did horrible things to them to try to get the player to feel both loss and the sense that the world was actually dangerous. We left a lot of ambiguity in the story to allow the player to write the story however he wanted to, from what he was experiencing.

Asked to discuss the primary differences between creating a PC game and a console game—from a game design point of view—Newell ponders the question, then responds:

> The demographics for the console audience are quite different from the PC audience, so you need to make sure you understand who the game is for. Consoles have almost no variation in system configurations or performance, whereas the PC has a huge range of configurations you have to deal with. The

design of the game has to reflect the differing user inputs (mouse and keyboard on a desk versus console controller held in hand), as well as the difference in resolution, contrast, and color saturation between a monitor and a TV.

In addition to all of these differences in hardware, the customer, and usage scenarios, there's also a set of "cultural" issues you have to take into account. For example, consistent frame rate is viewed as being a lot more important for a console title than for a PC title. I'm not really sure why that is, since it doesn't seem to be a function of genre or demographics, which is why I'd lump it into a separate set of "cultural" issues.

On the future of gaming, Newell adds:

It's pretty interesting to see that DSL installations were up 50% month-to-month lately. That's an incredible growth rate for anything, even the Internet. It's also going to be really interesting to watch Microsoft and Intel make their move into the living room to make sure one of the console vendors doesn't steal away the low end of the marketplace from PCs. The price/performance improvements in CPUs, 3D accelerators, and hard drives have been even more mind-boggling than normal, and it certainly seems likely that this will enable a new class of game types that we haven't seen before.

Finally, Newell offers some advice on how best to break into the gaming biz:

Good game developers or designers are very hard to find. They need to have "good enough" technical skills, "good enough" art skills, a sense of what a target audience will find entertaining, and a personality that works well in the type of small group that typically builds games. I'm not sure *chutzpah* actually makes for a good designer, although it certainly is what gets some people the title of "game designer" at the larger game companies. When I've met with some of the great game designers, I've almost always been struck by their humility and the seriousness with which they've approached game design. Game promoters, as opposed to game designers, certainly seem to have a lot of *chutzpah*, but unless there is somebody else delivering on all of the hype, I'm not sure it doesn't backfire pretty quickly.

In Valve's Half-Life: Team Fortress 2, there are nine classes of players to chose from, each with their own particular skills: Commander, Light Infantry (Scout), Medic, Heavy Infantry, Rocket Infantry, Sniper, Commando, Spy, and Engineer. (Half-Life: Team Fortress 2 is a registered trademark of Sierra On-Line, Inc. Images used with permission. Copyright 1999-2000 Sierra On-Line, Inc. All Rights Reserved.)

For more on getting a job at a game development studio, turn to Chapter 20.

SHINJI MIKAMI, CAPCOM

As the manager of the R&D department (#4) at Capcom, Ltd. in Japan, Shinji Mikami has worked on the celebrated survival horror series *Resident Evil* as well as the 1999 PlayStation hit *Dino Crisis*. Mikami's future aspiration is "to make sure the new *Resident Evil* games become the best ones imaginable."

Concerning general game design, Mikami was asked to list the three most important considerations for budding game designers to keep in mind. His answers are as follows:

> Make it crystal clear what you want to achieve with your game.
>
> Think in advance of the most effective way to shape up the initial game specs so it fits within various limitations/restrictions (development time, hardware specs, etc.).
>
> Never give up. Patience is the key.

Mikami believes that much of the success of the *Resident Evil* series is due to the fact that he followed the above three rules strictly, and because "it was easy for a person to convey the horror factor in *Resident Evil* to his/her friends, orally," says Mikami. That is, much of the success of the *Resident Evil* series can be attributed to the strong word-of-mouth advertising between gamers. Says Mikami, "I guess it was easy for a person to explain to others what they love about *Resident Evil*." Furthermore, Mikami believes the market must also be ripe for a game to be a huge hit, such as what the original *Resident Evil* did in the bourgeoning "survival horror" genre. "Few games keep a good balance between 'video games as an art' and 'video games as a business commodity,'" says Mikami. "That's the biggest problem, in my opinion, with many of today's games."

Resident Evil: Code Veronica (Biohazard: Code Veronica in Japan) on the Sega Dreamcast continues the story of Claire Redfield in her quest to find her missing brother. (Used with permission by Capcom Entertainment, Inc.)

Chapter 15 discusses various ways to test games in development to ensure a bug-free and balanced experience. Meanwhile, Mikami briefly touches on how he tests games such as the *Resident Evil* series and *Dino Crisis*:

> I usually test my game for a month before release. I first list all of the points in the game where a bug can be expected. Then I assign several different groups to each different "suspicious" part of the game and have them test it systematically.

CLIFF BLESZINSKI, EPIC GAMES

Beginning at the age of 17, Cliff Bleszinski developed games for Epic Games. In 1993, Cliff designed the popular platform title *Jazz Jackrabbit*; then he began work on *Unreal* and a sequel to *Jazz Jackrabbit*, both of which were released in 1998. At last check, Bleszinski was enjoying critical praise due to the success of *Unreal Tournament*.

Bleszinski says there are three things that he believes are key for designing and building a game:

NO ONE IS BIGGER THAN THE BAND

" Making a game involves an entire team of talented and dedicated individuals. No one person makes any product; much like a Super Bowl–winning football team is not all about the quarterback, a game is not about a programmer or designer. A good team works well together, hangs out together occasionally, and acts like a well-oiled machine. "

As an example, Bleszinski reveals that building *Unreal* took 20 people from start to finish. "Games are far more complex and involving than ever before."

DESIGN DOCUMENTS AND CONCEPT ART ARE INVALUABLE

" They outline your game plan and provide a "to do" list for the entire team. If anyone ever finds themselves twiddling their thumbs during the development cycle, you can just refer them to the documents or concept art for direction. A game needs a central starting point—although the team builds the game and makes it great, it needs focus and direction, and design documents and concept art do this. "

Epic Games' Unreal Tournament garnered commercial and critical success when it was released to eager action fans during the 1999 winter holidays. (Used with permission by Epic Games, Inc.)

THE ABILITY TO SEPARATE GOOD IDEAS FROM BAD IDEAS IS HIGHLY UNDERRATED

> You can sit down and dream up "the most incredible game ever," but can it be done realistically in a development cycle? Do you think you can really make 40 guns that all interlock and make infinite combinations of weaponry? Be realistic, and don't be afraid to shoot down an idea you don't like or an idea that's not feasible in the timeframe. Remember, every month your project is delayed is a month that you're paying a team and not earning money back.

DAVID PERRY, SHINY ENTERTAINMENT

As game designer and president of Shiny Entertainment, David Perry has been responsible for many adored games, such as Disney's *Aladdin*, the *Earthworm Jim* series, *MDK*, and most recently, *Messiah*. Although most of Perry's input for this book is found in Chapter 4, he shares some words on general game design here:

> A good hook is essential. A good hook means that you can describe your game in one sentence. For *MDK* it was, "He has a weapon so accurate, you can shoot your enemy in the eye from a mile away"—sniper mode was born.
>
> A good ambiance. Take the gamer off into a world that he can explore and have fun in. It can be the real world, but if so, he must be able to do things that he doesn't personally have the skill to perform. If it's a fantasy world, make sure that everything makes sense and has consistency.
>
> Keep the gameplay challenging, but don't let players get lost or blame the game for their problems. A good game designer always knows what the players are thinking and is looking over their shoulders every step of the way.

Perry continues:

> I think design is all about vision—seeing the game in your mind—being able to see at a glance when something is wrong. When someone asks you what would happen in a complex situation, you have the answer. When you play other games, you question why things are done the way they are. AND THE MOST IMPORTANT THING—you have solutions! Many "designers" complain and moan, but rarely have a solution. I have met gamers who are true visionaries and they don't even know it. Just listen to their comments as they play—you slap yourself on the head and think, "D---, why didn't I think of that? It's obvious!"

Shiny's Messiah took many years to develop because of its ambitious gameplay objectives and scalable hardware requirements. (Used with permission by Shiny Entertainment, Inc.)

Having created games for both PC and console platforms, what are the primary differences from a game design point of view? What are the challenges for each platform, and how do they differ? Perry ponders the question, then answers in the following four paragraphs:

> Designing games for the PC is fantastic because you have lots more RAM. So you have lots more storage space for graphics, sound effects, speech, world topography, etc. These are all really good things to have in a designer's toolbox if they can provide freedom. The dark side of the PC world is the fact that there is such a spread of hardware prowess around the world. We have to design our game for some guy in Greece playing on a Pentium 166 so that his old machine gives him a great experience, yet the latest Intel 1000 Mhz machine also needs to get a great experience.
>
> How do you design a game for both? The answer is scalable engines. That means that the game internally says to itself, "This machine kinda [stinks], let's just have 50 particles in the explosions instead of 500." Or, "Instead of 8,000 polygons on this character, let's just use 1,000." The latest engines do this in real time. Another great benefit is that now you can add lots of characters onscreen. As the machine begins to choke, it just removes polygons to keep the game speed constant.
>
> It's a fantastic tool for a designer's toolbox because it means you don't have to always design for situations with a maximum of just 5 or 6 guys. If you want 75 guys to get in a giant fight, that's just fine. You can also use this technology on console. It doesn't help you with the different processor speeds because, for example, the Sony Playstation2's all share the same heart. But it will give you the ability to have maybe 100 characters with you at one time…great for *Braveheart* scenes!
>
> Another great benefit of PCs is the hard disk. The [Microsoft] X-Box will bring that to the console world. This gives you the ability to load quickly, stream movies/audio/textures *into* the game world, and [even] to modify the game permanently. So if you dig a hole, it's there forever.

Finally, Perry is asked whether any recent technological advancements have made—or should have made—the gaming experience richer. He answers:

> Storage space has greatly increased with CD, then DVD, and now hard drive space…we really cannot complain anymore. Processors are insane also. The excuses are over. 3D hardware is jaw-dropping. I think every part has moved forward so much that it's up to us to take the leaps forward in pushing ourselves. To stop accepting things because "that's the way it's always been done." The one thing that still needs attention is control devices and voice recognition.
>
> Then I will be blissfully happy.

David Perry's personal Web site is at www.dperry.com; Shiny's official site is at www.shiny.com.

JASON RUBIN, NAUGHTY DOG

As co-founder of California's admired Naughty Dog development studios (alongside Andy Gavin), Jason Rubin was the lead designer on all the *Crash Bandicoot* titles for the Sony PlayStation platform, including, in reverse chronological order: *CTR* (*Crash Team Racing*), *Crash Bandicoot: Warped*, *Crash Bandicoot 2: Cortex Strikes Back*, and *Crash Bandicoot*. Naughty Dog has created three of the top five PlayStation titles in America and is the only American developer to sell over a million units of software in Japan in the history of video games, with *Crash Bandicoot: Warped*.

While most of Rubin's advice can be found in Chapter 4 on creating a hit character, he is asked to list the three most important considerations for a newbie game designer to keep in mind. He prefaces his response by clarifying that these tips are to make a "popular" game:

> You are making the game for the tastes of the masses, not for your own tastes.
>
> You are making the game for a wide variety of skill levels, not for your own skill level.
>
> You can test your success in executing the first two points above by massive amounts of game testing during the creation process, making changes accordingly, and testing again.

On the *Crash* series, Rubin says part of the success of the games relied on "quality gameplay that both challenged and rewarded." He explains: "Most people who played *Crash* games will tell you that they 'were good' and that they 'got pretty far,' although how good they were and how far they got in the game varied greatly. This lead to a great amount of positive buzz about the product and word-of-mouth sales."

Crash Team Racing was the first Naughty Dog game to combine the popular Crash Bandicoot characters with white-knuckle racing. For more info, drop into www.naughtydog.com. (Used with permission by Sony Computer Entertainment of America, Inc. (SCEA))

Rubin also says that *Crash* has maintained its popularity by keeping the gameplay fresh. "You never knew what to expect in the sequels. *Crash* might get a jetpack (*Crash 2*) or a jet ski (*Crash 3*), but you knew that whatever it was, you would have fun!"

In Naughty Dog's opinion, what's the biggest problem with games today? Rubin believes there is "too little attention paid to the quality of the engine and gameplay." Says Rubin, "You might have a great license, or a great main character design, or the coolest background art, or a really good story—but without the tightest engine and smoothest gameplay, you don't have a good game."

Be sure to flip to Chapter 4 to read Rubin's advice on creating a popular mascot such as Crash Bandicoot.

JORDAN MECHNER, FREELANCE GAME DESIGNER

Over the past decade, Jordan Mechner has earned a reputation as one of the world's premier computer game designers by bringing cinematic techniques to the small screen in games like *Karateka*, the *Prince of Persia* series, and *The Last Express*. Mechner's passion for visual storytelling has now led him to a new career as a screenwriter and filmmaker.

In 1999, Mechner was too busy finishing Red Orb/Mindscape Entertainment's *Prince of Persia 3D* to partake in the first of edition of *Game Design: Secrets of the Sages*, but he was eager to offer his advice this time around. Asked where budding game designers can look for inspiration, Mechner responds as follows:

> Once you've chosen the basic idea, everything becomes grist for your mill—other games, movies, books, real-life experiences, everything. You are always keeping one eye out for things that can work into your project somehow.

On his first game, *Karateka*, Mechner discusses its genesis:

> *Karateka* drew inspiration from a number of sources—Paul Stephenson's game *Swashbuckler* was the first game I'd seen with large and identifiable characters, not just tiny stick figures. I was also impressed by the smooth scrolling and illusion of 3D depth in Dan Gorlin's *Choplifter*, as well as the lifelike animation of the tiny little fellows. I hoped to achieve the lifelike feeling of *Choplifter* but with characters the size of *Swashbuckler*'s. I didn't want my game to look like a direct copy of *Choplifter*, so I made it bare-handed karate fighting instead of sword fighting. That was the basic idea as far as what kind of game it would be, what it should feel like to play.
>
> From that point on, my inspiration mostly came from further afield—not from computer games. The medieval Japanese setting was inspired by my favorite film, Kurosawa's *Seven Samurai*. The "Way of the Warrior" philosophy in the prologue came from Mushashi's *Book of Five Rings*. I wanted to make the actual fighting as realistic as possible, so I took karate classes and read karate books. Once I'd worked out which moves would work best with the game and interface, I got the local sensei to execute the moves for me in proper style, filmed him with a movie camera, and rotoscoped the action frame by frame—that is, I put it on the Moviola and traced each frame onto tracing paper. Rotoscoping was a technique that had been used by Disney in the 1930s in the early days of animation. It hadn't been used yet in computer games, and it gave the animation an uncannily lifelike quality—for the time. Today it looks primitive. The view of Mt. Fuji in the background, which gives the illusion of 3D depth, was adapted from a woodblock print by Hokusai. So nothing is wasted.

On his critically acclaimed PC adventure game *The Last Express*, Mechner says he was influenced by both Brøderbund's mega-hit game *Myst* and European comic books. He explains:

> I liked the simplicity of *Myst*'s point-and-click interface, the fact that it didn't look or feel like a computer game. It wasn't really a game—more of an immersive world where you didn't know right off the bat who you were or what the goal was, and I thought that was an interesting direction for games to go.
>
> I'm a big fan of artists like Hugo Pratt, Francois Schuiten, Enki Bilal, and others who are well known in France but not so much yet in the U.S., who have used the comic book form to tell adult stories, sometimes very dark stories with a lot of moral ambiguity and a very non–Disney take on the 20th century. I was intrigued by the idea of using cartoon characters to tell a non-cartoon story, and I wanted to try that in a computer game. I wanted to see if it was possible to do a computer game without a happy ending—it always seemed fake to me that at the end you're told that your actions have saved the world or won the war or got the girl or whatever, and that's supposed to make the player go away happy. Movies can be just as satisfying with a tragic or ironic ending—*Romeo and Juliet*, *Gone with the Wind*, *Titanic*, to name a few—so why not a game? That was the starting point for *The Last Express*. The train setting was inspired by another of my favorite films, Hitchcock's *The Lady Vanishes*. I love spy stories—*The 39 Steps*, John Le Carré—and a luxury train like the Orient Express seemed to me the perfect setting for a game: a contained environment with a finite cast of characters, which would enable us to create a real, immersive world in great detail—but a world that was always in motion. World War II had been done to death, both in computer games and movies—maybe because the Nazis were such easy villains. So to be different I chose World War I.

Mechner explains how he continued to shape *The Last Express* once the core idea was established:

> Once the train got moving (so to speak), inspiration came flooding in from everywhere. Research was very important—I can't stress that enough. This includes reading novels from the period, newspapers and magazines that tell you how people spoke and what they thought at the time; watching every train movie ever made to learn all the clichés so you can go them one better; visiting actual railroad cars from the period, riding trains, having dinner on trains, to learn what it was really like; and digging up original documents—blueprints, railway timetables, conductors' rulebooks of the period. This might sound a bit like busywork, but the more you become expert in the minutiae of the world of your game—regardless of whether it's a fantasy world, a futuristic one, or a world of the past—the more it wakes up your mind to dream. The look of the characters was inspired by Art Nouveau, a graphic style in vogue at the turn of the century, in which characters were drawn as realistic but stylized ink line drawings, with flat washes of solid color, very little shading. The early Disney films like *Snow White*, with their flatly drawn cartoon characters against richly dimensional, painterly backgrounds, were another touchpoint.

Drawing from his own experience, Mechner was asked if there were any do's and don'ts when it comes to game design. "Don't get too caught up trying to second-guess what publishers want, or what you think will sell," begins Mechner. He expands:

> There are too many people already employed in this industry trying to do just that. Obviously this is a business and everyone would like to produce a hit game that will sell millions of copies. But as a game designer, you should be asking yourself what you would want to see in a game, what would excite you. Because if your concept doesn't thrill you, it probably won't thrill anybody else. It's very tough to get a game made and brought to market. A lot of things can go wrong along the way. If you are passionate about your project, if it is a labor of love, then even if it doesn't hit the jackpot commercially, you will still be proud of the work you've done. So don't get too caught up in worrying about how many copies it will sell, or how much you're getting paid. The work is its own reward; focus on the work.

Secondly, Mechner acknowledges this may sound like a bit of a contradiction to his first piece of advice—but he insists it's not—try to retain ownership of your own work to the greatest extent possible. Says Mechner:

> Usually when you sell your idea to a publisher or development company, you become their employee, which means that from that point on, you own nothing. What they offer you in return, usually, is money—salary, bonuses, option or purchase payments. This can be very tempting, especially if you're broke and/or unemployed, but don't let the up-front money turn your head. If at all possible, hold out for a deal that will let you retain some degree of ownership. This can be a royalty, equity, stock options, or percentage of the profits; it can involve your retaining some kind of contractual creative approval, or requiring them to credit you publicly as creator of the game. This may mean that you end up making less money in the end, but it's worth it.

MICHAEL BÜTTNER, X-AMPLE ARCHITECTURE

Mission: Impossible was a popular action game for the Sony PlayStation published by Infogrames in early 2000. It was developed by a German development studio known as X-ample Architecture. Lead designer on the project Michael Büttner discusses a number of topics, ranging from general game design to working on console versus PC games, and what it's like to create a game based on a popular franchise.

Off the bat, Büttner says a wise game designer will keep these points in mind:

- An "open" design will allow for changes on the fly.
- Direct communication and teamwork between programmers, graphic artists, and designers is extremely important.
- A small and efficient team is best.

Büttner expands on each of the three points:

> The "open design" concept is the most important issue because it's easy to add or remove things (large stuff like scenarios or minor things like some in-game sequences) on the fly according to the time left, without violating the game design in general. Next, on teamwork, a good, small team allows the direct communication that is at least as important as the design itself, because only the people actually doing the game know what's impossible and what's possible and how to achieve the latter. We are a relatively small team with everybody putting their thoughts, experience, and ambition into the project. If we encounter something impossible (technically or time-wise), we always find a good solution to get around the problem, and this is where new ideas and possibilities find their room. We try to catch up and integrate all those ideas from the whole staff. In fact, this helps the whole team to learn and gain experience.

Büttner says X-ample has learned this throughout the company's short history:

> The progress between *Tunnel B1* (1997), *Viper* (1998), *Mission: Impossible* (1999), and our current spy game (due out in late 2000) is extremely large while still developing for the same platform (PlayStation). This constant progress and development allows us to improve the game design further and further. Ideas are always present in a large number, but the platform restricts them. But our concept is to make the best version of a game even on the weakest platform. The engine is designed to run on all systems and needs only a short timeframe to be ported to even new machines. This technical background gives the level designers the freedom they need to let their ideas become reality.

So what exactly are the pros and cons of developing games for the PC versus console games? Büttner offers these comments:

PRO	CON
PC	
Technology is moving very fast	Time-consuming development because of different target systems and drivers
Almost no testing time because of lack of approval	Large number of competitors because everybody with a PC can develop games
Limited number of platforms (DirectX and OpenGL)	
CONSOLE	
Fixed hardware for each console	Expensive development kits
A big market worldwide	Loads of restrictions
Limited number of competitors	Time-consuming approval
	Support of new hardware can be time-consuming as well

Since we're on the topic, what about the pros and cons of working with a well-known license, such as *Mission: Impossible*, compared to starting a new franchise from scratch? Büttner begins with the cons and lists many off the bat. "It's always a tight schedule due to the expectations of the licensors, [and it's difficult dealing with] the prejudice that licensed products have [poor] quality due to the publisher relying on the product to sell well even with a weak gameplay. The licensor and publisher interfere with the game design, a license can have a negative image, and there's a much harder approval process."

The pros, according to Büttner: "Getting the offer to develop a license product means being esteemed, as the publisher has a large risk due to the amount of money being spent for the license itself—so he will never give this project to an unstable developer. The scenarios are predefined so it's easy to add the game; it's less work than inventing a new and interesting game universe. Everybody already knows what the game is about, so you don't have to sell your idea to the publisher, [and] Marketing has loads of stuff from the first day on. It's less work for the developer to come up with marketing materials, and it's extremely easy to motivate the team because everybody wants to work on a 'license title.'"

In Chapter 15, Michael Büttner explains how he and the rest of the development team at X-ample Architecture approach the testing process.

ALAN PATMORE, SURREAL SOFTWARE

Alan Patmore is the president and design director at Surreal Software, the company behind Psygnosis' action/adventure title, *Drakan*, where he served as lead designer.

In a lengthy interview, Patmore touches on game design recommendations, where to look for inspiration, and the issue of 2D versus 3D games:

> Game design has been evolving over the past four years. Traditionally, designers would create a design document and sketch the levels. Artists and programmers would then build the game based on the design. *Doom* changed the way games are designed by providing easy-to-use tools that combined the art and programming, creating a level. This took gameplay to the next level; gameplay iterations took minutes instead of days. Surreal has followed this model by building tools specifically designed to allow for maximum gameplay iteration. With all that said, game designers at Surreal are both environment architects and gameplay gurus.
>
> The first thing you need to do when designing a game is to get all of your ideas down on paper. Even with the most incredible tools, it's important to have a well-thought-out game. This means writing everything down before diving in and building the game. By sketching out levels before you build them, you eliminate a lot of potential design problems.

According to Patmore, the next step is to build a demo, the first real implementation of your design. He explains:

> While building the demo, it's important to tackle the major game mechanics. If you're building a third-person action/adventure, you need to figure out how the camera is going to work. Implement the control system and combat system, figure out the world scale. When this is done, you will have a really good feel for how the game will play and feel.
>
> Once in full development, the most important thing is to figure out what your game does well and build on it. The best games are usually based on five or six play mechanics that, when combined, create the basis for the majority of the game. Essentially, stay focused! It's very easy to "feature creep."

"If you want to be a designer, there are several things you need to ask yourself," advises Patmore.

> First, do you LOVE games? You really have to eat, sleep, live games to survive in this industry. You will have no life other than games. Do you like to work long hours? The game industry is not a 9-to-5 job. It's not uncommon to work 100-hour weeks when under the gun. Do you take criticism well? If you answered "yes" to all of these questions, you may be able to survive a job in the game industry.
>
> The next step is to figure out what you want to/can do in game development. All too often I receive résumés from people who don't have the slightest idea what they want to do: "I program a little, but I want to design and do animation." Focus! Focus! Focus! The best game designers I know focus on game design. That's all they want to do. The best programmers program. Everybody has input into the game. It's important to figure out what you want to work on for the game and focus on it. The best way to get into design is to get the latest *Quake II/Unreal/Half-Life/Drakan* editor and build levels. With complete levels, you can demonstrate your ability to create 3D geometry, your mastery of level flow, creature placement, and game balance.

Surreal Software's Patmore recommends getting a prototype of your game up and running as fast as possible. "It was a snap pitching Drakan to publishers with a playable demo," says Patmore, because "there were no questions; the gameplay had been implemented." (Used with permission by Psygnosis, Inc.)

What about inspiration? Where does it come from?

> Ideas for games come from everywhere. When I play games I think, "Wouldn't it be cool if they did this?" or "Why didn't they do this?" That sort of thing. Movies, books, and simply imagination are the greatest sources of inspiration. I am always daydreaming about alternate worlds. That's how *Drakan* was created.

After *Drakan* was conceived, what was the next step in the game design process? Has the vision of the game remained the same over the past two years?

> *Drakan* has had two distinct designs. Originally it started as a fast action dragon shooter. That's right, Rynn wasn't even in the game. We chose this direction more from publisher pressure than our own creativity. Early in development, while we were creating a playable demo, we realized that the current design of the game wasn't going to have the depth that we desired. Our publisher, Virgin, was going through financial problems, and wasn't treating us very well. They eventually told us to start shopping the game around. We took this opportunity to start fresh. We redesigned the game, and the world of *Drakan* was created. We immediately created a demo demonstrating the new play mechanics, the look of the world, combat system. From there we took the play mechanics that we had established and built on them. *Drakan* was always an action game, so we focused on air combat first.
>
> After getting the flight mechanics tight and solid, we focused on the ground section of the game, i.e., Rynn's combat system. This was the most difficult part of the game to design. We chose to develop a system that had not been implemented by any other game, so we had no model to use as a baseline.

Do games need to be in 3D these days? Does a 2D game have a chance at succeeding? Patmore says games don't need to be 3D, and titles such as *Starcraft* and *Diablo* are perfect examples of 2D games that have been incredibly successful. That said, Patmore suggests the following:

> However, with 3D cards standard on all new machines, and the power and flexibility that 3D allows the development team, there's really no reason to build a game in 2D. 3D allows you to create environments that are much more immersive than 2D. After all, we live in a 3D world. There are tried-and-true 2D game mechanics that transition well into 3D. *Mario 64* is a perfect example of how 2D platform elements can work incredibly well in 3D.

Patmore says he's been an avid game player and designer since he was eight years old. (Hence the fantasy game where you can ride the back of a dragon?)

DAVID WALLS, HASBRO INTERACTIVE

As creative director at Hasbro Interactive over the past two years, David Walls had the opportunity to design and direct many games, such as *Frogger*, *Centipede*, *Game of Life*, *Jeopardy*, *Wheel of Fortune*, *Clue*, the *Tonka* series, and more.

Concerning general game design, Walls says to adhere to the following rules:

STUDY GAMES

> Don't just play games, study them. Many people play lots of games, but the key to game design is understanding them. Why do some hold you for hours while others have you running back to the store to return them? Why do some games have a look and feel that makes you want to play them, while others disgust you at first sight? The problem is that there are really no tried-and-true

rules to game design; in fact, many great games are designed by feel alone. But by studying games and trying to pick out those things that work and don't work, you can begin to develop a feel for game design. But, remember, this feel doesn't come from just playing alone; you must actively think about the design of the games, the reasons they do what they do.

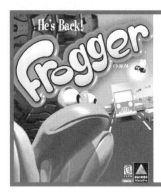

Walls and company at Hasbro Interactive decided not to toy too much with the winning formula that made the original Frogger such a hit in the arcades nearly twenty years ago. (Used with permission by Hasbro Interactive, Inc.)

In addition, don't just play one type of game, play all types. Many people are just like, "Dude, I'm an action guy," or "I only play the hardcore strategy games." I feel that you definitely limit your thinking by playing only one style of game. You can gain so much by playing lots of different games. Here at Hasbro Interactive, we work with everything from *Candyland* to *Frogger* to *Axis and Allies* to *Civilization*. It's awesome to be surrounded by so many great games because you can learn so much from different styles of game. You discover that even a game like *Sorry!* can teach you something about great multiplayer game design.

So play everything from console to PC to board, from action to strategy to family. Go from an action game like *GoldenEye* to a strategy game like *Civilization*. Think about what works with these games, find similarities. Find things that work for one type of game but not for another, and discover the reasons why. Study as many games as you can and you will begin to get the *feel*.

DEVELOP WRITTEN SKILLS

More often than not, game design ends with a design document. This is a doc that outlines the whole game: rules, style, interface, characters, story, etc. As much as possible should go into the design doc before the project begins.

This requires that game designers have good written skills, especially the ability to organize information in a document form.

DEVELOP VISUAL SKILLS

Most designers use game design docs to communicate the vision, but visual skills are very important. Now, you don't necessarily have to go out and become an artist, but the ability to draw and/or use a drawing program such as Visio is important to outline interfaces, levels, maps, character design, game structure, etc. Words are great, but a picture of how something works is always better. The ability to think visually is key.

Is it easier or more difficult to work with a well-known franchise, such as a board game, arcade game, or TV show? What are the pros and cons? Walls responds simply with the following: "It's fun to work with well-known franchises that are great games, but it's really hard work to get it right." He expands:

You would think that working with well-known franchises is easy, but they often prove to be just as challenging as developing a new game from scratch. At Hasbro Interactive, we work with many well-known games in different forms. We develop games from many sources, such as *Frogger* and *Centipede* from the arcade world, games such as *Monopoly*, *Scrabble*, and *Clue* from board games, *Jeopardy* and *Wheel of Fortune* from TV, and even *Tonka* from the world of toys. Each of these formats has its own challenges, but the trick is to remain true to the brand, the play pattern, the look and feel, while updating where necessary for the computer games market. Here are some examples and lessons learned.

ON FROGGER

Sometimes, the biggest mistake, and the one that is always easy to make, is to really "blow out" the game and try to update it too much. *Frogger*, as many remember, is really just a simple but addictive game where you hop little Frogger across the road. We were given the task of taking this game and "updating it for the 90s." Fun? Yes. Simple? No. *Frogger* started with the concept "*Frogger as Mario*"—a hop-everywhere sort of frog that you could steer in any direction. After all, who would want to play that old game as it was? We need to update the gameplay! Sounded like good strategy, but we quickly discovered that this just didn't feel right. It just didn't have the frantic *Frogger* feel. So we said okay, let's give him an eight-way hop! That sounded good—Marketing could probably put it on the box: "*Frogger*! Now with Eight-Way Hop!"—and it would make the game feel updated. But even that just didn't work gameplay-wise to allow Frogger to hop diagonally. So we made the grand leap—do nothing. Stick to the basics: forward, backward, left, and right, and keep the levels in a grid format. And that did the trick—it was *Frogger*! (of course).

But the big question was, "Would people still want to play a game with these simple controls?" After selling a million-plus copies, the answer was definitely "YES!" and there was a reason for that. A game like *Frogger*, that has simple, addictive gameplay, is still a blast to play!

There were many lessons learned from creating *Frogger*. First, when dealing with classic properties, sometimes it's best to stick with the core gameplay and resist the urge to fit it into today's gameplay design. Second, as more people get computers, the audience for computer games is becoming wider, and games that have a combination of ease of use, ease of control, and simple, yet addictive gameplay patterns have the potential to become huge.

ON JEOPARDY AND WHEEL OF FORTUNE

> TV shows and movies have their own set of challenges. The primary urge is to re-create the show on the computer. For example, with game shows, you would get video contestants, do lots of different cuts, shoot lots of video, make a full-blown interactive television show. When we started *Jeopardy* and *Wheel of Fortune*, I'm sure we would have gone down this route had it not been for two games: the previous computer rendition of *Jeopardy*, and *You Don't Know Jack*.
>
> When we started, we sat and played each game. In the old *Jeopardy*, the game tries to mimic the show and features video contestants. But since you're playing the game through characters, you never really feel "in the game." It just didn't flow. *You Don't Know Jack*, on the other hand, talks to you. It's first person. You are the contestant. You are playing. Everything is directed at you as "the player." We quickly arrived at the conclusion that the *Jack* format was the way to go with the new *Jeopardy* and *Wheel of Fortune*.
>
> But wouldn't people want that "watching the TV show" experience? Don't we need video contestants? Don't we need Vanna spinning the letters? The answer was no, people want to play the game, and they don't want to watch TV when they're playing a game. Beyond being great TV, *Jeopardy* and *Wheel* are awesome games, tons of fun to play, and anything that gets in the way of that game-playing experience just gets in the way. So our direction was: These are not the television shows, these games are computer games. Approach it from the point of view that the game knows it's a game and it knows that the players playing are sitting around a computer. Avoid anything that bogs down the game.
>
> This approach freed us from many binds. By relying on the power of the games themselves, we didn't need lots of video footage, we didn't need video contestants, we didn't need tons of bells and whistles, we didn't even need Vanna spinning the letters (fun to watch on TV, but murderous to game pacing). This approach allowed us to make very playable games.
>
> Lesson learned: When designing games, always look at it from the player's point of view. Avoid anything that doesn't support the gameplay. Make things "player focused."

In conclusion for this thought, Walls says while it's challenging getting the right mix of brand essence, gameplay, and look and feel, working with these *old* games is great fun and a real gamer education. Says Walls: "There is a reason why these properties are still around; they're all simply amazing games!"

Walls was asked how he and the creative folks at Hasbro Interactive come up with new games. That is, are they brainstormed in a meeting or individually conceived? Walls says both, "but it's good to go to many sources for inspiration." What sources?

> **Other games:** Depending on the genre for which you're making the game, it's good to immerse yourself just playing games in that genre to get you in the right frame of mind. But instead of just jumping into making the game, question everything about the current games. Try to go beyond the current thinking.

This is always hard to do. Sometimes it helps to do crazy mental exercises to free your mind. For example, "I'm making a first-person shooter; what if I had to do that without any weapons?"

Other people: Get a bunch of people together and brainstorm. Believe it or not, at this point, include everyone: producers, programmers, sales, marketing, executives, anyone with ideas. But always start the meeting by saying that this is a brainstorming meeting. No bad ideas, but also no decisions. It's just an "idea collection factory." These type of meetings are great, but you want to avoid designing by committee.

Hard thinking: Most great ideas come from just plain hard mental work. It's good to lock yourself up in a quiet room with a pad and pencil and just think. Image what the game will be like from the title screen on. Think about characters. Think about gameplay mechanics. Try to think of the game as a whole entity. And then challenge your assumptions. Got something good? Try to make it incredible. Got something incredible? Shoot for amazingly amazing.

What is Walls' take on 2D versus 3D? He retorts: "3D only matters if you need 3D to make a great game. Can a 2D game make it in [2000]? If it's a great game, yes."

So why do people tend to run to 3D? According to Walls, it depends on the genre and demographic: "Action currently is about 3D. Strategy can take or leave it. Families don't want 3D because they typically don't have the hardware to run it."

And finally, what about multiplayer gaming? A must-have these days? "Again, depends on the game," answers Walls. He continues:

There will always be an audience for the single-player game. If *Half-Life* had shipped without multiplayer, it probably would still have been successful, because the game was about an action/adventure story. The multiplayer to that game was just a bonus. But other games are beginning to be defined as multiplayer-focused games, such as *Quake III: Arena*. It's all about the online competition.

David Walls says his future aspirations are to continue to make top-quality games for Hasbro Interactive—and along the way, add some original games to the mix.

JAY WILSON, MONOLITH PRODUCTIONS

Monolith's Jay Wilson, who was responsible in part for games such as *Shogo: Mobile Armor Division* and the *Blood* series, had plenty of axioms to share with newbie designers when asked "What makes a great PC game?" These assorted pointers are as follows:

1. Play a lot of games, understand them, and love them. "This seems obvious," begins Wilson, but says it's a necessity. "If you don't, and all [involved] don't, then there will be an imbalance in the group; you all have to have the passion to take it one step further. The gaming industry is very competitive and everyone must want to do it."

2. You *can* improve on a good thing. Wilson draws the analogy to movies, where there are large categories, such as action, drama, or comedy, but the implementation of each is very different (slapstick comedies, dark comedies, dry comedies, and so on).

> It's a young industry, so everyone has their own idea on reinventing the wheel. It's evolutionary, not revolutionary. With *Blood 2*, we added RPG elements to the action game genre; with *Shogo: Mobile Armor Division*, it was an animé element to the action game genre.

3. More importantly, ask yourself what's realistic. Mirroring other designers' opinions in this chapter, Wilson says it's key to understand whether you can realistically pull off what you plan to do. "You may want to make an online role-playing game—do you have the resources to do it and compete against others? You either have to scrap your idea if it's not realistic, or change the idea."

4. And finally, "Organization is key. I can't stress this enough," asserts Wilson. "I believe in that saying, 'work better, not harder.' Know exactly what you're going to do when you're making a game, and everything will run much smoother."

JON ZUK, RAVEN SOFTWARE

Gathered from his experience as lead designer on *Heretic II* and as one of the creators of the controversial *Soldier of Fortune*, Zuk says he certainly has some advice to pass onto junior designers. He offers these three quick pointers:

> I believe that the number one thing to keep in mind when creating a game is whether or not it's fun. No matter how good your idea or how many little extras you manage to stuff into your game, if it's not fun, it won't last. We spent time every step of the way to ensure that *Heretic II* would be fun. We had focus groups on the character, we tested key configurations, we tweaked the camera over and over, and so on. We as a development team knew that it wasn't the hook that was ultimately going to make the game successful, but the fun factor. The hook only gets people looking at it and trying it out. People most likely aren't going to play *Broccoli 2000: The Garden Simulation*, because it doesn't sound fun.
>
> You'll notice that I brought up the word "hook." While fun is most important of all, the hook is probably second. What's going to make people look at your game over the other 4,000 on the market? If you really think about it, there aren't a lot of original game ideas out there. So how do you make it stand out from the other 20 *Quake*-killers, or 50 racing games, or 100 real-time strategy games? The hook. Games always need a hook and a style of play that people can relate to. Take for example *Heretic II*. The hook is that it's a third-person action game. It's not *Tomb Raider*, and it's not *Quake*. The style, though, is closer to *Quake*, and people can relate to it.

Finally, after you know (or think you know) your game will be fun, and you've got that perfect product hook, you need a team. Team chemistry is very important. At Raven, almost everyone gets along well with each other. If there is someone who doesn't, at least everyone is professional. I've heard and read stories about other companies that have terrible chemistry. There's constant infighting, the managers yell at everyone, and no one wants to work. This causes schedules to slip, and the game to suffer as a whole. If you're going to put a team together to make your dream game, make sure you can put up with them for a year or more.

"For a bad team-chemistry example," concludes Zuk, "go to www.dallasobserver.com for a story on ION Storm."

STRATEGY GAMES

SID MEIER, FIRAXIS GAMES

There is a very good reason why Sid Meier is one of the most accomplished and respected game designers in the business. He has pioneered the industry with a number of unprecedented instant classics, such as the very first combat flight simulator, *F-15 Strike Eagle*, then *Pirates*, *Railroad Tycoon*, and of course, a game often voted number one game of all time, *Civilization*. Meier has contributed to a number of chapters in this book, but here he offers a few words on game inspiration.

"Find something you as a designer are excited about," begins Meier. "If not, it will likely show through your work." Meier also reminds designers that this is a project that they'll be working on for about two years, and designers have to ask themselves if this is something they want to work on every day for that length of time. From a practical point of view, Meier says, you "probably don't want to get into a genre that is overly exhausted."

To Meier, it all boils back down to passion:

What do you get excited about and what are you good at? Do an RPG, not an action shooter just because it's in style. Perhaps find something new and fresh—publishers want to be leading edge, too, so they're usually receptive to new ideas. But remember, for every 20 guys who walk into the door, maybe only two ideas are worth considering.

Meier's last two releases were *Gettysburg!* and most recently, *Alpha Centauri*. Be sure to flip to the chapters on user interface (12), testing (15), and breaking into the industry (20) for more from Meier.

PETER MOLYNEUX, LIONHEAD STUDIOS

Peter Molyneux is a household name for hardcore gamers because of his string of continuous successes at Bullfrog Productions. At this U.K. development studio, Molyneux served as a game designer, programmer, and often producer for the following international hits: 1989's *Populous*, 1990's *Powermonger*, 1991's *Populous 2*, 1993's *Syndicate*, 1994's *Theme Park* and *Magic Carpet*, and last, 1997's *Dungeon Keeper*. His number one current aspiration is to make Lionhead Studios' first release, *Black & White*, "the best computer game ever."

When asked to offer advice for budding game designers, Molyneux responds with the following:

> The art of game design is not so difficult as people might imagine. The first piece of advice I would give anyone designing a game is use every source of inspiration available to you—from films, books, and music to everyday life. For example, I got the initial inspiration for *Dungeon Keeper* after seeing the films *Pulp Fiction* and *Interview with the Vampire*, where the bad guy was the hero. Once I've been inspired and have the idea, then I always spend at least six months turning it around in my head. Personally, I never write anything down; once I do that, it seems to solidify, and I'd rather keep it developing until I'm completely happy with it. Once this happens, I write down the idea, keeping to two pages and just listing the exciting parts of the game. (If you need more than two pages to do this, your idea is too bulky.) Only at this stage do I feel ready to reveal my idea to friends and colleagues, and if they're excited by that idea then I know I'm onto a good thing. In conclusion, I would point out that my game ideas are evolutionary, as they grow as the game is developed.

For more from Molyneux on breaking into the industry, see Chapter 20.

RICK GOODMAN, STAINLESS STEEL STUDIOS

While at Ensemble Studios, a company formed in 1995 with his brother Tony, Rick Goodman was the lead designer on the tremendously popular *Age of Empires* for Microsoft. He has since left to form another development house, Stainless Steel Studios, and is currently working on an epic real-time strategy (RTS) game known as *Empire Earth*.

Goodman offers us his "Ten Commandments of RTS Game Design," here in its entirety. Thou shalt pay attention:

THE HEALTHIEST PLANTS HAVE THE STRONGEST ROOTS

Goodman says to know your roots, whether they're comic books, sci-fi, board games, puzzles, toy soldiers, chess, *Dungeons & Dragons*, or anything else, for that matter.

PAPER NEVER REFUSES INK

The key here is how to separate your good ideas from bad, otherwise known as the ol' "Hey—I have this great idea for a strategy game."

Goodman says anyone can write a good design document, but there are four keys to success: Play the game through in your head, model everything in a spreadsheet, prototype user interfaces, and compose your "strike team" of play testers. In fact, Goodman used the Internet to recruit 12 savvy *Age of Empires* players and uses them all the time for guidance on *Empire Earth*, and to flush out bad ideas. Goodman reminds designers to welcome advice from others, with the adage "It's hard to see the picture when you are inside the frame."

A PERSON WHO WALKS IN ANOTHER'S TRACKS LEAVES NO FOOTPRINTS

To innovate or to clone? Goodman reminds budding designers that we tend to criticize clones, then religiously follow up with new ones. He cites a phrase coined by Sid Meier, "innovative continuity," who came up with this term to not preclude him from doing anything he wanted. "Balance is key—add some innovative new things but make players comfortable in the game's surroundings so that they understand the rules and won't have to read the manual."

Finally, Goodman says to "enhance the positive, eliminate the negative, and don't fiddle with the middle."

If a game is too realistic, does it take away from the fun factor? Goodman pokes fun at his own Age of Empires by asking "Where are the women? Doesn't anyone eat food?" and "Soldiers always fight to the death?" (Used with permission by Ensemble Studios, Inc.)

IF I REALLY WANTED REALITY, WOULD I HAVE BOOTED UP THE COMPUTER?

The point of this commandment is to reinforce the fun factor over reality. Goodman refers to *Computer Gaming World* magazine polls that suggest fantasy strategy games are often more popular than historical or reality-based ones. He reminds game designers that even though *Age of Empires* is a historical strategy game, not everything is realistic: priest conversions, moving catapults, naval units attacking land units, and so forth.

IF I HAD BEEN PRESENT AT CREATION, I WOULD HAVE GIVEN SOME USEFUL HINTS

Goodman advises knowing your limits—look at yourself, try to recognize your strengths and passions, and take advantage of them. For example, Goodman knew his knowledge of board games was very strong when he approached *Age of Empires*.

BY THE MILE IT'S A TRIAL, BY THE INCH IT'S A CINCH

Creating a game usually follows a top-down methodology, with game vision on top of the pyramid, game ideas and features in the middle, and low-level game mechanics on the bottom. Goodman explains:

> There *is* a method to this process. The top is where the vision is generated (e.g. "How about a game where you're on a desert island?), the middle is the game's features ("And this is what we'll do on this island") and the bottom, the most crucial out of the three, is how to implement these ideas in the game.

According to Goodman, many game designers concentrate too much on the top two levels and not enough on how the play mechanics will work in the game. "The bottom level is the hardest; the implementation of the details is key," says Goodman. He also says most design docs seem to rely on the first two levels, when the emphasis should be on the implementation of the ideas into the computer and not just the ideas themselves.

TAKE NOTE OF THE FUTURE; YOU ARE GOING TO HAVE TO SPEND THE REST OF YOUR LIFE THERE

Basically, Goodman says for the RTS genre to move forward, there has to be more to the game, and not just more of the same. He cites 3D action shooters as a genre that has evolved graphically, but not in gameplay, barring a few recent exceptions. With RTS games, try to foresee what will come down the pike and work toward bettering the genre.

TREES THAT ARE SLOW TO GROW BEAR THE BEST FRUIT

"Time is your friend," says Goodman. "Use your project schedule well. *Age of Empires* was a 1,000-day project; 500 of those were spent internally at Ensemble Studios, the other half play testing by Microsoft.

"Beware—the only thing that can kill a good game is a great game." Be realistic at the beginning of your project and keep in mind many of the great RTS games, such as *Starcraft* and *Age of Empires*, took longer than average to complete, but look at the outcome!

COMMUNICATE YOUR VISION

One of the most important considerations while developing a game is communication. This is not only between a designer and his team, but between a designer and publisher, the public, marketing, game critics, and testers.

NEVER PUT A GLAZED DONUT ON A MOUSE PAD

"...and other lessons learned the hard way," says Goodman. Some of his other lessons are "Schedules are not more important than quality," and "'Let's not tell them and maybe they won't find out' always backfires; it's no different than when you were a kid."

For more information on Empire Earth and the design team at Stainless Steel Studios, visit www.stainlesssteelstudios.com.

BRUCE C. SHELLEY, ENSEMBLE STUDIOS

Bruce Shelley is a senior game designer at Ensemble Studios who helped shape the mega-successful *Age of Empires* series. Prior to moving to Ensemble Studios, he co-designed many games at Microprose, including *Railroad Tycoon*, *Covert Action*, and the one and only *Civilization*, alongside Sid Meier.

Before diving into game design advice, Shelley was asked to discuss how he goes about researching a game, such as *Age of Empires I* and *II*. (Ever see the bibliographical references in the game?) Must it cost a lot of money? Shelley responds with the following retort:

> For most games, don't go into great detail in your game. Don't try to amaze gamers with your deep knowledge. The player should have the fun, not the designer or researcher. The information in your game should be at a level of detail accessible by the average person. I begin researching games in the children's section of the local library. This works because children's books include a lot of graphics and computer games are intensely graphical. You can pick up graphic hints as well as research information. The level of detail regarding history presented in children's books is very well suited for mass market games. If you want to do a detailed simulation for only the hardcore, then you have to dig into more detailed sources. Eventually I do read a lot of adult books as well, to help with the overall understanding of events and the period.
>
> Research should not cost a lot of money. Microprose had a very limited budget for books and other sources. I learned this business making do with what I could find at the library. Ensemble Studios has been much more willing to buy books and videotapes to help our designers and animators. We have two bookshelves full of resources for *Age of Empires II*.

Shelley believes too much research is definitely a risk because people have preconceptions of historic topics based on movies and TV, in large part. If you stray too far from that paradigm, you risk frustrating them. The following is an expansion of this suggestion, and an example:

> When the game plays differently from what they expect, they're confused and begin to question the game. Always give precedence to creating fun over re-creating history. That's the clear lesson of entertainment media, especially movies and TV.
>
> An example from *Age of Empires* would be the catapult unit, which is able to move and fire with an area effect. There was nothing like this in ancient times, to my knowledge, but it worked for our game and stayed in. Also in *Age of Empires*, we adjusted the range, number of attacks, and movement of the different units so that there were interesting relationships between the units. We approached this balancing from the play test side, not by calculating real ranges and movement speeds. Flight sims designed for fun usually compress the time flying from base to dogfight and back because that's no fun. They

usually also allow the player to carry way more fuel and ammunition than they do historically. This is to emphasize the fun part of play, which is combat, versus just flying in formation for hours to the engagement.

I reminded Shelley that it can be quite intimidating as a new designer to create a game with so many great titles on the market. Is there any advice he can give to ensure success? Shelley offers this assorted collection of general game design tips:

Design games that you want to play and hope that a million people or more have the same taste.

Try to make the game attractive to both hardcore and casual gamers; hardcore people create the buzz, but the big sales come from the casual market. Blood, gore, and foul language kill much of the casual gamer interest, and severely limit the potential sales of your game.

Provide the player with interesting decisions, not trivial or random ones. This is the essence of gameplay.

Analyze what the competition is doing very well and plan how you will meet or exceed them; determine where the competition is weak and plan how you can be very strong in those areas. For *Age of Empires*, we determined that none of the other RTS games had a non-cheating AI, random maps, or multiple victory conditions. Including those features in our game helped differentiate our product and went a long way toward creating the perception of value that made *Age of Empires* successful.

Avoid random events that adversely impact a player. These just increase frustration and add very little of interest.

Work toward two goals: maximum player fun (gameplay) and minimum player frustration (random events, poor interface, bugs).

And finally, Shelley's last truism is possibly the most poignant:

A new design (perhaps not a franchise sequel) has to have a great first 15 minutes. *Age of Empires* did, but many of our competitors didn't.

When it comes to balancing units in a real-time strategy game, are there any do's and don'ts a new game designer should bear in mind? Answers Shelley:

There are no real do's and don'ts. You simply rely on your instincts and thousands of hours of testing by different types of game players. Fix things people complain about, and leave things alone where they don't. If people don't find a unit useful, you improve it. If everyone wants to use only one unit, you scale back its effectiveness. We use this evolutionary process because it gives us the best chance of developing a game that's a lot of fun to play and is deep. The downside of this process is that it's very hard to predict. We don't know when we'll be done until we get very close to being finished. For most publishers, this is unacceptable because they must plan ahead for marketing, advertising, budgets, etc.

For *Age of Empires II*, we wrote a small routine that lets us quickly set up battles between different types of units. They fight it out in high speed and we quickly get empirical evidence of how they fight against each other. It can be a difficult problem to solve when you see A always defeat B one-on-one but 10 B's always defeat 10 A's.

Strategy game designers interested in learning more about unit balancing should read Chapter 9 for additional advice on this important matter.

BRIAN REYNOLDS, BIG HUGE GAMES

"Okay, here are a few general thoughts," begins Brian Reynolds, former vice president of software development of Firaxis Games. Before leaving the company in early 2000 to start his own development studio, Big Huge Games, Reynolds' first release at Firaxis was the highly-anticipated *Sid Meier's Alpha Centauri*. Reynolds breaks down his advice into three main compartments:

Being a professional game designer (probably much like being a professional anything) is not nearly so *difficult* as you might think; it's more a question of scale and the amount of time you put into it. If you're good with a computer, you can probably already write a simple and fun game in a weekend or a week. Now imagine hiring 10 more people and spending an extra year or two polishing it—that's really the main difference between doing it strictly for fun and doing it for both fun and profit. So all of the tricks that professional game designers use work just as well for games written at home. In fact, you have a lot of advantages—the most successful professional game designers are usually the ones who both design the games and write the code personally. If you've got a cool idea for a game, no one can bring it to life the way you can.

Secondly, Reynolds says to get in there and make something you can play right away. He expands:

Don't try to write everything out on paper or make fake interface screens, thinking you'll come back and write some code for it later. Try to put something simple together that you can actually *play* right from the very beginning. Play your game and see which parts are fun, what the strong and weak areas are. Then get back into the code, improve the strong points, and eliminate the weak points (or sometimes start all over with a different idea entirely). At Firaxis, we created a working prototype in the first few weeks of a project, and then [would] play-and-revise-and-play-and-revise-and-play-and-revise for the rest of the project. We called this "prototyping" and the "iterative design process," and it really works. If you want to end up with a game that's really fun, there's no substitute for playing it yourself.

His third and final piece of advice covers the fun factor, interaction, and challenges:

One way to describe a computer game is "a series of interesting decisions." Computer games are so much fun because they allow us to interact with a story rather than simply sit passively and receive it; so when you're creating a game, try to present the player with lots of opportunities to react. I've seen lots of games, even some famous ones, make the mistake of creating an elaborate "game system" that nonetheless leaves the player with nothing important to do. If a game spends most of its time performing elaborate calculations to simulate complex events, but doesn't spend much time allowing the player to participate and control the process, we say that "the computer is having all the fun," and that's bad—the player isn't getting to make enough interesting choices. Likewise, if a game leads you along one particular linear path, essentially forcing you to make particular decisions in order to succeed, we say that "the game designer is having all the fun," and that's bad too, since a decision where A is always the right answer is really a non-decision, and isn't much fun. That's why we say a game needs to be a series of interesting decisions. When you present the player with three different options, each option should be a plausible path, and you should be able to succeed and win (at least sometimes) using each option. If you present your players with the choice "Fight, Bribe, or Flee," then each choice should lead to victory in at least some circumstances. The best games allow the player to call the shots: The *player* picks a strategy, and then makes choices to bring his or her goals to fruition. If your game can be won using not just one, but a whole variety of strategies, people will want to play it more than once.

As you can see in the bio appendix at the end of this book, Brian Reynold's computer mastery is all self-taught.

TREVOR CHAN, ENLIGHT SOFTWARE

Hong Kong's own Trevor Chan founded Enlight Software in 1993. Under his leadership, the company has received numerous accolades from the industry and has become one of the world's leading developers of strategy and simulation games, with its *Seven Kingdoms* series and *Capitalism* franchise, respectively.

Chan takes some time out of his busy schedule to contribute some of his commandments of good game design:

First, a game designer shall have a vision of the game design at the outset and shall follow it through. Next, a game designer shall not be afraid to innovate and scrap ideas that initially look promising but then turn out to be bad ones after implementation. And thirdly, a game designer shall have a firm belief in his own design when the game is still in its infancy.

To support his advice, Chan was asked if he could provide examples from his own experience at Enlight Software:

When I started developing *Capitalism*, I wanted it to be the most realistic business simulation game ever made. I made no compromises along the way and maintained the insistence on the realism of the game. The game ended up not only winning the acceptance of gamers but educational professionals who have elected to use the game for teaching proposes in such respectable institutions as Harvard and Stanford universities.

The *Capitalism* development was an experience that I found extremely valuable for learning how business activities can be simulated in a game. The attempts to simulate some businesses were successful and they became part of the final product. However, a considerable number of attempts to simulate businesses (like banking) were not equally successful and they were eventually scrapped after implementation. A game developer shall not be deterred by his inability to turn a game idea into fun gameplay. Instead, he shall only become more eager to innovate and come up with new ideas, as the past failure experiences actually mean elimination of impossibilities and increase of odds of success for new ideas.

On his third commandment on believing in one's own ability, Chan recalls:

Due to their complexity, *Capitalism* and *Seven Kingdoms* did not get all of their pieces glued and work well together until very late in their development. Prior to that, many people were skeptical of these games' playability and negative comments were not uncommon. With firm beliefs in my design, I was able to follow through on my vision without changing the core elements of the game design.

But where exactly does a game designer look for inspiration? Chan says a game designer should not be bound by the hot trend of the day, or any other existing frameworks of game design. He elucidates:

Although it is natural to relate a new game to an existing game or genre, a new game does not necessarily have to fit into any of the existing genres or feature gameplay that most gamers are familiar with. Currently, I am working on a university simulation game called *Virtual U* that is unlike anything else on the market. The game puts the player into the role of a university president and challenges the player on issues like student life and academic performance. From a traditional perspective, few game designers will choose a subject like this for a game. However, with the thought that this game may not be played by the average hardcore gamer, but by university faculty, the idea of introducing gaming to the academic community and allowing people to use it as a tool to learn [how to run] a university is indeed an exciting one.

Finally, Chan was asked what's most lacking with today's PC and/or console games. He responds as follows:

In my opinion, games these days lack diversity. While there are a great number of titles released each year, they get increasingly similar to each other. *Tomb Raider* clones and *Diablo* clones alone account for a big percentage of the releases. To address this problem, more independent developers must be able to get their non-mainstream games published. For this to happen, game developers must be able to get access to game distribution independently, without the blessings of big publishers. Distributing games via the Internet is one of the hopes. While it is still premature, the hope is highly promising and I continue to look forward to its full realization.

To learn more on releasing your game via the Internet, turn to Chapter 19.

CHRIS TAYLOR, GAS POWERED GAMES

By the time Chris Taylor launched his own company, Gas Powered Games, he had been in the gaming industry over 11 years, working at Electronic Arts for most of this time. Five years ago, he hooked up with Ron Gilbert to begin work on *Total Annihilation* at Cavedog Entertainment. Now, he's hard at work on *Dungeon Siege*, a strategy game to be published by Microsoft sometime in 2001.

Though he was on his vacation in his native province of British Columbia, Taylor was eager to share his knowledge on game design, inspiration, and how to become market sensitive. He begins as follows:

> Well, the first [principle] has to be an overall vision of the game that they're about to design. It's really hard to design something if you just have the mandate to make a great game. The second is that implementation is very important and that you have to find the right team of people to build the game. Third is understanding a long list of principles when designing. Principles like not designing it all up front, working with the team, experimentation, paying attention to the market, breaking some rules, not being afraid of copying what the competition has proven to be fun, and not being afraid of throwing stuff away if it [stinks]!

On inspiration, Taylor says that it often comes from the gamer inside of yourself:

> What do you like? What makes you nuts? How could you change something to make it better? I play games and always ask myself those basic questions. I also try to learn from movies, books, and music. These are areas where artists struggle to create new ideas, tell new stories, or evoke emotions that have never been felt before.

Taylor offers the genesis of *Total Annihilation* as an example:

> After playing *Command & Conquer*, I wanted to do an RTS game, but in 3D. I didn't know how much of the game would run in 3D at the time but I knew that if I could get the units to render at any angle, then things like being able to shoot while retreating would be possible. I also knew that if the units were 3D, I could have many more of them in memory than if they were all pre-rendered bitmaps.
>
> When I told Ron [Gilbert] about the idea, he immediately liked it and supported the project by having me join Humongous [Entertainment, Cavedog's sister company] and start working on it.

Kirkland, Washington's Gas Powered Games was founded in May 1998 by Chris Taylor, creator of the award-winning Total Annihilation. Its first release is a fantasy strategy epic, dubbed Dungeon Siege, to be published by Microsoft in 2001. For more images, visit the game's official site at www.dungeonsiege.com. (Used with permission by Microsoft Corp.)

Being market sensitive is often an important determinant of a game's success, believes Taylor, and he explains how to achieve this without having to compromise the designer's original vision.

> Well, first of all, let's define "market sensitive." I see this as meaning "paying attention to what people are buying, what people are ignoring, and an extra sensory perception of what people might want if it were there to buy."
>
> I think if you have a strong vision of the product you want to build, nothing will get in the way. Even a market with a constantly shifting focus.
>
> I don't think it will ever pay to jump off the deep end and deliver a new experience that's so alien that [players] can't relate. Creating a means of allowing the gamer to relate to the game is one of the most important things that a designer should keep in mind. People need to feel comfortable with what they're seeing and interacting with.

Taylor was reminded that this book was meant to also cater to budding game designers with little or no money. How can someone begin building his/her development team on a shoestring budget? Answers Taylor:

> Well, if you have no money, then everyone involved should have another job to pay the rent, and a lot of spare time afterwards to devote to the project. If you have that, then you have a chance.
>
> Someone on the team should have the vision, someone else should be an ace at code, and someone else should kick some huge butt in the art department. Sound is important but that can come later, and be d--- sure they know what they're doing, because nothing can make a game come alive like sound and music.
>
> When you're working on something on the sly, you'll need to have something special, something that's brilliant and that makes the difference in a way that high production values won't. Think of an art film that captures the imagination of the audience for $100 grand, not $100 million. Even when you're in the business, you need to come up with tricks to cut corners and make a thousand dollars look like something that cost ten times that. Heck, I think that's where the magic can come from. A limited budget can help to focus you on the game experience and not all the expensive fluff that so many games have.

Taylor's extensive history is documented in the biography appendix. Betcha didn't know he worked on the first *Triple Play Baseball*.

ALEX GARDEN, RELIC ENTERTAINMENT

At barely 25 years old, Alex Garden has already been in the industry for 10 years as a game designer and programmer for a number of titles at Distinctive Software, EA Sports, Radical Entertainment, and, most recently, at Relic Entertainment, where Alex sits as the CEO and design director for the *PC Gamer* "Best Game of 1999," *Homeworld*. Published by Sierra Studios in the fall of 1999, *Homeworld* has won over 50 awards in total.

In the following passage, Garden talks about general game design concepts and how they helped him create such internationally renowned products.

THE TEAM

> I guess the first thing is to remember that you're part of a team. You have to understand the strengths and weakness of each person you work with. You have to understand how to create an environment where each person can excel and where each person can feel respected. Without that kind of development environment, people invariably feel a lack of enthusiasm and a lack of ownership on the product.
>
> If I look back at the development of *Homeworld*, the foremost reason it was a success was the team that built it. The commitment to excellence that the *Homeworld* team aspired to was really quite incredible, and that kind of focus is where truly great games come from.

THE FUN FACTOR

> Secondly, you have to understand that what's fun for you isn't necessarily fun for gamers. Know your market—what they like and dislike, what they buy and what sits on the shelf. Then it's simple: Give the people what they want! The most successful games are the ones that understand their market, and cater directly to their market. If you're an artiste, you're going to be critically acclaimed but you're going to sell very few units. If you're a game designer, and you know your market, you're going to be very successful.
>
> With *Homeworld*, I think the fun aspect speaks for itself. It's fine to say, "Well, the game isn't fun now, but you just wait till it's done! It's going to rule!" but there comes a point at which you have to ask yourself "Is this still a good idea?" This is probably the hardest *and* most vital part of the process. I think that the best game designers are the ones who can objectively ask themselves this question.

VISION

> Finally, understand your vision, and know your limitations. If you don't feel like you can clearly articulate every point of your idea, then spend more time with it. Write it down, and try to approach your design problems from more than one area. Listen to your team (this is where the respect issue comes in). Chances are, they're going to solve most of your problems for you. The best advice I've ever received is "Figure out what you're good at, assume you're lousy at everything else, hire people to do all the things you're lousy at, and get out of their way."

Even though Homeworld was a relatively diffi-cult game and was a true "genre-buster" by fus-ing various kinds of gameplay together, it still went on to sell over 500,000 units within six months of its release. (Homeworld is a regis-tered trademark of Sierra On-Line, Inc. Images used with permission. Copyright 1999-2000 Sierra On-Line, Inc. All Rights Reserved.)

" This is the "glue" that binds the team together. Fortunately, at Relic we have a culture where every person can contribute to the direction of the game. Particularly on *Homeworld*, that culture was one of the main reasons the game ended up being so deep. The real trick is to have a culture that allows this kind of collaboration while ensuring that one person is the driver behind the process. One person has the totally uncompromising vision for the prod-uct. At Relic, we call this vision "The Thread." The Thread is the thing from which all answers regarding the game flow. It could be a piece of music, it could be an image, it could be a story, whatever. The most important part about this Thread concept is that you can point to it, and say "That's *Homeworld*." For us it was the theme song for *Homeworld* that really defined the feel of the game. "

Finally, Garden was asked if he could cite any recent technological and/or design innovations in the gaming industry. He answers, "Clearly the biggest recent inno-vation in design and technology has been the nearly universal move to 3D gam-ing." He continues, "We're also seeing huge advances in AI, sound, and scope of games." Garden also says a close second on the innovation side (and one that's becoming more and more important) is the online, Internet component of today's games.

In Chapter 20, Garden also offers his insight on how to be best equipped to score a job at a game developer, such as Relic Entertainment.

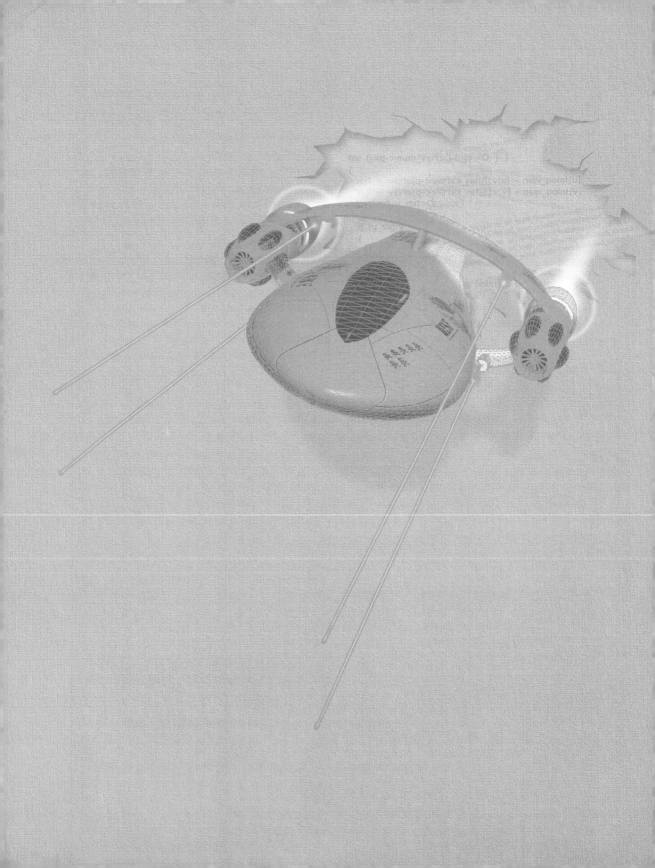

CHAPTER 3
GENERAL GAME DESIGN: ADVENTURE, RPG, SPORTS, PUZZLES, AND SIMS

This chapter continues the discussion of general game design and inspiration from Chapter 2, heading into the rest of the game genres: adventure, role-playing games, sports, puzzles, and simulations.

ADVENTURE GAMES

HUBERT CHARDOT, GAMESQUAD

You may not be familiar with Chardot's name, but this French game designer was responsible for one of the most celebrated PC adventure games of the 1990s: *Alone in the Dark*. After designing for Infogrames for five years, Chardot left in 1997 to launch Gamesquad (founded with three of his close friends). Most recently, Chardot was a consultant on *Alone in the Dark 4*, *The Ring,* and *Faust*, while working on his own projects, *Devil Inside* and *Agartha*, a future Dreamcast game to be released sometime in 2001.

Chardot was asked to explain to budding adventure game designers what's important about the craft and what isn't. He responds as follows:

> First, it seems to me important to describe and show a strong and powerful universe where the gamer will have pleasure and emotions to visit, experiment, and interact with. Second, the challenges the gamer have to succeed must remain clear and simple to understand, but surprising. I always try to be the first player (in my mind) of the game I write...if I'm astonished by the story I write, it's supposed (but only supposed) to be good. Third, try to do your best, and if you're lucky and work with a good team, you could (maybe) make something good.

Are there any examples from Chardot's history that reflect this advice? On puzzles that should be "clear and simple to understand," Chardot explains that in *Alone in the Dark 2*, Carnby (the hero of the game) was supposed to get into a locked door and Chardot devised a puzzle that he thought was simple enough to figure out. He was wrong. Recalls Chardot, "The guys at Infogrames' help line had hated me for weeks, especially in the U.S., because no one was able to figure this one out."

Chardot thinks back further to the team vibe while creating the original *Alone in the Dark*:

> The first game was a piece of cake to write...there was no tension between the team members; every guy and girl really wanted to do their best, not for their ego but for the sake of the game. This particular state of mind created a very challenging mood and the gamers must have felt that while playing the game. In a way, the game absorbs the atmosphere created by a team. I'll never forget when Philippe Vacher (the sound designer) had come with the sound of the riot gun reload click, [co-designer] Frederick Raynal and I were mad about this metallic noise and the *blaaam* produced when you press the trigger, not to mention the animation of the zombie dying. At that moment, we had felt something different happen to us, something important: The game was more than we planned. It instantly became more than the sum of our time, work, and stress.

In Chapter 8, Chardot offers a few programming tips for novice coders.

As with his thriller Alone in the Dark, Chardot's next project, dubbed Devil Inside, will be a third-person perspective action thriller set in a haunted mansion. Get more info at www.gamesquad.fr. (Used with permission by Gamesquad, Inc.)

BOB BATES, LEGEND ENTERTAINMENT

Legend Entertainment studio head Bob Bates started his career in 1986 writing games for Infocom, the popular computer game company that specialized in text adventures. Since then, he has written many award-winning graphical adventures, including *Eric The Unready* and, most recently, *John Saul's Blackstone Chronicles*.

In the following composition, Bates divulges his strategies and secrets for creating successful adventure games:

ENTERTAIN THE PLAYER FROM MOMENT TO MOMENT

> The worst crime you can commit as a game designer is to bore the player. More specifically:
>
> a) Don't make the player perform a complex action twice. Once he has completed the steps to a puzzle, if he needs to do it again give him a single input that will perform the entire sequence. I'll give you two examples:

If you have a combination lock on a safe, once the player has opened it the first time, don't make him reenter the combination thereafter. Just give him an "Open safe" command.

If you've created a maze that takes a 20-move sequence to get to the center and recover the sacred *foo*, when the player starts to go out, take him all the way out automatically. Don't make him go through that 20-move sequence in reverse. And if he decides he wants to go back into the maze later, take him right to the center.

b) Don't create long action sequences where the player has to do a bunch of tricky stuff without being able to save, and then, if he fails, make him go back and do it all again.

c) Make it easy for the player to move around. If you have large environments, build in shortcuts to get from one end to the other, and don't design your puzzles so the player has to continuously crisscross your world.

d) Similarly, if you have rendered transitions in the game, let the player hit the Escape key or right-click to bypass them. There's nothing worse than being forced to sit through the same cut-scene over and over. God gave us the Escape key for a reason. Use it. And restarting the game is another spot where we often cause the player tedium. I know you've created the most beautiful intro movie known to man, but hey—he's seen it already. Let him bypass it.

If you eliminate these and other boring activities that most game designers put players through, what you'll be left with is a tight, fast-paced game that will hold the player from start to finish.

Bates says *foo* is a generic word game designers use to stand for any object, such as "thingamabob."

DON'T TRY TO WRITE IF YOU DON'T KNOW HOW

It turns out that writing well is hard. People spend a lifetime learning to do it. If you've never really given writing much thought, don't do it. This doesn't mean you can't be a good game designer, or that you can't do good puzzles. It just means that when it comes to writing your text and dialogue, you need to get someone else to do it.

Good writing is an art and a craft. It's a lot like game design, in that you're trying to create the maximum effect with the minimum output.

My own personal litmus test is this. If you've never read Strunk and White's *Elements of Style* [Allyn & Bacon], you shouldn't be writing your own text. If you've never studied writing, if you've never struggled to learn the difference between good writing and bad, then bring in someone else.

PLAYER EMPATHY

> When people ask me what it takes to be a game designer, I tell them the single most important skill is what I call "player empathy." You need to be able to put yourself in the player's shoes. To anticipate what he's thinking, what he's feeling. To know what he'll want to try and to let him. To know what he or she will think is exciting. To know what will feel boring and to cut it out.
>
> Without this ability, I don't think you can make it as a game designer—in any genre.

RON GILBERT, HUMONGOUS ENTERTAINMENT

This gentleman is personally responsible for many of our best-loved computer games, such as *Maniac Mansion*, the *Monkey Island* series, and a handful of children's adventure games for Humongous Entertainment. Here he talks about the root of it all—inspiration. Says Gilbert:

> Sometimes it comes from playing someone else's game; it may come from watching a movie or reading a book—just something will give you a spark. Adventure games are built on stories, and you must approach the game design from that angle, as if you were writing a script or a book.
>
> Also, be aware of who the audience is; if you're making a game just to please yourself, you may not be too successful unless you're really in sync with the market. But, at the same time, it has to come from your heart and not your head. If you do market research, it may come out too much from the head.

Are there any examples Gilbert can give, based on his past works? How did the *Monkey Island* idea come about? According to Gilbert, it was a bit of market watching (there were no pirate games of this kind) but was more of a personal preference:

> I wanted to make a fantasy game, since *Maniac Mansion* was set in a contemporary world, and I liked pirates. It took me a couple of years for *Monkey Island*, actually. I wrote five stories before I settled on one. But on the other hand, *Monkey Island II* was done in less than a year.

We hear from Gilbert in the next chapter on creating a hit character, as well as Chapters 12 and 15 on user interfaces and testing.

DAVID CAGE, QUANTIC DREAM

At the tender age of 30, David Cage is the founder and CEO of Quantic Dream. He was also the lead game designer on the action/adventure hit *Omikron: The Nomad Soul* (published by Eidos Interactive). His aspirations at Quantic Dream are to produce ambitious products and link video games to the other media industries—namely the movie industry, the music industry, and comics.

Asked if he could share any advice on creating adventure games for those who are just starting out, Cage replies, "We receive tons of email messages every week with people saying 'I have a great game idea.'" He acknowledges that some of them probably are great, but most of them aren't. He explains the difference:

> A lot of people misunderstand what a good game idea is. It's quite easy to write a great synopsis or build an interesting world, but this isn't what games are about. Games [are] about interactivity. If what you want to do is tell a great linear story, you would work better in the movie industry. Game concepts are the most important thing to ask yourself: What is there to play in my game? Why is it fun to play? Why would anybody want to play my game? What's appealing? Having a good story, solid characters, and an original world are of course essential, but [you also need] a clear vision of the interactivity.

Secondly, Cage says budding game designers should keep in mind that "games are for people." What exactly does he mean by this? Cage clarifies, "Games are not only for you or your neighbor, not even for people in your city or your country, but for people worldwide. Finding ideas that can draw the attention of a large number of people without being their lowest common factor is quite difficult."

The last pointer offered by Cage is simple: "No matter how good your game design is, the quality of the final product will depend on the talent of the development team." Cage says that in the past he has seen very common game designs turn into extraordinary games because the team was incredible, and excellent game designs resulting in very poor games because the team wasn't there. He expands on this:

> The game designer plays a role in this: First, he needs to be able to communicate his vision and enthusiasm to the team. Second, he must be able to understand the technology enough to design a concept that's just a little bit ahead of what can be done today. If he's too far ahead, the technology won't follow and it will result in conflicts with the team (and often, game design on the fly); if he's late with the technology, the game will be outdated and won't use the power of today's hardware. The last thing (but not the least) is to feel the right compromise during the development. A good game designer must feel when he must hang onto his idea to preserve his vision, or when he must change his plans.

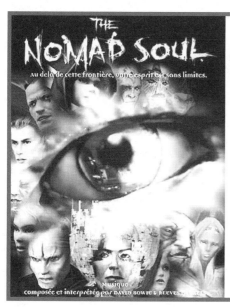

Rock legend David Bowie wrote eight original songs for Quantic Dreams' action/adventure PC and Dreamcast game Omikron: The Nomad Soul. He also made virtual appearances as a character named Boz. (Used with permission by Quantic Dreams and Eidos Interactive, Inc.)

For more information on Cage and the rest of the talented team and their projects, point your browser to www.quanticdream.com.

ROBERTA WILLIAMS, SIERRA ON-LINE

We're privileged to hear from this veteran game designer throughout this book, but here she comments on game inspiration and ties her advice to a couple of fairly recent projects. Williams says a successful game designer is part marketer. She expands, "It's important to make a game you want to make, a game that will please you, but you must also know your audience, and, at the same time, know what niches can be filled."

With Williams' latest, *Kings Quest: Mask of Eternity* (*MOE*), she explains why she made a few changes with the game's design:

> I was getting the sense that people were growing tired of slow-paced games, or "plodding" through an adventure game, and it seemed there was a need for more "instant gratification." I didn't think *King's Quest: Mask of Eternity*, if created in the same vein as past *King's Quest* titles, would fly in today's world. Therefore, I did something to spice it up—adding an action element and making it in 3D, with no limitations. Again it goes back to understanding the marketplace. Although I think *MOE* straddles the fence well to appeal to longtime fans of the series, while attracting a new audience…it's very tough, but I wanted to inject some new blood into the adventure game genre.

As an additional example on niches that can be filled, Williams sheds some light on her design behind *Phantasmagoria*:

> I realized there was a popular genre going on in books and movies—horror—but this niche wasn't being met in the computer game industry. So *Phantasmagoria* became an interactive horror movie using full-motion video, with real actors.

ROLE-PLAYING GAMES (RPGS)

HIRONOBU SAKAGUCHI, SQUARE, LTD.

It is a great honor to welcome Mr. Hironobu Sakaguchi, executive vice president of Square Co., Ltd. and president of SQUARE USA, INC. Sakaguchi is responsible for all Research & Development aspects of the company, with his most famous work on the internationally renowned *Final Fantasy* series, which has sold in excess of 26 million (!) copies worldwide since its inception. Presently, Sakaguchi is working on the development of the official *Final Fantasy* CGI movie at the SQUARE USA Honolulu studios (scheduled for a Summer 2001 release).

On general game design tips, Sakaguchi lists the three most important considerations for game design:

- **Understanding and grasping the player's psychology.** According to Sakaguchi, it's important to ask yourself, "What will the player feel from the images, sounds, and movements?" He claims it's also necessary to take into account and predict how the player will react in response to those stimuli.

- **Degree of freedom.** Says Sakaguchi, "Consideration must be taken so that the players feel that they can freely move about the world. There will be constraints, of course, but the key is to create movements within the system and the game itself so that the constraints and limitations are not felt by the player."

- **Characters.** Sakaguchi says this is the most important factor in terms of storytelling and visuals: "A setting that allows the user to relate to the characters is necessary."

Asked how he creates such memorable characters in a video game, such as Cloud or Squall, Sakaguchi points to "the uniqueness of the character, romance, a character that can become a master and someone to protect." Indeed, this is all true if you think about the protagonists for the *Final Fantasy* series.

The pre-rendered cinematics in Final Fantasy VIII are absolutely stunning, and serve as key turns in the ongoing saga. Will gameplay one day look this good? We're getting pretty close…(Used with permission by SQUARE USA, Inc. and Electronic Arts, Inc.)

What's lacking with today's console or PC games? Lack of originality? Poor control? Not enough emotion? Answers Sakaguchi:

> There are many factors that are lacking in today's games. They range from the constraints of the hardware itself to problems stemming from the network or user interface. Of course, the story, characters, and world settings aren't being given much thought either. But this is part of the evolutionary process of the industry in which we work. It gives us reason to evolve, to do better each time around. Actually, to be in the process of evolving may be the best place to be because of the excitement associated with thinking about the future and how things will change.

When asked about user interface and control, Sakaguchi answers in light of the external and in-game limitations of today. He clarifies:

> In the household, we have been limited to the NTSC, a simple stereo environment, and the joystick. I believe that if the images were all 3D and we had a

physical sensation system (with chairs that slant and shake), it would be much more fun, but I guess that's not realistic at present. But I believe that the interface within the screen, the GUI, is very important. Even if the story and game system are good, if the GUI is not created well, such as in the menu system, there are times when the game cannot be enjoyed and appreciated.

For more on graphical user interfaces, flip to Chapter 12.

BILL ROPER, BLIZZARD ENTERTAINMENT

As senior director of developer relations at one of the most prestigious game software developers in the world, Bill Roper has helped shaped such instant classics as (in chronological order): *Warcraft: Orcs and Humans*, *Warcraft II: Tides of Darkness*, *Warcraft II: Beyond the Dark Portal*, *Diablo*, *Starcraft*, *Starcraft: Brood War*, and most recently, *Diablo II*. Says Roper, "I have had the good fortune of working on some fantastically talented teams to create some great titles and I look forward to making even more memorable games in the future."

Roper was asked to list the most important considerations when creating a hit game franchise, such as *Warcraft*, *Starcraft*, or *Diablo*. His response is revealing:

> While game designers have to keep a lot of balls in the air at once, the single most important factor is your audience. Never lose sight of who the game is made for and what they want and expect out of the product. Knowing your gamers is vital if you are to create a game that's going to excite and challenge them without being too hard or not hard enough. *Starcraft* is a good example of this in that we had a very strong core fan base of people who played and loved *Warcraft II* and had specific expectations of our next strategy title. We looked not only at what we wanted to do, but also at what had worked—or not worked—for us in the past. We also play a lot of games at Blizzard and viewed them with a critical eye for ideas, both good and bad. During every phase of the design process, we kept our audience in mind; core gamers who demand longevity with involving strategic gameplay and more casual gamers who need to be able to play the game just by sitting down with the keyboard and mouse. Our goal was to make the game easy to learn but difficult to master, so that gamers at many different levels of expertise could enjoy the play experience.

A simple and easy-to-use interface is key to making the game accessible to as many players as possible, says Roper. He expands:

> You should never have to fight against the interface to play the game—it should be as intuitive and clean as possible. *Diablo* has a very simple interface in that you just point and click. The whole game was extremely playable by using just the mouse, especially since mouse actions were intelligent in their execution. If you clicked on a monster, you attacked, while right-clicking cast your ready spell. If you clicked on an NPC [non-player character], you automatically activated their trade or talk menus. If you clicked on an item on the ground, you picked it up. If you clicked on a chest, it opened. We worked hard to make the interface as transparent as it could be, so that it was a natural extension of what the player wanted to do with his character.

> The UI [user interface] also needs to provide as much information as possible. *Starcraft* does this very well in that every button has a form of pop-up help so that if the icon isn't clear enough, you can always read what the button does. Also, all of the buttons have keyboard shortcuts for advanced players, making the game user-friendly for beginning and advanced players alike.

For more on designing a good user interface, flip to Chapter 12.

Finally, Roper maintains that his third point is one of the most critical, yet one of the most overlooked. According to Roper, "It is the simple design credo that the game should be *fun*."

> Developers tend to make the mistake of letting the technology direct the course of the gameplay, and this works in very few, if any, cases. Many people argued about whether *Diablo* was a true RPG or some action/RPG hybrid. What no one ever argued about was whether the game was fun. In *Warcraft II* we had an idea that the catapults should have to be manned in order to fire. We envisioned battles pivoting around who could control these machines of war and, while that's what developed, it simply wasn't any fun. You have to be willing to throw out ideas—even ones that are near and dear to your heart—if they don't advance the gameplay or they stop the game from being fun. Never forget that you are making a game and not a technology demo.

In light of these rules of game design, what is this "Midas touch" that Blizzard seems to have, and how can a budding game designer learn from it? Says Roper:

> We have always been focused on creating the best games possible and have remained dedicated to not releasing a game until it meets the standards that both we and our fans have set. While this is a very difficult path to follow, especially when the end of the year approaches and the game just isn't done, it is the guiding tenet of our company and has served us very well if the sales and followings that *Diablo* and *Starcraft* have generated are any indication.

The Sorceress puts her enemies on ice with Frost Nova (left) while the Diablo 2 box is sure to cause heat at retailers when it's released in the summer of 2000. (Used with permission by Blizzard Entertainment, Inc.)

Next, Roper was asked, "How important is a multiplayer component in 2000?" He responds as follows:

> This may be the single most important aspect of gaming for the next five years. We have reached a point where we almost can't keep up with technology and game developers have little or no problem getting hardware that can run programs and drive graphics that were unthinkable just a few short years ago. What we are seeing now is an evolution in connecting gamers that will only get bigger and better over the next few years. It is a main focus of the next-generation console systems such as the PS2, and we are seeing more and more companies either ally themselves or start their own online gaming services. Blizzard attributes much of the success of *Diablo* and *Starcraft* to their play over Battle.net [www.battle.net], and, while we have always been focused on multiplayer games, we know that this will only be of greater importance in the years to come.

Is there anything that annoys Roper when playing games developed by other companies? In what areas should newbie game designers stay alert, so they could possibly avoid them? Answers Roper:

> If I had to pick one thing that makes me crazy, it is that games are laden with bugs when they are released to the consumer. As a game buyer and fanatic, I wait for two or three years to get a game that I have been anticipating, only to have it crash during installation. Worse yet, I get a few minutes or even hours into the game and hit a bug, so that it's impossible to complete the game. Many gamers have become complacent and now expect this from developers and, since they're being allowed to release this kind of software, developers are simply "fixing it in a patch." As an industry, we need to be willing and supportive of developers taking the extra day, week, or month required to make the game as bug-free as possible.

Speaking of bugs, most Blizzard games don't seem to have very many. Roper was asked to comment on Blizzard's alleged rigorous testing process. Roper lets it all out with the following:

> We maintain a permanent QA staff of about 15–20 testers at Blizzard, raising that number to between 30–40 when we get near release. We have always felt that we need to make the game as bug-free as we can, and that stems from our days as a console developer, where you simply don't have the luxury of patching. The QA team is responsible for finding and reporting bugs as well as ensuring compatibility with available computer hardware. In addition to that, QA is responsible for providing qualitative feedback on the functionality of the product, including level of difficulty, unit or class balance, overall game enjoyment and balance, and finally questioning intended functionality. The team is split into groups that specialize and focus on different aspects of the product, from the installer to testing the quests, and each of the team leaders talks directly with the programmers as needed. It's a very interactive and iterative process that we feel gives us the best chance at finding and fixing as many bugs as possible.

For more on game testing, turn to Chapter 15.

For more on Blizzard's game design protocol, keep on reading...

MATT HOUSEHOLDER, BLIZZARD NORTH

Blizzard North recruited Matt Householder to produce *Diablo II* and bring onboard a hand-picked group of programmers, artists, and sound/music artists for the project. Householder has worked in the gaming industry for many years and on varied platforms. As a special treat to this chapter, Householder has written a large set of assorted truisms for game designers to follow. The list applies not just to RPGs, but to all genres.

HOUSEHOLDER'S AXIOMS OF INTERACTIVE GAME DESIGN

Design for the target market—the players. Well, it may be obvious, but sometimes this basic principle gets lost during the dynamic process of game implementation. Of course, this axiom is true of all products, games or not.

Game design is an incremental process—you make changes to the game's code, artwork, or sound. Then you evaluate whether the changes improved the game or not. You try to predict which changes will be most valuable, of course, to avoid wasting time on things that add little/no/negative improvement to the game while requiring significant time or effort. In this way your game design "climbs the ladder of fun."

All design elements in a game must be judged by the standards of the target market. After all, players are going to spend most of their game budget and game-playing time on things that they enjoy. The best way to ensure that all your design decisions *increase* the amount of fun in your game is to test each one on the target market. But this is impractical for two reasons. One, the target market is huge. And two, it takes too long to get feedback. To make testing of design changes practical, you must choose a subset of the target market and poll it instead. Then the problem becomes one of choosing the best, most representative subset that can be *quickly* polled. The only subset that you can poll quickly enough is your game design/implementation team. So it is essential that your team represent as faithfully as possible the target market. That is, they must know games and know what is fun.

When you get into the beta process of bug-fixing and game-tuning, widen your market subset to include a well-selected group of beta testers. The Internet is probably the best way to find and communicate with these beta-testers.

Study the classics of game design. For coin-ops: *Pac-Man, Centipede, Asteroids, Defender, Robotron 2084, Joust, Street Fighter, NBA Jam.* Computer games: *Pinball Construction Set, Jumpman, John Madden Football, Doom, Quake.* Handheld/console: *Mario, Zelda, Bomberman, Tetris.*

Take something familiar to the audience and combine it with something novel. Beware, though, of an idea so original that you've never seen it in a game. Maybe it's such a bad idea that any game containing it is a guaranteed failure—kind of like a fatal genetic mutation.

Don't frustrate the player's desire for perfect control within the game world. Any sense by the player of lack of control (however brief) can be fatal.

The user interface must be intuitive and consistent. This makes it easy for new players to learn and encourages experienced players to become experts.

Reality is vastly overrated. Don't try to re-create reality. After all, if reality were that much fun, people wouldn't play games.

Don't interfere with the player's suspension of disbelief. And try to keep the game world (and interaction with it) self-contained and self-consistent. Although in this post-modern world, maybe the audience is only pretending to suspend their disbelief.

Make sure your player character is likable. If your audience looks at the character they control onscreen and thinks "Is that me? I don't like me!" your game won't sell well. Game players tolerate neither bad art nor the nagging feeling that they don't get the joke.

Make sure the frame rate is high enough and consistent. This is more important (and harder to do) for action games than strategy or simulations.

If you can't compute it, pre-compute it. Don't make the programming job even harder by calculating unnecessarily during runtime. Whenever possible, pre-calculate algorithms into tables and just look up the results at runtime.

Make everything (that must be) in the game adjustable.

An important part of game design and implementation is deciding how to model the game world—that is, the game variables and how they interact. Anyway, put these variables into tables. This includes all the attributes of the players, enemies, and environment.

Balance the game by adjusting everything until it's maximally fun. Obviously, this is easier said than done. And economic realities will force you to stop sooner or later.

Have fun.

If all goes well, you will get to try it again.

TIM CAIN, TROIKA GAMES

Before leaving Interplay to launch Troika Games in 1998, Tim Cain became one of the most recognized role-playing game designers for two of his most famous works: *Fallout* and *Fallout 2*. Currently, Cain is developing an original RPG dubbed *Arcanum*, to be published in late 2000 by Sierra Studios.

On role-playing game design, Cain outlines a few strategies, with the first being "an idea that looks great on paper may not be so great when implemented." Says Cain:

I have read features that seemed brilliant in the design document, but when I implemented them they were not very useful or enjoyable in the game. Sometimes you have to try variations on your ideas, and sometimes you have to just throw ideas away. Never be afraid to experiment.

Next, Cain maintains, "It is impossible to foresee every necessary feature in a design document." He clarifies:

> This is not to say that you shouldn't try to make a design document as complete as possible. But you should never view the design document as written in stone. Instead, you should be open to adding, improving, and (most importantly) removing features as the game's development progresses. Your vision of the game may change as it's developed, and the design document will need to reflect this change.

Troika Games was founded April 1, 1998 by Tim Cain , Leonard Boyarsky, and Jason Anderson. They're currently working on their first project, Arcanum, to be published by Sierra Studios. (Arcanum is a registered trademark of Sierra On-Line, Inc. Images used with permission. Copyright 1999-2000 Sierra On-Line, Inc. All Rights Reserved.)

Finally, Cain reminds us, "No game is designed in a vacuum." What exactly does this mean? Says Cain:

> The days of the one-person development team are over. You will be making games with a team, and sometimes other people on the team will have better insight into the game than you. Remember this, and be open to their ideas. To someone just starting out as a game designer, I would recommend learning to code or to create art, so that you can reduce the number of intermediaries between your idea and its final implementation. Remember, ideas are a dime a dozen. Unless you can implement your ideas, your only recourse is to describe these ideas in excruciating and well-written detail, and then you hope the person who actually implements your idea will understand your vision.

Cain goes one step further and extracts examples from his past work to support the aforementioned game design recommendations. In particular, he discusses his work on *Fallout*, the successful post-nuclear RPG developed and published at Interplay in 1997, and how it influenced *Arcanum*, a Tolkienesque fantasy RPG currently in development at Troika Games. Says Cain:

> *Fallout* was the first game where I worked on the original design rather than accept a predesigned game to complete, and it was the first game where I worked as a producer as well as programmer. I put many of the principles I described above into practice on *Fallout*, and I assembled one of the best development teams I have ever had. *Fallout* won numerous "Best RPG" and "Best Game of the Year" awards, and I am very proud of the team's achievement.

Arcanum is a radical departure from the standard "dark ages" fantasy RPG, and I have tried to give it the look and feel of late 1800s Victorian era Europe. Technology and magic have reached an unstable equilibrium, with technology being on the rise in the last several decades, and magic being in decline from its once penultimate position in the world. Being a true fantasy world, *Arcanum* is populated with elves, orcs, humans, dwarves, ogres, gnomes, and halflings. However, with the advent of technology, the races' roles in society have radically changed, bringing additional tension to the world and giving ample opportunity for adventure.

In many ways, *Fallout* was a stepping stone to *Arcanum*. Many lessons were learned, for good and for bad, on *Fallout*, since it was my first project. *Arcanum* is the culmination of everything I have learned to date about making games. I have great hopes it will be as successful.

In an interview with Gamespot.com, a popular online gaming magazine, Cain told the journalist that *Arcanum* "is the RPG I've been waiting 15 years to make." What does this mean, exactly? Does Cain have a problem with some of today's RPGs? He answers as follows:

Freedom is the element missing in most games. In an RPG, especially, I want to play many different types of characters—an evil priest, a super-smart gadgeteer, a weapons master, a wealthy aristocrat. I want the freedom to play games the way I like to play them, and the onus is on the game's designer to make sure the game reacts to my playing style in a consistent and enjoyable fashion. I am not saying I want to be able to grow wheat, grind flour, and bake bread, but I am saying I want choices to make throughout the game, from character creation to the big endgame finale, that are reflected in the world of the game.

Finally, Cain was asked where a game designer looks for inspiration:

Some designers draw on their life experiences, others like to watch movies, and others play their competitors' games, but for myself, I read a lot. I read fantasy and science fiction novels, as well as historical essays, humor books, and old game-adventure modules. You would be surprised at where you can find inspiration.

Are any of these literary influences found in *Arcanum*?

Indeed. I am reading a ladies home journal published in 1883 called *Demorest's Monthly Magazine* (the January issue, Vol. XIX, No. 3, for those who care). The magazine is providing me an incredible window into the last century, especially into how people lived day to day: how they worked, what they ate, and how they viewed the world at large. The issue is full of grandiose advertisements, romantic short stories, fashion tips, and lightly covered world affairs. My favorite section is "Kitchen," which is full of recipes for foods like pickled oysters, mincemeat pies, and homemade mayonnaise sauce, all to be washed down with Beef Tea. It is amazing what you can find on eBay these days…

For more information on Cain's *Arcanum*, visit www.sierrastudios.com.

RAY MUZYKA, BIOWARE

Baldur's Gate, released at the tail end of 1998, proved to be one of the true instant classics in the computer gaming industry. And successful, too—over 200,000 copies of the game sold through its first two weeks. Dr. Raymond Muzyka, one of the three founders of BioWare, is here to discuss what it's like to work with a licensed property (that is, *Forgotten Realms* and *Advanced Dungeons & Dragons*), and whether it helps or hinders game development and consumer recognition. The following is Dr. Muzyka's response in its entirety:

" Interesting question. A little bit of both at the same time, generally. I suspect that the answer will vary greatly depending on who you are licensing the property from, as well as the type of property. Wizards of the Coast (and TSR, which WOTC purchased two years ago) have been great to work with, actually (our publisher, Interplay/Black Isle, holds the license of *Forgotten Realms* with them, and BioWare developed *Baldur's Gate* in this universe). WOTC/TSR were very receptive to most of our ideas. If they had been difficult to work with, this would have made things a lot more complex—thankfully we didn't have to worry much about that, since we had a lot of fun working with them.

One of the things we did early on was to involve WOTC/TSR in the design process—several representatives from TSR flew out to BioWare to see some of our art, design, and writing, so that they became more comfortable with the direction that we wanted to take with *Baldur's Gate*. They actively participated, suggesting things that would help out with the storyline. This ensured that they knew what we wanted to do, and also ensured that we knew how they felt about different design directions—we had to take care to develop the property in a manner consistent with their internal developments. It seemed most useful to talk to them frequently—not only at the outset, but a few months into the project and again a few months later, so that they could stay involved and comfortable with how we were treating their property.

Now, certainly, developing a licensed property is not a simple task. One of the first hurdles we encountered with developing in the *AD&D* world was complying with TSR's strict code of ethics—and this did limit some of the design a little. However, it didn't prevent us from coming up with a novel concept for the storyline, and in the end it didn't really impair any of the development. It was more something we had to stay aware of at all times.

We definitely benefited from the large variety of areas and characters that were already well developed in the *Forgotten Realms* universe—it simplified the task of picking locales, and we used the source books very heavily in this regard. We placed towns and cities, buildings, characters, and even scenery in *Baldur's Gate* according to how they were laid out in the sourcebooks for the game. Yet, this didn't constrain us too much because there was still a lot of scope for new characters or areas to be added in.

One of the largest hurdles was figuring out how to actually implement the *AD&D* rule system on a computer. We made the task more challenging for ourselves because we elected to make the game real time, rather than turn-based. We also decided early on to aim to not change any rules that we didn't need to change. Since *AD&D* is largely a series of exceptions to rules rather than merely a set of rules, this caused a lot of headaches. In the end, though, the benefit of staying true to the complete rule set became evident in the QA process: The game was largely balanced using all of the statistics of creatures and items "as is" out of the sourcebooks. If we had changed a lot of rules, the game would have been a lot more difficult to balance.

Finally, there are cost considerations. I'm not at liberty to say how much it cost for Interplay/BioWare to use the *Forgotten Realms/AD&D* license, but suffice to say, it wasn't cheap. A big-name license will cost a fair amount.

Overall, the process of developing a licensed property has both good and bad aspects. Certainly we plan to work (via our publisher, Interplay) with WOTC/TSR in the future, so in our case, at least, it was a very good collaboration.

TIP From a consumer standpoint, developing a game based on a well-known and loved franchise can work for you and against you. On one hand, the customer is already familiar with the characters (e.g., Fox Interactive's *X-Files* game), the environments (e.g., the *Star Wars* or *Star Trek* universes) and the rules (such as *D&D*). Therefore, the game may fly off the shelves faster because of the instant recognition, and the game may be easier to understand. On the other hand, there is a level of expectation by the consumer that, if not met, will surely disappoint the player more than an unknown set of characters, environments, and rules would.

GREG ZESCHUK, BIOWARE

Also at BioWare is Dr. Greg Zeschuk, another cofounder and CEO, who accompanies Dr. Muzyka's contribution to this book by discussing game innovation, what it's like to develop for the PC versus a console system, and what the future holds for the interactive entertainment industry.

On where innovation can be found in creating a unique computer game, Zeschuk comments:

Each new game represents a completely blank canvas lacking limits or constraints; game designers have the ultimate freedom to create their wildest dreams. Their greatest challenge is to create a unique game rather than follow the mass of average and uninspired games released each year. Without perceived limits, though, it is difficult to find a balance between functionality, technology, and personality in a game. Technology fortunately limits our creativity to reasonable paths, and creativity causes us to stretch the boundaries in unprecedented directions. Actual innovation within a game can be found practically anywhere. The visual style, the interface, or the core game idea can be innovative in both minute detail and broad sweeping vision. Innovation can also be achieved be refining or redefining existing standards of gameplay. Often, the entire package, rather than any single element, can be considered innovative. A truly unique game can also be built out of an aggregation of small, discrete advances.

At the time of interviewing Zeschuk, *MDK2* had just gone gold for the Sega Dreamcast, while *Baldur's Gate II* was half-completed for the PC. He was asked what are the primary differences in designing games for different platforms, and the challenges for each:

> Console and PC players have markedly different philosophies in how they approach and play games. PC players generally are more impatient than console players. PC players loathe repeating a game sequence, while console players revel in the chance to repeat something until it's perfect. My analogy is that of PC players having less free time than console players—they are less willing to spend their time doing repetitive activities in games. These ideas directly influence how to approach the design of both PC and console games. From a purely technical perspective, I would argue it's easier to make a console game than a PC game because the creators don't have to worry about different hardware setups on the consoles. At the same time, consoles are more challenging in the initial stages of development because of their unique and quirky architectural design.

Zeschuk was asked to cite any recent innovations in technology and/or game design:

> Some people would say 3D hardware acceleration is the most significant advancement in the last couple of years. It has completely changed the way we make games and it has caused technology to become the primary concern for most development projects. "Everyone" is obsessed with the latest and greatest 3D technology, while the average game-buying consumer doesn't really care about 3D acceleration. *PCData*'s 20 top selling PC games for 1999 had only one 3D game in the top 10 and only 5 3D games on the list. Sure, the future is in 3D, but we haven't realized that the present isn't there yet. The real innovation is in Internet and multiplayer features. Massively-multiplayer games featuring thousands of concurrently connected users were inconceivable a few years ago. Even the concept is mind boggling: Thousands of people all playing together at any given time! The key will be discovering how to get all of these thousands of people to interact online rather than live out their solitary lives in a digital world.

On the future of gaming, Zeschuk adds: "It's a wired, online future. Everything will be available over the Internet. All forms of entertainment will converge into a common digital entertainment signal that will enter every home in a big fiber optic pipe. And games will be a big part of it."

Turn to Chapter 20 to read Zeschuk's advice on breaking into the industry.

TOM HALL, ION STORM

Before leaving to work on his RPG *Anachronox*, Tom Hall, the always-informative game designer extraordinaire at ION Storm, cofounded id Software, the birthplace of 3D shooters.

Concerning general game design, Hall admits there are many things that are important, but following are three good ones:

THE GAME IS FOR THE PLAYER

> It's cool if you want to tell a story with the game, or have things go a certain way, but it needs to be fun and under control of the player as much as possible. It's okay to have arbitrary rules (like you can carry only four widgets), but never let them feel led by the nose. Never let the player see the man behind the curtain. They should always feel they're participating. If they ever feel they're watching and can't do anything about it, you've lost them. And what you actually get to do must be fun. Some designers seem preoccupied with the new or bizarre or detailed aspects of the game, and forget that the player is supposed to be having fun somewhere in the process.

GRAB THE PLAYER IN THIRTY SECONDS

> Within the first half-minute of gameplay, you should really have an idea of the coolness of the game. If you're stuck in boring exposition, or you have to do boring things to get to any cool stuff, again, you'll lose the audience. What you want to hear when they start, and every few minutes after:
>
> "Oh—no way! Cool!" *Half-Life* did this well.

YOUR FIRST TEN GAMES WILL [STINK]

> Get them over with. Make a bunch of small different games and learn your craft. I must have made 50 little games before working at Softdisk. Just finishing a game is a great accomplishment. It teaches you the whole process, and gives you incremental confidence.

To learn more about *Anachronox*, visit www.ionstorm.com.

WARREN SPECTOR, ION STORM

Also at ION Storm is Warren Spector, a veteran game designer who produced a number of award-winning PC classics such as *Ultima VI* (alongside Richard Garriott); *Wing Commander* (with Chris Roberts); the *Ultima Underworld* series (with project director Doug Church); *Ultima VII, Part 2: Serpent Isle, System Shock* (again with Doug Church); *Wings of Glory*; and many, many more. He is currently readying an action/role-playing game entitled *Deus Ex*, to be published through Eidos Interactive sometime in 2000.

When asked to offer advice on general game design, Spector had plenty to say on the matter (and later apologized for rambling, but we welcome his words of wisdom!). The following are his rules of engagement in its entirety:

SPECTOR'S GAME DESIGN TIPS 'N' TECHNIQUES

> (a) Give players tools and information enough to make and execute a plan in response to problems you set up. In the end, that's what gaming is all about. Just as important, though, make sure you provide enough feedback so players

know why their plans worked or didn't work. In *Wings of Glory*, we played a simple, wood-creaking sound effect when you were nearing the limits of your World War I biplane's structural limits. Seems utterly trivial, but think about it—we were telling you that your plan (out turning or out diving your foe) was about to fail and giving you the opportunity to formulate a new plan. Now, if your plane was taking heavy damage and your windscreen was shattered and so on, maybe you kept taking the risk, maybe not. The key thing is that we had a variety of visual and audio cues to give players information about the condition of their plane and then feed back the results of their actions.

(b) Make sure the world responds to player actions in direct and observable ways—ways that players expect and can comprehend. If there's a computer monitor in your game world, and it's constantly playing annoying Big Brother messages, sooner or later players are going to try bashing them. And if they *can't* bash them, they're going to feel thwarted and just a little bit frustrated. Worse, they're going to be reminded that they're just playing a game. And then you've lost them. In *System Shock*, if you banged on a computer screen, it made a nice satisfying pop sound (as you'd expect), went dead (as you'd expect), and cracked (as you'd expect). A nice, simple—some would say trivial—thing made you feel like you were in a real world. Nice…

(c) Know what you want players to *feel* as they play. You can't be sure what players will see or do (that pesky interactive thing, you know…) but you can set up situations designed to evoke certain kinds of feelings—fear, paranoia, tension, sadness, etc. To be honest, I've come to this realization fairly recently, largely as a result of playing *Thief: The Dark Project* and *System Shock 2* (the former a game I had something—but not much—to do with, and the latter I had no hand in at all). This is an area where I don't think I've done a particularly good job and I'm not sure how I'll work this into my development process. (Hm—maybe I shouldn't be admitting this in print! Nah! When I stop learning with each game I'll know it's time to find a new line of work…) Anyway, in the future, I intend to pay much more conscious attention in pre-production to the emotional state I want the player to be in as he or she plays. When I figure out how, I'll let you know!

(d) Abandon reality and put gameplay first (and last and everywhere in between). Recreating the real world is a seductive goal and something we do a little better every day. The question is, *should* we do it? Verisimilitude can be a powerful tool in the game developer's arsenal, but it's not the only one. Use realism sparingly and you can suck players into your game world in powerful ways. Fall victim to realism's seductive charms and you almost always end up with a game that's just not much fun. This is a lesson learned during the course of developing *Deus Ex* (which started out with the phrase "Real World Role-playing" as its motto). It took much Warren-beating by lead designer Harvey Smith and others to convince me we had to shift our focus from Reality Simulation to Believable Simulation. Man, were they right!

(e) Don't think of your AI as a tool to beat the player. The role of AI is to act as the player's foil—there to challenge players, not defeat them, to make them sweat but, ultimately, to make them feel cool and powerful. Yet another lesson

I learned (embarrassingly recently), this time from Doug Church, project director on *Underworld* and *System Shock*. Given that we've worked together for about the last ten years, you'd think I would have learned long ago. I didn't. Argh. On *Deus Ex*, we made our AI-controlled enemies way too tough, at first. We wanted them to behave like real, highly trained terrorist and military units. Because of that, we went through a period where players screamed in frustration as they failed miserably to avoid detection or got blown to smithereens when they chose to engage the enemy. Fixing the problem wasn't so much a matter of "dumbing down" the AI as it was tuning for believability rather than realism (see above!) and for maximum challenge—we wanted players to end combat exhilarated and exhausted, with one bullet left in a gun…we wanted players to work hard and break a sweat evading and hiding from a pursuing enemy…we did *not* want players getting killed all the time by our super-realistic super-spies and having to load a saved game every ten minutes!

(f) Accept and exploit the limitations of the medium and be prepared to junk your favorite ideas. There are all sorts of things you're going to want to do but, because of technological limitations, you're just not going to be able to do them. You don't want to be too conservative but you do want to be realistic about what's possible and what's not. Identify the "not possibles" early and don't fight them. Working within limitations is a time-tested aspect of commercial art and mass media in general. One of the few things that's true in movies and in games…Specifics? How about this: We had a mission in *Deus Ex* that called for the player to rescue a couple hundred prisoners from what amounted to a concentration camp. Uh, sure. What was I thinking? No *way* you can pull that off convincingly. You're lucky if we can show ten characters onscreen at once!

(g) There's no such thing as a one-man show in gaming. Sages don't make games; team make games. *System Shock* would have amounted to nothing without project director Doug Church; programmers like Art Min, Rob Fermier, and Marc LeBlanc; designers like Tim Stellmach and Dorian Hart; and audio guys like Greg LoPiccolo and Eric Brosius. *Serpent Isle* was the work of more than 30 people; *Deus Ex*, the work of 20-plus. The *Wings of Glory* team was about 20 for much of development and, at the end, came down to a half-dozen folks working their tails off. Individual attention to game designers is nice, but it's more of a marketing tool than anything else. Individuals don't make great games— great teams make great games.

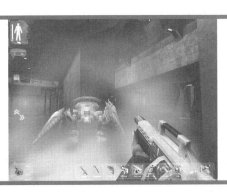

Deus Ex is Spector's latest and arguably most ambitious PC project. To read more on the background of the game, visit the official Web site at www.deusex.com. (Used with permission by Eidos Interactive, Inc.)

Spector says, "One of the goals with *Deus Ex* was to 'put power back into the player's hands—confront them not with puzzles, but with problems.'" What does this mean? Answers Spector (in essay form, no less):

> What this means is that we have to stop paying lip service to the notion that interactivity is what sets gaming apart from other media, and actually start making games that are interactive, where we really do abdicate authorship or, at least, share it with players. Maybe some examples will help make this clearer.
>
> How interactive is it in an adventure game when you're confronted with a puzzle and have to guess the solution before you can make further progress? Not very interactive, I'd say. How interactive is it when the *only* way to defeat an enemy is to guess that the designer wants you to throw some smelly sweat socks and moldy cheese into a vat, light a fire, and then stir the melting mixture with a broken tree limb that magically transforms into a Wand of MegaDeath? Again, not very. And how interactive is it if all players are doing is finding all the pieces of a designer-created puzzle before being allowed to assemble them? I think you can guess my answer…
>
> And just about every game puts you—the player—on rails like that. Just about every game forces you to play Guess What the Designers Intended, which isn't really much fun, to my mind. Sometimes we let players pick the order in which they do things, but very few games let players actually decide what to do. And deciding what to do is what real interactivity is about.

Spector goes on to say that he believes there are two issues stopping game designers from accepting players as coauthors (in other words, accepting that players must be given some real choices about what to do during minute-to-minute gameplay). He expands:

> First, game developers (to say nothing of players and critics…) have a hard time letting loose of the idea that there has to be one person—an artist or storyteller or someone—who creates an experience, creates challenges for players, leaving players with little more to do than navigate this creator-centric *gamespace*. This artist-centered view of the world is ingrained in all of us, thanks to millennia of cultural conditioning. From the first day a guy squatted in front of a fire in some cave somewhere and told the story of that day's mammoth hunt, we've been trained to accept art as the work of an artist. Why should gaming be any different from every other medium of the last several millennia?
>
> Second, computer gaming is a terrifyingly difficult medium to work in, if for no other reason than that everything you see and hear has to be generated by hand by someone. If a writer doesn't write the right words, a character can't say them, no matter how appropriate it might be for that character to do so. If an artist doesn't generate art for a charred tree, you can't burn that tree down, no matter how much you want to or how powerful a fireball spell or flamethrower you may have. If the game isn't set up to tell the difference between a whispered comment and a shouted one, players won't be able to whisper or shout. And this raises issues of time and money to generate, well, infinite content and storage space for delivering it. You just can't take into account everything every player/coauthor might want to do. Put these issues together and you have a recipe for disaster, interactively speaking.

So, how does one get around the problem? Spector offers the following:

> You can, as we're trying to do in *Deus Ex*, offer players a variety of solutions to minute-to-minute game problems—not an infinity of solutions, but a healthy variety. So, for example, there might be a half-dozen ways to get through a locked door—blow it off its hinges, find a security panel from which you can override the lock, talk a non-player character into giving you the key, use your lockpicking skill and a set of lockpicks, climb up to the roof and come in through a skylight—bypassing the door entirely—and so on and so forth. Extend that kind of thinking to every situation in the game and you have (I hope!) a richer experience than people are used to in gaming. And there's no "right" or "wrong" answer, only different answers...
>
> Take that thinking just a step further and you can attach different consequences to each of those approaches to door-opening. Blow the door up and attract every guard in the area. Hack a security panel and risk discovery by someone on the Net who's a better hacker than you are. Get the key from an NPC and risk having that character tell his boss, who alerts Security. Use your lockpicks and risk having someone see you engaging in an obviously illegal activity. Climb to the roof and risk falling off or being spotted when you drop from the ceiling.
>
> The key is that the solution to the problem is in the player's hands and the consequences all follow logically from each player's choice. And that's just in the case of a single door. Apply that thinking to an entire game and you end up with something really special. No one's made that really special game of "choice and consequence" yet—of sharing authorship with players by putting power back in their hands—but we're getting closer all the time.

We would all like to know how *the* Warren Spector comes up with the ideas behind his celebrated games, so he was asked where he, and others, can look for inspiration. His answer is straight and to the point:

> I guess it's like any other creative field—you find inspiration everywhere. I guess what I'd tell people is not to be limited, as so many developers seem to be, to games or the Web or fantasy and science fiction novels. Look to movies and music. Read a newspaper once in a while. Do some living. As in all creative endeavors, there's no substitute for life experience.

Any examples from your past or current work, Mr. Spector?

> Way back in 1989, I produced a game called *Martian Dreams*. It was set in the 1890s. People thought I was nuts (and they were probably right), but I was obsessed with that period. I saw some incredibly interesting parallels between the late Victorian era and our own. It bugged me that no one remembered some truly remarkable historical figures. So, out of that wacky, intensely personal interest came the game's milieu and cast of characters (to say nothing of look and feel).
>
> *Deus Ex* was kind of a similar story. I was so tired of working on fantasy games ("You're the guy locked in a dungeon who has to save the kidnapped princess!") or clichéd science fiction games ("The aliens are invading and

Only You Can Stop Them!") Bleargh! So I started thinking about something more, I don't know, believable…Adult, maybe. Whatever, the point is I realized that gaming didn't have to be limited to the sort of niche genres we typically draw on for inspiration. We could move away from geek fiction and plug into stuff that was floating around more generally in the cultural zeitgeist. I mean, where were the James Bond characters and *Die Hard*-style games? Or the Tom Clancy-style games? (Remember, this was several years ago. I think people started twigging to this a few years back…) Anyway, I said to myself, let's do a game set in something resembling the real world, where you're the guy who gets called in when the CIA and FBI can't handle the job (inspiration from popular movies and novels). Then along came *The X-Files* (which my wife is totally obsessed about) and I figured, "Let's see what happens when James Bond meets *The X-Files*." (Inspiration from popular television show.) And by that time we were at the turn of the millennium and there was all this millennial weirdness and conspiracy theory stuff just sort of floating around in the air. (Inspiration from the Web, nonfiction books, etc.) And I just reached up and grabbed a handful of it because I thought it'd be so cool in a game. Next thing you know—*Deus Ex*…

Conversely, Spector was asked if any games or game trends irked him these days, and why?

Well, there sure are a lot of sequels out there these days, which says maybe we're not stretching as much creatively as we might. And lots of games, sequels or not, seem to spring from the fertile minds of people whose entire experience is other games (with the occasional comic book thrown in for good measure). And while I love a good comic book and, obviously, I love games, you kind of have to broaden your horizons to do really good work—gets back to my earlier point about drawing inspiration from a variety of sources.

So that's one thing. Another thing is how painfully limited our graphic range is. It's almost as if every game made had a single art director or something. I mean, characters all look like they stepped off the pages of a comic book. Give me a hero who isn't proportioned like The Mighty Thor™ or a heroine who doesn't look like she jumped off the pages of *Playboy*—please! And does everything have to be portrayed in bright, highly saturated colors or (the only other option, seemingly) the somber browns of the first-person shooter? Let's have more *Parappa the Rapper*s! Gimme something different, will ya?

Finally, it'd be hard to argue that we're doing a good job of portraying the full range of human emotion. Shooters and other action games do a terrific job of eliciting a rush of adrenaline from players. And some puzzle games and sims get people focused, intellectually, on some astonishingly complex tasks. That's all to the good. What we don't see much of is sadness and laughter in games (and when we do, it's usually of the sort "My wingman died and I cried when they played Taps," or "Wasn't it funny when the dog farted?"). In fairness, some role-playing games—notably Japanese games like *Final Fantasy* and *Suikoden*—make you really care about their characters, but the price is in limited interactivity. It's relatively easy to elicit emotions in the context of a linear narrative—humankind's been doing that kind of thing for millennia.

I'd love it if we could portray and elicit deeper, more complex emotions in the context of a genuinely interactive game. I'm waiting for someone to make a love story or a human comedy with the player's choices driving the virtual relationship and/or humor. Or how about a tragedy where the player's choices really make a difference? Where's our "King Lear" or "Death of a Salesman"? When we achieve something along these lines, we will really have accomplished something. Until then, we're just this adolescent medium struggling to find its feet, going for thrills, chills, and spills. There's more to life than that. I hope, someday, there'll be more to games as well.

Point your browser to www.ionstorm.com to read more on Spector's highly anticipated *Deus Ex*.

While we've heard quite a bit about role-playing game design from most—if not all—of the gaming industry's biggest names, are there any major conceptual differences when developing a massively-multiplayer online RPG? You bet. Ever hear of a little ol' online RPG known as *EverQuest*?

BRAD MCQUAID, VERANT INTERACTIVE

Brad McQuaid serves as vice presidentof California's Verant Interactive, developers of the smash hit massively-multiplayer online role-playing game (MMORPG) *EverQuest*. McQuaid was the producer on *EverQuest* and for the first official expansion pack, *The Ruins of Kunark*. Before becoming producer, McQuaid was lead programmer on *EverQuest* for a brief period of time.

McQuaid is keen to share his words of wisdom with any budding game designer considering an MMORPG as a project.

Getting enough content into the game is the most important challenge to designing an MMORPG, says McQuaid. "It takes an author perhaps six months to write a novel, but the reader a week to read it. Players consume content at a rapid pace, and the game designer must create a system and environment in which content is self-generating but not repetitive."

The second big challenge is to create and maintain a balanced game, McQuaid comments. "MMORPGs change and evolve, both due to new content being added and also because the game's player base is constantly changing and advancing. This means constant tweaks must be made both before and after commercial launch."

Verant's critically-acclaimed EverQuest is a true 3D massively-multiplayer fantasy role-playing game. Hundreds of thousands of gamers pay to "live" in this virtual community each month. (Used with permission by Sony Computer Entertainment of America, Inc. (SCEA) and Verant Interactive, Inc.)

Finally, McQuaid says the elements of persistence and nonlinearity must be at the core of the game design for a successful MMORPG. "Unlike a traditional single-player game, there is no 'end' to playing an MMORPG—there is no all-encompassing storyline that the player follows from introduction to conclusion. And, of course, MMORPGs must keep players playing for periods orders of magnitude longer than single-player games, which means the focus needs to be on character development, in-game ownership, and building relationships with other players."

McQuaid also talks about writing missions for MMORPGs, the importance of a solid user interface, and proper game testing, so be sure to read his advice in Chapters 7, 12, and 15, respectively.

SPORTS GAMES

SEAN HOUSE, ELECTRONIC ARTS

Sean House is an associate producer at Electronic Arts, in charge of the award-winning *Madden NFL Football* series for the PC. He says his advice applies to sports games as well as other genres. The three top things to keep in mind as a new game designer? House says it's "detail, conciseness, and innovation," with the emphasis on the first point. He continues:

> The main factor to successful design is detail. Programmers and artists will take something that's unclear and always put their own spin on it, often in a different direction than that of the designer. A design that runs on with little focus will be hard to read and unsuccessful. Many of the main points will be clouded by the ramble. A design that's innovative will grab the attention of those who need to interpret it, and will have the greatest chance of being put into a product.

As an illustrative example, House recalls his experiences while working on *Madden NFL Football '97*:

> We had given the developer a rough idea of a main screen's functionality. We wanted it to function similar to the Windows 95 dialog box with tabs (Display Properties uses this). The rough idea we had given them was quite rough, although we did go over what we were looking for at length in a meeting. We also told them we wanted it to have a "metallic look" and to make "metallic sounds" when you clicked on it. A month or so later, we got a screen that had a standard 3D Studio metal texture (dull with no reflectivity, no texture, very drab looking) and sounds that were similar to a musical triangle instrument (very high pitched and tinny). The main thing we were looking for in the screen was a hard, strong feel of steel with sound effects that were low-toned, sounds you would hear in a steel mill or something, all of this depicting the hard, brute force of the NFL players and the game. What we got was a nice clean-looking screen that had some interesting sound effects, but something that would have been suitable for a techie application or something. Moral of

the story—if you have a particular idea about something, chances are that without a detailed, concise, and innovative design about it, you will get something out of it that is exactly the opposite of what you are looking for.

House was asked how important cheat codes, secrets, and Easter eggs are in games. He says, "Coming from a PC background, I would say they're not very important," but admits that's merely his opinion. At the same time, he acknowledges the benefits:

Cheat codes provide replay value. After people get bored playing a game with the default players or something, they can use the code to get a little more enjoyment out of it, and it makes them feel a bit more in control of their own game. This is what I have heard from our customers, and not a personal opinion of mine regarding my views on the games I play.

EA's Sean House believes detail and the implementation of the detail by talented members of a development team will ultimately lead to a better game. This is a shot from Madden NFL Football 2000. (Used with permission by EA Sports)

In closing, House says his aspirations include "moving up the proverbial ladder, taking on more responsibility, and developing new and innovative entertainment software."

STEVE COALLIER, ELECTRONIC ARTS

This software development manager works for an in-house development group (Scoreboard Productions) at Electronic Arts. He has worked on a number of games at EA, from action titles to space sims to sports games. Coallier was asked to give his opinion on the current status of sports games and what a game designer should bear in mind while creating one. He responds as follows:

Well, I don't think I've seen any sports game at all for the PC that I thought were well-tailored to the platform. There's a vicious circle with sports products: They don't sell well on the PC, so companies don't devote much effort to developing them, which affects their quality, so they don't sell well, etc. I believe the key to developing a successful PC title is to take advantage of the capabilities of the PC: There should be a well-developed network multiplayer version, there should be downloadable sets of stats, users should be able to import their own bitmaps to texture the players with, the graphics should push the PC envelope. Currently, just about all PC sports titles are not much more than you would see on a console system, and that's sad. This includes some of EA's own titles, such as *FIFA* and *Madden*, and it's an important thing that we're thinking about as we try to capture more sales going forward.

As for console games, it seems like the focus of effort in most of the games is on providing a million features, which is a mistake on a console system because of the hardware limitations involved. We were somewhat guilty of this on the last game I completed (*NCAA March Madness '99*)—everyone felt that the 1998 product, which launched the franchise for EA, was fairly thin in hindsight, and so we sought to add anything you could possibly want in a college basketball game. As a result, we didn't have time in the end to do some of the polishing and tweaking that should be a part of any game's development.

So what's the answer?

A game should have a limited but extremely well-done scope of features, with most of the effort spent on the time the user spends actually playing the sport involved—keeping it fast and intuitive to control, with the user feeling like a part of what's being played. Our NBA Live franchise is an excellent example of this. They know that it's going to be an every-year product, and so they settle on a reasonable number of improvements each year. One year it might be adding plays to the AI and refining the Create Player feature; another year it might be adding facial animations and more dunks. You add enough each time to add value, and make it worth buying over last year's game without the updated stats, and then you add those as well. If you tailor what you're trying to accomplish to the schedule you're trying to accomplish it in, you're going to come out a lot better in the end.

Coallier's last point ties the two platforms—PC and console—together:

All of the time spent (on any platform) making a game look good, or sound good, or including every conceivable feature—all of that is simply wasted if the game is not fun and engaging to play. Take *Doom*—the number of features was extremely limited. Instead, they focused entirely on making an immersive, entertaining product, and because they kept that focus, they succeeded.

MARK DICKENSON, TEAM .366/3DO

But what about developing baseball games? Is designing games for America's favorite pastime any different than for other sports titles?

You may have not heard of the developers Team .366, but undeniably, if you're a video game sports fanatic, you're aware of their award-winning franchise, *High Heat Baseball*. In fact, Mark Dickenson, executive director for this sports line at 3DO, says *High Heat Baseball 2000* on the PC won many "Sports Game of the Year" awards from many publications, including *Computer Gaming World*, *PC Gamer*, *PC Accelerator*, *Computer Games*, and *Gamespot*, to name a few.

When it comes to designing a game such as *High Heat Baseball*, what should a young or newbie game designer keep in mind? Dickenson answers with some general game-design advice:

Game design is about knowing exactly what's going to make your game compelling. If you can get this, you can compromise and sacrifice on many other issues. When it comes down to it, the thing you should be grabbing hold of is the "fun factor." What's going to make this thing fun? After all, that's truly the goal of a game. Everything else is just icing.

As for starting out on a sports title, I think you need to first be passionate about the sport. After that, you need to find out what's missing from your competition. By this, I don't mean features. What is it that the competition is just not getting right in your target sport? When we started on High Heat, our competitors were not doing simple things like intentional walks and pinch running with their AIs. Find out what little things are integral to the sport that are missing and then get to work. Always remember, sports games live and die with their on-the-field gameplay. Get this right and you will get loyal fans!

Whoa, that was a close one! Sammy Sosa High Heat Baseball 2001 and Sammy Sosa Softball Slam were both developed by Team .366 and published through 3DO. (Used with permission by 3DO, Inc.)

Are there any examples from developing the High Heat series to support these words of wisdom? Says Dickenson:

The first thing is that in *High Heat Baseball 1999* we took the "concentrate on the gameplay" aspect to the limit. Basically, all you could really do in *High Heat Baseball 1999* was go out on the field and play. However, the team took time on the details here. Our computer manager was doing things that baseball game fans had not seen in games for a long time. We had double switching, pinch running, late-inning defensive substitutions, etc. The manager AI was playing to win. This was just missing from the products that were available at that time. Plus, there were basic things (such as walks, correct number of doubles, and even some triples) that the competitors were not getting in their games, and these were integral to the sport. While *High Heat Baseball 1999* was not a large commercial success, fans did take note of the things the game was doing, and it laid the foundation for the franchise.

Dickenson was asked candidly what he thought of today's sports games, and, more importantly, what's missing in them. His answer? "The essence of the sport." He clarifies:

> Everyone gets caught up in graphics and feature lists. Most of the things that make a sports game great cannot be listed on a fact sheet. Everyone is chasing the Holy Grail when all they need to do is study the sport. Details of the sport are far more important in a great sports game than features. Fans will forgive a missing feature, but they will not forgive missing the basics.

On developing for the PC instead of consoles, Dickenson says the advantages of the PC are also its shortcomings:

> The PC is very flexible, and this is its strength *and* weakness. There are too many permutations to the box to get a large game to run on everyone's machine. The processing power of the machine combined with storage space provided by hard drives give you a lot of freedom. However, you know it's going to be a nightmare to bring home. With console boxes, you can really focus on the game. You know what the box can do and you know that every box is the same. You don't get caught up chasing down specific hardware issues. This frees time that can be spent polishing the game.

Dickenson talks about the importance of releasing a free game demo to the PC community in Chapter 17.

PUZZLE GAMES

ALEXEY PAJITNOV, MICROSOFT

This famous game designer, who is now creating puzzle games for Microsoft, is best known as being the author of *Tetris*, one of the most popular (and most imitated) video games of our time. During a telephone interview with Pajitnov, he divulged his top three game design secrets and admits he adheres to them when creating puzzle games.

NOTHING IS TOO SIMPLE

Pajitnov says nothing is too simple for players and mentions this first because "when you get too close to your work and you're involved with it for so long, things tend to look simple to you." With the puzzle games Pajitnov has worked on in the past, everything looked to be trivial after a while, but he later realized that someone who hasn't seen the game yet would likely find it challenging.

DON'T NEGLECT THE HARD PUZZLES

No matter how difficult the task, there will be the player who figures it out," says Pajitnov. He admits this is contradictory to the first point, but they're both correct. "Don't neglect the hard puzzles because you don't think someone will figure them out; there will always be a smarter gamer than you."

IS THE GAME FUN?

Finally, Pajitnov believes if you don't get fun from your game, nobody will. "I tell all three of these things to my team all the time."

What about inspiration? Is there a way to find it? Pajitnov says, "Inspiration cannot be rationalized. It usually comes during the work. I am never waiting for it."

Do puzzle games need to be in 3D these days? How about multiplayer games? Does a single-player game stand a chance in the 21st century? Pajitnov's reply:

> 2D games still have great chances: The technology has been changing dramatically for the last 10 years, but not the human brain. And there are lot of people enjoying the Solitaire games, but multiplayer mode is such a great advantage that it's a crime to skip it.

Alexey Pajitnov knows a thing or two about puzzle game design. After all, he was responsible for getting the world hooked on Tetris. Pictured here is his latest brain teaser, Pandora's Box. (Used with permission by Microsoft Corp.)

HARRY GOTTLIEB, JELLYVISION

Surely you've played one of the many incarnations of the clever *You Don't Know Jack* series, and if there's one person you should thank (or blame, for that matter, for the hours wasted playing these games!), that's Harry Gottlieb, founder and principle designer at Chicago's hip developers, Jellyvision. One of the top-selling PC games of 2000 was also created, written, designed, and produced at Jellyvision: *Who Wants to Be a Millionaire?* (in partnership with Disney Interactive).

While Gottlieb takes more time discussing the ways Jellyvision's puzzle games are tested in Chapter 15, he says while Jellyvision adheres to many important game design "rules," two of the most important would be that: a) the star of the show isn't *on* the screen, but sitting in front of it, and b) the greatest games help us enjoy each other's company. Surely, a single play of any of *You Don't Know Jack* (*YDKJ*) supports both of these credos.

Gottlieb was asked to comment on why the *YDKJ* series has been so popular. His answer is, simply, "the writing, the writing, the writing." 'Nuff said?

FRANZ LANZINGER, ACTUAL ENTERTAINMENT

An independent game developer for nearly 10 years, Frank Lanzinger is responsible for games such as *Gubble 1* and *2*. Now with Actual Entertainment, he offers some comments that may be more sobering than you would want to hear, but it's the truth, according to Lanzinger.

From a creative standpoint, what are the three most important things a budding game designer must keep in mind when creating a puzzle game such as yours?

" First, make your puzzles easy early on. This helps beginners and gives players a chance to learn the game mechanics. Many designers fail here and think that their early puzzles are easy, when in fact they're not. "

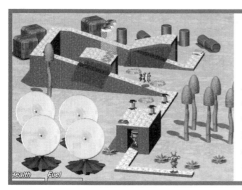

Franz Lanzinger advises, "Even if you're absolutely sure that the game is really easy early on, don't forget to test this with young kids and adults who don't play many games." This screen is from Gubble 2. (Used with permission by Actual Entertainment, Inc.)

" Second, if you must make ridiculously hard puzzles, make them optional. You'll still get support calls about them, but not quite as many. Or better yet, include cheats or hints in the product itself. After all, nobody sells crossword puzzle books without the solutions!

Third, whenever possible use the game itself to teach your players how to play it! In *Gubble* we were concerned that players wouldn't know how to fly and would get stuck on levels where it was necessary to fly. Game designers often solve this kind of problem by putting a note in the manual or by putting text or even speech into the game to teach the players. This is okay, but there's a better way. For *Gubble*, we created a level whose whole purpose was to teach players that there was a fly button, and that they had better use it or they would have no chance at completing the level. "

SIMULATIONS

WILL WRIGHT, MAXIS SOFTWARE

In early 1999, when the esteemed Will Wright was approached to contribute to the first *Game Design: Secrets of the Sages*, he reluctantly turned down the offer because he was hard at work on *The Sims*. This game later became one of the most celebrated and ingenious PC games of 2000. Instead of building and maintaining a city, as with Wright's most popular game series (*SimCity*), this time around gamers are encouraged to manage a family of characters.

Wright takes the time out of his arduous schedule to chat about game design, innovation, and the possible reasons behind the immense popularity of his games.

Concerning general game design, what are the three most important pieces of advice for budding game designers? Wright says they're as follows:

> **1.** Games are about players having fun, not about programmers solving the problems they want to solve.
>
> **2.** Be open to inspiration from unusual sources.
>
> **3.** Know as much about every aspect of game production as you possibly can (especially programming).

Wright was asked to support these "rules" with his own personal examples from his past or present work at Maxis. He responds as follows:

> *SimEarth* was a great example of why rule #1 is important. In this game we created a really cool simulation that we (the programmers) were very proud of. Unfortunately, this cool simulation we made was not very fun to play with.
>
> From rule #2: *The Sims* was originally inspired by a rather academic book on architecture (*A Pattern Language*). The final game bears very little resemblance to the book but owes a lot to it.
>
> As for rule #3, you need to understand the nature of your materials (code, art, sound) before you can become a good artist. Imagine trying to be a master painter while not knowing how to mix colors or stretch a canvas. As you begin to understand both the limits and the possibilities of your materials, the full range of creative possibilities becomes much more visible to you as a designer.

The Sims may have been influenced by a book on architecture, but where else do you find inspiration?

> I mostly get my inspiration from books, both fiction and nonfiction. I really enjoy learning new subjects. When I find a new subject that's especially intriguing, I try to design a game that will help spread my fascination with that subject to the game players. Sometimes the game that emerges from this process seems very removed from the original subject, but that's okay, too.

As examples of inspiration, Wright says *SimCity* was inspired by train sets and a book by Stanislaw Lem, dubbed *The Cyberiad*; *SimEarth* was inspired by many science fiction books, evolution, and climate; while *SimAnt* was inspired by Wright's backyard!

Is there a tangible reason why Wright's games are so sought-after? We asked the designer himself, and he responded with the following:

> I think one reason these games are so popular is because they allow the players to be creative in their gameplay. Many games are structured with a more linear or branching topology. This means that the problems that are encountered in the game have a very small number of possible solutions and are solved mostly the same way by different players. In contrast, a more open-ended game (like *SimCity* or *The Sims*) allows each player to find creative solutions to the problems that maybe no one else has found.

The Sims is one of the most innovative and imaginative computer games of the 21st century. Be sure to read Will Wright's words of wisdom on creating such unique and fresh games. (Used with permission by Maxis Software and Electronic Arts, Inc.)

The upside of all this is that the creativity helps to promote empathy in the game. I care more about my City or my Family because no one else has one just like it. Not only that, but I remember all the good things and bad things that happened to it and how I managed to deal with those issues. It seems more "real" to me.

On the other side of the coin, what's missing with many of today's computer games? Wright comments, "I think in the future games will be more about the story that the player is constructing through the play process and less about the story that the game designer is trying to tell through the design process. *The Sims* was an early attempt at just that, to make the players become the script writers. I believe this will push empathy even further in the player's mind as we draw them into these complex little microworlds."

ADAM LEVESQUE, BLUE FANG GAMES

Before leaving Papyrus to become President of the newly formed Blue Fang Games, Adam Levesque served as a 3D artist on *IndyCar Racing*, a producer/designer on *NASCAR Racing 1* and *2*, and an executive producer on all Papyrus products. Levesque was asked for three pieces of advice he can offer a budding game designer who wants to create a racing simulation. His reply is as follows:

DECIDE WHO YOUR MARKET IS

> If you're going after the hardcore sim market, make sure you understand what they want. The game will have to be realistic. The physics model, the rules of the racing (especially if modeling a real racing series) will all have to be spot-on. On the other hand, if you're going after the casual gamer, make sure that the game is easy to get into and not too complicated. Give the player early success and build from that. Also, the physics model will probably be more arcade-like; it's important to keep the frustration factor very low.

DO LOTS OF RESEARCH

> Learn the type of racing you're trying to model. This follows more for modeling an existing race series like *NASCAR* or *Formula 1*. If you're inventing a new series, this is less important. Make sure you know all the rules of the series inside and out. Make sure you understand all the little nuances of the series—who are the best drivers? what are the most difficult tracks? etc.

STICK TO YOUR DESIGN GOALS

> This really applies to all games. At the beginning of the project, come up with a set of goals (usually no more than five) that the game *must* follow through on. Make sure every team member knows the goals and buys into them. Then, when a major decision about the game must be made, refer to the goals to help make the best decision.

Levesque provides an example of this five-goal rule as it pertains to *NASCAR 2*:

> Our goals were to: a) make the interface easier to use, b) add the spotter feature, c) add the crew chief feature, d) make the race weekend more realistic, and e) improve the graphics to current standards. I think we stayed pretty true to those goals. The degree of success we had on each varied (in particular with the race weekend) but for the most part we achieved what we set out to do.

When Levesque created *NASCAR Racing*, did he look at older racing sims and think, "Hmmm...I think I can make one that's better"? In other words, should game designers try to reinvent the wheel, or is it possible to simply improve on a good thing? Answers Levesque:

> No matter what type of game you're making, to some extent you're always getting inspiration from other games, past and present. The challenge is taking those designs and adding your own interpretation on them. I believe it's critical for games to have their own *twist* to them. I mean, who cares if someone does a game that's essentially a copy of EA's *Need for Speed*?

> Wouldn't it be better to take that concept and add a different *twist* to it? Maybe make it a game about racing those sports cars across country, dodging other vehicles and the police. Maybe about racing those cars around major cities in the world. With regards to *NASCAR*, we knew we had a good thing with *IndyCar Racing*. We also knew that *NASCAR* was an up-and-coming series. Heck, there was an old game called *Bill Elliott's NASCAR Challenge*

(not regarding it as a stellar game) and it sold very well, because it was *NASCAR*. The main thing with *NASCAR* was to build on the success of the *IndyCar* engine, and make sure we were as true-to-life with the representation of the sport as we could be.

NASCAR 2 was a similar process. We knew we had a good franchise, and we wanted to make sure we could add some new and different things to it. That's why I'm pleased we were able to get the spotter/crew chief feature in the product. Not only was it something that could really help the player, but it was something they really *do*. In fact, it's a very big part of the sport.

In closing, Levesque says the most important thing is to identify the goals of the project and stick to them. "In addition, add something new to the genre. Don't just rehash the same old stuff."

Levesque left Papyrus to start his own company and work on other genres. He and his team are currently working on *Dragon Hoard*, a strategy/RPG in which the player takes on the role of a dragon.

CHRIS SAWYER, FREELANCE

Believe it or not, the best-selling PC game in the United States for 1999 was not a Barbie or hunting title! In fact, it was Hasbro Interactive's *RollerCoaster Tycoon*, an addictive little business simulation where the gamer must build and maintain a theme park. The game was created by industry veteran Chris Sawyer, who in the past has designed and programmed the popular *Transport Tycoon*, along with many PC conversions of Amiga games: *Frontier Elite 2*, *Xenomorph*, *Conqueror*, *Campaign*, *Virus*, *Goal*, and *Birds of Prey*, to name a few. His future aspirations are to continue to create original construction/simulation-style games.

From his office in the U.K., Sawyer takes the time to answer a number of questions on game design, innovation, and technological achievements.

First off, Sawyer says the most important considerations where designing a computer game are to make it fun to play, challenging, and rewarding. Adds Sawyer, "Many other things are important, such as subject matter, visuals, interaction, etc., but none are as important as these three."

By using *RollerCoaster Tycoon* as an example, Sawyer walks the reader through his three main pieces of advice and applies them to this smash hit:

FUN TO PLAY

Building things in a theme park environment is fun—most people enjoy building things, designing rides, even planting trees and gardens. Even if there wasn't a challenge or a reward involved, it would still be fun to just build things.

CHALLENGING

Without a "challenge," a game wouldn't be a game, it would be just a simulation or a construction set. If the player has to achieve something, or aim for something, or compete with something, then it creates more of a structure to the game. A good game is all about restrictions, not freedom—give the player limited resources, or define strict rules or limitations that have to be followed, and it turns a "toy" into a "game." A very different example of this is the game of chess—without the rules and restrictions it would not be particularly fun, but the rules that restrict movement are what turns it into an engrossing game.

REWARDING

If there's a challenge, there needs to be a reward. This doesn't need to be major, but something is needed. For example, in RollerCoaster Tycoon, there are minor rewards all the time while playing; just watching your well-designed roller coaster in action is one reward, and there is also the reward of gaining access to different scenarios and parks if you achieve a particular objective in the current one.

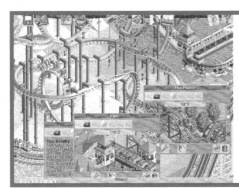

Thousands of RollerCoaster Tycoon gamers from around the world have logged onto www.rollercoastertycoon.com to download new rides, extra scenarios, and other freebies. How has Chris Sawyer achieved this level of success? Be sure to read his entry in this chapter. (Used with permission by Hasbro Interactive, Inc.)

I think *RollerCoaster Tycoon* appeals to so many people because it draws on two of our fundamental human instincts. We all like building things, doing something constructive, creating our own little world, and as humans we also like to look after or "nurture" our creations. This is what *RollerCoaster Tycoon* is all about. You spend hours building up your park piece by piece—designing the rides, placing the footpaths, and organizing everything—and then you feel it's *your* park and you want to look after it, keep it running well, keep everyone happy. You become personally attached to your park, and you become happy when the guests are enjoying your rides, and sad when things go wrong and your guests are unhappy.

What about game innovation? Does it exist today? Where can it be found? Answers Sawyer:

I don't think there's much scope for major "innovation" in computer games at the moment, but perhaps someone else will prove me wrong! Most games nowadays take established concepts and develop them in different ways or with enhanced graphics, sound, or features, so any innovations tend to be in the technological side of the game, rather than the design itself. My own games could hardly be described as innovative, but I think most people would regard them as "unique," due to the character, gameplay, look and feel, depth, and longevity of the games. It's difficult to create something completely new or different, but what you can do is take an established concept into new areas or give it a different focus, and you can then end up with a very different kind of game.

On technological innovations, Sawyer adds the following:

3D graphics get faster, smoother, and higher resolution, sound becomes higher quality with surround sound, realism is improved due to faster CPUs and larger memory (though I think realism should not be the ultimate aim for a game design). Even multiplayer games have been around since the 1980s—it's just that they no longer need a mainframe computer! Of course, there have been many minor innovations, and probably every game developer out there will be able to tell you why his or her game is "innovative," whether that's because it uses a new method of smoothing polygons in a 3D view, or improved animation by the use of motion-capture methods, or improved AI by the use of a unique algorithm. On the game-design side, most of the truly innovative game designs just don't work out—they may have been great ideas, but just didn't make it as a finished game, or were too ambitious, or just weren't any fun to play.

Asked if he has any beefs with today's games, Sawyer responds by saying perhaps the biggest problem with many games these days is they try to impress graphically, and often to the detriment of gameplay. He expands: "Graphics are of course very important, but often much more goes into the graphical aspects of a game than the gameplay side. This can create a wonderful 'looking' product, but the gameplay is often shallow and lacking depth."

What does Sawyer predict that the future holds for gaming? He hopes games will become more diversified:

Personally, I hope there will be diversification, in both game design and "look and feel," much like the car industry is currently doing. After years of creating cars that all started to look and function so similarly, the car industry is now much more creative in their designs, going after niche markets, and deliberately making their products different. I think the game industry will revisit some of the neglected game designs from years ago, and will also take advantage of new technologies like permanent Internet connections, but beyond that I don't know.

Finally, though Chapter 15 focuses solely on proper game testing, Sawyer offers a few bits of advice on that subject here. To him, game testing is vital, both for testing gameplay and for locating bugs. Says Sawyer:

> Early on in the development of *RollerCoaster Tycoon* I tested the game out on various people, always while I watched, so I could see what they were doing, what problems they were having, what they enjoyed, what they didn't enjoy, and just generally get a feel for whether the game was heading in the right direction. Perhaps a major milestone in the development of *RollerCoaster Tycoon* was when I arranged for my neighbor's young daughter to try the game. And I watched for no less than nine hours nonstop while she played, refusing to stop for meals or anything else, just totally engrossed in the game. I knew then that the game was heading in the right direction.

CHAPTER 4
CREATING CHARACTERS, STORYBOARDING, AND DESIGN DOCS

Lara Croft. Mario. Sonic. Pac-Man. Earthworm Jim. Crash Bandicoot. Leisure Suit Larry. Duke Nukem.

What do these words have in common? The answer is simple—all of them are household names, but they're not famous actors from a Hollywood movie or some hit TV show. They're not Saturday morning cartoon characters (okay, some of them went *on* to that) and they're not the latest doll craze for kids. These are the video game heroes, the stars of the interactive screen whose marketing potential has kept them in the limelight for many years, and lined the pockets of their creators with green.

Many developers and publishers have tried desperately to create the next billion-dollar game icon, but a catchy name or cute look often isn't enough. So what's the secret? This chapter contains words of wisdom from the creators of many of those aforementioned characters. But that's not all we're going to explore here.

If there was a common theme running through this chapter, it would be "how to get your ideas down on paper." Some game designers prefer to sketch out rough characters or backgrounds on paper (or work with artists to do so); others draw sequential storyboards to help shape the vision and flow of the game; and in other cases, designers write fiction or game screenplays (usually for adventure games or RPGs when there's a lot of dialogue). *Design documents* are often lengthy paper reports used to communicate the entire blueprint of the game, covering all its features, story elements, characters, locations, dialogue, puzzles, artwork, sound effects, music, and much more. These documents are usually designed in a modular fashion so they can be updated and modified if the design of the game takes a new form.

This chapter highlights how some of the more famous characters in the gaming industry were born, plus we talk with game designers and artists about storyboarding, script writing, design documents, and other ways to flesh out your hit game before you type your first line of code.

AL LOWE, RETIRED

Al Lowe has been a game developer for Sierra On-Line since 1982, and it was five years later when he introduced a lovable loser of a character, Leisure Suit Larry. Eight games have been created based on this successful franchise; the latest is 1998's *Leisure Suit Larry's Casino*. Unfortunately, Mr. Lowe retired altogether from the gaming industry in 1999 to become a Webmaster of www.allowe.com. But at least we've got his immortal words of wisdom to live by!

Lowe was asked if he can offer any tips for those who want to create a successful lead character such as Leisure Suit Larry. He replies:

> Clarify the character in your own mind before you begin. Describe him in writing, in great detail, fleshing out his background, his hopes and dreams, his desires, his strengths and weaknesses, his personality, etc., etc., etc. (Of course, I did none of this for Larry. Instead, I just made things up as I went along. But look at how he turned out!)

But where exactly did Lowe find the inspiration for him?

> Inspiration, hell! I had to ship a game in six months from start to finish, with nothing but a set of locations and weak puzzles to start with. It wasn't so much inspiration as pure unadulterated fear!
>
> That said, I'll give you a little more detail. In late 1986, I felt the time was ripe for a game that I didn't see anywhere else. Something that dealt with mature subject matter, and was funny. At the time, every computer game was terribly serious: save the princess, save the galaxy! And all were set in fantastic settings: medieval times or other planets. I thought the world was ready for a funny game set in modern times, with modern people. Larry's loser image grew as I developed the game. Was he based on someone I know? No, he's based on the jerk everyone knows. (Well, okay, there *was* this guy who worked for Sierra as a traveling software salesman…)

When Al Lowe created Leisure Suit Larry, he said he wanted to create a character that people could laugh at, but the difficult part was to make him someone they could relate to. It's that balance that made Larry a success. (Leisure Suit Larry is a registered trademark of Sierra On-Line, Inc. Images used with permission. Copyright 1999-2000 Sierra On-Line, Inc. All Rights Reserved.)

Lowe says sketching out a lead character prior to writing the game is essential:

> If you can't write it down, you don't really know it yet. And if it's not written down, how can anyone else know what you're talking about? Every game I've done (at least since the old days of "Al does everything including the art") has had a game "bible," containing everything about everything in the game. The only exception to this is the actual dialogue, which I write later, while the art and programming are progressing.

Was the first *Leisure Suit Larry* game storyboarded?

> In a way. *Larry 1* was based on a text-only game called *Softporn* that Sierra published in the Paleolithic period of home computers (1980). Sierra wanted an updated, fully graphical version of that design. When I examined it carefully, I realized I just couldn't do it. There was no protagonist at all! The writing was terrible. It took its mission seriously: Your goal was really to "score three chicks." It was so out of touch, I said there was only one thing I could do: parody it. Mock it. Laugh at it. So I created a hero so out of it, he thought leisure suits were still hip.
>
> So was there a storyboard? No. Mark Crowe and I determined all the elements that were needed in a scene, he drew it, I programmed it, then I wrote dialogue to fit what was there.

The rest, as they say, is history.

TOBY GARD, CONFOUNDING FACTOR

Toby Gard is the creative director at Confounding Factor, but most gamers know him as the creator and designer of *Tomb Raider* and the Lara Croft character, when he was employed at Core Design.

When creating a lead character for a video game, Gard says to be sure you really like what you've designed; then other people have a good chance of liking it too. He expands:

> If you aren't sure about your character, dump it. If you experiment all the time, drawing without any particular purpose, and explore avenues that look good in a fairly freeform sort of way, at some point you'll get something that you just instinctively know works. Then, you see, you'll start to love the character, and that will shine through in your work because the character starts to take on its own personality through your drawings. I think that's probably it—you need to design and redesign again and again, until you can't anymore. Then just draw that character about a hundred times (having fun with it) and you'll be there. Well, that's the method I use.

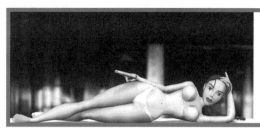

Think you can create a revolutionary game icon such as the lovely Lara Croft? The digital diva's creator, Toby Gard, says a winning character will start to take on its own shape and personality after ample experimentation. (Used with permission by Eidos Interactive)

Are there any specific do's or don'ts Gard can offer when creating a hit character like Lara Croft?

> Make a character simple and clear; look at comics to see why. Your art should be an iconic piece of graphic art, as well as a nicely rendered piece of art. Example: gray, black, and yellow = Batman. Bold sections of color and a simple overall design. Whatever style you draw him in, Batman is always Batman because he's so iconic he's almost a logo in his own right.
>
> Do something radical. Almost everything can work equally well turned on its head. Most people are sick of seeing the same sorts of characters, so break the rules.
>
> If you want people to take to your character, then you should have respect for it; i.e., it should have admirable qualities, it should be something you kind of wouldn't mind spending a few hours stepping into the shoes of.
>
> After all, that's the whole point, right?

SHIGERU MIYAMOTO, NINTENDO

The honorable Mr. Miyamoto is a living legend cin the interactive entertainment industry. He has conceived some of our most beloved electronic characters, such as Mario and Link. When asked how to create such internationally recognizable and deeply loved characters, Miyamoto says it all boils down to the fun factor:

> Making games "fun" is our only objective, and we are always making an effort to accomplish this goal. I believe that the creation of game characters is simply one of the processes to achieve this goal. If Mario games hadn't been fun to play, the character wouldn't be popular at all.

To probe further, Miyamoto was asked to explain what makes a character fun, exactly. Is it solely based on its appearance? A cute voice? Ease of control? Why do many game developers fail to create a memorable character? Answers Miyamoto:

> I am not sure why some fail to create a memorable character. Players can emotionally relate to the video game character as his/her other self, which is the decisive difference from the characters in other media. Mario, for instance, can be a character with a completely different meaning when he is driving a car and when he is jumping. The other design elements are solely at the discretion of each designer's taste. I think a number of game players feel, "If Miyamoto's characters had cooler appearances, I could love them." All I can say to them is, "I am sorry."

Characters such as Link must be fun to play above all else, says Shigeru Miyamoto. This seems obvious, so why are there so many lackluster characters in computer and console games? (Used with permission by Nintendo of America, Inc.)

The big questions remains: Where does Miyamoto get inspiration for his beloved games and characters? How exactly did Mario came to life?

> The inspirations come from all over: my childhood adventures, the stories I heard growing up, the legends in Japan. After all, we can get inspiration from the ordinary things that everyone is experiencing in their daily lives, by looking at them from a different angle, that is. In the case of Mario, back in or around 1980 when we could not reproduce sophisticated designs on TV game machines due to the technological limitations, I had to make his nose bigger and put in a moustache so that players could notice he had the nose. I had to let him wear overalls so that his arms' movement became noticeable. Mario was the result of these rational ideas, plus the Italian design touch that I loved.

Miyamoto also warns that designers may not be able to objectively comprehend how the actual players will feel when they play the game for the first time, because they're so close to the project themselves.

JASON RUBIN, NAUGHTY DOG

Of course you know who Crash Bandicoot is, but creating a hit mascot doesn't happen overnight. In the following passage, Naughty Dog's cofounder and lead game designer Jason Rubin shares some words of wisdom on designing a lead character/mascot.

Asked if there is a "winning formula," Rubin responds:

> No, I don't think there's a winning formula in character design. With all we learned during the creation of the four *Crash* games, creating a new character for our next game has become *harder*, not easier. There are so many things we wanted to improve upon with *Crash*. But getting everything right is so hard. The best suggestion that I can offer is to ask a lot of opinions during the process, and be open to opposing opinions. Maybe after a few more times through this process I will be able to make broad sweeping generalizations about directions that work and don't work. Right now, we are still learning.

What the heck is Crash? According to the Naughty Dog Web site, Crash is a Perameles gunnii, of the order polyprotodonta, family Peramelidae, commonly known as the Eastern barred bandicoot. (Used with permission by Sony Computer Entertainment America (SCEA), Inc.)

Speaking of Crash, if had to summarize it into a paragraph, what would Rubin say is the key to his success? He ponders the question, then answers:

> Crash Bandicoot, the character, appeals to the broadest variety of people; young and old, male and female, Japanese, North American, or European. Most first time *Crash* purchasers, regardless of nationality, are buying from advertising, promotional material, or the box cover. If the character fails, then the game fails. *Crash* excelled in this department thanks to both a good original design and Sony Computer Entertainment's amazing worldwide marketing campaign.

If you haven't flipped through Chapter 2 already, jump back to read additional advice from Rubin on game design.

DAVID PERRY, SHINY ENTERTAINMENT

President of Shiny Entertainment and game designer extraordinaire David Perry has brought to life a number of hit characters over the years. This includes protagonists from the *Earthworm Jim* games, *MDK*, *Wild 9*, *Messiah*, and others.

Perry was asked to provide three (in)valuable pieces of advice on creating a successful game character, and all three of his answers are thought-provoking:

> 1. Humor is a very important part of entertainment. So if you can make it amusing, that's the easiest way to go. Unique abilities are also good. Earthworm Jim's suit would use him to achieve its goals. Funny stuff like that adds spice to the characters you're creating.
>
> 2. Somebody once said that a great character has a unique silhouette—if you can identify a character just by its outline, you know you've made something that will stand out in a crowd.

3. New and interesting weapons are also important. Nothing is worse than playing a game with a leaky peashooter. So great firepower is a good way to pat a gamer on the head.

Finally, how important is storyboarding a game? Perry says it depends. "Storyboards dictate the direction of the game and the pacing, but it ultimately comes down to how well the game plays. Storyboards make a great starting point, but you can't rely on them 100% of the time. What works for films doesn't always work for games."

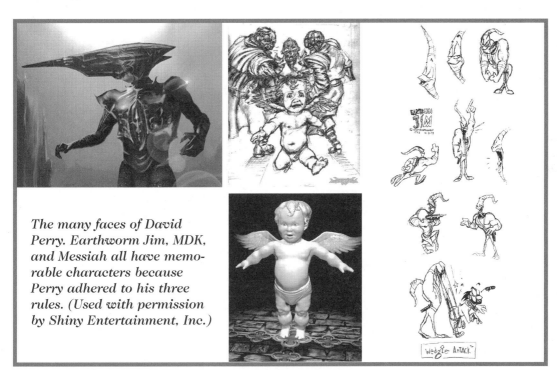

The many faces of David Perry. Earthworm Jim, MDK, and Messiah all have memorable characters because Perry adhered to his three rules. (Used with permission by Shiny Entertainment, Inc.)

GEORGE BROUSSARD, 3D REALMS

George Broussard is the president and partner of 3D Realms, one of the most sought-after development studios in the world. After all, they created the franchise known as Duke Nukem, and they're currently working on their fourth official title, *Duke Nukem Forever* (six if you count the PlayStation and Nintendo games they licensed).

What are the most important pieces of advice Broussard can give to someone trying to create a successful lead character in a game?

It really depends on the type of characters you want to make. We typically create over-the-top characters that lean more toward what you might find in comic books or high-action movies. Characters that are larger than life, and for those types of characters there's a pretty basic starting point.

Broussard says you can break down any character into the following characteristics:

- **Personality traits.** This defines the character's personality and how he or she reacts to situations.

- **Appearance.** There should be a distinctive look to your character, so people will learn to recognize the character from appearance alone. Examples: Lara Croft, Superman (almost any super hero), Darth Vader.

- **Motivation.** Why do your characters do what they do? What drives them? Once this is established, your characters will get stronger from doing things the way people expect them to.

- **Catch phrase.** The best characters become famous and well known for a simple catch phrase that sticks in people's minds, and usually becomes part of pop culture. Remember the "Where's the Beef?" commercials for Wendy's? Examples: "What's up, doc?" (Bugs Bunny), "Up, up, and away!" (Superman), "Holy hand grenades, Batman!" (Robin), "I'll be back" (The Terminator), "Go ahead, make my day" (Dirty Harry).

- **Name.** A character's name should be "catchy" and unique in some way, so people hear the name and get an instant image in their mind. Rhyming and alliteration are good tools to come up with a catchy character name. Examples: Duke Nukem, Sonic the Hedgehog, Earthworm Jim.

To illustrate his point on the personality, appearance, motivation, catch phrase, and name of a distinguishable character, Broussard provides three excellent examples:

> See if you can guess the character before the name is given, simply from the basic elements.
>
> **Personality trait:** Egotistical
>
> **Appearance:** Sunglasses, red muscle shirt, bandoliers, blond flattop
>
> **Motivation:** Kick alien a--/score with babes
>
> **Catch phrase:** "Come get some"
>
> **Name:** Duke Nukem
>
> **Personality traits:** Determined, inquisitive, loner
>
> **Appearance:** Black suit, white shirt, tie, cell phone
>
> **Motivation:** FBI agent/uncover conspiracies
>
> **Catch phrase:** "The Truth Is Out There"
>
> **Name:** Fox Mulder, from *The X-Files*
>
> **Personality traits:** Lazy, devious, self-centered, meek
>
> **Appearance:** Middle aged, gray hair
>
> **Motivation:** Space explorer, shirk duties, cause mischief
>
> **Catch phrase:** "Oh, the pain"
>
> **Name:** Dr. Smith from *Lost in Space*

Duke Nukem is one of the few characters to make a successful leap from a game to action figures and movies. (Used with permission by 3D Realms, Inc.)

Says Broussard, "The above is merely a starting point for developing your own characters, and you can make them more or less complex depending on your needs. But in the end, these characteristics are needed for a really memorable character."

When it comes to artwork, how do you translate your sketches to real characters in the game? Is it necessary for a series such as *Duke Nukem*? Broussard responds:

> As video games have gotten more and more complex, we've started to adopt the ways that movies do things. A lot of games today have scripts much like a movie, where all the action, cut-scenes, and dialogue are carefully laid out in every detail. Another thing that has been adopted is the idea of concept sketches. These sketches serve to solidify the look and feel of elements in the game, such as characters, locations, and action sequences.

The old adage "A picture is worth a thousand words" is certainly true.

This is a concept sketch for a character known as "Gus" in Duke Nukem Forever. Next to it, you can see how it translated into the game. The sketches provide the 3D modelers with a solid base to build on. (Used with permission by 3D Realms, Inc.)

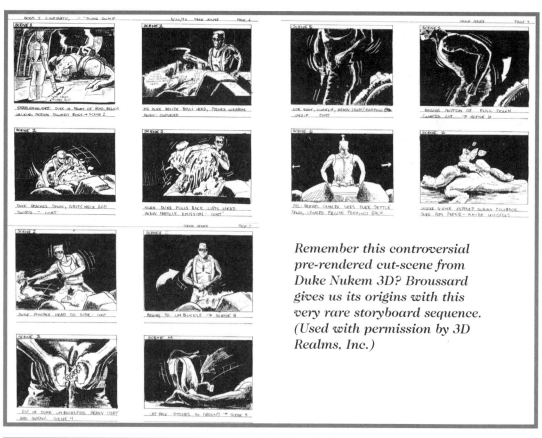

Remember this controversial pre-rendered cut-scene from *Duke Nukem 3D*? Broussard gives us its origins with this very rare storyboard sequence. (Used with permission by 3D Realms, Inc.)

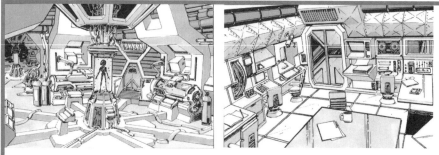

Here's an early representation of some locations in the highly anticipated Duke Nukem Forever. These room sketches aid the level designers considerably in the construction of levels. (Used with permission by 3D Realms, Inc.)

But what about design documents? Does Broussard think they're necessary for all types of games?

> Let me tell you about design docs. *Duke 3D* didn't even have one. We did stuff as we went, adding bits that were cool and discarding ideas that didn't work. Look how the game turned out. All we had was a vague notion that the game would be based in a future, seedy L.A. The rest came from a dynamic development process.

Duke Forever had substantially more on paper from the start because it's a much more cohesive and large game. But people who write 300-page design docs beforehand are wasting their time. The game design process (for most) is an evolutionary process. You refine and redesign as you go, learning and making things better. It's insane to write a 300-page doc, then just make the game. There is no way you can think of every cool idea before you make the game, and you have to be flexible enough to roll with the punches and add and refine ideas as you go, all according to the timeline.

Speaking from our experience, design docs are merely a general guideline that gets more and more polished as you go. You just try to stay 3–4 months ahead of things as you go. The design doc isn't done until the game is.

Also bear in mind that 3D action games are not that complex. They have bad guys, guns, items, and level locations. Not exactly rocket science, or something needing 300 pages.

Be sure to read all about the exciting *Duke Nukem* happenings at 3D Realms' official Web site (www.3drealms.com).

JANE JENSEN, SIERRA ON-LINE

As a game designer at Sierra On-Line, Jane Jensen has created one of their most memorable identities—*Gabriel Knight*—and has had plenty of experience in writing scripts for her award-winning adventure games. She joins us here to talk about designing characters and writing stories.

I think this is a very similar process to writing in any medium. Yes, I do try to work through the characters' backgrounds and motivations, as well as, hopefully, having some change in the character that results from the story.

I do maintain a fairly tight control on characters during production. I review the character models, write the dialogue myself, and participate in the casting. It's critical to get the characters right. There are also some greater challenges and rewards, specifically in interactive characters. On the downside, you must do voiceover messages and responses to a lot of unimportant details (like the door or magnifying glass) and remain in character. There usually are also dialogue paths that lead nowhere. On the plus side, using these kinds of messages—which are not really story-related—you can really flesh out a character for the player in a way that might be difficult in a book or movie, where you have to stick directly to story-related events.

There must be considerable storyboarding in the *Gabriel Knight* mysteries, no? "We do some storyboarding of the large scenes for artistic reasons," answers Jensen, "to get the animation and cameras right. But most things are not storyboarded." So how then does it all come together?

The design process goes something like this: My first job is the design "bible" or story outline. Usually this ends up being about 100 pages and takes me five months. It lays out every scene and what happens in that scene. The big puzzles, such as the treasure map in *Gabriel Knight III*, are laid out in this document, though smaller ones often will be added later.

The team reviews this document and any necessary changes are made. At this point, I do "room descriptions," which lay out each location in the game and describe everything in the location and what animations take place there. This is for the background artists. I then begin the scripting process. We have a tool in-house that's like a Microsoft Access database. Each scene, whether a large story scene or a one-line voiceover message, gets its own entry. These are keyed by noun, verb, case, sequence number, in that order. For example, in the location KITCHEN you might see an entry for STOVE LOOK ALL 1 "It's a stove." Or:

CHIMNEY CLIMB NOT_HAVE_ROPE 1 "How would I do that?"

CHIMNEY CLIMB HAVE_ROPE 1 "I guess I could try it."

CHIMNEY ROPE FIRST_TIME 1 "I guess I could try it."

CHIMNEY ROPE FIRST_TIME 2 <Gabriel takes out the rope and throws it up the chimney.>

CHIMNEY ROPE FIRST_TIME 3 <Gabriel climbs up the rope. CUT TO: Rooftop>

CHIMNEY ROPE OTHER_TIME 1 "I don't need to go back up there."

In this fashion, each interactivity in the game is laid out with the logic (what triggers the response and under what conditions), the dialogue, and the description of the action for the animators and programmers.

After I see the art that's done for the backgrounds, I also add "incidental messages," that is, simple LOOK messages or whatever, for items that the artists put in the room that I hadn't called for (or sometimes I'll have them take it out if it's too leading or confusing).

Here's a shot of Gabriel Knight in the third incarnation of Jane Jenson's popular adventure game series. For the uninitiated, Knight's a charming, rakish New Orleans resident who has a way with women when he's not (and sometimes when he is) tracking down supernatural forces. (Gabriel Knight III: Blood of the Sacred, Blood of the Damned is a registered trademark of Sierra On-Line, Inc. Images used with permission. Copyright 1999-2000 Sierra On-Line, Inc. All Rights Reserved.)

Jensen says many people wonder how to tell a real story interactively. In fact, she has been to conferences where Hollywood types claim it can't be done. She explains why they believe this is:

The reason is this: A real, defined plot and story are by nature linear and inflexible. People ask why *Gabriel Knight* (*GK*) doesn't really have the ignorantly lauded "multiple endings." The answer is simple. It's because a *real* story has a natural flow and a natural termination. If in *GK I*, for example, I decided that the hero died at the end or the "bad guy" lived or some such variation, the players would have been frustrated—they would know that was not the "right" ending. Indeed, *GK I* had a "false" ending in which the hero died; players instinctively knew this was not the "right" ending and that they'd done something wrong. They would even write to me in those words: "I saw the wrong ending once but then I replayed and got the real ending." Take, for example, the movie *Clue*. It had multiple endings, but most of them seemed pretty fishy. You knew the last one was the "real" one. And even to provide those multiples, the story was not so much a story as a series of red herrings.

Another problem is the natural linearity of storytelling. Gabriel can't confront his mistress with her sins until he has learned about them. And she can't threaten his life until he has confronted her. And he can't respond to that threat until she has threatened him. And so on. A story, by its nature, is a sequence of action/reaction, with the stakes and the pressure building more and more at each arc. How, then, to make it interactive?

The answer is the old "string of pearls" approach, which was first described to me by Roberta Williams when we were working on *King's Quest VI*. The idea is to picture each major plot point as the beginning of a pearl on a string. It has one central point, which is fixed. This could, for example, be the beginning of the game, or the beginning of a chapter or time block. You know where the player is at this point, you're in control of what he knows, and you convey the next large chunk of story. After this comes the "wide part" of the pearl. There may be 3 or 8 or 15 different little scenes or actions the player can trigger, and he can trigger them in any order. Thus, these smaller actions are "nonlinear." But once the player has done all of these things (or, at least, all that are required for the story—some might be optional), the game registers this fact and comes back to a central point—ending the chapter or section of the game by giving another big story chunk and thus "closing" the pearl.

As an example, Jensen offers the following:

The first chapter of *GK II* opens with a scene in which the villagers of Rittersberg come to ask Gabriel to take on a new *Schattenjäger* case: the hunting of an alleged werewolf that has killed a young girl. I know where the players are mentally—they have just started the game and as of yet know nothing. So the scene is simple; it's just like the opening scene of a book or movie. After the scene ends, Gabriel is left in the farm house of the murdered girl's parents. At this point we are "interactive." The player can move Gabriel around and explore the surroundings. During this chapter, [you as] Gabriel will do the following plot points:

■ Read a newspaper that tells about the case, mentioning that wolves that escaped from the local zoo are the suspected culprits and giving the name of the detective on the case.

- Write to your assistant and mail the letter.

- Examine the crime scene at the farm; take a cast of a wolf-like print and pick up some animal hair.

- Go to the zoo and look around at the wolves in the habitat—eventually interviewing a boy who feeds the animals and the man in charge of the animals, and getting in to examine a wolf up close in order to get some hair for comparison.

- Go to the police station and ask to see the detective in charge.

- Take the samples of the wolf hair along with the hair and print from the crime scene to a local lab for analysis.

- Look up your family lawyer and ask for help translating some German you find.

- Follow the man from the zoo to a men's club and figure out a way to get in.

"This is all greatly simplified," admits Jensen, "but it illustrates how things are linear or not within the body of the chapter or the 'wide part' of the pearl." Keeping with the examples from *Gabriel Knight II*, Jensen expands on the "string of pearls" analogy:

Gabriel can't get to the zoo until he's read about it in the newspaper, so those two actions are linear. However, he can do the zoo sequence independently of the police station sequence and writing to his assistant. He can't accomplish much at the lab until he's completed the zoo and gotten the hair sample, but he can go there and have the crime scene finds analyzed even if he doesn't have the hair from the zoo. The lawyer can be visited at any time, though you need the German note to get him to translate it. You can go through the entire zoo sequence without ever having found the hair and print at the crime scene. And so on. What all these actions lead to is getting into the men's club. That needs to be disallowed until all other actions are done, because that's where we "close the pearl" and end the chapter. This is taken care of as follows: You can go visit the club, but in order to be admitted you need family papers from your lawyer. You can visit the club earlier (after visiting the man at the zoo and asking your lawyer for the German translation, which gives you the name of the club), but the concierge asks for these papers. If you go to your lawyer to request them, he accepts the request but claims that his secretary needs to "find them in the file and Xerox them." No matter how often you go back to the lawyer, these papers will not be ready until the game finds that all other actions have been done (write to assistant and mail it, visit police station, etc.). Once all these things are done, the lawyer will give you the papers, and with these you can get accepted into the club. At this point (Gabriel gives papers to concierge), I once again know where the player is in the story—he has completed all actions for the chapter, so now we "close the pearl" and have the chapter close with a large story scene in which Gabriel meets the members of the club. This completes the chapter as well as setting up the intrigue for the next chapter (by introducing many new characters that the player will want to check out). It's not, perhaps, infinitely nonlinear, but it does provide enough variety and freedom for the player to explore in his own manner and learn things in a number of different ways. More importantly, it allows us to have lesser and greater plot points, which, in turn, allows us to tell a story.

Jensen has published novels based on the *Gabriel Knight* series, and she also gives us a special treat—excerpts from the design doc of the latest *Gabriel Knight* adventure, dubbed *Gabriel Knight III: Blood of the Sacred, Blood of the Damned.*

EXCERPTS FROM THE GABRIEL KNIGHT III DESIGN DOCUMENT

Examples of fleshing out characters:

Detective Mosely

Mosely is from the New Orleans Police Department and is an old friend of Gabriel. Mosely just happens to be in Rennes-le-Château, having come on a "treasure hunt" vacation package. "It sounded like a lark," he says, but his behavior is decidedly strange. He keeps disappearing, for one thing. For another, he seems a little too interested in Gabriel's case. Mosely further bewilders by insisting that Gabriel not let anyone on the tour know that he's a cop, which, to Gabriel's thinking, is the only remotely interesting thing about him. Why does Gabriel get the feeling he's not *really* as "off-duty" as he claims?

Madeline Buthane

Beautiful, strong-willed, and erotically French, Buthane has down cold the mix of outdoorsy-yet-quintessentially-feminine womanhood that few men can resist. She certainly has her nearly all-male tour group wrapped around her little finger. Still, she is *awfully* enthusiastic about—one might even say *obsessed with*—the Rennes-le-Château treasure. Could the tour group be a ruse? A way to get free labor for a personal mission or get frequent access to the region for her own purposes? And is her interest in the ideas of every male she runs into really coquettishness? Or is she hunting for something specific?

John Wilkes

Wilkes is an Australian of the exceedingly macho variety (as if there were any other kind). In his late 40s, Wilkes has been all around the world—at least the desolate parts of it. He's a real treasure hunter, that's quite obvious. Although he won't talk about it unless exceedingly drunk or well seduced, Wilkes believes he has the secret of the treasure of Rennes-le-Château. He believes the secret will make him incredibly wealthy. He's dead wrong about that.

An example of a scene and puzzle:

Catch Emilio spying in hallway (3D puzzle).

When talking to Mosely about the case, if you zoom in on the keyhole in Mosely's door during the conversation, you can see an ear.

When you go outside after the conversation, you can see Emilio just stepping away from the door. He has a glass in his hand. He pretends to finish drinking what was in it (the glass was actually empty); then he puts it down on a service tray in the hall and walks away.

> If Gabriel misses this scene, he can still get the glass, as it will be on the tray when he exits.
>
> Take glass from hall tray.
>
> The glass goes into inventory.
>
> This glass can be used on any of the hotel room doors at any time to see if someone is in the room or not. (We'll play various sound effects to indicate their presence in the room.)

And finally, an example of a conversation tree:

> Jean, the hotel desk clerk
>
> Talk to Jean
>
> Topic: Rennes-le-Château
>
> Jean recommends that Gabriel check out the museum.
>
> Topic: Two men with a trunk
>
> He wasn't on duty last night so he doesn't know how people came in or what luggage they had, but there are only seven rooms and a tour group takes up the other six rooms (besides Gabriel's).
>
> Topic: Tour group check-in
>
> Jean only knows that the rooms were reserved and filled, not what time people arrived.

The official *Gabriel Knight III: Blood of the Sacred, Blood of the Damned* Web page is at www.sierrastudios.com/games/gk3.

A very well-written and informative guide to writing design documents is available on the Gamasutra Web site. It's written by DigiPen's Tzvi Freeman and was originally published in *Game Developer* magazine in mid-1997. To access the guide, go to www.gamasutra.com/features/game_design/091297/design_doc.htm. Special thanks to editor Alex Dunne for the link!

ROBERTA WILLIAMS, SIERRA ON-LINE

During a telephone interview, Williams gives her take on storyboarding and creating characters.

> Storyboarding works when you're creating a cut-scene or intro movie, when there's less (or no) inventory. Storyboarding seems to interfere with gameplay since it's hard to show all the options visually.

Williams says she has done very little storyboarding and writes more in script form for her games, such as the *King's Quest* series or the *Phantasmagoria* titles. The design document is written rather than drawn and will describe with words what a character or room should look like. Concept artists may take it over from there to sketch the visuals. Williams also writes in a language so that the programmers will understand what she wants at that spot in the game.

Williams fleshes out the history of the other characters in the game much more than the main protagonist—the one that the player assumes the role of. Why is this?

> This is so you can put yourself in their shoes. Main characters are the least fleshed out in the game, so you don't know where they're from or who they are, really. I make them more open to interpretation."

For more on how to create a great design document, flip over to Chapter 20, "Breaking Into the Industry."

RON GILBERT, HUMONGOUS ENTERTAINMENT

The gaming genius behind many of our most lovable characters, such as *Monkey Island*'s Guybrush Threepwood, *Maniac Mansion*'s Bernard, and Pajama Sam, believes that "there has to be something about the character that is visually recognizable, and simply understood." Gilbert continues:

> We don't have the bandwidth yet for complex characters like in film, so we simplify and often rely on stereotypes, and then we build them up through storytelling. In action or RTS [real-time strategy] games, we rely on these stereotypes for you to instantly understand who the character is. The story is secondary, more of an afterthought, but not for adventure games, of course.

Many of Gilbert's latest and greatest characters can be found and downloaded at www.humongous.com.

TOM HALL, ION STORM

To continue with our roundtable of game designers and artists, ION Storm's Tom Hall takes some time out from working on *Anachronox* to give his opinion on creating a successful computer or console game character. He comments:

> Good lead characters must have recognizable motivations, have personalities that are engaging, represent a player's fantasy, and have an interesting quirk/Achilles' heel/pet object that makes interesting. Their humor should be from within. Cracking jokes is cool, but if you hear them again and again, they wear thin. If something is funny because "that guy is just being that guy," then it's funny every time. Ben from *Full Throttle* is consistently cool. Any jokes or comments make sense within his tough biker world. And the free life on the road is a common fantasy—the player wants to be Ben. His pet object is his cool bike.
>
> Manny Calavera and other Tim Schafer lead characters always have wonderful references and non-sequiturs that keep every interaction interesting. They also have wonderfully expressive faces, which most games lack. This helps the players, because you don't have to tell them how the character is feeling, or use excessive voice work or exaggerated body movement—they can just look dejected. Tim is very good at presenting characters that are very unique and instantly familiar at the same time.

Manny Calavera and the other memorable personalities from Tim Schafer's ingenious Grim Fandango are great examples of rich, expressive characters, says ION Storm's Tom Hall. (Courtesy of LucasArts Entertainment Company LLC. © 1998 LucasArts. All rights reserved. Used by permission)

> On the action game front, Duke Nukem is always crass and full of *machismo*—a refreshing break for many people when times are so politically correct. He's basically Arnold mixed with Ash from *Evil Dead 2*.
>
> Lara Croft has that wonderful accent, the tough adventuring female angle (like a British Ripley [from the *Alien* films]), and the ridiculously proportioned measurements, which are the stuff of teenage fantasy. For men, you want to adventure with her, and be with her. For women, she's a strong female role model—a rare thing in gaming.

"Another great thing is a sense of mystery," continues Hall. "If there's more to their story than just what happens in the game, that's great." What exactly does he mean by this? Answers Hall:

> If you give the character a history, even if you don't mention it, the character and your writing will feel deeper. And if you do have foreshadowing, like Cloud freaking out once in a while in *Final Fantasy VII*, questions are raised in the player's mind. This is wonderful, and makes the player yearn to know what happened, and what's next.

Are there things a game designer should not do when creating a lead character?

> I would say don't rely on punchlines, and don't just trot out the usual stereotypes. Make something new. If you steal a recognizable stereotype, give it a twist that makes it fresh. If you're going to have an old Gabby Hayes prospector, have him knowledgeable in quantum mechanics. Have your action hero brake for pets. Have the old lady confess her torrid love affair with the character's father. Set up expectations and go against them, and you'll always get people's interest.

JOE SELINSKE, WESTWOOD STUDIOS

To complete this chapter on "getting ideas down on paper," Westwood Studios' Joe Selinske offers an example on fleshing out a character's dossier prior to creating a game. Before moving over to Las Vegas' Westwood, Selinske was responsible for creating Elexis Sinclair, the femme fatale from Ritual/Activision's *Sin*.

Joe Selinkse submits Elexis Sinclair's dossier as an example of how budding game designers can breathe life into game characters. Sinclair was the deliciously evil character in Ritual Entertainment's 1998 shooter, Sin. (Used with permission by Activision, Inc.)

The following is an excerpt from her file:

> Name: Elexis Sinclair
>
> Sex: Female
>
> Age: 31
>
> Eye color: Green
>
> Hair color: Black
>
> Marital status: Single
>
> Occupation: Bio-geneticist, chemist, and head of SinTEK Industries
>
> Distinguishing marks: Tattoo on right buttock, tattoo around ankle, and navel ring
>
> Family relations: Thrall, father (whereabouts currently unknown). Diane, mother (living in Europe).
>
> Background history:
>
> Born in the sumptuous suburb of Freeport to Dr. Thrall Sinclair and Diane Kettle Sinclair on April 12, 1996. Elexis' mother abandoned them when Elexis was two to go out and "find herself." Her father, Thrall, a university professor and research scientist for a large pharmaceutical company, raised Elexis. She attended various boarding schools until the age of six, at which time her mother returned to partake in Thrall's good fortune. Thrall gathered up all of his and Elexis' worldly possessions, liquidated all of his assets, hid his money, and disappeared into the wilds of various jungles to escape from his estranged wife.
>
> Not much is known of this time in Elexis' life, except that they both traveled around the world while Thrall studied all of the mystical and wondrous native sciences. For four years they traveled, learned, explored, and studied. One experience changed all that when Elexis contracted a rare sickness that was running rampant through one of the towns that they were currently in. Thrall feared for his daughter's life and rushed his little girl back to Freeport and the best medical help that money could buy. Elexis underwent extensive medical treatment and almost died due to complications.
>
> Thrall wept by her bedside as she lay at death's door. This should never happen to anybody. Death is the cruelest of masters and on this day he vowed to

find some way to prolong or even conquer this specter. He returned to his work with a newfound passion: to conquer death.

Many new challenges and situations help mold the woman that Elexis would become. Her mother's return (yet again), the problems and pain that Diane caused Elexis and her father. The fights over money, the struggle over control of Elexis' upbringing, and the tearing of her poor fragmented soul into a million pieces. She turned her attention away from family and began to study. She was soon swept up in a new passion—a passion for knowledge. She grew up fast and never looked back.

She had an affinity for the sciences and worked long and hard to learn everything there was to learn at the university. She graduated in three years with degrees in both chemistry and biology and entered into the masters program that summer. In only a year and a half, unheard-of at this or any other university, she completed the masters programs for both chemistry and biology. She manipulated her way into a lucrative research project that she was then able to use to obtain her Ph.D. in biochemistry and genetic engineering. She had become an equal to her father in cunning and talent.

She joined her father again and together they brought the smaller but growing SinTEK Industries to the forefront of the medical and scientific community. They diversified the business even more and expanded their market into the global economy. They stunned the world with a new product, Vanity, which seemed to stop and almost reverse the aging process. Their lives were set; Thrall quietly retired from the scene, and Elexis leaped to the forefront of the media to continue to push SinTEK Industries.

Little is known about her current genetic research. Rumor has it that she is experimenting in areas where many scientists fear to tread. SinTEK Industries is a virtual fortress, so even the local law enforcement has had no luck in getting even remotely close to speaking with Elexis about this. You can be sure that, whatever Elexis is involved in, it's something that's not even close to moral.

She's a gorgeous and mysterious woman. A genius who uses every faculty at her command to control and manipulate the situations to her benefit. She has her finger in so many different places that even an octopus would be envious.

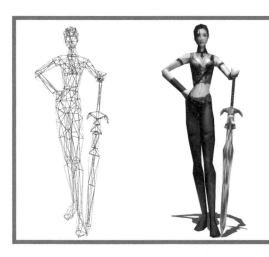

Is sex often used to sell a game character? It's hard not to argue that sex appeal had something to do with the success of Sin's Elexis Sinclair, Tomb Raider's Lara Croft, and pictured here, Drakan's slender but big-busted Rynn. Why should games be any different than movies, TV, music, or comic books? (Used with permission by Activision, Inc.)

CHAPTER 5
PUZZLE DESIGN

You look through the keyhole into the next room and there it is—the book of spells you've been yearning to find throughout this treacherous journey. With this precious collection of magic potions and chants, you will surely be able to get past the grunts guarding the castle up ahead. Alas, the door is locked, but a second glimpse into the keyhole reveals something sticking out of the other side. It's the key! You hastily look around the room, to find a scrap piece of paper lying on the table. And then it hits like a bolt of lightning. You slide the paper halfway under the locked door and bang your fists on it until the key falls out of the keyhole and onto the paper. Slowly sliding it back toward you exposes the key, and into the room you go to snag the book.

This hypothetical example is meant to illustrate *puzzle design*. That is, a game designers' sneaky way of inserting a challenging obstacle the player must solve with brains and not brawn (usually) to continue playing the game. These kinds of puzzles are found in adventure, role-playing, and some action games. There are usually different kinds of these puzzles littered throughout games:

- *Environmental puzzles* can be solved by analyzing and often altering your surroundings in the game. In Nintendo's *Legend of Zelda: Ocarina of Time*, the player must light torches on each side of a door to enter a new area of the cave.

- In *inventory puzzles*, objects in your possession may solve the puzzle. It's fair to say that environmental and inventory puzzles work together quite a bit, such as in the example above (or in a game like LucasArts' *Day of the Tentacle*, where you must place your bottle of wine in a time machine and pick it up in the future if you need vinegar).

- *Conversation-based puzzles* are usually solved by saying the right piece of dialogue when conversing with a character, or perhaps recalling an exchange between characters in the game that may be used in the present situation. An example of this is Mindscape/Legend Entertainment's *The Blackstone Chronicles*, where the ghosts of tortured psychiatric patients must be talked to in order for the player to find his/her kidnapped son.

- Finally, many adventure games, especially those that came out in the mid-1990s, used puzzles that had no relevance whatsoever to the task at hand. For instance, in DreamWorks Interactive's *The Neverhood Chronicles*, the player must solve a sliding tile puzzle in one instance and play a game of *Concentration* in another, though it had nothing to do with the game.

BOB BATES, LEGEND ENTERTAINMENT

Bob Bates is the studio head at Legend Entertainment, and he shares the duties of running the organization with Mike Verdu, who has been his partner at Legend since they founded the company in 1989. Altogether, he has written, co-designed, or produced over 20 games that have won more than 30 industry awards.

Bates begins by explaining how puzzles relate to gaming, and the best ways to insert them smoothly into the game world:

> When you set out to write a game, you first design the major structural elements—the story, the setting, the characters, the major threat to the player's world, and the final goal that the player is striving for. Once you've done that, you've got to put obstacles between the player and his goal. These are the puzzles, and they must flow up naturally out of the setting you've created and the story that you're telling.
>
> Some think this requirement is unique to the adventure game genre, but it's not. Putting obstacles in the way of the hero has always been a fundamental part of storytelling. Ulysses didn't get back from the Trojan wars in a weekend.
>
> The important thing is that each puzzle be appropriate to its setting, that it be reasonable for the obstacle to be there, and that, when we solve it, we know why what we did worked.

Bates believes that the villain should be at the center of the puzzle. He explains:

> Probably the single most useful piece of advice I can give about designing puzzles is to think about the villain. Something doesn't want your hero to succeed. Whether it's a person, the gods, the government, or the ultimate bad guy—whatever that thing is, is the villain. The villain is in active opposition to your hero/heroine. He's the one creating the obstacles. He says to himself, "I do not want the hero to succeed, and I will stop him by doing this." The material he uses is material from the environment. His purpose is clear, and it's up to the hero/heroine to overcome the obstacle. So when you're designing a puzzle, ask yourself why it should be there. Who would have put it there? Why? Who is this bad guy and why is he threatening your hero/heroine?

The villain in John Saul's The Blackstone Chronicles is the spirit of the player's deceased father, Malcolm Metcalf, as pictured in this painting on the asylum wall. By understanding Malcolm's ways, it may be easier to get out of the many puzzles inherent in the sanitarium. (Used with permission by Mindscape, Inc., All Rights Reserved)

"And remember to have your puzzles make sense," reminds Bates. "Give the player enough clues to solve them, don't make them too hard, and make sure that every puzzle advances the story."

Bates gives an example of a character-based problem to solve in order to advance the story:

> For example, think of a locked door. Sure, you could put a "move the blocks around" combination lock on the door. But what if you had a woman sitting on the floor in front of the door, crying? Clearly you need to talk to her to learn why she's crying. And then you're going to have to solve her problem to get past her.
>
> So suddenly we have introduced character development. Probably the very same bad guy who is making your life miserable did something nasty to her. The player learns more about her, the environment, and the villain—all because you designed a really good puzzle.

Bates concludes by suggesting that story and/or character-related puzzles may be the best way to go when creating an adventure game. "If you think of each puzzle as a storytelling opportunity, then it will fall naturally into the game, and your players will accept it as an integral part of the story, instead of an arbitrary roadblock put there to slow them down."

JANE JENSEN, SIERRA ON-LINE

Jane Jensen has talked with us quite a bit throughout the pages in this book, offering her expertise in many areas, including game design and character development (Chapter 4), and now she wears the hat of puzzle designer extraordinaire. Her flagship series for Sierra Studios is the *Gabriel Knight* (*GK*) franchise.

Jensen says it helps to choose a story concept in the first place that's inherently loaded with "puzzles." She explains:

> Detective mysteries work well. What does a detective do? He examines evidence at the scene, tracks down and interviews suspects, perhaps follows people, gets news back from the lab, looks up the files on his suspects, etc. All of this natural work is easily converted into puzzles. "Quests" of the kind that *The Odyssey* or *Sinbad* made popular work for similar reasons. It's in the nature of a quest to explore foreign lands, have fights with bad guys or monsters, find treasure, and so on. A love story is a good example of a genre that's harder to make puzzles from. This is not to say that every game should be a detective story or a quest, but do be aware of how the puzzles will flow from your story before you spend a great deal of time writing it.

Jensen believes that puzzles are best when they flow naturally from the plot. Why is this, exactly? And why have so many game designers added puzzles that don't make any sense in relation to what's going on? Is there room for both?

> A story with a bunch of logic puzzles (like *7th Guest*) has its place, but it probably won't be much of a story. It's not realistic to have your detective keep running into Chinese boxes and complicated puzzle locks. Of course, one or two aren't bad. In fact, you must put in more interesting puzzles than simply interviewing people and finding keys or reading letters. Just try to integrate them with the story.

In *GK I*, there was a clock in Gabriel's grandmother's attic that used to belong to his grandfather (now deceased). The clock was a German mechanical clock and it looked like it might do something, but what? On the outer dial was a series of images: a dragon, a lion, a moon, etc. To open the hidden drawer in the clock, you had to set the dragon to the top (12:00) position and set the hands of the clock to 3:00. A puzzle? Yes. But it was worked into the plot. "Three snakes" was a recurring theme in Gabriel's dreams—dreams he shared with his father and grandfather. This imagery was a key one to their enemies, being a sort of sacred symbol to them. This little puzzle not only emphasized the importance of this image in Gabriel's family dreams; it acted as a hint to a later, more important puzzle where "three snakes" had to be set in the enemy temple to get back the family talisman. Thus the "three snakes" ideas provided two very "logic puzzle"–type puzzles, but it was also an important plot point and felt like part of the story—not a tack-on.

Also in *GK I*, Gabriel could visit the tomb of Marie Laveau in New Orleans. He finds odd symbolic marks on the tomb that he can copy. By copying these marks, he can find a voodoo expert to tell him that it's a code and translate the message for him. It's a direct letter-for-symbol translation, and the message is a hint pointing toward a suspect—but nothing definitive. That's because that first message is not the main point of this puzzle. Later on in the game, Gabriel finds a second message left on the tomb that he can copy (but not have translated at that point—the "expert" is now unavailable). Still later, he needs to have the voodoo cult take something specific with them to a meeting. How to accomplish this? He can leave his own message on the tomb, which will be assumed to be from the code writer. The problem? To leave the message, he needs some letters that weren't used in the first, translated version. But by transferring the letters he knows from the first message to the second message, he gets something like this: "I would l_ke to h_ve." Thus giving him by deduction the symbols for *i* and *a*. Now he can leave his complete message. This is a hard puzzle sequence, quite complex. And yet it does work with the story.

In *GK III*, I found a story idea that was naturally chockfull of puzzles. The story was about an obscure little place in France called Rennes-le-Château. The real-life mystery involves a number of riddles that supposedly point the way to buried treasure in the region. Not only was this a great mystery plot idea, but it provided the game with a main body of puzzles (deciphering riddles, laying out a treasure map) that were inherent to the story.

LOUIS CASTLE, WESTWOOD STUDIOS

We now turn our attention to Louis Castle, vice president of creative development at Westwood Studios. This experienced producer, programmer, artist, and art director explains how some of the creative puzzles were conceived for *Lands of Lore 3*:

The storyline and the gameplay evolve hand in hand. We try to map out the emotional experiences the player will have while playing the game. Puzzles figure heavily into this, since they will slow down a game and take the player into a different range of emotions than the action sequences. The story and the puzzles are usually thought of in the abstract first—"At this point we need a task that will help the player improve *xyz* skill." Then each designer reaches into his or her bag of tricks to offer some ideas on how to accomplish the goal.

Many times a designer will have a great idea for a puzzle but can't find a place for it. I encourage designers to flesh out their ideas and set them aside. It's amazing how the need for that idea will come up within a few weeks.

Castle says that puzzle designing is really a collaborative effort:

We have in-house writers and have used contract writers. As long as the designers know the emotional beats of the story and the basic actions that take place, the writers can go to town on characters and situations. Many times a puzzle or task comes out of reading and interpreting the story.

In *Lands of Lore 3*, you have the opportunity to travel to the underworld, where spirits are trapped in limbo due to the circumstances of their deaths. You meet a maiden who bemoans her fiery fate and that of her sisters. She implores you to end her suffering. As you explore the house, the rooms catch fire, and you're caught in an inferno that spreads down the halls and into the sleeping chambers. The puzzle? To find the lamps and empty the oil before the event begins. As with all quests in *Lands of Lore 3*, care was taken to reset the events should you fail and "perish" in the flames. In this case, the flames are but phantoms—in all cases there is a way out of your position so that no situation is a dead end, where the player is stuck with no way to progress. This prevents players from feeling they have to restart the game to succeed. It's always possible, although sometimes far more difficult, to finish the game.

Instead of punishing the player for failing to solve this real-time puzzle in Lands of Lore 3, the designers at Westwood Studios have written an alternate way for players to beat the situation. (Used with permission by Westwood Studios, Inc.)

ROBERTA WILLIAMS, SIERRA ON-LINE

"Designing good puzzles is an art. To jog the player's mind without giving it all away or making it so tough that they give up—that perfect balance is a very fine line." Williams should know; after all, she's often referred to as the godmother of graphical adventure games. *Mystery House* was one of the first graphical adventure games, released on the Apple IIe in 1980.

Williams maintains that being obtuse isn't bad, but "it's how you give messages and arrange your clues, dialogue, inventory, and environment." Williams believes it's important to "remember to repeat hints, in case the player missed the first one; do this until the puzzle is solved, then the clue can go away."

 Ever play an adventure game and, because you couldn't figure out a puzzle, you "cheated" by finding a walkthrough on the Internet or calling a hint line? The most frustrating part of all this is when you find out the answer to the puzzle was related to something you didn't notice onscreen. Because of this, Roberta Williams says when she's writing environmental puzzles, she always makes sure that the object that must be noticed is twice the size it should be, and center screen, if possible. She also believes in "message clues" through dialogue or through items that say something when you click on them.

Following suit with the other members of this chapter's puzzle-writing round table, Williams says she prefers real-world puzzles to abstract ones, and she cites Trilobyte's *The 7th Guest*, where the puzzles have no relevance to the story.

An example of a good environmental puzzle (and one that relates to the story) can be found in Williams' latest adventure, *King's Quest: Mask of Eternity*. Explains Williams:

> At one point in the game, you have to look for a Stone of Order. It was stolen and it must be retrieved, as it [represents] law and order for these people.
>
> Later on, the stone is found, but it's high up on an altar with lava below, and the player is on a plank suspended above the lava. Between the gamer and the stone hang seven gong-like objects. There are also message clues when you click on objects such as the stone in the distance, your inventory, and the gongs, which allude to the solution. The player then realizes that his bow and arrows can be used to shoot at these gongs. When a gong is hit, a musical tone plays and color flashes. If the player hits the right one, the platform extends out toward the stone. If the second one is wrong, it brings the game back again.
>
> The solution can be figured out by trial and error (for example, writing down which one is first, second, third, etc.), but the tones also represent a musical scale beginning with C, and they go in order up the scale, and the colors represent the seven colors in the rainbow. Hence, the "Stone of Order."

Roberta Williams says some of her puzzles in King's Quest: Mask of Eternity may be solved in different ways, with plenty of messages given to the player as feedback. (King's Quest: Mask of Eternity is a registered trademark of Sierra On-Line, Inc. Images used with permission. Copyright 1999-2000 Sierra On-Line, Inc. All Rights Reserved.)

For a playable retrospective of Roberta Williams' fruitful career, be sure to pick up Sierra's *The Roberta Williams Anthology*.

CHAPTER 6
LEVEL DESIGN

The worldwide PC gaming community hasn't been the same since id Software's *Wolfenstein 3D* was unleashed in the spring of 1992. More than a quarter million people scrambled to download this racy, 700KB shareware game from their local bulletin board system (BBS), and thus, the first-person perspective 3D "shooter" was born.

The next seven years yielded many memorable shooters—*Doom, Dark Forces, Duke Nukem 3D, Quake, Jedi Knight, GoldenEye 007, Unreal, Sin,* and *Half-Life*—and in so doing, it launched a specialized and necessary art form known as *level design*. Loosely speaking, level design pertains to creating the architecture of maps in the game, plus dealing with object placement, mission or goal of the map, and often mini-missions within the level as well.

So what makes for a well-laid-out and challenging level to complete? What are some of the more common mistakes found in amateur level design? Is there a science to it? You bet. This chapter features the world's top level designers and their invaluable opinions on what makes or breaks level architecture in 3D shooters. Keep in mind that many of these pointers can also apply to other 3D games, such as third-person perspective action/adventure hybrids (e.g., *Tomb Raider*).

The classic Wolfenstein 3D almost single-handedly diffused side-scrolling "platform" games on the PC. But with this new perspective came new obstacles...(Used with permission by id Software)

TIM WILLITS, ID SOFTWARE

As level designer on *Ultimate Doom* and *Quake* and lead level designer on the legendary *Quake II* and *Quake III: Arena*, Tim Willits has gathered quite a bit of knowledge (and respect in the industry) on how to create a successful map for 3D shooters. He shares with us his words of wisdom on this exciting facet of 3D game development. Before Willits sits down to create a map, he asks himself, is this going to be a single-player map or Deathmatch map? He expands:

> Before you can do anything, you need to figure out what kind of level you want. It's a lot easier if you stick to either Deathmatch (DM) or single player (SP). Though it can be done, making a map great for both DM and SP is a very difficult task. Usually if it's great for DM it'll be too circular for SP, and if it's a fun SP map it's usually too straight for DM.

 Deathmatch, or *DM*, refers to non–team-based multiplayer maps typically played over the Internet or on a LAN with other human players. It's a "kill or be killed" scenario where the goal is to stay alive and rack up as many *frags* (points) as possible. Kill a player, get a frag; die yourself, lose one. Hence the name "Deathmatch."

While many of the same principles can be applied to creating both SP and DM maps, Willits breaks up his advice into separate groups for SP and DM.

SINGLE-PLAYER LEVELS

According to Willits, there are a number of rules to adhere to when devising successful single-player levels. The following are the most significant rules to keep in mind.

FOCUS AND CONTINUITY

Of the utmost importance in Willits' opinion is focus and continuity of the task. And, as he explains, it can be easy to lose both during a game's cycle:

> Every game has one overall mission or goal. The game then is made up of many single levels. Every level in turn must also have one overall mission. And every map must have a reason why it exists. It's important that the designer doesn't forget this—it happens a lot. A designer will be working on a level with a goal in mind. And then something happens—sometimes a technology is introduced into the game or a technical problem arises and the focus of the map shifts. Sometimes the designers don't even realize that they've lost focus on their original goals of the level, but they have. When this happens, the designers must step back, look at where things are going, and focus more attention on the overall design and goals of the level, sometimes reworking areas or changing the goals to accommodate the map's mission. Basically it's crucial that designers stay focused on their ultimate goals in designing a level.

As a side note, Willits reminds level designers that there must be one person who focuses on the entire design process, to ensure that levels don't stray too far from their original goal. A fresh set of eyes from someone not too close to the level designing is ideal for all games.

ARCHITECTURE DESIGN AND GAMEPLAY ELEMENTS

According to Willits, SP maps require a pretty linear flow, and they need to guide the player through the level with both architecture design and gameplay elements. To clarify, *architecture design* is basically how the areas are constructed. There should be natural breaks in levels that separate the major components of that level, as well as the level's mini-missions (Willits gets to this in a moment). *Gameplay elements*, on the other hand, follow the events orchestrated by the story of the level within the game. Willits cites an example:

> If the player's mission on the power station level is to destroy the nuclear reactor, then the level may be broken down into areas such as the control center, waste pumping station, core reactor, and coolant subsystems. Each one of these areas must look like it's supposed to look, as well as perform some function in the overall level. The player may need to enter the security codes in the control center to grant access to the coolant subsystems. Once in the coolant subsystems, the player could drain the core reactor's coolant, causing an unstable heat exchange within the core. Finally, the player could reverse the waste in the waste-pumping station, creating a chain reaction that would destroy the entire nuclear reactor.

RISKS AND REWARDS

Risks and rewards must be peppered throughout SP maps to challenge the gamer while plowing toward the end of a game. Willits believes it's essential that each new area contain these kinds of obstacles. Here's an example:

> The player enters a new area of a map and there's a slime pool that's too far to jump across. On the other side of the slime pool is a button that extends the bridge, but it's guarded by a monster. The player's mini-mission is to extend the bridge. The obstacles to accomplishing that mission are the monster and the fact that the button is on the other side of the slime pool—too far away to push. To accomplish this mini-mission, all the player needs to do is shoot the button from his side and then avoid the monster while crossing the bridge; that's it. Simple. It may not seem like a mission, but it is. It's a challenge that the player must face and overcome in order to continue with the game. A single-player level is a collection of these mini-missions tied closely around unique areas in some cohesive manner.

Levels should contain mini-missions within them—that is, obstacles and objectives aside from just enemies. In this example from Quake II, the player must get across this broken bridge somehow without landing in the molten lava. (Used with permission by id Software, Inc.)

As an example of *not* rewarding the player enough, Willits recalls:

> I once played a game where there was a tower in the middle of a courtyard with some monsters in it. It looked important and it was a centerpiece of that courtyard. I killed the two guys in the upper portion and navigated to the top.

> I was pretty disappointed when I finally reached the top and there was nothing there. Every time you have an area in the map that looks important and there's a fight to reach it, you need to reward the player with some "goodie."

ENVIRONMENTAL FEEL, TEASERS, AND FLOW

An important consideration of an SP map, according to Willits, is the overall environmental feel. Aside from looking good and playing well, what does he mean by this?

> A designer must make the level look the way the player expects it to. If the designer calls a map a *warehouse*, then there better be some crates lying around, because players will be looking for them. Also, a designer must try to make the level seem like it fits into the rest of the world. Don't mix time periods if you're not traveling in time, don't mix construction materials along similar time periods. For example, don't build your first map out of sheets of metal and have the follow-up map made mostly of brick and stucco. Players want consistency; they're comfortable with it because it surrounds their everyday lives.

Another nice touch in creating a good environmental feel is to build the map with the hint that there's more out there. "Create fake facades that can be viewed through windows but unreachable on foot. Have boxes come out of walls and vanish through other walls on the other side of the room. Create architecture that sweeps out past the playing area," says Willits. If these items are placed in the levels by the designers, players will feel like they're involved in something "bigger."

Along with these "teasers," a few outstanding visual scenes or landmarks will also help capture the environment that the designer wants to create, says Willits.

> Spend some time developing a spectacular view. Maybe a grand entrance, a detailed outer building, or even a super advanced control center. Make players turn a corner for the first time and say to themselves, "Wow." It stays with the players, and they remember the level long after they completed it if they were impressed by something cool-looking. This isn't so important in DM maps, mainly because once you run past it no one cares what it looks like time after time. Don't spend too much time on something visually stunning in DM; spend more time on flow.

In terms of flow, the levels need to start out pretty easy and then advance in difficulty, maintains Willits. As a rule, he builds the first level as a training level.

> If you want to build some cool objects that move or some sort of complex geometry to showcase the engine, put it out of the path of the player. For example, air vents with spinning blades look just as good horizontal behind grates. Or moving pumps along side walls is another good use of moving things that are non-threatening. I know you want to add a lot of interesting things in the first couple of levels, but just keep them as non-intrusive as possible.

Perhaps you're only interested in creating top-notch multiplayer maps? If that's the case, pull up a chair to Willits' DM 101 and a few pointers on *Capture the Flag*–style games as well.

Check out the detail on these characters from Quake III: Arena. All of this graphical eye candy, including the use of curved and reflective surfaces and dynamic lighting, adds to the all-important immersion factor. (Used with permission by id Software, Inc.)

DEATHMATCH LEVELS

There are basically five popular styles of Deathmatch levels: arena, circular, linear, location-based, and theme-centered. Many of these styles can be included in one map, and some have crossover traits, according to Willits.

ARENA

In a nutshell, arena levels usually have one central area where most of the combat takes place. Most of the hallways and passages either lead from this central area or to it. Says Willits:

> The map has very few other large rooms or areas of significance. The arena style of DM is very focused, very refined; the maps are quickly learned and easy to master. Players will always know where they are and should never get lost navigating the hallways around the arena area. Players will find these maps fast paced with high frag limits, which will be reached quickly. An example level is MAP07 from *Doom II*.

And a word of caution to designers:

> Try not to make the arena areas too architecturally complex. This is the area where all the fighting occurs, so it has to run fast. Complex architecture may look good, but it only slows down the game. Try to build this area as simple as possible.

CIRCULAR

As the name suggests, these maps are circular in design, or as Willits says, "built in such a fashion that the player would never need to stop and turn around along its main path." He expands:

> Build with as few dead ends as possible—they're best built with none. Use numerous entrances and exits around its central core, which would allow free-flowing movement without hitches. The map would also need good weapon distribution, where either side would not have an advantage. There would be as little holding ground as possible. (*Holding ground* is a place where a player can stock up on health and ammo in a room and camp.) An example level here is DM6 from *Quake*.

LINEAR

Linear maps are built with only a few alternate paths. Willits amplifies:

> The architecture becomes a roadmap, where people instantly know which side of the map they're on. Nice open areas or wide hallways where players can enjoy jousting-type combat. Even weapon distribution to force players to move back and forth. Have the ammo for the weapons on the opposite side of the map, forcing players who want to stock to travel. An example level is E1M1 from *Doom*.

LOCATION-BASED

> Location-based DM allows players to always know where they are. You may not be able to figure out how to get somewhere else fast, but you immediately know your location. These maps are not free-flowing as in circular or linear maps, but instead are made up of many unique identifiable areas. Each area should have some distinct combat areas or mini themes included in it. For example, in DM3 from *Quake* is a water area for swimming, a thin staircase for vertical fighting, and a computer room made for close fighting. Each area has a special weapon or power-up that fits the environment. These maps are great for team games.

THEME-CENTERED

And last on the list for DM maps are theme-based maps. As Willits put it, a theme-based map uses something unique to combat and over-exaggerates it all over the map. Perhaps this is better explained by an example:

> An example of this is E1M4 from *Quake*, a.k.a. The Sewage System. This map is covered with water; most of the fighting is in or around water. Everywhere the player looks, he sees water or something related to water. In almost every area, the player can enter or exit the water. The water is the "theme" or the special combat characterization throughout the map. Theme maps are great for players who enjoy something totally unique. Theme-based maps are also more difficult to navigate through, and should only be used for medium or advanced play. Themes need to enhance gameplay, not detract from it.

 NOTE Good id Software examples of theme-based maps include wind tunnels (*Quake*, E3M5); low gravity (*Quake*, E1M8); low light, such as the mine levels in *Quake II*; hazardous materials such as lava, slime, or pits of death (*Quake*, DM4); torturous devices such as spike shooters or security lasers (*Quake II*); wide and open areas (*Quake II*); teleport craziness (*Quake*, DM1).

CAPTURE THE FLAG

"Capture the Flag" is a popular team-based multiplayer game where the object is to steal the other team's flag and bring it safely back to your own base. There are now many new custom variations of Capture the Flag (CTF) games. In the following section, Willits offers advice on creating maps for CTF fanatics.

SYMMETRIC LEVELS

With CTF games, it's important that levels be nearly mirrors of each other to make things even between the two teams. Willits maintains, "In theory it's possible to have two bases look different, but even in practice this has rarely worked." He cites a bad example of a CTF map from *Quake II*, and why:

> *Strike* is a fairly big failure in that regard due to BFG and teleporter placement (putting red team at a large disadvantage). Also, there are more methods of entering the red base than the blue base, making blue base easily defensible. This map also has uneven ammo and weapon placement; the blue base has far better resources within. All this is solved very easily by making both sides identical.

ASYMMETRICAL LEVELS

Willits says if the level is not symmetrical there should be a balanced strategy that needs to be employed by each individual team. For example, if one side is largely covered by water, the team should be given rebreathers. Similarly, protective environment suits should be accessible on the slime side.

RANDOM TIPS FOR CTF MAPS

Willits grants us an assorted medley of tips on creating CTF maps:

> There should be a good supply of weapons and ammo near a base, but don't overdo it. This makes the base too easy to defend and difficult to attack. If a designer is using power-ups, they should never start off within the base.
>
> While still making it defensible, there should be multiple entry points and exits to a base.
>
> Centralized placement of major power-ups is a good idea. The power-ups still need to be located far enough from each other to prevent players from using a single power-up and crushing everyone on the map.
>
> Create some good sniper locations, but, if players are going to snipe, they should be vulnerable in some way, too.
>
> There should be obvious color coding of areas, but don't rely on colored lighting, since colored lighting tends to neutralize player colors and you can't see what team they're on. Use colored textures instead.
>
> Focus on good weapon placement and think it through. Weapon placement may be more important in CTF than normal DM because it can greatly shift the balance of power from one side to the other.

DAVE "ZOID" KIRSCH, THREEWAVE SOFTWARE

Dave "Zoid" Kirsch will be forever immortalized by the devout members of the *Quake* community for designing a modification that would revolutionize the way 3D multiplayer action games were played. The mod was simply known as *Capture the Flag*, or *CTF*, which is now part of the *Quake III* core game. Zoid has also been commissioned by the gurus at id Software to convert the past three *Quake* games into Linux. In Chapter 8, Zoid offers many programming tips, but the following takes a quick look at his thoughts on level design.

Zoid begins by stressing that there are two major issues a level designer needs to keep in mind: appearance and flow. *Appearance* is the architectural design behind the level and its "look and feel." *Flow* is how the level plays. He expands:

> Appearance is a long topic itself. The level designer needs to focus on effective use of textures and a good design that feels like some sort of representation or abstract representation of a real place. Design that doesn't look convincing doesn't work.
>
> The reason you see so many crates and gothic church levels is they are easy to build and fun to design. They are also tested and "trustworthy" designs. It's a lot more interesting to escape into a musty old church or a high tech base with lots of flash and perhaps crates around than to Deathmatch in mundane locations like a representation of your local mall.
>
> A lot of level design is escapism and this is reflected in building designs of cool places that aren't something people encounter in normal life.
>
> As for flow, this can only be achieved with play testing. A good level designer realizes he may have to rebuild, redesign, and even sacrifice some of his architecture design in order to make a level that plays well and "flows" during gameplay. I've seen a lot of people make gorgeous masterpieces that just aren't any fun to play. There are also people who make the world's ugliest maps that feature amazingly fun and exciting gameplay. The best maps are the ones that combine both elements.

We'll return later to the masters at id Software. But first, we've got some divine intervention. Bow your heads because next up is The Levelord.

THE LEVELORD, RITUAL ENTERTAINMENT

Much of the excitement and anxiety experienced during bouts of *Duke Nukem 3D*, *Quake: Scourge of Armagon*, and *Sin* can be directly linked to The Levelord's miraculous touch. So what's his secret for keeping you awake until 4 a.m.?

The Levelord's three commandments may seem obvious, but according to him they're quite often neglected or overlooked: the "fun factor," game action/player interaction, and authenticity of setting.

The Levelord has requested that we keep his written material the way it was submitted, so this is the Lord speaking throughout. Hear ye! Hear ye!

THE FUN FACTOR

" The first and foremost question to be answered about any game, whether it's a shooter or whatever, is "Is it fun?" This applies to the game itself, of course, but it also has great bearing on each and every component of the game, including level designing. As a game is developed, this question should be answered many, many times.

The Fun Factor is often forsaken for cutting-edge flash, and much effort is taken away from the game itself due to the ever-increasing computer performance on which games are played. Nonetheless, it seems paradoxical that many games simply are not fun; they look great, but they aren't worth playing. Cutting edge is indeed fun when it adds cool weapon effects and faster game performance, but it's not cool when a developer spends too much time with research and development, only to forget the main purpose of a game: fun!

The Fun Factor is also frequently back-seated to realism. This is not to be confused with a game being realistic or authentic, but is rather a seeming side effect of the "reality" portion of our games' virtual reality. Too often fun ideas and features are shelved because developers say things like "Hey, you can't change momentum in mid-air in real life!" or "A real bullet doesn't do that!" when the more important statement at hand was "That was so much fun!"

There are no defined rules for fun and the only way to ensure the Fun Factor is to play test. The easy part about adding the Fun Factor is that most all of us have the same concept of fun; that is, if you the game developer think it's fun, then the game audience is likely to think so, too. The Fun Factor is not transient or ephemeral, either. It should survive countless trials and tests and still be entertaining in the end. This is the only way to ensure that a game is fun— to play test it over and over. "

GAME ACTION AND PLAYER INTERACTION

" First-person shooters are no longer the simple "shoot, find the key, and shoot some more" games that they were a few years ago. These games are now fully interactive environments, and what used to be considered randomly placed and sparse Easter eggs are now the standard norm. If a level has a phone or computer, they had better be functional, and the player had better be able to blow them up.

The player must be able to destroy just about everything! As a level designer, I spend a lot of my time making things destructible, but it's always worth the while. Take the time to become a good demolitions expert, because destroying things is not only good action, it is also never-ending fun.

Another important aspect of the action in a first-person shooter is puzzle solving. A good level should be a series of challenges and rewards. The challenge can come before the reward, or after, but don't just haphazardly strew goodies and bad guys through your level. The players should feel as though they are being run through a gauntlet of contests and prizes. "

Puzzle-solving is an integral part of 3D level design, says The Levelord. This "heated" scene is from Scourge of Armagon, the first official add-on pack for Quake. (Used with permission by Ritual Entertainment)

" All of these forms should be as animated as possible to improve feel of action. Make the player work for the rewards. Do whatever you can to make the player say "Ah ha!" Make as many secret areas as possible, too, as discovering secrets is one of the most fun puzzles in a game. "

AUTHENTICITY

" Related directly to level designing, the third question to be answered is "Are you there?" First-person shooters in particular rely on the sense of immersion. The most important duty you have as a level designer is to bring the player "into" your level. It's not until after this submersion that issues like action, gameplay, and even the Fun Factor enter the game.

The more of your level to which the player can attach himself via familiarity, the stronger the player's sense of "being there" will be. Real-world situations usually make good levels because it's easier to capture the reality. "

A strong sense of authenticity is the groundwork of any killer level. Remember the movie theater or football stadium in Duke Nukem 3D or the opening bank sequence from Sin? Here's a look at Sin's jungle level. (Used with permission by Ritual Entertainment)

" The closer that the player can relate to your level, the deeper the player will be submerged into the level.

Continuity is also an important factor of a level's immersion. Continuity is related to the level's main theme, and this theme must be maintained throughout the entire level. Too often I see levels that are patchworks of various themes. Your level must seem like a continuous place. "

The almighty Levelord has spoken, and deems these as the true foundations of any killer level. "These seem apparent, but they can be the biggest burdens a game designer, especially a level designer, can face…without them, most every other aspect of a level will be missed or forgotten, and the game as a whole will suffer."

Littering your maps with secrets is also an important consideration in level designing, deems The Levelord. Anyone find this in Duke Nukem 3D? (Used with permission by 3D Realms, Inc.)

PAUL JAQUAYS, ID SOFTWARE

Paul Jaquays is a "jack of all trades" (check out his bio in the appendix), but at id Software he provides level design for *Quake II* and *Quake III: Arena*. Now who *wouldn't* want to be in his shoes, eh? When Jaquays heard about this *Secrets of the Sages* project, he wanted to offer a large collection of do's and don'ts on level design, as well as more general advice on the art of map creation. Without further ado, let's first jump into his collection of handy design tidbits.

JAQUAYS' 26 LEVEL DESIGN TIPS

1. Know what you want to do with a level before you start. Don't expect a map that you start as a single-player map to be easily changed into a multiplayer map. The reverse holds true for trying to make a Deathmatch map into a single-player challenge.

2. Sketch out a diagram of the map to use as an initial guide.

3. Don't start with grandiose projects. Try making something fun with a few rooms.

4. If possible, build your level with a "gimmick" in mind—some tricky gamism bit that players will remember. Popular gimmicks that have been used in the past include wind tunnels, numerous portals, lava maps, trap maps, water-filled maps, maps with large, slow-moving hazards, and low-gravity maps.

5. Try to be fresh and original with every new design. Do something that you haven't seen done before.

6. Test gimmicks of gameplay, tricks, and traps in test levels before building them into your game level.

7. Do architecture and texture studies ahead of time to establish an architectural style. Stick to that style.

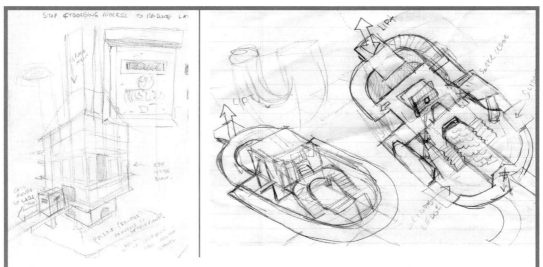

Left, Jaquays roughly sketched out a complicated puzzle and trap for Quake II, involving modularized, moving prison cells as a part of the Laboratory sequence. The concept was not implemented in the final game. Right, Jaquays began one of his first Quake III arena maps by roughly sketching out the major game features and their relationship to each other. The final version of this arena map carried several of the original concepts through to fruition, even though much of the layout and geometry was changed. (Both images used with permission by id Software, Inc., copyright 1998)

8. Block out your level with large pieces of geometry. Think of the architecture you'll use, but concentrate more on how gameplay will flow through the level. At this stage, I try to keep my map grid at the largest possible setting (in *Quake II* or *Quake III*, that's the "64" grid). Avoid fussy details at this point and go for massiveness. At this stage of development, try to keep your frame-rate speeds well below the amount allowed by the game (for *Quake II*, we aimed to be below a maximum count of 500 triangles of architecture in any view). A good rule might be to try for no more than a third of your total possible polygon count in the worst views in and near your larger rooms.

This 64-player map is taken from the Quake II DM Pack 1: Extremities expansion CD. Jaquays reminds level designers to make sure that large maps have distinctive, memorable play areas. (Used with permission by Activision)

9. Once the flow is established, you can start adding architectural detail and refining hall and room shapes.

10. Build in a modular manner. Make prefabricated pieces that be can fit together easily to make your level. Build tricky pieces of detailed architecture (such as door frames, complicated cornices, or furniture) once and set them outside the boundaries of your map. Clone them as needed for placement in the map.

11. When designing architectural elements, study the real world. Try to duplicate the look and feel of impressive works, but with less complicated geometry. Set yourself challenges in this regard.

12. Strike a balance between the use of real geometry and textures that imply three-dimensional depth when building architectural details. Textures that appear to be 3D should be used with caution. When viewed from a distance, they can fool the eye into believing that the architectural geometry is significantly more complex than it actually is. But the same texture viewed up close and at eye level completely destroys the illusion of depth.

13. Compile the map often. Don't wait until everything is placed to see what things look like (or if you have leaks in the map hull).

14. Complete your map geometry before adding monsters and items.

15. When building single-player game maps, don't put every game feature in the level. Having every monster possible in the game in a single game level is a glaring sign of amateur work. Generally speaking, the only place you're going to see all the monsters at once is in the AI programmer's test level.

16. The same goes for tricks, traps, items, weapons, and power-ups. Unless your map is as massive as the 64-player DM maps created for *Quake II*, restrict the number of different items you put in the map. Use a few things cleverly, rather than many poorly.

17. Small maps can be relatively similar throughout. Large maps should have distinctive, memorable locations that the player can use to orient himself in the map. "City64," a large DM map for *Quake II*, featured a huge canyon area, a massive alien temple, underwater caverns, a vast deep tank with water in the bottom, and numerous stretches of twisty corridors. The corridors were often similar, but they ended in distinctive large play areas.

18. For DM maps, give the players frequent opportunities to avoid pursuit and dodge for cover. Long hallways with no exits are bad. Avoid forcing players to make long trips to dead-end rooms—even to get good power-ups.

19. Place lights to achieve drama. If you have a choice between under-lighting an area and over-lighting it, err on the side of darkness. Just don't go overboard. Dark levels may look nifty, but stumbling around in the dark while playing gets old fast.

20. Light as you go—even if you're only placing temporary lights.

21. Don't forget the audio elements of a map. Sounds can provide important game clues.

22. If possible, allow multiple solutions for puzzles. You can still reserve the greatest rewards for players who solve them in what the designer has decided is the "best way."

23. Give the player a variety of game experiences and challenges in each map. All combat or all puzzles can get old quickly.

24. Be kind to your players; don't over-challenge them unnecessarily. Well-placed environmental hazards add to the tension of gameplay, but falling into lava or slime every third step or being crushed to death by falling weights every time you turn around quickly becomes frustrating.

25. Study maps you like and make an effort to duplicate or even improve situations and settings.

26. Finish what you begin.

As many other programmers, artists, animators, musicians, and level designers have stated elsewhere, this last point on finishing a project instead of starting 10 new ones is essential, and not easy for beginners.

PAUL'S ADVICE ON GAME DESIGN

Throughout his career in the gaming industry, Jaquays has accumulated quite a bit of knowledge on the art of game design. While he covered many individual points in the preceding section on map creation, the following details serve as more broad advice on game design, drawing from his own personal experiences as well.

STOP IMITATING YOURSELF

I started in the game business as a designer of game adventures for the new (at the time) game called *Dungeons & Dragons* and later for the game called *Runequest*. There was a time when I was considered one of the best adventure writers in the field. One of the reasons that I quit designing pencil-and-paper–type role-playing games was I found that I had started to imitate myself, rehashing the same storyline over and over. I was no longer fresh. Thankfully, I had other career options within the game business that I could pursue. But the problem still remains: how to keep your ideas alive and new.

CHOOSE THE UNCONVENTIONAL SOLUTION

There's a tendency in game design to use familiar or tried-and-true solutions to design. In the latter part of the Golden Age of Video Games (the *classic* 8-bit years), the solution for nearly every game based on a character or movie license was to create a side-scrolling game. During my tenure at Coleco, we were given very few opportunities to create new games. Most of our work was to analyze and translate arcade titles.

The *WarGames* movie license gave us the opportunity to create a game that broke the mold. The conventional solution would have been to make a side-scrolling "solve the puzzles, find the hidden goodies, and avoid the bad guys" game until at last you confronted the computer in the last scene. At that point, the game would start you back at the beginning and ratchet up the level of difficulty a notch. After seeing a special preview screening of the movie *WarGames*, I was inspired by the sequence near the end of the movie in which the computer runs simulated scenario after scenario in which the outcome was always the same: nuclear war and complete world devastation. I was taken by the graphics that plotted the arcs of missiles as they approached their targets. If I could convince the powers-that-be, that short sequence of the movie would be our game. The actual gameplay derived from several unrelated concepts. The goal of the player would be to stop bombers, subs, and missiles (which were drawn on the fly as lines—no simple trick in the 8-bit pattern tile game systems of the day), from reaching their targets on a map of the United States. In a way, it had similarities to the popular arcade game *Missile Command*, where the player fires anti-ballistic missiles at incoming missiles dropping down from the top of the screen. Unlike the arcade, the play took place on six separate maps simultaneously. Like the juggler who keeps numerous plates spinning at once atop thin sticks, the player had to rapidly switch his attention between a radar map showing the whole USA and six sub-maps that contained closer views of target cities and military installations. The player had to rapidly commit resources (missiles, interceptor planes, and attack subs) to deal with enemy attacks, then shift to the next map and do the same. If the player had the right stuff, he or she could defeat the game.

BLENDING FLAVORS

Some of the most popular foods are those that blend unlike or even opposite flavors together in one tasty package. Sweet-and-sour Chinese dishes and Chicago-style hotdogs are just two examples. What does this have to do with game design? One of the products of which I am most proud is a book series called *Central Casting*. The purpose of the products was to create vivid back-stories or histories for characters in role-playing games. I created separate books that covered three distinct genre groups of games: fantasy, science fiction (or futuristic), and 20th century games. Players rolled dice and compared the results against a series of tables and lists. Roll by roll, they selected events and personality traits that they could use to define their game characters. Quite often, the results of dice rolls would seem unlikely to be combined together, but with a little creative thought the widely disparate events would blend together, like the myriad of flavors in a Chicago-style hotdog, into a uniquely original result.

MAKE IT REAL

Even if you plan on making your game setting wildly fantastic—that is, nothing you would ever see in the real world—take care to make it seem real. This is something I learned as a fantasy illustrator, painting covers for games and books. The way to make the fantastic elements of a painting believable is to realistically paint the mundane things in the picture. This establishes a setting that appears as if it could actually exist somewhere. You then paint the fantastic elements in the painting with an equal amount of care so that they partake of the *reality* of the rest of the painting. The same holds true when making 3D game levels. Give the player one or more familiar elements that he can relate to. By comparison with the *real* elements, the *unreal* things in the game should seem more real, or perhaps a better explanation is that they seem more plausible. And by contrast with the mundane, they will seem that much more fantastic.

Be sure to read more on Paul Jaquays in the biography appendix at the end of this book.

JOHN ROMERO, ION STORM

"A level designer has a very responsible position, because maps are where the game takes place," says John Romero, game designer, chairman, and cofounder of ION Storm. Having worked on such 3D shooter classics such as *Wolfenstein 3D*, *Doom*, *Doom II*, *Heretic*, *Hexen*, and *Quake*, Romero has plenty of opinions to share regarding level design, so let's get to it.

First, Romero maintains that the inevitable breaking up of responsibilities at a development house can take away from the overall vibe and consistency of the level. "Some companies do their maps in stages, with many different people handling different tasks—there's architecture, texture placement, object placement...and this [specialization] can take away from the 'cool' factor."

Although most of his suggestions on what makes a good level are fairly universal (such as providing the gamer with landmarks throughout the map to give it personality, making the player totally immersed in this fictitious world, and so on), Romero also proposes an interesting rule that's broken more than it's obeyed, in his opinion. "The gamer must be in constant fear," believes Romero. "It's extremely important to keep gamers on their toes when playing shooters, with plenty of traps lying around so they're constantly in fear of dying..."

 Landmarks can serve a dual purpose in well-designed maps: They can add to the immersion factor while offering navigation cues to players, helping them know their direction and location in the level.

Romero cites specific examples such as *Quake*'s E2M5 ("Wizard's Manse"), where players get locked into a cage and it slowly descends into water with no way out. Another *Quake* map, E2M6 ("Dismal Oubliette"), also has a slow vertical sink, inspired by Disney World's Haunted House "elevator" ride. "The player panics because he's stuck in this room and after it stops completely, a Shambler is teleported into the room, spikes shoot out, then there's a Fiend to fight, and then Zombies. It's just one thing after another," says Romero with a smile. "This is key in good level design."

Romero will be able to show off these helpful tips with *Daikatana*—his first game since leaving id Software—when it ships in mid-2000.

CLIFF BLESZINSKI, EPIC GAMES

At a mere 25 years old, Cliff has made quite a name for himself as a game designer and level creator on the award-winning PC titles *Jazz Jackrabbit*, *Unreal*, and *Unreal Tournament*. Although he agrees with Romero that fear is an important element of level design, he believes that it's only a fraction of what makes a solid level. "Pacing is far more important. If the player is constantly in fear, then he'll become numb; if he's constantly surprised, then it will wear off and not be effective," explains Bleszinski. "The key to scaring the player in a level is knowing when, where, and how often to spring a surprise. If there are, say, five minutes of idle time exploring and chatting with peaceful aliens, then, when the door bursts in and a lava monster stomps in screaming bloody h---, you can bet the player will be shaking in his boots. This is why good horror movies don't spring surprise after surprise on the audience—because it loses its impact."

Being chased by a deadly Skaarj adds to the fun and excitement of the level, but Bleszinski warns that fear should be used sparingly to break up the pace of a level. (Used with permission by Epic Games)

> Good pacing is a skill that applies to every element of level design. Pace your flow of monsters, and have areas where the player feels like he is being engulfed by less intelligent "cannon fodder" foes, as well as areas that have just a few devious baddies that are hard as nails to take out. Know how often to reward the player with goodies or health. Don't cover the level with items; rather, give him the prizes after monsters are killed, doors are opened, or a ledge is reached.

Bleszinski recognizes that there's a lot more to level design than the fear factor and good pacing, so he also provides his very own five-step crash course in good level design. Pencils in hand? Here we go…

GEOMETRY BUILDING AND WORLD TEXTURING

> Naturally, you need to construct your environment first. Ideally, the texture artists should have a head start on the level designers so that the level designers have content with which to texture their areas while building. Then the level designers can tell the artists, "I need a 32 × 128 girder with three bolts on it and no directional rust, and please put it into the FACTORY texture set!"

LIGHTING THE ENVIRONMENT

> The right kind of lighting can make or break a beautiful scene. Low lights tend to illuminate monsters more dramatically, while bright rooms reduce fumbling around in the dark. A level designer needs to be creative with his lighting; if the player is going deeper into a volcano, then the lighting should get "hotter" the further you go by getting brighter and more orange and red; or, if you're sending him through a swampy area, use drab, depressing colors, such as green and gray.

Pancho Eekels, one of the level designers Cliff Bleszinki works with, has managed to make this room well lit, yet moody and colorful. This shot is from Unreal Tournament. (Used with permission by Cliff Bleszinski)

> Using the *Unreal* or *Quake* engine gives a level designer amazing control over realistic shadows. Building architecture that allows for shadows is essential; try putting support beams beneath a skylight to encourage sharp, moody shadows on the floor, or put a flame behind a polygonal grate to cast harsh shadows on the opposite wall.

TRICKS, TRAPS, AND PUZZLES

> Never force the player to learn by dying. Always give him a chance to figure out a puzzle without slapping his wrists. Remember, the person playing your game is playing it for fun, not for work. If you want to have slicing blades pop up from the floor of your Incan temple, make sure that you put some blood splotches and body parts around the exact spot that the blades spring forth, so that the attentive player will not be killed. Even if the player is killed, he will think "Oh, I should have seen those warnings, how stupid of me!" instead of "This game cheats! How was I supposed to know there was a trap there?"
>
> If the primary objective of your game is to kill and kill fast, then don't slow the player down with boring, cumbersome puzzles. It's one thing to have three switches that need to be turned on in order to pass; it's another to have twelve switches that have a combination code three levels away that the player must physically write on a piece of paper to remember.

MONSTER, AMMO, AND HEALTH PLACEMENT ("GAMEFLOW")

> During the course of *Unreal*'s development, I harassed the level designers to always make their monsters patrol a local area, or to have them spring out of the dark, or even crash through glass at the player. If the player walks into a room and the monsters are just standing there waiting for him, he's not going to feel that this is a very believable world. However, if he walks into a room and his foe is just walking past him to go work on a computer terminal, he'll appreciate the extra effort that has been taken to further the believability.
>
> Ammunition is always tricky to get right in a level. Too much ammo and the gamer breezes through the level without a sweat; not enough ammo and your gamer is running around the level hacking at your foes with his default weapon while pondering looking for cheats online. Right when the player is thinking, "Boy, I'm going to be needing some ammunition soon," there should be a box of bullets waiting for him. The same rules apply for health.

DRAMA!

> In *Unreal*, we're trying to create a sense of being in a hostile alien world. This believability is greatly helped by what I refer to as *drama*. Hearing a scene occur behind a locked door. Watching an evil alien punish a friendly alien who assists the player. Witnessing the murder of a comrade before your eyes. Real events that occur real time in the game, many of which the player can interfere with. Well-done drama will stick in the player's head for years to come.

So how important is level design, anyway? Why is this such an integral part of the game design? "Level design is where the rubber hits the road," are the first words Jay Wilbur, former "biz guy" and CEO of id Software, told Cliff Bleszinski, during their initial telephone conversation a couple of years ago. This has stuck with Cliff as an "absolute truth." He expands on the analogy:

> Game development can be compared to building a car. You have all these different parts that are created by talented people—programming, modeling, sound, and artwork—and at some point, everyone's hard work on a car comes together, and the tires hit the road. With a game, everyone's work is held together by the levels that use all of that, and they'd better be exceptional or the game falters.

MARC LAIDLAW, VALVE SOFTWARE

Valve's first release, *Half-Life*, was a major evolutionary step in the history of the first-person perspective action genre. The game excelled in all key areas: storyline, art, animation, sound, music, pacing, and level design; combined, it made players feel like they were part of a living, breathing, populated world. The level design was instrumental in pulling off this effect, and even during the last third of the game, while on another planet with alien architecture, maps maintained their focus with lush outdoor and indoor environments and challenging obstacles to overcome.

Marc Laidlaw, the level team coordinator at Valve, was responsible for overseeing the six level designers who worked day and night to create *Half-Life*. Did you know there were a whopping 96 BSPs in the game?

 BSP is an editing tool that converts map files into *Quake*-compatible level files. *Half-Life* is based on the *Quake/Quake II* engine, so they call the mini-levels in the game BSPs.

Laidlaw takes some time out of his busy schedule to discuss his own personal approach to level design:

THE GOAL

The first on the list is the goal of the level. That is, the point of it all in the grand scheme of things. Says Laidlaw, "Everything in the level should somehow contribute to that goal—even detours, diversions, and distractions should figure into the overall scheme, thematically."

THE GAMEPLAY

Consideration of the gameplay is also important. What will players be doing as they go through the level? "Is this something that will engage, immerse, and interest them to the point that they absolutely cannot stop playing until they've accomplished their goal?" asks Laidlaw.

THE ATMOSPHERE

Laidlaw asks, "What kind of mood are you trying to create in the player? One of horror? One of pure action? Are you trying to create a mood that contrasts with preceding or subsequent levels?" The goal is to select and invent details that suit the mood you want to get across.

Marc Laidlaw stresses that you must understand the goal, relevance to gameplay, and atmosphere for each level when making maps in a 3D shooter. These two images, from the "Office Complex" and "Questionable Ethics" levels of Half-Life, accompany the extensive descriptions provided by Laidlaw for each of the two areas. (Used with permission from Sierra Studios)

The following is a look at how Laidlaw's emphasis on the goal, gameplay, and atmosphere can be applied to some of the key levels in *Half-Life*.

"OFFICE COMPLEX"

The "Office Complex" level of *Half-Life* is a deliberately drab environment composed of offices, laboratories, corridors, and stairways. In other words, fairly mundane locales about as far removed as imaginable from the usual fantastic trappings of a science fiction action game. With that in mind, Laidlaw applies the level to each of his three approaches to map design:

Goal: The goals in "Office Complex" are fairly obvious ones, such as exit doors, in plain sight. The layouts of the maps are simple and, in essence, linear. However, by imposing obstacles, we force the player to take a devious route to the destination. For instance, you can peer through a pane of glass in a fire door and see your exit at the far end of a corridor; but since the fire door is locked, you'll need to explore other avenues. Clever use of obstacles can turn a completely obvious route into a complex non-obvious route. This technique was used numerous times in *Half-Life*. What's important is to make the goal obvious from the first, in order to give the player a start on solving the problem of how to get there. And if they forget their goal somewhere along the way, they will experience a jolt of recognition when they finally gain the far-off door.

Gameplay: "Office Complex" occurs fairly early in *Half-Life*, and therefore gameplay was slanted toward the player who is still mastering basic skills, while preparing him for more dangerous encounters ahead. We force the player to crawl, dodge, and fight in tight quarters against ambushing headcrabs. Slow monsters, such as mawmen, give a steady sense of horror and menace, and allow the player plenty of opportunities to learn to team up with allies. He can talk to non-player characters (NPCs) and solve various small-scale room-based puzzles (such as shutting off switches to deactivate deadly turrets and electrical threats). In addition, we knew that the subsequent level would drop him into combat with extremely tough human soldiers, and in order to give him some experience fighting against squads of creatures with long-range attacks, we set up encounters with squads of vortigaunts, which are fun to fight and fairly easy to kill, thus allowing the player to develop some of the skills he'll need to survive encounters with human soldiers.

Atmosphere: The banal office atmosphere provides a perfect background for scenes of carnage and horror—the contrast with gruesome images is all the more striking because of the familiar setting. Most of the details were selected to evoke feelings of dread in the player. Scientists are dragged to their doom in airshafts; mawmen feed on corpses in the cafeteria. The one crucial atmospheric element that can't be conveyed in screenshots is that of sound. The first time the player steps into the walk-in freezer, he triggers music that evokes cold, echoing emptiness. And the claustrophobic echoing sounds not only reinforce the realism of the environment, but add to the sense of menace: Echoes are creepy.

Laidlaw uses another level in the game for contrast. This section of *Half-Life* takes place in a research and development lab, where the player catches a glimpse of some of the experiments that were in progress when disaster struck the Black Mesa Research Facility.

"QUESTIONABLE ETHICS"

The labs served numerous purposes in the game: To deepen the sense of conspiracy and cause the player to question what was actually going on at Black Mesa; to give the player access to a high-powered weapon that's crucial for battling powerful enemies in subsequent levels; and to force a style of puzzle-solving focused on protecting and working with human characters (scientists) rather than simply throwing switches.

Goal: This section of the labs is quite nonlinear in layout, although judicious use of locked doors again gives it a linear flow the first time through. Nonlinear areas tend to work against the usual dramatic virtues of pacing and rhythm and timing, and give rise to plentiful opportunities for boredom and confusion. They also make it easy for the player to miss or forget his goal. When designing the labs on paper, we decided that the player should see his goal (the exit) immediately upon entering the lobby. There's a scanner next to the locked exit, and by this time the player has been taught that only scientists or other NPCs can operate a scanner. Presumably the player will carry this knowledge with him as he moves away from the exit and fights his way through the other areas of the map, and by the time he encounters a group of hiding scientists, he'll understand that he's supposed to escort one of them through the labyrinthine labs back to the scanner. (To further aid the player in understanding the goal, we added a security guard to give a short briefing on the way into the area.)

Gameplay: Puzzles were built around a variety of enemy encounters, traps, and scientific devices, and assembled from elements that have some logical place in the environment: sterilizers, laser equipment, caged monsters. Getting certain weapons is tricky in that it requires exposing oneself to monsters, and then quickly working with the environment to neutralize the threat. The player must open a cage full of sharks, then retreat into a sterilizer control room in order to vaporize them before he is overwhelmed. In addition, the presence of enemy soldiers adds a constant threat and gives contrast to the alien menace. In some circumstances, the canny player may choose to wait out battles between aliens and other humans, and then deal with the weakened victor of those battles. In such cases, the player's best strategy is patience. This puts a twist on the usual action game tactic, where players usually can expect to solve all problems by direct, aggressive attacks.

Atmosphere: We selected details that seemed appropriate to the research environment, and that added to the underlying story. Certain areas were tailored specifically for the study of alien creatures, which tends to raise questions about how long the researchers at Black Mesa have known about the aliens, and what exactly they were doing with them. As much as possible, the details also provided opportunities for gameplay; for instance, sterilizers that were used by researchers to cleanse rooms of biohazards turn out to be just as effective at vaporizing pursuing soldiers. Since we wanted a mood of high-tech horror to pervade *Half-Life*, we avoided a lot of opportunities for wacky comedy, and instead tried to set up situations for suitably dark and ironic humor. The "Tau Cannon," for instance, is given to the player at the end of a macabre sequence. And as a bonus, in addition to the weapon itself, the player is "rewarded" with a unique piece of music that punctuates the action and puts a weird spin on the otherwise relentless mood of horror.

ON LIMITATIONS OF TOOLS

All of these aforementioned objectives must be accomplished with the tools at your disposal, and within the limits of your game engine. Laidlaw explains:

> Working within your limitations can seem restricting at first, but it also allows you to plan in advance and really get creative. It would seem as if having a team of programmers available to constantly implement new features would be utterly liberating, but sometimes this makes it hard to just get down to work and use what you have. It's very hard to anticipate what you might have one day. Level designers who have built a lot of *Quake* maps are used to working with known quantities; they know the limits of the *Quake* engine, they know the entities they have to work with, they know how to create spectacular effects that take both these factors into consideration. When the rules suddenly change, and a lot of new entities and features are in the works, and the engine itself is altered, a kind of paralysis can creep in. This is a predictable stumbling block for people who are moving from mapping as a hobby to level design as a profession; but being aware of it in advance, you should try to stay aware of your strengths and the known quantities, and master the new quantities a bit at a time.

HAVE A PLAN

Laidlaw says if you can keep it all in your head, fine. But putting your ideas on paper is good.

> Sketches are helpful. You can evaluate your overall scheme more easily when it's clearly stated. If you can't sum it up in a few words, or sketch it out so that someone else will understand it, you might be painting yourself into a corner when you've put a lot of work into actual level construction.

DON'T WORK IN A VACUUM

Mirroring much of the sentiment offered by the other talented contributors to this chapter, Laidlaw urges budding level designers to bounce ideas off a few like-minded people:

> A few brains working on the same problem will often come up with more interesting and varied ideas for gameplay than one person working alone. Each person tends to favor a particular style of gameplay, a particular design approach; in the course of a long game, you'll want to represent a variety of styles, to keep things fresh.

Finally, Laidlaw recognizes that it's important to study and learn from your favorites, but says to use them only as a springboard to invent something new.

> Everyone starts out trying to re-create the great game experiences they loved, and this is a good way to learn the basics. But you won't get anywhere rehashing old ideas. Try to think in terms of the game you would love to play, if only someone out there would finally make it.

> Then make it yourself.

PETER HIRSCHMANN, DREAMWORKS INTERACTIVE

From swank offices in Bel Air, California, producer and writer Peter Hirschmann has created some of the most memorable levels and moments ever to grace a Sony PlayStation game, with the action thriller *Medal of Honor*. As Hirschmann cites from a glowing review of the game at IGNPSX.COM, "Authentic and original to its core, *Medal of Honor* is an example of how the DreamWorks team took the *Saving Private Ryan* sentimentality into its development studio and showed everyone that first-person shooters don't have to follow the standard route."

Many real-world WWII situations and locales were re-created to give gamers the ultimate experience. Famed Hollywood military consultant Captian Dale Dye (USMC, retired) was also brought on to test the game's authenticity. (Used with permission by DreamWorks Interactive, Inc. and Electronic Arts, Inc.)

So how exactly did the team at DreamWorks approach level design when creating *Medal of Honor*? Would this protocol be the same regardless of the game genre? As a special treat, Hirschmann chronicles the complete development approach to game design for *Medal of Honor*. Here it is in its entirety:

> Process is incredibly important, and what that process really depends on is the kind of game you're trying to make. Our goal with *Medal of Honor* was to create an environment that felt as authentic as possible, though not necessarily

realistic. One of our rules during production was that when it was fun versus realism, fun won. There were several well-established gaming conventions that we embraced, like the fact that despite the caliber and country of origin, weapon types (i.e., pistols, rifles, submachine guns) all shared the same ammunition; you could carry over 100 pounds of gear and never get tired; and (most importantly) you could come back to life as many times as you wanted after you've been hit in the head with a German Panzershrek bazooka.

The process for building each *Medal of Honor* level was long, complex, and, ultimately, very rewarding for the team. During the first few months of production we just immersed ourselves in the subject matter, reading all the reference material we could find (Stephen Ambrose's *Citizen Soldiers* being a team favorite and providing a lot of personal inspiration); building scale models of tanks, half-tracks, and field artillery; and (most importantly) working with (read: getting our butts kicked by) our consultant, Captain Dale Dye, USMC (Ret.). A quick tangent: I often get asked about how many war movies we watched, and I think it would surprise people how few we actually viewed together as a team. Watching a movie about a subject that you're researching can sometimes have a detrimental effect, as it can irrevocably influence you on how something should look, as opposed to what your imagination might come up with on its own. The exception to this was obviously *Saving Private Ryan*, which we all saw for the first time about nine months into production. It was a moving experience, because it was head and shoulders above almost the entire canon of WWII cinema.

We were continuously prototyping the engine code, creating concept art (both 2D and 3D), and testing character animation during this research phase, so after a few months we had a good idea of where we wanted to go with the game both in terms of scope and design. The next step was formalizing the gameflow, which was ultimately organized into seven missions, each composed of three thematic levels: infiltration, mission execution, and exfiltration. This breakdown came directly from Capt. Dye, who early on pointed out to us that the hardest part of any mission is usually getting back home. This structure lent itself beautifully to gameplay, as it has a ramping naturally built into it. Infiltration levels tended to emphasize more stealthy gameplay, as you're trying to sneak into wherever it is you need to get to (e.g., creeping through giant pipes into a heavy water plant). The Mission Execution levels were generally where one actually accomplished the primary goal of the mission (e.g., sabotaging the heavy water plant), made up of some more intense combat and complex mission objectives. Finally, there was Exfiltration (e.g., escape from the heavy water plant through the snow), levels consisting of all-out combat from start to finish against the toughest of that particular enemy (e.g., Arctic troopers armed with Panzershreks).

Once this structure was in place, the team went about filling in all the blanks. The player character of Lt. Jimmy Patterson and his story of a C-47 transport pilot-turned-reluctant OSS agent was fleshed out early on, and our wish list of missions was whittled down to the seven that ultimately appeared in the game. From there, each mission was broken down into its three levels (and sometimes a level was split in two parts to accommodate art needs), and the designers got to work.

Here are the three key things we learned, in ascending order, that went into making a successful single-player mission for *Medal of Honor* (*MOH*):

1. **Start with a good, well-developed idea.** Seems like common sense, but it's very easy to get excited about a cool-sounding idea that ultimately won't work within the parameters of your game. The list of rejected *MOH* levels ranges from a fight aboard a Zeppelin to being caught in a POW prison riot. Both of those have some nifty potential, but could never be pulled off in the original *MOH* game engine. One that did work successfully was the "Scuttle U-4901" mission, where Jimmy has to sink the prototype of a new, giant class of German U-boat submarines. Laid out by co-lead designer Lynn Henson, this mission takes what everyone on the team agreed was a cool idea (doing something on a U-boat) and fleshes it out into an epic *Medal of Honor* adventure. You start out in disguise mode on a ship taking you to the submarine facility in Germany where the U-boat is being built. After disabling the ship's engines, you have to disembark via a cargo crane, then sneak along the rooftops of the bustling port and into the U-boat production yard. Once inside, you have to secure plans to the sub you're about to sink, then get aboard as she departs on her maiden voyage—ultimately blowing the sub's dive controls to smithereens before escaping out the conning tower as she sinks to the ocean floor...

    Thinking things through before pen is put to paper and polygon is rendered onscreen will inform the countless decisions you have to make in the course of bringing a mission alive. Here's a partial list of the U-boat mission objectives: Find wrench, gain access to engineering, jam engine, exit ship through cargo hold, locate smuggled weapons, secure deployment timetable, blow up truck with demo charges, find hatchway to production facility, find engine specs, procure hull blueprints, destroy sea door control, locate and board U-4901, radio coordinates to Allied intelligence, lock fins to dive setting, destroy fin controls, blow ballast to surface boat, find exit hatch. All in a day's work, eh?

2. **Design with an emphasis on ramping.** Not just ramping difficulty, but new objectives, new enemies, new mechanics, and new terrain (both indoor and outdoor). Tell a story through the level design. As you work your way through the sub pen (Level 3.3: "The Hunter's Den," built by lead artist Dmitri Ellingson), you initially see only welding tanks and scattered industrial equipment. As you move further, though, you begin to come across drive shafts and propellers, torpedoes and fuel—even a pair of half-finished submarine hulls. Travel even deeper and you discover a complete U-boat in dry dock, along with its well-armed crew on deck. This is not your final destination, however. If you survive and make it to the end of the level, you discover the gargantuan U-4901 prototype ready for launch.

3. **Enemies are everything.** For *Medal of Honor*, this was the key. You can have the prettiest graphics in the world, the slickest level layout, the coolest mechanics—but if you don't have smart enemies, you don't have anything. *MOH* was about the tactical relationship between the player and

the enemy Germans he or she encountered, so the animation and AI systems were where we always poured the bulk of engineering resources. The amazing enemy behavior states created by animation director Sunil Thankamushy, combined with incredibly robust message handler scripting done by co-lead designer Chris Cross, lead to the polygonal army that populated the *MOH* universe. Things like getting enemies to pick up grenades and throw them back to you took a lot of time, but without that effort our virtual European Theater 1944 would not have been worth the trip.

As one last piece of advice, Hirschmann offers, "Always keep your quality bar raised as high as Mount Everest." He explains, "The nuts-and-bolts of game production are incredibly diverse and complex, but there's no secret to making a game other than it's hard and it takes a long time. However, if you have a passion for seeing it through, getting up and going to work everyday will feel like a privilege."

ERIC BIESSMAN, RAVEN SOFTWARE

As project coordinator, lead designer, and level designer at Raven Software, Eric Biessman has received many email messages from those who want to know how to create breathtaking levels, as seen in *Heretic II* and *Soldier of Fortune*. Here he sets the record straight:

- The level must be fun. This is a game, after all.

- Make sure that you have the level planned out before you start designing. To design in a vacuum usually means that you'll have a large amount of wasted time.

- Pay attention to the world around you. Find ideas in everything you do. Make sure that you aren't just making a level that plagiarizes another game. Detail is the key, but it has to be from your own imagination, not someone else's.

Is it worth sketching out levels, as advised by other designers in this chapter? Biessman answers:

I definitely sketch out ideas on paper first, but not the entire level. Usually, I will design smaller areas that are very important to the game and then go from there. I also like to flowchart the entire level before I even think about sitting down to the editor.

Key areas such as the Silverspring Docks in Heretic II should be sketched out on paper first, says Biessman. (Used with permission by Activision, Inc.)

Beissman says having the talent to create levels is important, but a serious dedication to improving your skill is even more critical:

> Be persistent. The more you practice, create, and build, the better your levels are going to be. Make contacts in the industry and touch base with them regularly. Play as many games in as many different styles as you can, and learn from them. Turn your hobby into a passion. If you can't do this, then you probably should think of another way to release your creativity. Dedication pays off 90% of the time, but you still need to have creativity. Otherwise, there's really nothing that can be done.

PAUL O'CONNOR, ODDWORLD INHABITANTS

As lead game designer on *Oddworld: Abe's Oddysee* and *Oddworld: Abe's Exoddus*, Paul O'Connor has learned quite a bit about game design (not to mention that he's been designing games in some form since 1981). O'Connor provides a different take on this chapter, since the first two *Abe's* games are "side-scroller" platform games, in 2D. But do the same principles apply? What are the three most important considerations of a level designer?

THE PLAYER'S EXPERIENCE

O'Connor asks, "Will the player understand the level, puzzle, or situation? Is it clear to the player what he must do to solve the puzzle? Is it fun?"

RELATIVE DIFFICULTY

> As each *Oddworld* designer works on his own levels, and as the order of those levels sometimes isn't determined until late in production, how does this particular level fit into the overall game flow in terms of difficulty and what you're demanding of the player? If this level requires mastery of a specific [mechanism], has that [mechanism] already been introduced earlier in the game? In other words, are the level design and difficulty level appropriate for the anticipated placement in the final game?

NARRATIVE

Finally, O'Connor says to ask yourself, "How does this level advance the story of the game? What vital information does the player gain by completing this level? How does it connect with the preceding and following levels?"

O'Connor comments on sketching out levels:

> I do occasionally [sketch out levels] if the situation is novel. The level editor we used on the two *Abe* games was flexible enough for use as a composition tool. Usually, I'd just sit down in front of the editor with a rough idea of how many screens the budget would afford for this portion of the game, and a notion about the type of play I wanted to accomplish in this area, and then go from there.

CHAPTER 7
MISSION DESIGN

Mission design is an integral part of strategy games, simulations, RPGs, and, most recently, many action/adventure titles as well.

Whereas Chapter 6 deals with *level design*—that is, how a map is laid out architecturally (and the objects placed within it)—*mission* or *scenario design* refers to the specific objective(s) the player must carry out during the game. They can be historical in nature, such as in WWII combat flight sims or turn-based strategy war games, or purely fictional, as found in fantasy role-playing games. In many cases, each mission may have a number of smaller goals to complete. And it follows that the missions are part of a grander story.

Campaigns in a game refers to a string of single-level scenarios or missions, often in a sequential order to complete an overall goal. For example, Blizzard's mega-hit sci-fi strategy game *Starcraft* contains three campaigns for the different races—the Zerg, Protoss, and Terrans—each containing 10 scenarios, for a total of 30.

Dynamic campaigns means that the success or failure of missions is factored into the campaign, and should impact the future of the campaign as a result. For example, if Saddam Hussein's radar bases are destroyed in northern Iraq, it may be harder for them to detect U.S. and British forces approaching from eastern Turkey in future missions. Naturally, this breathes some life and additional satisfaction into the game experience, instead of the player feeling like he or she is part of a canned script. Hundreds of games a year fall short in this area, and the player often stops playing because of repetitive missions/campaigns, confusing situations, or missions that can be too easily completed or are painstakingly difficult.

Games such as Microprose's European Air War offer a dynamic campaign so the missions (and situations within missions) will change as the player progresses through the game. (Used with permission by Hasbro Interactive, Inc.)

This chapter contains advice from hand-picked professionals on what can turn your average game into a veritable masterpiece.

ROB PARDO, BLIZZARD ENTERTAINMENT

Rob Pardo is a producer and designer at Blizzard Entertainment who was in charge of unit balancing on *Starcraft*. On the famed *Starcraft: Brood War* expansion pack, he became the lead designer. Pardo has a number of guidelines for his mission designers, and asks that they adhere to these rules closely:

KEEP IT SIMPLE

Whatever the gimmick of the level is (countdown timer, must rescue a troop, etc.), make sure that it's very clear and that you don't use more than one. When designers try to put too many different gimmicks and/or goals into a level, the focus and objectives become confusing to a player.

DESIGN ON PAPER FIRST

You should always sketch out your level first and write down how the level should flow. This process will save you many hours in the long run, since it's much easier to change something on paper than it is to change in a mission editor.

ARTISTICALLY PLEASING LEVELS

While the gameplay of the level is of primary importance, don't neglect the aesthetics of a game level. In *Starcraft*, there are a few guidelines that we follow:

- **Lay down the terrain in isometric patterns.** *Starcraft* tile sets are built along diagonal/isometric lines, so you don't want to have vertical or horizontal cliff faces for long stretches.

- **Use a variety of tile types throughout the map.** My general rule is that, on any given screen of map, if you can only see one tile type (water, dirt, etc.), then it's too much.

- **Good doodad use.** Doodads are important to make your map unique and interesting. It's very important, though, that they not be placed in a player's way. Keep them along terrain edges that the player will not be directly traversing frequently (cliff edges, water edges, etc.).

CLEAR BRIEFINGS AND OBJECTIVES

After players have seen the briefing and read the objectives, they should be able to start the level and make progress very easily. If you have more than three objectives, I would classify this as "not clear." Players should never be frustrated with a level because they don't know what to do next. This is a major failing in many levels—and full-blown games, for that matter.

AVOID PAUSING THE GAME FOR STORY ELEMENTS

" Any time the designer pauses the game on the player, it takes away the immersion factor of the game experience. If you have a "major" story point that you want to get across or you're changing the level objective, it's acceptable, but make this the exception, not the rule. On another note, though, it's perfectly fine to have a scripted cut-scene at the end of the level. This is a reward, and the player is usually pleased to sit and watch the story unfold at this point. "

RAMP UP THE DIFFICULTY APPROPRIATELY

" No matter what the relative difficulty for a given level, it should ramp from the beginning of the level at one point and become gradually harder as the level progresses. Try to avoid "killer" attacks that wipe out a player 30 minutes into a level. "

SPACE OUT THE MINERAL PLACEMENT (STARCRAFT SPECIFIC)

" Due to the pathing algorithm that *Starcraft* uses, worker units can easily get stuck while harvesting unless the map designer places the mineral chunks in a pattern to prevent this. It's a good idea to play test every resource node before pronouncing the map "done." "

PLAY TEST, PLAY TEST, PLAY TEST

" You should be constantly play testing your own levels to be sure that they work correctly and that they have the proper difficulty throughout the level. Levels at Blizzard are play tested by everyone in the company at the end of the project to make sure that we never release a level that's not up to our own quality [standards].

Also, be aware that you as the designer will be very close to the level and can't always be objective—get a friend who has never played your level to play test it. You may discover your friend never picks up on an objective that you thought was easy to understand, and he becomes frustrated with the level. "

STAGES OF STARCRAFT: BROOD WAR CAMPAIGN DESIGN

Pardo offers us a chronological overview of how they created the campaign for *Starcraft: Brood War*.

" 1. **Write the back-story.** Our first stage was to write the story for the campaign. It was important, though, to write a general story that could be modified as time goes on. This process was to give us a starting point from which to think about the campaign as a whole.

2. **Define the campaign structure.** The Brood War campaign is a linear campaign that progresses through each of the three races, telling one unified story. We had to decide in what order the player would play the campaign. In our case, we chose to start the player as the Protoss, then go to the Terran, and end with the Zerg.

3. **Plot major story nodes.** Now we wanted to define the major events that were going to happen in the story: what characters were going to die, where betrayals were going to happen, etc.

4. **Start first-pass mission design on paper.** All the level designers would sit in a room and brainstorm on a level-by-level basis. When doing brainstorming, no idea is a bad idea. It's important for everyone to participate and to just get a ton of ideas down on paper. We would spend about 15 minutes per level just talking about the story for the level, how big the level should be, ideas for gimmicks, what units the player should have, and so on.

5. **Second-pass story design.** After the first round of discussions on a level-by-level basis, we found it necessary to tweak different parts of the story to accommodate certain goals we wanted to accomplish with the levels. In one case, it was necessary to add two more levels to the last campaign to better tell the story to the player.

6. **Second-pass level design on paper.** It was time to start locking things down. We went back through each level and talked about what the level should look like, where the player would start, how large was the enemy force, how we would program the AI and triggers. It's important to note that we had yet to lay out one level in the editor at this point. All work had been done in a conference room on paper.

7. **Start laying out levels!** Now it was time to divvy up the workload among the different designers and start work. Each designer would be responsible for laying out, placing enemy forces, and programming their own trigger actions.

8. **AI programming.** The AI programmers would take over the level and make the AI perform in interesting and different ways, according to the paper design and appropriate difficulty for the level.

9. **Play test.** For a level to be pronounced "done," it would take two to three weeks of testing and iterating on the level, based on feedback. (Once a level is finished, don't touch it! Even if it's a minor change, it isn't worth the chance that you could break something else and ruin all the effort that you placed into your level.)

ON UNIT BALANCING

One of the weakest and ironically one of the most critical elements of a real-time strategy game is proper unit balancing. In the following discussion, Pardo explains its importance and offers some advice on ways to be sure that units have the proper "rock, paper, scissors" effect.

> For games like *Starcraft*, unit balancing is the most important aspect of the multiplayer games. If this game isn't balanced for each race, then there's no point in having different races, since everyone will only play one race. An entire book (or at least a chapter) could be written on this subject alone, so understand that these guidelines are not meant as a comprehensive list but rather as a starting point.

EARLY GAME UNIT PRODUCTION FAIRNESS

> Every race needs to have the same opportunity to get early military units and/or defenses. If one race can get units substantially quicker than other races, you'll end up with one race winning a lot of games in two minutes.

PURITY OF PURPOSE

> Every unit should have a primary purpose. For example, in *Starcraft*, the Zealot is tough ground attacker, the Queen is spell-caster so doesn't have an attack, etc. The units that don't have a "pure" purpose are always the toughest units to balance (Hydralisks, Marines, and so on).

NO INVINCIBLE UNIT COMBOS

> It's extremely important that you find any unit combinations that are unbeatable by another player. It's acceptable if there is a powerful strategy, but it should never be unbeatable if a good player is prepared for it.

AVOID REDUNDANT UNITS

> In *Starcraft* we made a conscious effort not to have any unit duplicate another unit in the same race tech-tree. What I mean by this is that, while a Marine is the first troop you can build in the Terran tech-tree, it's still useful at the end of the game because no other Terran troop does the same job as the Marine.
>
> Be aware of when new units become available. In each race's tech-tree, you must be aware of when a new powerful troop becomes available and make sure that the other races will have a counter to this new super unit at the same point in the game. Another *Starcraft* example: We found that Mutalisks were coming so early in the game that the other two races were not able to properly defend against them, so we increased the build time of the Spire (the building that allows Mutalisks to be built) to compensate.

MAKE BABY STEPS

> It's very important not to overdo a change. It's surprising to most people how one point of damage can make a huge difference in real game situations. Even if you feel that a larger change is warranted, it's always better to err on the side of a small change; otherwise you now have a balance problem in another area—and before you know it you have caused a chain reaction of changes that have unbalanced the game.

EVALUATE ALL EFFECTS OF A CHANGE

> The obvious change is not always the right change. Whenever you're going to make a change to a unit, look at all places that this new change will impact. As a *Starcraft* example, we at one point changed the size of the Dragoon to medium, thus changing how much damage it took from large and small-sized troops. This had the positive effect of making Dragoons more susceptible to attacks from Vultures and Firebats (a previously underutilized troop) but also had the unintended effect of making them take less damage from Tanks. This in turn led to a new Dragoon rush strategy, and we had to undo the change.

TIM STELLMACH, LOOKING GLASS STUDIOS

As senior game designer at Looking Glass Studios, Tim Stellmach's latest and arguably most impressive work is *Thief: The Dark Project* and *Thief 2*. For these titles, Stellmach was responsible for training and managing junior designers and overseeing the design of gameplay systems and missions. Who better to invite to talk about mission design? After all, *Gamecenter*, a popular Internet e-zine, awarded *Thief: The Dark Project* the "Best Story Line" award for 1998. That's right—an action game, of all things. And tightly woven in the story are the individual player missions, so let's begin.

Stellmach first defines scenario design and how he approaches it. In this segment, he also explains the differences between scenario design and puzzle design (discussed in Chapter 5).

"I'd say the most important thing is just healthy amounts of playing time and willingness to adjust your work," says Stellmach. He also warns there's such a thing as getting "too close" to your work to make an accurate judgment. (Used with permission by Looking Glass Studios, Inc.)

> In any mission-based game, scenario design involves a mission objective, a description of the space in which the mission occurs, some obstacles, and the tools for overcoming those obstacles. Note that the actual solutions to the player's problems aren't on that list! That's the difference between a *scenario* and a *puzzle*. A puzzle has a solution designed into it, and that's really the only valid way of approaching the puzzle. One thing you see in a lot of games is missions designed as a set of puzzles the player has to "solve" in order to achieve the objective. There are games where that really is the point, of course, but you have to question that assumption. Can you design more than one solution? Could you enrich your game by making an environment in which the player can experiment and improvise?

The "campaign" in Thief is a work of fiction that holds the missions together and motivates them. Most action games involve a predetermined sequence of missions, so the campaign doesn't serve any interactive function. Instead it serves the interactivity in a support role. The fiction enhances the individual mission objectives by making them part of a story the player cares about. Success is its own reward, of course, but with a compelling fiction the player also feels like his success has achieved something meaningful.

Stellmach explains how to wrestle with mission design for a game and speaks on the common problems inherent in creating a successful game:

Well, design in the first place implies setting goals, and planning and implementing solutions. People tend to forget what it means to do things "by design." It's important to stress the role of planning because in a creative business it's all too easy to get swept up in your ideas and just improvise as you go along. Generally this leads to work that's sloppier and less focused than what you're really capable of. Think about what you're trying to do overall before you even start work on any individual part. Don't go off half-cocked.

A corollary to this rule is to organize your work in iterations. Any job that's too big to understand all at once should be broken up into phases, each of which improves on the previous step. It's not actually possible to know exactly what you want to do from the beginning, so you have to be able to grip the problem as you go along, and adapt your plan. In designing a mission, this means starting with a written plan, doing a general floor plan of the area first, and not working in details until they're necessary. The more detailed a construct is, the harder it is to rework, and everything you do will need to be reworked at some point. Plan ahead for prototypes and demos. Nothing is more useful in understanding the thing you're making than a working model.

That's all about getting work done in the first place—not wasting your time or straying off-track. To get good work done, I'd say the most important thing is just healthy amounts of playing time and willingness to adjust your work. This applies particularly to your communication with your play testers. There is no way for you to maintain your objectivity while working on a game day to day, for months at a time. When in doubt, the other guy is probably right, because you're too close to the thing to see it clearly. Build relationships with play testers who are good critics and good communicators.

Thief: The Dark Project was quite a unique action game in that the emphasis was not on annihilating everything in sight. Rather, its focus was on cunning stealth and subtle operation. Asked to comment on hurdles in light of the game's mission design, Tim replies:

The biggest obstacle was the amount of Thief that we were inventing ourselves. Nobody had done a first-person action-adventure game before where things like hiding in shadows and creeping around were so important. Or one where sound was really so basic to understanding the environment around you, rather than just being window dressing on a world that's essentially visual.

It's hard to design missions around gameplay experiences you haven't really seen before. In production, it wasn't even really clear to us which parts of playing the thief character people would respond to. So there's all sorts of opportunities, not just to sneak around, but to pick pockets, ambush guards, defeat traps, and scout around eavesdropping and such. That led to a lot of richness in the game, but at times it was hard to get a grip on it all.

The key to dealing with this was a lot of game playing and critique up front to get a better understanding of the gameplay we wanted to see. Even many of the most original ideas have elements of a lot of previous work in them; there's no such thing as working in a creative vacuum. So there's elements of *System Shock*, *Prince of Persia*, *GoldenEye 007*, and a lot of other games in there. And we thought about similar-seeming games we didn't want to emulate, and what we wanted to do differently, and why. We asked a lot of sort of goal-level questions like "What are the tactical situations that make stealth necessary?" and "What are the emotional buttons those situations push, and how do we capitalize on that?"

In closing, Stellmach confirms that this all boils down to the antecedent strategies: plan ahead, get the gameplay prototyped as early as possible, and get as much feedback from players as you can.

GREG STREET, ENSEMBLE STUDIOS

Dr. Greg T. Street, game designer at Ensemble Studios, worked on the *Age of Empires: Rise of Rome* expansion pack and *Age of Empires II: The Age of Kings*. On these two products, his responsibilities included designing campaigns and random map types, helping contribute to unit and civilization balance, and providing historical background when needed. Street discusses the distinction between scenarios, campaigns, dynamic campaigns, and branching campaigns as they pertain to real-time strategy games. He alludes to his work for examples of each:

A *scenario* in an RTS game puts you in interesting situations where you must solve a certain mission rather than just build up and crush a generic computer opponent (although that often happens in scenarios). Scenarios rely on interesting maps, unusual victory conditions, unique art or sound additions, and attempting to tell a greater story.

A *campaign* is a string of scenarios in the way that a book is divided into chapters or a play into acts. In *Age of Kings*, one of the campaigns follows the battles of Joan of Arc. In one scenario, you must emancipate the city of Orleans, being held by the wicked British. In future scenarios, you attack Chalons and Paris.

In a *dynamic campaign*, events in one scenario directly affect future scenarios, often by carrying over the health and status of your units to the next scenario. (*Warhammer: Dark Omen* is a good example.) *Branching campaigns* are those in which you have a choice of which scenario comes next in the story, either by directly choosing on the user interface or by your actions or degree of victory in a previous scenario. Personally, dynamic campaigns are not my favorite. Players often feel like they must not only win a scenario, but win by overwhelming odds in order to beat future scenarios. As a game designer, it's very hard to balance. Branching campaigns are a little easier to do successfully, but you're often committing to twice the number of scenarios in a campaign, many of which a particular player won't even see. In fact, one of the problems with branching campaigns is that players often choose to try both scenarios off a particular node, just to make sure they aren't "missing anything."

For games such as Age of Empires Expansion: The Rise of Rome, historical accuracy was an important consideration, so Street researched the zeitgeist of the time. (Used with permission by Microsoft, Inc.)

Game designers who would like to learn more about creating successful missions and campaigns should heed the following advice.

Make the scenario interesting. Why would a player want to go through your scenario instead of just playing versus other humans or on a randomly generated map?

Try to tell a story. Most players respond better to a scenario if they think that capturing the Assassin's mountain fortress will unite all the Saracens in a common front against the Crusaders than if they're just pitted against yet another bad guy. What are the two sides of the war? What is the historical significance of this battle? Will the outcome change anything? I've said this before (and you probably heard it before that), but "Red called you a monkey—go destroy his town" is not the stuff of epic literature.

Play test. Play test. Play test. Play through your level over and over, and then have friends, enemies, random Joes from the Net, your parents, and your pets play through the scenario. You would be amazed at the goofy things people come up with that will break all your best-laid plans.

Are there any specific do's and don'ts Street can offer? Why do so many strategy games and sims have weak mission and campaign structure? Street offers us over a thousand words of advice in the following primer:

PLAN AHEAD

I always say that when designing a scenario, you should know exactly what's going to happen at any given time. Don't just plop enemy units down on the board and hope that they'll provide an interesting challenge. You should know that there will be a rush 5 minutes into the game, followed by a prolonged battle 20 minutes later, and that the entire scenario will take about 90 minutes for an experienced player.

THE FINE LINE BETWEEN HUMOR AND SOLEMNITY

Try to land on the continuum somewhere between cheesy melodrama and slapstick humor. If things are too sweeping, too desperate, too clichéd, then you can easily lose the mood and the player's desire to get through the campaign. (As a side note: FMV [full-motion video] and voice actors always tend to push you a notch or two closer to cheesy.) On the other extreme, backing so far away from an epic story that everything becomes one big joke won't push people onward either. A little tension break is good once in a while, but don't let the player feel that he or she is just a straight man for a bunch of zany events. *Warcraft II* was quite humorous, but it never detracted from the grittiness of the story. If you have to make silly units because you're burned out on the story, consider making them cheats or Easter eggs.

FREE TOOLS

Make whatever tools you use to develop scenarios available to the fans, preferably with the retail product. Having a well-documented editor is almost a must in the RTS franchise these days. The fans are very supportive of powerful editors.

DON'T SACRIFICE QUALITY FOR QUANTITY

People who play scenarios are very sensitive to repetition. If every mission feels the same, it's probably worth scrapping or merging a few. Alternatively, try to alternate scenarios where you basically build up to attack, fight a set-piece battle (a situation where you can't produce any additional units and must budget your starting resources), sneak a few units around a puzzle-type map, or have some other nontraditional victory condition (such as defending a weak unit, escort missions, etc.)

Use as many different victory conditions as possible. If the player just wanted to build up and crush the AI, he or she would use random maps. At Ensemble Studios, we strive to provide every scenario with a *hook*—something unique about the scenario that makes it fun. In the *Rise of Rome* expansion pack, one of the most popular scenarios that I made was the siege of Syracuse. The goal was to capture the Greek mathematician Archimedes in the center of the city, while avoiding the dreaded mirror towers that Archimedes designed to defend his city. (According to legend, the mirrors focused sunlight with enough intensity to ignite a trireme. There is some debate about whether this actually happened, although historians agree that the physics are believable.) The hooks for that scenario were being careful not to kill the weak Archimedes with indiscriminate catapult fire, and having your navy avoid the virtually unbeatable mirror towers protecting the Syracuse harbor.

One other caveat: Based on experience, prolonged sieges of an entrenched enemy sound really epic on paper, but the gameplay can be tedious as you slowly take out all of an enemy's defenses. The enemy should always be counterattacking. Don't let the player have more than a few seconds of peace, unless you are purposefully trying to prolong the tension.

MORE BANG FOR THE BUCK

> Make it easy for fans to have access to additional scenarios not included in the main game. There are always retailers or periodicals eager to have some exclusive "bonus level." Make additional scenarios available on your company's Web site or encourage and facilitate the fan sites to trade user-submitted scenarios. Some of the *Age of Empires* fan sites literally have hundreds to thousands of scenarios.

INCLUDE EXTRA TOUCHES

> Use unique terrain, units, heroes, art, music, voiceover, or any other embellishment that encourages people to want to explore the map and play through just to see the next scenario. Including legendary heroes such as Alexander the Great and Hector of Troy in the *Age of Empires* campaigns and in the scenario editor was very popular with the fans.

USE SCRIPTS BUT DON'T OVERDO THEM

> Do use scripts or triggers, but don't use scripting as a crutch. By *scripting*, I mean forcing an action as the result of a condition being met. Scripts or triggers can really enhance the single-player experience. An example would be receiving reinforcements when you reach a certain area or defeat a certain enemy, possibly with a chat message or voiceover text.
>
> However, if the human player feels that the computer opponents are merely responding to a specific set of actions (such as attacking every five minutes or attacking when the human player builds a certain type of building), the AI becomes very predictable and the human player feels that he or she has lost any chance to make real decisions. Blizzard's *Starcraft* did an excellent job of using triggers without overdoing them.

TRY TO EVOKE EMOTION

> Try to evoke emotion in people playing through your scenarios or campaigns. I read once that good nonfiction conveys information but good fiction evokes emotion. Players should feel fear if they know they're up against a powerful enemy that can strike at any moment. Players can feel redemption or justice if they're beating off a predator from a victim or avenging a comrade's sacrifice. Even the map layout can convey emotion. Empty, barren battlefields speak of desolation, while cramped, jumbled surfaces can suggest paranoia.

ON DIFFICULTY, HINTS, AND BALANCE

> Don't rely on a save-fail-retry mentality. It's very frustrating. Don't allow a player to stumble blindly into a battle from which he can't possibly survive, unless you're punishing him for making a bad choice. It should always be possible, if difficult, to win a scenario on the first try. If you plan an ambush, use some foreshadowing such as skeletons or crushed vehicles, or possibly burning buildings or fleeing refugees. If there is a right and a wrong path at a fork

in the road, provide some hint for the right way to go, preferably "in story." Best of all, don't set up right-versus-wrong choices. If one path is more deadly, there should also be a reward hidden within. The classic tradeoff is lengthy but less difficult versus short but dangerous.

DON'T FORGET ABOUT THE SINGLE-PLAYER GAME

Multiplayer is very compelling in most RTS games, but I think designers sometimes forget the numbers of customers who don't yet have access to a reliable multiplayer connection (although that number is decreasing every day). When working on the *Age of Empires* franchise, scenarios were up against a strong multiplayer experience plus a random-map generator and tolerably good computer AI, so it would have been easy to neglect single-player campaigns. One of my responsibilities is to see that we don't!

The AI of the computer player can also prevent single-player scenarios from being very robust. Until very recently, it was typical in RTS games such as *Warcraft II* and *Age of Empires* for the AI not to build walls! Obviously that makes it pretty hard to defend.

JON ZUK, RAVEN SOFTWARE

Raven Software's Jon Zuk, the lead designer for the popular action/RPG *Heretic II* (published by Activision in late 1998) and *Soldier of Fortune* (published by Activision in 2000) says there are different ways to create a mission or a goal for the game, and uses one of his projects as a prime example:

Heretic II has one large "mission" or goal that needs to be completed. Many games follow the idea of a large all-encompassing mission to win the game. Some games, however, use small individual missions. Take a racing game, for example. The user's goal is to win an individual race, but the other races don't really matter all that much. However, most games that have a large mission usually break that up into smaller, more manageable, and easier-to-remember goals. In *Heretic II*, the large goal is to cure the people of Parthoris of a plague. As you explore the first level, you meet a man who can give you a little information and a more immediate goal; meet the Celestial Watcher in the palace. Even though there's still that larger goal, a sub-goal has been introduced to steer the player in a direction.

"One thing I've noticed, though," continues Zuk, "is that in some games, there are too many sub-goals." He expands:

I can think of many recent role-playing games being guilty of this problem. What happens then is that the user loses touch with the larger overall goal and the focus of the game. It's easy to lose interest in a game when this happens. If you're going to have many missions reaching toward a large overall goal, make sure that they tie in together or at least keep the focus of the main goal.

Zuk warns, "Losing focus can make the game no longer fun, which I think is the most important thing in any game." Check out these action shots from Raven's controversial 3D shooter Soldier of Fortune. (Used with permission by Activision, Inc.)

BRAD MCQUAID, VERANT INTERACTIVE

As producer on *EverQuest*, arguably the most popular massively-multiplayer online role-playing game (MMORPG), McQuaid says that good RPG mission design is largely due to the AI (artificial intelligence). He explains:

> The real challenge in terms of quests and missions, whether in single-player RPGS or MMORPGs, is AI. Until some major advances occur in the realm of AI, interaction between players and NPCs (non-player characters controlled by the game) is going to remain pretty limited. Typically it consists of interacting in basic dialogues, asking simple questions, and being assigned "missions" or "quests" that usually involve bringing an item to another NPC, or saying something to another NPC, or perhaps even escorting an NPC somewhere. And no matter how many times RPG game developers say they're going to go beyond this method in their "next game," I've not seen a significant change in years.

"I think EQ keeps players playing for so long because we've provided strong and varied game mechanics that support both character development and community," says McQuaid. "Players spend a lot of time interacting with others and building their characters by gaining experience, game knowledge, acquiring items, etc. (Used with permission by Sony Computer Entertainment America (SCEA), Inc. and Verant Interactive, Inc.)

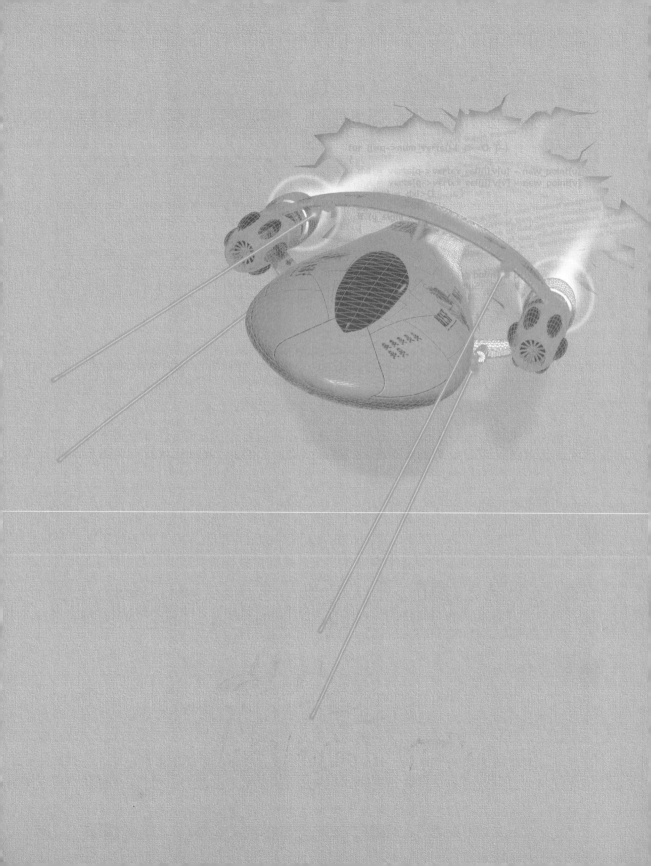

CHAPTER 8
PROGRAMMING

In this chapter, we get down to the meat and potatoes of game design—programming.

Programming, of course, refers to designing and writing a computer program, and, in our case, a game or game engine. It's the programmer's job to decide what the game needs to do, develop the logic of how to do it, and write instructions for the computer in a language that the computer can translate into its own language and execute (such as Microsoft Visual C++).

Another definition of programming is "the most fun you can have with your clothes on, although clothes are not mandatory." (Okay, that's debatable, but it is a real secondary definition at the FOLDOC Web site, the Free On-Line Dictionary of Computing at www.instantweb.com/~foldoc/contents.html!)

Call 'em what you want—code-crunchers, number-munchers, algorithm analysts—programmers are the talented folks who create the backbone of the game. As an analogy, think of the game as a building under construction. Programming represents the girders or the skeleton that forms the shape of the structure. All the beautiful art on the walls or incredible music pumping through the P.A. system will not substitute for poor engineering. A game, like a building, must be built on a solid and secure foundation.

There's a lot more to programming than graduating with a degree in computer science and hacking around with some code on your PC. Game programming takes cunning, patience, and an intangible *savoir faire* developed after years of practice, discipline, and a passion for the trade.

Over the next couple dozen pages, we'll hear from savvy programmers who want to share with us their years of experience on programming games, and how to overcome the tribulations inherent in this growing profession.

KURT ARNLUND, ACCOLADE

Before leaving Activision to become lead programmer on Accolade's *Slave Zero*, Kurt Arnlund worked on such PC hits as *Mechwarrior 2: NetMech*, *Interstate '76* (all incarnations), and *Heavy Gear*. When it comes to programming a computer game, Arnlund says there are three key things a budding game programmer should bear in mind: the balance between time and ambition, the importance of specificity, and short versus fast routes to solving problems. He expands:

THE BALANCE BETWEEN TIME AND AMBITION

> A game designer needs to walk the fine line between dreaming of this amazing game that goes so far beyond today's technology, and the time it takes to create amazing technologies. If you're too ambitious, you may be asking to create a game that can't be made in the industry standard timeline of a year. If you slip by six months because of a too-ambitious project, you run the risk of someone outdoing you before you can even come to market. On the other hand, if you scale your ambitions back too far, you run the risk of releasing a game that has been outpaced by your competitors long before you reach market.

BE SPECIFIC, VERY SPECIFIC

> As a game designer, it's your job to dream up coolness, then put it to paper in as exacting a way as possible. The programmer must then take this design document and make your dream a reality. A good programmer is going to go through your design and come across details that you hadn't anticipated. There are few things more frustrating as a programmer than realizing that the designer didn't put a lot of thought into creating a thorough design. This results in lost time and lost efficiency on the programmer's side because he may have already started coding your idea before the flaw is discovered. The more time you spend fleshing out every minute detail of your idea, the happier everyone will be. And as an added bonus, you'll get a killer game.

THE SHORT WAY VERSUS THE BEST WAY

> Game programmers are generally lazy individuals. That's right. It's true. Don't let anyone tell you otherwise. Since the dawn of computer games, game programmers have looked for shortcuts to coolness. We almost always try to take the shortest route from point A to point B. Sometimes when we look at a problem all we see is the shortest route to completion. What's the point of all this? Well, I'm going to let you in on a little secret. Sometimes the shortest route isn't always the best. As much as I hate to admit it, it's true. The more you, the game designer, know about programming, the more you're able to walk up to the programmers and say, "Hey, I think what you did is cool, but couldn't you have done it this way? That's what I really want." Better yet, if you really know what you're doing as a game designer, you can ask for a specific implementation right from the get-go.

> You may be tempted to ask us programmers, "If you know that the shortcut isn't always the best, why don't you always do things the best way?" And my answer would be, "Because the best way isn't always the shortest." Actually, you should be quite happy that most game programmers think this way, because this means that things will get done on time. If we coded everything the most accurate way possible, we'd all end up with games that take three times as long and have one third as many features. Worse yet, we'd wind up with some over-budget, late, un-fun, technological showpiece like *Trespasser*.

Left, a pre-rendered screen shot from Activision's popular Interstate '76 combat racing game. (Used with permission by Activision, Inc.) Right, Accolade's Slave Zero. (Used with permission by Accolade. Inc.)

What about licensing an existing game engine, such as the *Quake II* or *Unreal* engine? Is it worth the greenback or should a programmer create his own?

> That's a tough call. I know a few programmers who wouldn't dream of working with a licensed engine because they think they'd lose working on all the cool engine details that they love so much. In the end, it probably doesn't matter too much. If you make an engine from scratch, you have to create and work on a whole lot of details that you don't need to work on if you license an engine. When you license an engine you can probably begin prototyping very quickly, but eventually you're faced with learning and possibly debugging all the details of the licensed technology if you want any hope of making the most use out of the technology. Because everyone codes differently, your licensed engine can range from indecipherable code to a beautiful masterpiece, but it'll most likely be somewhere in between.

Arnlund provides tips for newbie programmers who want to break into the industry:

> If you want to be a game programmer, a Bachelors in computer science is a must. You don't have to go to fancy, expensive schools—just try to get a firm grasp of math and a bit of physics, and you'll be set.
>
> The best tip I can give to someone starting out is that if you really have a passion for games and you really want to be a game programmer or designer, then stick with it. Let everyone know that this is what you want to do. You never know who's going to be talking to a recruiter or who may know someone in the industry. Save up your money and attend a Game Developers Conference, or volunteer to work there and get a pass for free. Meet as many people in the industry as you can, and eventually you'll get lucky. I got lucky because a friend of mine who was seeking the same kind of work gave my name to a recruiter. Everyone in this industry has their story.

In closing, Arnlund suggests you set your goal, work hard, and hang in there. "Many people have gone from being testers to being designers or producers. Just stick with it and eventually it'll happen."

TIM SWEENY, EPIC GAMES

Tim Sweeny is the founder of Epic Games and the programmer behind the *Unreal* engine, which powers such games as *Unreal Tournament*, *Duke Nukem Forever*, *Deus Ex*, and *X-Com: Alliance*, to name a few. Being the talented workaholic he is, it took quite a bit of arm-twisting to get Mr. Sweeny to take time out for an interview, but at last he gave in (thanks to some extra *nudging* from coworker Cliff Bleszinski!).

Sweeny was first asked what are the most important rules to keep in mind when programming an action game, and what are some of the biggest obstacles he has faced (and how they were overcome). He begins as follows:

MAKE A FUN GAME

> This seems obvious, but this simple goal so often gets lost in the game industry, with so much attention being paid to technology, features, and the difficulty of developers obtaining a publishing deal. If you look at the very earliest successful games, like *Pong* or *Donkey Kong*, they have nothing in common with modern games in terms of technology or design. The only common ground is that they're fun to play.
>
> If you look at all of the gaming industry's biggest screwups, for example Rocket Science Games' collapse, you can always trace it back to the simple fact that the developers weren't focusing on making a fun game.
>
> But having a fun game can often save you from other problems. For example, our first huge development project, *Unreal*, ran into major delays as the engine was rewritten, updated, and fine-tuned—the game shipped over 18 months late. The thing that saved us all along was the fact that we had a really fun game. Before *Unreal* was released, there was a lot of bad press and publisher frustration over *Unreal*'s delays. But when the game shipped, it turned out to be a really good, fun game. Now when people look back at *Unreal*, they remember the fun game that sold a million units. In the end, gamers and publishers and magazine reviewers forgave us for our other mistakes with the project, because we came through and delivered a good game.

DON'T PROGRAM YOURSELF INTO A CORNER

> There's a great saying: "Complex programs that work start out as simple programs that work, not as complex programs that don't work." So many games are canceled after protracted development cycles because the programmer made a bad decision early on—often seen as a very minor decision at the time. As you're building the foundation for your game, think about all the future ramifications of your decisions.
>
> You often hear about a game that is highly anticipated and soon to be released. Then months go by and you hear nothing. Then more months go by. After a year, the publisher announces that the project was canceled. This scenario is

common in our industry, and the reason is hardly ever something like "The developers weren't working hard enough" or "The game's artwork was late." It's almost always caused by a simple, early programming mistake that became impossible to extricate from the engine.

Epic Games' programming mastermind Tim Sweeny cautions budding game designers to try to keep the code as modular as possible to fix errors later on in the development process. (Used with permission by Epic Games, Inc.)

KEEP YOUR CODE FLEXIBLE

If it's easy to replace a component of your game, for example the physics collision system, then you are insulated from the danger of screwing up your initial implementation. The worst that can happen is a small delay if you rewrite the flawed code. But if the component is hopelessly entangled with the rest of your game, then it could later come back and haunt you—or kill your project.

Flexibility saved *Unreal* from disaster many times. I rewrote the texture mapper from scratch seven times during the development cycle, each one invoking major new design decisions. I rewrote the collision code three times. I rewrote the networking twice. I rewrote the sound interface twice. In each of these cases, only the final implementation was commercially viable. My first six rendering engines had fatal flaws which, if left unsolved, would have prevented the game from shipping.

Think about that for a moment. I'm a smart guy. You're a smart guy. Now, speaking statistically about the demographics of readers of this book, you are probably not significantly smarter than I and, if you are a first-time game developer, you are less experienced than I was. And it took me seven attempts to get *Unreal*'s renderer good enough to ship. Do you think you're going to get your game's renderer perfect on your first attempt? Or even your second or third?

So, since we're all imperfect programmers, and the nature of our projects forces us to make design decisions long before we have enough data to back up those decisions, flexibility is the one thing that saves us from disaster. *Unreal*'s rendering code was modular enough that writing a new renderer and fully integrating it with the engine took an average of one month per renderer. A month is a long time, but it's only 1/24th of a typical project's duration, so it is actually quite reasonable to expect to spend a few months rewriting and revising old code after you see more of the "big picture."

You wanted the best, you got the best. Next we'll hear from Jay Stelly, responsible for coding a little ol' action game called *Half-Life*...

JAY STELLY, VALVE SOFTWARE

Jay Stelly is a senior software engineer at one of the hottest development houses in the gaming industry—Valve Software. This talented team of game designers, programmers, artists, animators, and sound engineers produced *Half-Life*, one of the most talked-about games of 1998 and 1999.

Asked to address the many facets of game programming with which a software engineer must be concerned, Stelly answers the broad question with a short essay on frame-rate issues and memory limitations for 3D accelerator card support. The example is drawn from the *Half-Life* engine, a *Quake/Quake II* technology first licensed from id Software and modified greatly by Valve:

> Any game engine you can create or buy will have a set of technical constraints. You can choose some of these constraints, such as your target platform (CPU, memory, disk space, etc.), and target performance on that platform (frame rate, loading times, etc.); others are imposed by what hardware your audience owns. These choices do have consequences, of course. Let's look at an example.
>
> In *Half-Life*, we chose to support 3D accelerator cards for PCs. This allows people with additional 3D hardware to have higher image quality and frame rates. On the surface, this seems like an easy choice to make, but it comes with constraints of its own. One of the biggest challenges we faced was the fact that many of the 3D accelerators on the market only had access to 2MB of memory for storing textures. To make matters worse, the cost of swapping old textures with new textures was pretty high on many of these cards, so using more than 2MB caused a large frame-rate decrease. What this meant for *Half-Life* is that we had to limit any individual scene in the game to a maximum of about 2MB of visible textures.
>
> Think of programming time as a resource for overcoming constraints. You can only spend a certain amount of it. A good engineer can estimate the difficulty of a problem and choose the correct set of approaches to consider as solutions to a big technical problem. Many of the defining decisions about a game are made as tradeoffs between different technical constraints. This was definitely the case with *Half-Life*.
>
> Early on, Valve recognized that managing texture memory for 3D hardware was going to be a big issue. Limiting ourselves to 2MB of textures per scene had tons of consequences. Not only did the environments themselves have textures, but each character in the game had its own textures. Also, each weapon the player could hold had its own textures, and the backgrounds in outdoor areas were made completely out of large textures. Because of the way our engine was designed, most of the lighting information in the world was also stored as textures. With that in mind, we spent programming time on managing this

problem. We knew that there were too many consequences to limiting ourselves to 2MB per scene. It wouldn't provide us with enough texture to reach the visual quality we were targeting. In fact, the problem was much larger than just a 2MB limit on some cards. As it turns out, almost all 3D cards on the market at the time *Half-Life* was released have dramatic performance differences that depend on how much texture memory you use, and whether your artwork is divided into textures with dimensions that are powers of two.

In the end, we chose a set of technologies and work that allowed *Half-Life* to use more than 2MB of textures and still run well on 3D cards with that limitation. Our artists reworked character textures and user-interface element textures by combining multiple textures into single maps with power-of-two dimensions. We added a subsystem for managing paletted textures, which allowed us to store more textures in the same amount of memory. We changed portions of the renderer to try and draw all polygons with the same texture at the same time wherever possible (to minimize swapping textures). For cards that still didn't have enough memory, we added a feature to automatically scale textures down—which reduces image quality, but improves performance.

Another quality that separates an average engineer from a good one is being able to spend the right amount of time solving a particular problem. We could have spent a lot more or a lot less time on this problem. Choosing the correct criteria for evaluating the solutions to problems like these is very important. Budgeting programming time is the balancing act that goes on when a game is produced. With good engineers, any piece of technology can be made better by working on it.

I feel that choosing the correct problems to solve and evaluating solutions well are two very important things that set *Half-Life* apart from other games.

What about the advantages and disadvantages to licensing a game engine versus creating one from scratch? How viable is it for newbie programmers to do it on their own? Stelly regards this as a very complex topic; to make this kind of decision, it's important to look at how game engines are developed.

The leading-edge engines for today's 3D action games are developed by teams of experienced programmers. Many of these programmers have built game engines before and have a good understanding of the challenges involved. Their engines represent many man-years of development effort. There are many games built on top of less complex (and less-often licensed) engines. As it turns out, most of these engines are built byv teams of experienced programmers as well.

Valve's Jay Stelly believes "one of the differences between an average engineer and a good one is the ability to think at a high enough level to choose the important problems to spend programming time on." (Half-Life is a registered trademark of Sierra On-Line, Inc. Images used with permission. Copyright 1999-2000 Sierra On-Line, Inc. All Rights Reserved.)

> Even though it generally requires a team of experienced engineers, it's often cheaper to build an engine than to license one. [However,] several factors make licensing desirable, even though it can cost more. Because they have been used in one or more shipping products, licensed engines are often more stable. You're buying not only the engine's technology, but the time and testing that have gone into it. These engines also have a lower opportunity cost. If you have a team of experienced engineers, you can have them build your game instead of the engine, or build solutions to technical constraints of the engine. There are also marketing and hiring advantages to licensed engines. People who have purchased products using your engine have positive expectations about your game, and you may even be able to hire team members who are already familiar with the technology. Not to be overlooked is the ability to prototype game concepts immediately because you're working with a fully finished piece of technology.

Jay Stelly's most current work can be seen—and played—in the multiplayer *Team Fortress 2* by Valve and Sierra Studios.

DAVE "ZOID" KIRSCH, THREEWAVE SOFTWARE

As an independent game designer/programmer, this Vancouver-based man of many talents has worked on a number of *Quake*-related modifications, namely: *ThreeWave Capture the Flag (CTF)* for *Quake*, Linux and other UNIX versions of *Quake*, *QuakeWorld* upgrades, *ThreeWave CTF for Quake II*, Linux and other UNIX versions of *Quake II*, *ThreeWave CTF for Quake III*, and most recently (you guessed it!), Linux and other UNIX versions of *Quake III*.

For the future, Zoid hopes to design and build some of the most advanced, complete multiplayer games around with fast action gameplay and acceptable Internet lag.

According to Zoid, the most important elements of programming a game are as follows:

KEEP IT SIMPLE, STUPID! (KISS)

> A simple design is easier to build, easier to maintain, and easier to understand than a complex one. One of the philosophies I have always had when building anything, especially games, is that doing things simple and right is more important than doing it incomplete, fast, or complex. Spend the time to understand what you're trying to accomplish and make sure you can break it down into small and simple units that can be written almost independently and combined together.
>
> If you're not the only developer on a project, make sure that you spend time discussing the design with the other developers. Make sure that you work together with them with a focus on simplicity of design, clean code, and well explained and useful interfaces.

USE CONSISTENT DESIGN THROUGHOUT THE PRODUCT

A game can be broken down into sections. For example, the games I worked on (*Quake*) could be broken down into six subsystems: file/resource management, renderer, network layer, server code, client code, and user interface code. It's important that the design of each of these sections use the same basic methodology as the others. The same basic types should be shared between them for passing pointers to resources, network packets, etc. They interact together and the boundaries between subsystems should have a consistent design and implementation.

For example, packets between the network subsystems and the client/server code should be identical, but on one end the client calls it, on the other end the server calls it. The network layer shouldn't concern itself much at all with which end [is making the call]; it should just worry about getting data between the client and server code (even if the code for each is on different computers). This consistency of design should extend to other subsystems, such as the file subsystem that offers handles or pointers to files or resources for the system. An example would be that a resource allocated by a call from the client subsystem should be able to be passed to the renderer subsystem without any changes in type or design.

Another consideration is when you're making changes or additions to a product, either as an upgrade or a third-party mod developer: Make sure you understand the design methodology, interfaces, and data types. Be consistent and use the ones that are already in place—in other words, don't reinvent everything with your own data types and abstractions if you're just making modifications. It's easier to understand and to remain consistent if you adhere to the established data types and conventions already inherent in the product.

CONSTANTLY STEP OUT OF THE CODE AND ACTUALLY PLAY YOUR GAME

Make sure the feel is there. Make sure the fun is there! A good example of this is when I was designing the CTF game. When I originally designed it, when a capture occurs the entire game gets "reset." Everyone resets and respawns in their bases for another round. I thought this would be ideal. But before I had finished writing the code and just got it to a stage of functionality, I fired it up and tested it with a few people. I found that resetting everyone wasn't fun—it didn't feel right. So I scrapped that code and went with simply resetting the flags.

My point is that I didn't invest a lot of time in designing the code to reset everyone. I only got a prototype of it working, and tested it before going for a full implementation.

It's important to make sure that the code you write is going to be an essential part of the game. There's no point in writing code that's going to be no fun and end up getting pulled out anyway. Prototype your ideas first and get a feel for how they affect the game in the long run. This can be anything: changes of weapon-switching methods, player movement physics, rules of the game, etc. Make sure you've got the design and feel you want before you do a complete implementation.

Zoid was asked to list a couple obstacles he faced as a game programmer and to discuss how he overcame them. "This one is tough," begins Zoid:

One of the biggest [obstacles] I had to face when I was maintaining the *QuakeWorld* project was the start of cheating. People were starting to hack the game to [gain] an advantage over other players. Some specific examples were stuff like hacking map files to remove walls so you would see through them, hacking the executable to allow cheat commands enabled during game-play, and finally, using a proxy between the server and client itself that would do automatic aim and firing.

In order to solve these, I began by implementing a checksum between the client and server for the data such as the player models—modified player models would not be the same as the default ones on the server. The server would notice this and either notify other players or disallow the client to play. As for the map hacks, I also instituted a checksum for map files to make sure it was the same for the map on the server and on the client.

Lastly, in order to overcome the proxy issue—modifying the packets between the client and server and doing stuff like auto aiming—I put a simple cipher over the data in the network packet in order to obscure it, but leaving the ability for the packets themselves to pass through firewalls or masqueraded (NAT) connections.

When designing cheat protection in *Quake III*, a more general method was used. Instead of just checksumming the individual data files (player models, maps, etc), an overall checksum was instituted over all of the resource data. Any modification of any of the resource data would result in failure and the server would boot you. This was made even harder to modify/forge [when,] rather than having the client enforce the checksum, the client had to provide the checksum to the server itself—the server would disallow the client if the right checksum result was not provided.

[Preventing cheating] via hacks of client data still isn't foolproof today. In a client/server design for something like a game, the client cannot be trusted since it's running on the end-user's machine. We can make it very hard for modified clients to successfully pass the tests, but there isn't an ideal solution. This continues to be a perplexing problem.

Another difficulty I faced when I took over the *QuakeWorld* project was that the player movement physics in *QuakeWorld* was not the same as in the original game. I felt that since *QuakeWorld* was simply a multiplayer upgrade to the existing game that featured more stable and playable Internet play, the player feel and physics should be as close as possible.

I spent several months in testing out new models of the player physics in order to get the feel right. This required a lot of testing since it was based on subjective feel. I couldn't simply clone the existing player physics code from the original game because the original code was designed for a non-predicted game model of network play. *QuakeWorld* featured client prediction, so the client would predict player motion of the server and the server would correct any differences in the motion [due to] collision later on.

One of the more tricky aspects of *QuakeWorld*'s multiplayer was the collision of other players in the predicted model. With the existing code (which didn't take this issue into account), you could end up literally walking through other players on the screen, only be "snapped" back to your original position when the server corrected your motion after the fact. This really destroyed the feel of the game, and it was something I wanted to correct or at least minimize.

So, after careful thought as to how to accomplish this goal, I added code to deal with extrapolation of other players and make educated guesses about their position when predicting on the client side. This took a lot of tuning, but after several test runs at high latency I finally got a model that felt really good to players—you hardly ever walked through other players, and the game felt much more solid and realistic.

These obstacles were solved by identifying the issue, designing a solution that was simple, and doing a lot of testing to ensure that the solution was the right one.

Since this book will also be bundled with a C++ compiler (Macmillan Digital Publishing's *Game Programming Starter Kit 4.0*), could Zoid offer any programming tips? He admits he has worked with C primarily and only recently began to toy with C++. That said, Zoid goes on to comment that one of the interesting challenges he faced when porting *Quake* to the X11 window system (used for graphic displays under UNIX) was that the display might not be in the correct color depth for *Quake*. Therefore, he had to write a routine that translated the 8-bit color values into either 16-bit or 24-bit color. Zoid originally wrote it like this:

```
void st2_fixup( XImage *framebuf, int x, int y, int width, int height)
{
 int xi,yi;
 unsigned char *src;
 PIXEL16 *dest;

 if( (x<0)||(y<0) )return;

 for (yi = y; yi < (y+height); yi++) {
  src = &framebuf->data [yi * framebuf->bytes_per_line];
  dest = ((PIXEL16 *)src);
  for(xi = (x+width-1); xi >= x; xi--) {
   dest[xi] = st2d_8to16table[src[xi]];
  }
 }
}
```

PIXEL16 is the 16-bit color pixel type; st2d_8to16table is a pre-computed table that takes an 8-bit color value as an index and returns the equivalent 16-bit color value, and framebuf points to the buffer where the bytes are to be translated in place.

This works, says Zoid, but it's not terribly efficient: "I did some research and found a really interesting method of optimization for this." Here's the new version:

```
void st2_fixup( XImage *framebuf, int x, int y, int width, int height)
{
 int xi,yi;
 unsigned char *src;
 PIXEL16 *dest;
 register int count, n;

 if( (x<0)||(y<0) )return;

 for (yi = y; yi < (y+height); yi++) {
  src = &framebuf->data [yi * framebuf->bytes_per_line];

  // Duff's Device
  count = width;
  n = (count + 7) / 8;
  dest = ((PIXEL16 *)src) + x+width - 1;
  src += x+width - 1;

  switch (count % 8) {
  case 0: do { *dest-- = st2d_8to16table[*src--];
  case 7:     *dest-- = st2d_8to16table[*src--];
  case 6:     *dest-- = st2d_8to16table[*src--];
  case 5:     *dest-- = st2d_8to16table[*src--];
  case 4:     *dest-- = st2d_8to16table[*src--];
  case 3:     *dest-- = st2d_8to16table[*src--];
  case 2:     *dest-- = st2d_8to16table[*src--];
  case 1:     *dest-- = st2d_8to16table[*src--];
    } while (--n > 0);
  }
 }
}
```

 This uses a method of unrolling a loop called a "Duff's Device."
This method was invented by Tom Duff while at LucasFilm
(www.lysator.liu.se/c/duffs-device.html).

This method is a lot more efficient because it lets the compile optimize it a lot
more since the loop is unrolled. Also, only three pointers and a count are
used in the loop now (n, st2d_8to16table, dest, and src) so the compiler can
easily stuff them into registers and perform quick optimizations on them.

I easily saw a 20% frame-rate increase directly due to re-implementing the
copy routine using this method.

See Chapter 6 for Dave "Zoid" Kirsch's level design tips in light of his *Capture the
Flag* game.

CHARLES GOUGH, BUNGIE SOFTWARE

Charles "Chucky" Gough has been programming on and off since he was nine years
old, when his father showed him the basics of AppleSoft Basic on the old Apple IIe.

Although he didn't work on the celebrated *Myth II: Soulblighter*, developed and published by Bungie Software, gamers will get a chance to see Chucky's work on *Oni* and *Halo*.

Chucky offers his opinions for beginners on programming computer games:

> **1.** Get your game up and running as quickly as possible. The sooner you have the basic engine and tools working, the longer you have to play and refine your game. It will also be easier for both your team and publishers to share your vision if they can see a working prototype.

> **2.** You have to be willing to make compromises in your code to achieve goals. For example, you might have an incredible idea for a rendering algorithm that would outshine everything currently available, but if it runs so slowly that it detracts from gameplay and takes so long to write that you lose your publisher, what have you achieved?

And a note to designers:

> The game has to be fun. For example, if you were making a role-playing game, it might be realistic to force the character to have to eat and sleep and defecate, but would it be fun? Sure, it might be funny the first time your character died of constipation because you weren't watching your crap meter, but it would get pretty annoying. From the beginning, making the game fun has to be the priority. The newest and best technology won't save a boring game.

Are there any good Bungie examples to support this advice?

> The *Myth* series is a good example of these rules applied to a genre that had seen only minor gameplay innovation. RTS [real-time strategy] games before *Myth* involved a lengthy buildup period before the action. And it was fun to watch your orcs smash the little humans, but other than the number and type of troops involved, you couldn't really affect the battle. The *Myth* team saw a lot of potential in the actual fight, and made the tactics of the battle the focus of the game. Jason Jones had a vision of what it would be like and decided to make a simple demo that involved a tiny 3D map, a dwarven grenadier, a troop of undead axemen, and the basics of a real physics engine. Originally he planned on having fully polygonal 3D characters and objects, but he felt that the frame rate would suffer and that it would take too long to develop. So he modified sprite code from *Marathon* and used that instead to quickly build his demo. This simple beginning was enough to get a cover of *Computer Game Strategy Plus*.

Understanding and adhering to tradeoffs (time vs. money vs. gameplay vs. technology) is a common theme in this chapter. Where does *Myth II: Soulblighter* fall into this common set of challenges?

> The biggest challenge was getting the game out the door less than a year after the original. We had a lot of things we wanted to change, improve, or add, but it quickly became apparent that there wasn't time to do it all. So we had no choice but to focus on those ideas that would have the most impact—like pathfinding, interface, and fire—while leaving out ideas like fully polygonal characters, non-bipedal units (cavalry and catapults), and burning trees.

When asked what reference material he finds beneficial to newbie game programmers, Chucky insists that, above all else, the most valuable resource is contact with experienced people and their code. "There's nothing more insightful than talking to someone who's written a few games, or looking at some real source code." Shy of that, Chucky suggests books as the next most useful resource, especially college textbooks, though it's "definitely hard to find good ones."

SHIGERU MIYAMOTO, NINTENDO

We've heard from the beloved and respected Mr. Miyamoto in Chapters 2 and 4 thus far, but he had a lot more to say for this second edition of *Game Design: Secrets of the Sages*. Here, he discusses a bit of theory behind Nintendo's programming protocol, commenting that a game designer should also have some understanding of code crunching, and vice versa. Says Miyamoto:

> I believe a game designer must also be an engineer...to have the necessary technological knowledge as well as being a designer. Whenever a new designer joins Nintendo, we make a point of letting him/her go through the technological lecture. By doing so, the designers can learn what they can do and cannot do in terms of the technology. Also, I am always telling our designers and programmers that we should be proud of ourselves for being the frontier of the unprecedented entertainment category called "interactive entertainment," and we must put our energies into the creation of new entertainment that no one else can make.

ORLANDO GUZMAN, EA SPORTS

As a producer on the coveted *Tiger Woods* golf series for EA Sports, Orlando Guzman talks about programming the unprecedented "Play Against the Pros" technology, allowing gamers to play golf online against real pro players such as Tiger Woods, in real-time.

In an industry first, computer golfers with EA Sports' *Tiger Woods 99 PGA TOUR Golf* (with the Monterey Courses add-on disc), *Tiger Woods PGA TOUR Collection*, or *Tiger Woods PGA TOUR 2000* can log onto the Net with the game, and, roughly ninety seconds after the real golf pro takes his shot in real life at a PGA TOUR event, players on PCs anywhere in the world can see where the ball lands in the game, and then can attempt to out-stroke the pro. To accomplish this ambitious feat live, EA Sports employed twenty-five "trackers" to record the data live from Pebble Beach and upload it online to the game's main server.

Guzman was asked to name some important skills required to program this new twist on multiplayer gaming. Was "Play Against the Pros" a programming nightmare? Guzman answers with the following:

> What I like to see in engineers is not only a good technical aptitude but a great ability to problem solve, especially in regard to design issues. I like disciplined engineers who can get a job done correctly the first time (this mainly comes from experience). Things for budding programmers to concentrate on are learning to engineer and design and not simply learning how to code in the coolest language out there (in other words, learn the process beneath programming, not just the logic of programming); have a passion for what you are doing (otherwise it's not worth doing); and keep up to date on current technology and consumer trends.

"I think when the history of interactive sports gets written, the [Play Against the Pros] technology will stand out as one of the turning points of how interactive entertainment and television should really work," says Guzman. "When I was tasked with this problem, I knew that, given my team's experience, they would be able to come up with a solution that would be straightforward and relatively easy to maintain." (Used with permission by EA Sports)

> I would guess that the only aspect of it being a programming nightmare was when we were asked to make this feature enabled for *Tiger Woods 99 PGA TOUR Golf* in addition to the newer *Tiger Woods PGA TOUR 2000* product. Any engineer will tell you that retrofitting a new feature once something is in production is never easy, especially when it wasn't designed for [the new feature] in the first place.
>
> I'd rather not get too technical simply because I believe in what Disney does (keep the magic "magic"). It's a little cheesy, but I will say that the "Play Against The Pros" server is a very early form of *Star Trek*'s holodeck. We're creating the environment and interaction based on real data that we gather in real time and transmit to the consumer as it's happening. They also have the choice of pulling up the data and interacting with it at a later time. In essence we're allowing consumers to relive and place themselves in a virtual environment and event that actually occurred in history.

But, as a budding programmer, is it best to license an existing game engine or to create a brand new one? Guzman believes it depends on the type of product you want to do. He explains:

> Game engines are generally created for very specific tasks/features/products. Development teams always have a goal of making engines as robust as possible for use in other products and licensing, but in practice that rarely works out. There are some good examples out there currently that do a good job it, *Quake* for instance. In the case of the *Quake* engine, though, you're still bound by some inherent design and programming limitations. Without a lot of work, for instance, I wouldn't be able to make a space shooter or sports game with the *Quake* engine; it just wasn't intended for those types of games. If you're just starting out, get products that will allow you to personalize and modify them somehow; then work your way into a product that allows you to create levels and do some game tuning and logic. If after that you still have the desire to do more, then take a crack at a product that allows you to do some basic programming and graphics.
>
> Robust game engines don't come cheap, so I honestly think that—unless you're independently wealthy—you have a huge, huge challenge ahead of you if you intend to do it yourself with no money. It's not impossible, but it'll be a challenge and a project you'll remember (good or bad) for the rest of your life. If you have the tenacity, I say go for it.

Finally, Guzman is asked to reflect on his history in the game-designing industry in order to give newcomers some valuable advice to save some time, money, and aggravation. He responds:

> Since my undergraduate studies, I've had a keen interest in how interactive products can be used to learn (whether it's process, content, or education). My graduate studies centered around managing, documenting, and teaching a course in interactive design and production (both for personal and professional reasons). Even if you intend on being an artist or engineer, if you learn to be a good problem-solver and you learn to manage process, you will be successful at your work. I use what I learned in school and what I've learned in the past 10 years here at EA every day, and every day I strive to learn something new. With each product, I try to instill creative thinking and innovation in myself and my team. Our consumers expect it, we demand it of ourselves, and we try to deliver on it each year with a fresh perspective.

HUBERT CHARDOT, GAMESQUAD

Having worked on the beloved *Alone in the Dark* trilogy (and as a consultant for the fourth game in the series), among a half-dozen other projects over the past eight years, Chardot offers this bit of advice for game programmers, based on his experience. Simply put, Chardot says, "The best way to avoid problems and misunderstandings is to be realistic with the code and the tools, and to communicate your vision to the team."

Chardot goes on to say that running into snafus is part of the process, and not to be discouraged. "During the programming of a video game, you have a better chance to meet Steven Spielberg and Boris Eltsine riding a Venusian shark than to never have a single bug in your code!"

Hey, who said game designers don't have a sense of humor?

GREG THOMAS, SEGA OF AMERICA

Greg Thomas, vice president of product development at Sega of America, brings more than a dozen years of experience to the table. As mentioned in his bio (see the back of the book), Thomas is considered the "mastermind" behind the award-winning Sega Dreamcast title *Sega Sports NFL 2K*, along with more than 20 other games throughout his prolific career.

When it comes to programming a sports game such as *NFL2K*, what are some of the biggest obstacles faced, and how did you overcome these obstacles? Says Thomas:

> The biggest obstacle we faced with these games was our collision system. For our collisions to be accurate, we had to do true 3D collision. In the past, we had only done simpler, cylinder collision, in which it's very easy to designate an object as a cylinder. But with *NFL2K* this was not acceptable; we needed to collide with all parts of the body properly. We did this by putting collision spheres on our player model and moved them as the model animated. This was a bit tricky but it ended up working well and making a large difference in the accuracy of our football game.

Any tips for newbie programmers who would like to create the Next Big Thing? Thomas responds by emphasizing that being a very structured programmer is extremely important. He expands on this notion:

> Games are getting to be huge projects. *NFL2K* had over 500,000 lines of code in it! And the place where structured programming is taught…is college. So even though I wouldn't have said this five years ago, today I believe going to programming classes in college is important in this regard.

Budding programmers should consider college for formal training, says Thomas. "You have to be a self-starter, [and] read lots of programming books (Code Complete is just one example). Programming games is not an easy job. It requires passion to succeed." Here's a gorgeous shot from Sega Sports' NBA2K for the Sega Dreamcast. (Used with permission by Sega of America, Inc.)

In Chapter 10, Greg Thomas discusses video game art in relation to Sega Sports' *NFL2K*.

MICHAEL MCGRATH, DYNAMIX/SIERRA

Michael McGrath is an engineer/programmer at Dynamix who was responsible in part for the popular WWI combat flight sim *Red Baron 3D*, plus other past projects including *Netrek* (public domain) and *Extreme Warfare* (Trilobyte). Over the next few pages, McGrath offers some pointed advice on programming and game design, while touching on many of today's most common blunders in the gaming industry.

DESIGN FIRST, PROGRAM LATER

Sitting down and writing a game, *ad hoc*, is one of the best ways to never finish your game. Most educated engineers can, in fact, write small projects in just this fashion, but written code ends up being a nightmare to use as "design notes" if you can't finish your work over a relatively short span of time. A good designer understands every aspect of his or her product long before it ever starts being written—because engineering and other design choices depend heavily on the job at hand. I've heard or been a part of too many projects that never got finished or went way over schedule—not because the engineers working on [the project] didn't know what they were doing, but because the lead engineers and designers clearly had no idea what exactly they were making until the project was nearly ready to ship. It *is* possible to design projects thoroughly beforehand, and if you don't, you pay the price.

Unfortunately, the games industry itself has its share of folks who don't understand this essential game-design philosophy. Take a good look at who you're working with before you start a project, and make sure they share the same philosophy with you. Unfortunately, many of the budding programming geniuses in the industry, who skipped out on the rest of college to write games, entirely lack the software engineering skills necessary to pull off a large game project efficiently. These people usually end up learning the hard way that programming is only a tool used by engineers to create things. Engineering skill is the real necessity. Practically *everyone* in this industry is at least a competent programmer. Which brings me to subpoint 1 of tip A: Finish college, if you haven't already.

Learn to *think* before you *act*.

KNOW YOUR AUDIENCE AND YOUR ENEMY

If you don't play games, you shouldn't be writing them. For that matter, if you don't play games, you shouldn't have anything to do with the games industry—except, perhaps, in a distant support role. Knowing how the industry works, how the audience thinks, and what the competition is doing are critically important to creating high-quality, successful games. It's also important to know your limitations as a game designer—and the kinds of games you sit down and play in an "addictive" fashion are *exactly* the kind of games you'd be good at helping create.

Don't pretend that you can design first-person shooters [if] you've been playing flight sims all your life, and recently got into your first shooter and loved it. To create and work on any game, you need to know every last incarnation of that genre, and be able to appreciate everything each instance has to offer.

Once you can reminisce about the "good ol' days" with people who have adored that particular genre since day one, then and only then are you ready to bring your masterpiece to the masses. Otherwise you're on course to become another "clone," and to be lost in the overwhelming sea of fish who get eaten by the shark who *did* do his/her homework.

This issue is *very* important for everyone in the industry, but more so to programmers in particular. The programmers breathe the essence of life into any game—no beautiful texture, 3D model, or epic storyline will ever make a game great without a program to give it to the user—the gamer—in the right way. In order to understand the "how's" of presenting a great story, you have to experience the works of the past—both the flops and the smashes. There's no substitute, and never will be. Period.

Conveniently, programmers and others who work on games they're interested in also tend to work faster, harder, and better. If there's a team of people to be had on a project, I would consider this kind of enthusiasm to be right up there, equal with sheer talent and people skills. Put simply, it makes for a (substantially) higher-quality product in the end.

ENGINEERING ISN'T EVERYTHING

Just because you can write blindingly fast code, 1,000 lines per day, and you *like* games, that doesn't mean you can do it all yourself. Writing computer games is all about telling and "living" a story—and although the engineers write the storyteller, you're still going to need a good story to tell. Everything [including] vivid artwork, an epic story, accurate physics engines, great multiplayer versus co-op teamplay, and moving music can go into making a great game experience. And in order to accomplish the task of creating a game, you need to understand each and every one of these things, from at least an appreciative perspective.

On top of understanding these things and their presentation, you need to understand their representation in the media you're using to tell the story. A 1-bit graphics pipeline will get you a great frame rate nowadays, but I doubt that anyone is going to really appreciate the visuals in your game if you decide to use such an engine. Part of understanding what's behind telling a great story in this fashion comes from experience—usually accrued from playing other games.

The last part comes from being able to work with and understand the people who help you (as any member of a game development team) tell these stories. You need to get good tools, you need to be able to teach others what they need to know to work with your technology, and, most of all, you need to have the patience and determination for doing all of the above. And to see it through to the end.

The games industry has no room for iron-fisted bosses, high-and-mighty anythings, or close-minded folks in any way, shape, or form. These kinds of people show up from time to time, and their games (and unfortunately their careers, and those [of the people] they work with) end up in the bargain bin…or, worse yet, never even make it out the door. If you ever find yourself working *for* someone, and not *with* them, you need to get away, because you're on the losing side in the (as of late) extremely competitive Deathmatch that is the games marketplace.

McGrath applies the aforementioned advice to Dynamix's *Red Baron II* and the problems that plagued the game. Says McGrath:

Red Baron II was a good example of over-engineering and lack of forethought in engineering design. In *Red Baron 3D*, most of the programming work involved fixing bugs and understanding the workings of the code, so we could add new features and technology. The original engineers no longer worked at Dynamix or had moved on to other projects when the conversion to *Red Baron 3D* began. The code was poorly documented, which caused us no end of trouble with the conversion—and, on top of that, we had no one to look to for assistance in understanding it. It would have been much simpler to convert (as a matter of fact, I believe the original team could have done it) if it had been designed well in the first place. But it was horrendously cryptic, being the work of many, many different people with no overriding design to guide them, in addition to being over-abstracted and over-engineered in places where the design *had* been thought through.

Red Baron II suffered the terrible misfortune of being developed first for DOS, then for Windows 95, then for DirectX, and then, finally, for hardware 3D. During its development, it was torn apart and rebuilt so many times that it became incredibly unwieldy in the end. The real problem was not the reconstruction itself, but rather that the engineering leads seemed to "over believe" in code reuse, and not in well-designed modularity. They would rip out [some] parts and keep others—tying them together with a mess of spaghetti that eventually rendered the code base very difficult to read and understand. If they had designed the pieces in a well-thought-out, modular fashion to begin with, they would have been able to finish the game far earlier than they did, despite the advancing technology that inspired the changes in the first place. That doesn't mean "if they had used C++," either—they did, actually. Object-oriented programming, with all its merits, can become a real nightmare when "abused" with poorly-thought-out design and corresponding makeshift engineering. Never ever let the "wow" factor of a programming language convince you that Ockham's Razor and legibility aren't important. Ever.

NOTE Thirteenth-century philosopher William of Ockham (also spelled *Occam* or *Occum*) coined this law of economy, known today as "Ockham's Razor"—the philosophical belief that the mind should not multiply entities beyond necessity.

In addition to chatting with others on Usenet and attending various conferences, McGrath suggests a few handy books that game programmers should consider:

- *Computer Graphics: Principles and Practice, Second Edition in C* by Foley, van Dam, Feiner, and Hughes (Addison-Wesley, 1996)

- The OpenGL programming guide (the "red book") and reference guide (the "blue book")

- The *Graphics Gems* series, edited by Andrew S. Glassner, James Arvo, David Kirk, Alan W. Paeth, and Paul S. Heckbert (Academic Press and AP Professional, 1993–1995)

- *Artificial Intelligence* by Patrick Henry Winston (Addison-Wesley, 1992)

JASON HUGHES, ORIGIN SYSTEMS

As advanced software engineer at Origin Systems, Jason Hughes helped program such games as *Wing Commander IV*, *Wing Commander: Kilrathi Saga*, and *Wing Commander: Prophecy*. On *Wing Commander IV*, he was responsible for everything that wasn't in space flight (roughly six CDs worth of data and lots of programming). On *Wing Commander: Prophecy*, he was solely responsible for all artificial intelligence and a fair percentage of the detailed special effects (cockpit jitter, all the missiles, and so on).

When it comes to creating a new game, Hughes says the most important considerations for a game programmer to keep in mind are as follows:

LIMITATIONS

> The real power of a game isn't in its incredible flexibility and options presented to the player; it's giving players an opportunity to explore what's possible with a limited set of options and contort those to suit their own purposes. Knowing the limitations of the game early on can give programmers a huge head start in knowing how to complete their tasks efficiently, both in terms of code and programming timeline.

KNOW YOUR AUDIENCE

> Sometimes a game can be fantastic, but miss its audience entirely due to game design or target hardware. Without knowing the audience the game appeals to, it's nearly impossible to make a hit game. And the target is constantly moving for each audience as well.

ATTENTION TO DETAIL

> Finally, a game needs to have incredible attention to detail. That can only happen when the designers don't have to wait on programmers. A lot of games these days have a graphics engine and an interpreter, and that's about it. The embedded interpreted language gives designers control over both high-level

and low-level details of the game. That way, if someone has a cool idea, they can jump in and do it, and show it to people without waiting a few days to a month to see it. For designers, it's similar to the traditional "interactive versus batch" argument. It opens up a whole world of interesting possibilities that are otherwise not available, especially with respect to third-party MODs after shipping the product.

Asked whether licensing an existing game engine is a good idea, Hughes responds:

These days, if you know what you're doing and have experience, you can build a decent 3D engine in a few weeks. However, every minute you spend writing your tools and libraries is another minute you take away from your game. Especially when you're working alone or with an under-funded small team, the *game* part is where the real payoff lies.

There's an awful lot out there that's inexpensive or free that works very well— unfortunately, 90% of the interfaces to these packages stink, and none of them resemble each other. Just write a clean interface that suits your needs; you can always change what happens behind the curtain.

Jason Hughes invites budding game programmers to visit his Web page, which contains many handy tips and tricks on working with Microsoft Visual C++ (http://flaredev.com/jh/progtips.html).

MATT PRITCHARD, ENSEMBLE STUDIOS

Matt Pritchard's title at Ensemble Studios, where he helped program *Age of Empires*, is Graphics Engine and Optimization Specialist. Pritchard is currently absorbed with *Age of Empires II: The Age of Kings*, but he takes a moment out of his busy schedule to share a few words for aspiring programmers. What are the three crucial things to remember?

1. You won't write an epic saga overnight; persistence and patience are your best tools.

2. Most things have already been done before; seek them out and learn what others can teach you.

3. Most projects are never finished; over-ambition and unrealistic evaluation of the tasks at hand doom them to being forgotten. Know yourself and your real limits, desires, and how far you will really take things.

What are the biggest challenges a game programmer must face? To Pritchard, there are two biggies:

■ Keeping up with technology. The only cure for this is to focus on what's important and invest the time and resources to stay current in your learning.

■ Discipline to manage the software-development process; i.e., to get things done on time and as planned. This requires experience. Books on writing solid code and *Code Complete* are an aid in breaking the problems down. This is an ongoing battle everyone seems to face.

Pritchard suggests game programmers should spend some time perusing the Usenet newsgroup rec.games.programmer to learn more about the art and science of creating and modifying game code. (Used with permission by Ensemble Studios, Inc.)

STUART DENMAN, SURREAL SOFTWARE

Stuart Denman is the vice president and technical director at Surreal Software, the hot development house responsible for Psygnosis' action/adventure game, *Drakan*.

Denman is no stranger to programming, and he says one of the single most important considerations when creating action games is watching the frame-rate speed. The three following memory strainers will ultimately affect frame rates unless you work on them religiously:

POLYGON COUNTS AND MINIMUM SPECIFICATIONS

> Designers must have minimum-spec machines available to test levels on, so that they can be sure that the game will run smoothly, even on low-end machines. A level that runs at 30 fps [frames per second] on a Pentium II 400MHz can run at 8 fps on a Pentium 166 with the same polygon counts. It's a balancing issue between look (high polygon counts) and feel (frame rate). Designers *should not* count on frame-rate optimizations later in the project.

ARTIFICIAL INTELLIGENCE

> Like polygon counts, AI contributes to CPU drain. Placing 30 enemies within the same area not only increases the polygon counts, but also increases the amount of AI computation required to maintain all those creatures. A limit on number of creatures should be established by the programmers once the AI programming is far enough along.

LIGHTING

> In *Drakan*, point lights are dynamically computed on objects and landscape areas that change. This means that any moving light source or moving object will have to be recomputed. Large numbers of lights and large drop-off radii will contribute to slower performance.

A game's frame-rate speed is one of the most critical factors to watch in game programming, says Denman. As seen here in Psygnosis' Drakan, enhanced lighting is one of the memory drainers. (Used with permission by Psygnosis, Inc.)

Other frame-rate issues of concern for programmers, says Denman, are making sure that models have lower levels of detail (to keep polygon counts low when objects are far away), and, as in *Drakan*, making sure that databases and parameters are organized efficiently. He explains:

> Databases include sound, behavior, model, texture, and scripting resources. Clean organization of these [elements] is critical to allow the team to work effectively with the levels. In *Drakan*, any object in the game has parameters that define how it behaves. They're also the mapping between resources in the database and the code, so it's critical that parameters are kept in their proper settings.

Denman discusses the pros and cons of working with an existing game engine versus creating your own:

> As far as licensing goes, it really depends on what you want to do. If you want to create new technologies not available currently, then licensing is not the answer. If you just want to create an original game with advances in gameplay and features, licensing an engine is a very good option. Licensing saves years of work, and can allow more time to make a better game.
>
> Surreal was lucky because we got initial funding for a project with only a small demo. Most development groups won't get this. I realize now (although I didn't at the time) that it's very hard to break into this industry if you've never worked in it. You need to prove yourself with either reputation or a knockout demo. Aspiring entrepreneurs can always come out of nowhere and create demos that rival those of professionals; so as long as that's still possible, there's hope.

Denman was kind enough to include a C++ technique for game programmers: "Every programmer must do this: Create a template for arrays. Don't use C-style arrays unless absolutely necessary."

NOTE   Denman clarifies some terminology for nonprogrammers. In programming, data is often stored in *arrays*—that is, strings of data. It's a frequent occurrence to access areas of memory outside of these arrays, which can produce an illegal operation in Windows—the General Protection Fault (GPF). For example, if the array has a length of five elements, and the program tries to access element 8, you'll get a GPF. To prevent these bugs, the following code warns the programmer when this problem has occurred so the bug can be fixed.

The template definition would look like this:

```
template <class Entry> class Array
{
private:
    Entry *pEntry;
    int iSize;
```

The template then has inline members to append (allocate) and delete entries in the array, and members like this to access the array:

```
public:
    // Allows access to an array entry...
    Entry &operator [](const int iIndex) const
    {
        Assert(iIndex >= 0 && iIndex < iSize);
        return pEntry[iIndex];
    }
```

The Assert function is important because it raises a debugging error if the expression in the Assert is false. This bit of code has saved us so many bugs, I can't even imagine living without it. Our Assert macro looks like this:

```
// Debug case:
#if defined(_DEBUG)
extern BOOL MyAssertFunc(BOOL, int, char *);
#define NatBreak() {_asm { int 3 } }
// Asserts that exp is true.
#define Assert(exp) \
    if (MyAssertFunc((int)(exp),__LINE__,__FILE__)) \
        NatBreak();
// Non-debug case:
#else
#define Assert(exp)
#endif // _DEBUG
```

In the release build, all Assert macros get compiled out. In the debug build, the function MyAssertFunc is included in a library. The function evaluates the first argument and brings up a message box with the line and file where the assertion happens (the last two arguments). The programmer can then choose to continue executing, or break. If the programmer chooses to break, the function returns true and the int 3 instruction causes the debugger to break on the Assert macro line.

To read more about Denman's Drakan project, drop into www.psygnosis.com/Drakan.

RICHARD MOE, HUMONGOUS ENTERTAINMENT

The next valuable submission to this chapter is from a savvy Humongous Entertainment programmer. Richard Moe serves as both a project lead and software engineer (among other duties). All Humongous games work in a proprietary language called SCUMM, which was developed by company cofounder Ron Gilbert. Some of the titles Moe has worked on here as designer and programmer are (in chronological order) *Junior Field Trips: Let's Explore the Airport*; *Pajama Sam in There's No Need to Hide When It's Dark Outside*; *Backyard Baseball*; and most recently, *Putt-Putt Enters the Race*.

Moe says each game brings its own set of challenges to a game designer and programmer. The following examples are from Moe's past experiences:

> For creating children's games, the most challenging aspect is balancing the difficulty level so the game can be as fun and easy to play for a four-year-old as it is for an eight-year-old. Obviously, the skill sets for these age ranges are vastly different. For example, in *Pajama Sam* we have a simple game of tic-tac-toe called "Cheese and Crackers" that can be played on one of three board sizes: 3×3, 5×5, or 7×7. The 3×3 board is simple tic-tac-toe—three in a row wins. The 5×5 and 7×7 boards need four and five in a row to win, respectively. It's plain to see that the first of the three is the easiest—fewer permutations—and the other two are successively harder. However, by providing all three, we've given a fun challenge to all ability levels. Moreover, the computer opponent (the AI code) tries to match the ability of the opponent. If the player wins, the computer plays smarter the next time. Similarly, if the computer wins, it next plays a little dumber.
>
> That tangent aside, I'd say the biggest issues for the designer in regard to programming are knowing the target audience and knowing current technology. The first point is related to the previous paragraph—if you're designing a kid's game, you've got to know what kids like. If you're designing a historical strategic war game, you need to figure out what war-game players like.
>
> Obviously, a good programmer needs to keep abreast of the current technology. There is no such thing as a "Renaissance man" in the field of computer game programming. Specialization is imperative. A good game programmer focuses on the areas that he or she is good at, and leaves the rest for someone else. I couldn't write a blit routine [copying a large array of bits from one part of a computer's memory to another part] if my life depended on it, but there are people here who can, so I let them do their thing and provide me a library to use.

Must a programmer be well versed in other areas of game design? Responds Moe:

> Budgets being what they are, oftentimes a game programmer needs to wear many different hats on a project, since the experts aren't always available to all the projects that need them. Other times, the specific problem is unique to the game and the engine being used. I can't get a good C++ programmer to write a routine for me to use in my SCUMM game. That's when the programmer gets to wing it, and it happens more often than not. I recently had this problem when working on *Putt-Putt Enters the Race*. At the end of the game, the player got to race Putt-Putt around a pseudo-3D course. To get this to work effectively, I had to keep track of things in a 3D world. I have had absolutely no experience in 3D transformation, and no other programmers

were available to help me. So basically I had to learn it and implement it myself. Luckily, I had a few experts' brains to pick, and thankfully, the results were good. It's no *Gran Turismo*, mind you, but then again, per the aforementioned point, I knew my audience (kids 3–8) didn't care about realistic physics models and real-time 3D rendering. Instead, I put in some funny-looking ducks that would quack and fly away if you drove too close to them.

And what's the best way to learn programming? "Plug your nose and jump right into the deep end," says Moe. "Start simple—a *Minesweeper* game, a *Tetris*-style game, or a *Space Invaders* clone. Soon you'll be making the next third-person 3D real-time action/shooter strategy game."

KURT PFEIFER, HUMONGOUS ENTERTAINMENT

Kurt Pfeifer worked on the megahit *Total Annihilation* for Cavedog Entertainment, and did the Sega Saturn port of *Duke Nukem 3D* and other PC games—*Microsoft Soccer*, *Powerslave*, *DinoPark Tycoon*, and *Magic School Bus Across the Solar System*.

Pfeifer offers a few indispensable pointers for those looking to create code for games in today's competitive industry:

MAKE A CLEAR DESIGN FOR YOUR GAME UP FRONT

If you want to complete your game anywhere near your scheduled delivery date, lay out what it's going to look and feel like up front. Game creation is a very inexact science, and usually is ad-libbed more than any other kind of programming. But if you can get a ballpark idea of what you're shooting for, it eliminates an amazing amount of guesswork and delays later on. Even just laying out storyboards to provide a visual reference is helpful, as any game has to be optimized for exactly what needs to be seen (for example, first-person point of view versus overhead, 2D versus 3D).

Pfeifer offers the following as an example:

One of the clearest designs you can program from is when you're porting an existing game to another platform. When we undertook the ports of *Duke Nukem 3D* and *Quake* to the Sega Saturn (when I worked at Lobotomy), we obviously had a clear design of what the game would need to be like. Instead of a design on paper that could possibly be modified or misinterpreted, we had the exact blueprint in front of us in the form of the PC game that had already hit the market. Every graphic, every sound, every nuance of the control system was laid out for us; we just had to squish it down to fit in the Saturn. We only had six months to complete the task (later upped to nine to allow for net link programming), so efficiency was crucial. This total understanding of the "big picture" of the design for the game allowed us to split up the tasks efficiently and plan our schedule effectively.

GET AS MANY PEOPLE AS YOU CAN AFFORD

> Easier said than done, as there are few schools out there to train you in this, and you need to find people with previous experience (of which there aren't many) or somebody who knows general programming and is eager to dive into gaming. Even the simplest programming tasks can add up to monumental ones, and if you're shorthanded all of the deadlines will start to slip.

ALLOW TIME FOR RESEARCH AND DEVELOPMENT

> [Allocating time for R&D] unfortunately is not done often enough due to a tight deadline. If you want to do something really unique, you have to sink in some time up front to research which off-the-shelf packages will fit some or all of your needs (3D modeling tools, paint programs, sound editors), and which tools you'll need to do in-house (often including map editors, scripting languages, and animation tools). This time can also be used for artists to create simulated movies or mock-up stills of what the game will look and move like, using existing 3D animating and 2D paint tools. This way you can see if everybody agrees on it up front, instead of finding out a year or two down the road that the publisher or designer had something else in mind.

Pfeifer believes that the biggest obstacles are ones most people don't consider when laying out a project: keeping interest alive and not getting overwhelmed. He continues:

> More than once I've been on a project where the designer loses interest after the first half of the project, when it's past the honeymoon stage and into the ugly detail decisions. In that case, I've played designer as well, and since I'm stretched thinner, the project is not programmed as effectively as it should've been. Getting overwhelmed is easier than ever now in game creation, with games (and their budgets) becoming bigger, and feature lists increasing dramatically every year.

In conclusion, Pfeifer reminds readers, "Just managing a project can become an immense task, but not an impossible one if it's planned out ahead and tasks are divided up properly."

MICHAEL SALADINO, PRESTO STUDIOS

After working at Mobeus Designs creating 3D graphics engines, Michael Saladino left to work at Volition (the creators of *Descent*), where he was promoted to lead programmer. Now he's an engine programmer at Presto Studios. Following is a list of Saladino's truisms, with explanation and support for each.

NEVER UNDERESTIMATE ASSEMBLY LANGUAGE

> With each generation of Intel processors to come and go, a new round of discussion on the future importance of assembly language is launched around newsgroups and development house water coolers. Even though it's true that

entire games for the PC being written in assembly language is a dead idea, it doesn't mean that assembly language can't often be an extremely useful programming tool. Tight loops that consume vast percentages of a game's total execution will always exist in one form or another. It used to be blit copying, then it was innermost texture-mapping loops. What's next? How about real-time tessellation of splines-based characters? A section of code that loops hundreds, thousands, or even hundreds of thousands of times per frame can often be sped up by assembly language.

I haven't seen a compiler yet that can understand the subtle nuances of a piece of code as well as an experienced programmer.

As a corollary to this rule, also remember not to rely entirely on assembly language to save the day. A slow algorithm will run slowly in assembly and in C. So remember to always start by trying to optimize the algorithm. Once you're secure that you've found a highly optimal solution (or you're down to the last five months of development and your producer won't let you rewrite your polygon-clipping algorithm for the fifth time), then you can focus on assembly in order to squeeze out the last bit of performance. And if you don't think it's worth it, what will you think when you realize that your game's direct competition had programmers that did think it was worth it, and their game runs just enough faster so that they could put in killer particle effects?

WE WILL OPTIMIZE NO CODE BEFORE ITS TIME

There is no need to optimize a section of code before you're sure that it's causing a significant slowdown. If you do, you can often waste time doing so, and slow down future code development when others need to interpret your assembly code. Here are some classic examples:

OPTIMIZING INITIALIZATION CODE

What's the point? It's run once at the beginning of the program. Granted, if your game startup takes 30 seconds because of some massive texture pre-processing, then something should be done (most likely making this stage a separate step in your level processing), but in 99.9% of the cases, if it's run once, it's not something to worry about.

OPTIMIZING BEFORE YOU PROFILE

With my experience in programming going all the way back to the age of seven working on an Apple II+, I still often make mistakes over what is and what is not slowing down my code. Luckily, profilers (especially Intel's Vtune) have become commonplace as a programmer's tool. It can tell you quickly and easily what functions or even what lines are causing your code to run like molasses. And by doing this, you're sure to never waste time optimizing something that's already fast enough.

OPTIMIZING BEFORE IT'S TOO SLOW

> I've often seen programmers converting perfectly readable C code into very obtuse (although often very clever) assembly language code when the program is already running at a constant 120 fps. I understand the desire to make your code as fast as possible, but this is too much. There is definitely something to be said for keeping your code readable by others, especially in a modern-day development house where sometimes dozens of people will have to look at your code at one point or another. In most cases, introducing assembly code into a game during the first half of the project is a bad idea. It makes updates and additions that much harder.

LOVE YOUR CODE, BUT DON'T *LOVE* YOUR CODE

> I've seen more time wasted at development houses over this issue than I care to estimate. Programmers who are so attached to their code that they're blind to any problems it might have. Writing code is fun, but try to remember that it's just *code*. If someone spots a problem in it, it's not a problem with you. Don't take it personally. Love the fact that someone has just spotted a way to make your code run faster. And from now on, that little trick he showed you is yours too.
>
> Also, don't get defensive over style issues. If I hear one more argument over whether to use tabs or spaces, I think I'm going to slit my wrists. I don't care where you put your spaces or brackets—just focus on the code. I think every office should make one of two decisions. Either everyone writes in their own style and no one is allowed to complain, or everyone must follow an exact standard.
>
> Programmers as a whole need to separate their own individuality from that of their code.

TODD JOHNSON, ODDWORLD INHABITANTS

Software engineer Todd Johnson worked on products including Genesis' *Sylvester n' Tweety in Cagey Capers*, *Demolition Man*, and *Izzy's Olympic Quest*, and PSX's *Oddworld: Abe's Oddysee* and *Oddworld: Abe's Exoddus*. As a programmer, Johnson says, the most important consideration is to recognize the limitation of the target system. He explains:

> I come from a console background, where we always struggle with a small amount of RAM. For example, Oddworld: Abe's Exoddus had to constantly swap animations, backgrounds, and even code into and out of RAM. On a PC, though, you might run into performance problems. Either way, some aspect of the target system will affect how the game is put together.

"Second, consider the player," says Johnson, because "after all, he is the one shelling out cash for the game."

> This generally means not to get too complicated. When we first started working on the emotions of the Mudokons in *Oddworld: Abe's Exoddus*, they each had their own personality and would react in different ways. From the user's point of view, though, it seemed entirely random because they all looked the same. We kept the emotions but scrapped the idea of personalities.

And last, "think reusability," suggests Johnson:

> It takes a while to code a design, so if the game is loaded with unique features it won't get done for years. The other extreme is complete monotony, so the trick is to balance the two. By adding simple parameters such as speed or timing to existing characters and mechanics, you can get a lot of mileage out of them.

What does Johnson see as the biggest obstacle for a programmer when trying to create a game?

> The biggest obstacle in game production is the communication gap. You have programmers, artists, and designers on a project, and each group has its own identity and realm of experience. It's much easier to communicate within the group than outside it, but that's the key to a successful project. Communication with someone from a wildly different perspective is one of those things that simply isn't taught in schools. That's at least part of the reason it's such a big problem—not only at game companies, but for any business.

GONZO SUAREZ, PYRO STUDIOS

Along with friend and business partner Ignacio Pérez, Gonzo Suarez cofounded Pyro Studios in January of 1997. It was here in Spain that *Commandos: Behind Enemy Lines* was born, later to become an international hit for Eidos Interactive.

Suarez provides a number of helpful tips for novice programmers, who may be starting to code their first game:

> Before anything else, ask yourself, "What do I want to play in this game?" The question seems obvious, but it contains a good 90% of the issues that will come up during the actual development. Curiously enough, most of the time this question is answered with blazing speed (I would be thrilled to have such a quick answer myself), but it usually brings up immediate concerns. Usually the answer is along the lines of, "It's an action game with strategy elements and a feeling of adventure, and it displays 30,000 polygons.'" Answering the question "What are you playing?" with an "It's a…" sentence is strange enough, but to mention the number of polygons is worthy of a Kafka novel.

> To hope that the answer will survive all through the project is a luxury that only experience can sustain (not only knowing the issues involved in a video game, but also understanding their impact during development). Most of the time, any lack of clarity when faced with the question will be justified by "open design" and "appeal to everyone," but to me this road leads to suicide.

As an example, *Quake II* and *Half-Life* could be considered games of a very similar nature. However, the emphasis placed on where, how, and when one shoots in *Half-Life* contrasts with the quick environment of moving targets and precise aim of *Quake II*; the powerful feel of weapons in the id Software game is opposite to the opportunities that *Half-Life* allows for stealth and sniper shots. All that also makes their network gameplay completely different.

During game development, one finds dilemmas where a sacrifice has to be made between conflicting options, all of which are attractive and can be given reasons for their validity. In other words, we all want the most beautiful car with the most powerful engine, best mileage, and lowest price, but the order in which we place these options can lead us anywhere from a BMW to a muscle car or [one that's] utilitarian.

After 15 years of programming and game design experience, Suarez says he heeds the following rules:

THE GAME

The main elements that build the gameplay logic are sacred over any other element. For example, the game logic criteria dictated that the graphics in *Age of Empires* would comply with the underlying grid world. In other words, game entities occupy one or several squares—they can never be shared with other entities, or placed in the middle of two squares. Distances and bearings in the game logic are measured based on the grid. Therefore the graphics must follow the same rules (more or less dissimulated). Despite this sacrifice in the graphical department, we have an outstanding game that couldn't have achieved such success without being faithful to these priorities.

A different example in game logic is *Commandos*. The logic game world is divided into irregular sectors, with any entity moving in continuous three dimensions and having volumetric information attached. This logic is what allowed the game graphics to be irregular and distinct (with the merits of a great art team exploiting it).

LOGICAL INTERFACE

The issues of communicating game logic elements from user to machine, as well as from the machine back to the user, would be the second most important element. A good example is the mouse pointer through which the user accesses the game world.

Anything that involves gameplay must be communicated to the user (more or less explicitly) in the *most effective* way; also, any actions the user may want to communicate (perform) in the game must be made simple well beyond intuition. In other words, a) if something can't be perceived by the user, it better not exist at all; and b) if something can't be made to happen by the user, it better not be offered as an option (much less a seemingly *attractive* option).

184

FEEL AND ALIENATION

" These [factors] encompass both the elements through which the game feeds back the user with sensations (visual as well as auditory), and the ability of the game to involve the player to the point that the player will believe himself to be inside the game (a 220-pound world-saving hero, for example).

Even though this seems to be the point most valued by players, I would keep it in third place in this scale of priorities. Otherwise, the outcome will be five minutes of awe, and then hours of disorientation. This is typically shown when the developer has created an amazing engine with this or that feature, so attractive that the developer forces it to be present in the game even though it doesn't blend well with the game logic.

Good examples of this include several cases (some of which could never be completed) where the programmer was so proud of the realistic and detailed physics engine, where everything rotated and collided just like in real life, that when these features were forced into the game they resulted in uncontrollable characters, and besides the first five minutes of curiosity playing with it, the rest was a plain nightmare. Going to the extreme, imagine a chess game in first-person 3D with each piece having a distinct face, battling in a beautiful valley where the ground has amazing grass animations, where the board squares can barely be distinguished. [You score] "10" in look and suspension of disbelief, " but I don't know who could design an interface to play such a monster.

FEATURES

" Features like technology, licenses, and other side elements that are important for glorifying the product during marketing—for example, displaying 40,000 polygons in real time—should be the last concern of the programmer. This should always be the slave of slaves, the last one to dictate criteria for a video game. In all my video game development experience, I have never seen a game made of features; however, this is the most common element on which people base their ideas about video games.

In a game-design document, it's disorienting to find pages full of pseudoscientific affirmations and no game ideas. I say "pseudoscientific" because, despite the underlying promises of exactitude, they're always vague in deep nature. What does it mean to say "moving 40,000 polygons"? Or "motion-capture"? Or "artificial intelligence"? Even though we believe we know what we're talking about, reality always has the last word. I remember when we pitched the *HeadHunter* project, Javier's [Javier Ignacio] technology prototype contained a host of jaw-dropping 3D features that have become commonplace ever since (flares, colored lighting, particle effects…). The people we met used to say "Looks great! Now you just have to put the game together with all this stuff!" " Piece of cake, *just* the game.

Suarez concludes by drawing on an analogy: "It's great to embellish a game with features just like it is to add spoilers, alloy wheels, and such to a car, but if the car doesn't fit its purpose well, all these accessories mean nothing."

TIP The World Wide Web has a number of handy resources for game programmers. Following is a short list of some of the more note-worthy sites to visit. (Game design sites are listed in Chapter 24.)

- Visual Basic Explorer
  www.vbexplorer.com

- Game Programming Galaxy
  www.geocities.com/SiliconValley/Vista/6774/

- Game Programming '99
  www.gameprog.com

- New Game Programmer's Guild
  http://pages.vossnet.de/mgricken/newgpg/

- Amit's Game Programming Information
  http://www-cs-students.stanford.edu/~amitp/gameprog.html

- GameProgrammer.com
  www.gameprogrammer.com

- Viper's C/C++ Page
  www.europa.com/~viper

- rec.games.programmer newsgroup

CHAPTER 9
ARTIFICIAL INTELLIGENCE (AI)

Artificial intelligence, or simply *AI*, may best be described as an attempt to model aspects of human thought and/or behavior on computers. In computer or console gaming, it boils down to making players feel like they're playing against real, intelligent opponents. Unfortunately, this has been one of the most difficult challenges of game programming, so this chapter will be solely dedicated to AI, instead of being lumped with the rest of the topics covered in the programming chapter (Chapter 8).

Another reason for giving AI its own chapter is that single-player gaming should not be neglected. With the growth of multiplayer gaming, many gamers fear a developer's time, money, and effort will be spent on tweaking the multiplayer code rather than improving the AI. After all, if the AI is predictable or dumb, many gamers will flock online to play against real people instead. The key is to make a game that offers both a hearty multiplayer component *and* realistic AI for those who can't afford to go online or prefer the solo gaming experience.

With a panel of AI specialists, each working in different genres, this chapter discusses different kinds of AI and how a game designer should approach this tricky matter.

BRIAN REYNOLDS, BIG HUGE GAMES

As one of Sid Meier's "star" pupils, Brian Reynolds went on to help create such PC strategy hits as *Colonization*, *Civilization II*, and *Alpha Centauri*. "Contrary to popular belief, you don't need any black magic to write AI for computer games," says Reynolds. "You don't need any patented algorithms, you don't need the latest papers on neural nets. All you need is a little creativity and a lot of persistence." The following sections describe some of his favorite techniques.

THE ITERATIVE DESIGN PROCESS

First of all, with AI, as with game design, use the "iterative design process." Start by just making a simple routine that moves the enemy pieces—even if your algorithm is nothing more complex than switch(rnd(4)). Then *play the game* against your AI and watch it make its moves. Watch until it does something dumb (shouldn't take too long at first); then think about a) what did the computer do that was stupid—e.g., moved its tanks slowly through the woods, or built only artillery units and nothing else; b) what you would have done instead (moved your tanks along the road; built a healthy mix of infantry, artillery, armor, and air); and c) what piece of information led you to (or helped you to) make that decision (road squares cost less to enter; you already had an artillery unit, but no infantry). Then just go back and revise your algorithm to incorporate this data.

Now play your game again and watch the AI; wait until it does something *else* stupid, and repeat this process. Repeat it over and over and over again, and your AI will get better and better. It's the poor man's version of the proverbial "AI that learns from its mistakes." Through your playing and revising, the AI is essentially building up "experience" and getting better and better at the game.

To illustrate his point, Reynolds shares with us an anecdote from when he was a young programmer working on his first game as a designer (*Colonization*). He recalls:

I was a little intimidated when it came time to start working on some AI. I mean, I had a game that you could play, move the pieces around, but the AI didn't know how to do any of that. Where was I to start? I can still remember Sid Meier's advice to me: Start by teaching it how to play one turn. Then teach it how to play two turns, and *then* worry about teaching it how to play 10 turns.

START SIMPLE

Start with simple building blocks. For instance, in a strategy game, a useful algorithm to have is a routine that tells a unit how to get from point A to point B, called a *pathfinding* or *go-to* algorithm. A go-to routine is a nice, compartmentalized project to start out with—just teaching a unit how to get from here to there, and worrying later about how to decide where "there" ought to be. I'm not saying it's easy to write a great go-to routine, but it's easy to start with a simple, adequate routine and work your way up to something more complex. Once you've got a go-to routine, you can have another routine that decides where on the map the pieces ought to move, and it doesn't need to worry about how they're going to go about getting there.

 Pathfinding refers to a unit or units moving from point A to point B, and what path is taken to get there. Ever noticed how, in older real-time strategy games, units at times will get "stuck" in some places, while at other times they take a longer or illogical route to their destination?

DOUBLING OR SPLITTING YOUR VALUES

Another excellent trick I learned from Sid Meier when I was getting started (and which, like almost all of our tricks, applies equally well to game design and AI): If you have a value or an effect, and you think you need to adjust it, then either *double* it or *halve* it. For example, if you think tanks are too cheap to build, double the cost. Spare yourself the frustration of increasing it from

10 to 11 and wondering whether you can tell the difference or not. Make it 20, even if that seems initially ridiculous, and try the game out that way. This will give you a clear-cut difference in effect and show you what the game is like with [items] that are definitely more expensive. If they feel too expensive, then you can cut back to 15 to fine-tune. If you think your computer AI is making too many infantry units, halve the likelihood that they will build them. I can remember countless times when I've doubled or halved something, thinking it would be too drastic a change, but wound up doubling or halving again before I really achieved the effect I wanted. All of this once again depends on using the iterative process.

Reynolds leaves off with this simple piece of advice: "Try stuff out, see how it works, revise, repeat."

MARIO GRIMANI, ENSEMBLE STUDIOS

Prior to moving to Ensemble Studios, Mario Grimani worked at 7th Level on *Dominion: Storm Over Gift 3*, among other PC titles. His latest work can be seen—and played—in *Age of Empires II: The Age of Kings*.

What are the most important things to remember as an AI specialist? Grimani responds:

- The amount of work in AI is not always directly proportional to how it's perceived by the user.

- Develop your AI through an iterative process. Implement a rough working system, test it, and improve the part that behaves the worst.

- Make your design flexible. Since you're most likely developing AI for the game that's in the making, you have to be able to modify it as the game progresses.

AI for *Age of Empires II: The Age of Kings* allows for controlling the computer player's behavior through an external, easy-to-use language. Computer players can play against humans or against each other. This gives us flexibility in modifying AI behavior during the game design process. It also makes it possible for AI features to be added late in the development cycle.

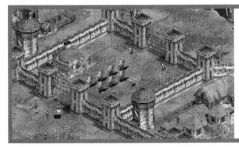

Mario Grimani advises making your game's AI modular, because it's likely you'll go back and make modifications during the game's development cycle. (Used with permission by Microsoft)

Grimani discusses the different kinds of AI and some of the problems in programming it:

> In game terms, *AI* is used loosely to describe solutions for a wide variety of problems that can range from simulating human behavior for characters in role-playing games to pathfinding in real-time strategy games (RTS).
>
> The main AI problems encountered in RTS games are unit pathing, unit AI other than pathing, group AI, and computer-opponent AI. Computer-opponent AI in itself has many parts: strategic AI, tactical AI, building placement, threat evaluation, terrain analysis, and many more.
>
> Some AI problems are more challenging than others. Any problem that has clear mathematical representation will be easier to solve than a problem based on concepts and abstractions. Unfortunately, the human mind is more likely to detect flaws in solutions to problems based on abstractions.

As an example, Grimani explains a common hurdle while working on RTS games:

> It's fairly trivial for a human player to determine whether a certain area is easily defendable. For a computer player, this is quite a task. On the other hand, the computer player can keep track of all individual units and their statistics much better than a human player.

So does Grimani think the growth in Web-based or LAN-based gaming will reduce the need for better AI? He responds:

> Multiplayer gaming is growing at a fast pace. This is mainly due to the fact that fast Internet connections are becoming available to more and more people. This doesn't mean that multiplayer gaming will replace AI. These are really two different gaming experiences. I personally enjoy multiplayer games and I've been playing them for a couple of years. Still, this hasn't taken away from my interest in single-player games.

MARC LEBLANC, LOOKING GLASS STUDIOS

Marc "MAHK" LeBlanc has been making games at Looking Glass Studios since 1992, with impressive design and programming credits including *Ultima Underworld II*, *System Shock 1* and *2*, *Flight Unlimited*, and *Thief: The Dark Project*. Currently, he is the lead engineer on Looking Glass Studios' RPG Engine Team.

Here, LeBlanc talks about coding good AI. Is there a "secret" to creating it? His response is as follows:

> It's a secret truth of game AI (so secret, in fact, that most game AI programmers fail to acknowledge it, much to their own peril) that *intelligence* and *realism* are not the goals. Game characters do not need to be perfect simulations of human behavior. Nor do they need to be ruthlessly competent opponents. Those things aren't even *desirable*. Game AIs need to be good babysitters. Or good playmates. The AI is there to *cooperate* with the player in entertaining ways.

LeBlanc offers *Thief: The Dark Project* as a shining example of this advice:

> The guards are canonical babysitters playing hide-and-seek with the player; they walk around constantly shouting about how they can't see you. If we wanted ruthless guards that searched and destroyed the player with maximum efficiency, we could have written them. They wouldn't have been any fun. Of course, game AI needs to be believable, but "believability" is not at all the same thing as "realism." Being believable is largely a matter of smoke and mirrors; it's about suspending disbelief, and if you give the player the right cues, then he'll cooperate with you.

STEVE POLGE, EPIC GAMES

In the popular 3D shooter genre, more and more games today include the option to play against computer-controlled AI bots to simulate the multiplayer gaming experience—offline. Arguably the most realistic bots are in Epic Games' *Unreal* and *Unreal Tournament*, and you can trace this savvy AI programming to Steve Polge, who wrote the AI and much of the game code for *Unreal* and *Unreal Tournament* (and before that, he wrote the Reaper bot mod for id Software's *Quake*).

Polge believes the overall goal is to make the game fun, so programming AI should lead to this objective. He explains:

> AI is one of the most important elements in making a game *fun*, and gameplay is what AI is about. Don't spend development time and CPU cycles on AI features that don't make the game more fun, or aren't obvious to the player. Focus on results, not sexy implementation. It doesn't matter if your creatures are being driven by a state-of-the-art adaptive neural network if it's not obvious to the player that they are (and in fact, it's a negative if you're sucking up CPU cycles that could better be used to implement some other feature). You can make AI obvious through the results (players are impressed and challenged by what the creatures do), and through visual and audio cues (you see them yelling and gesturing to each other as they coordinate an attack). These cues can be as important as the actual AI in making players feel like they're interacting with intelligent opponents or allies.

How does a programmer gauge the difficulty level of AI? Polge offers the following:

> Good AI should challenge the player intellectually, even in an action game. People enjoy feeling like they have to outsmart a computer opponent—but they don't enjoy playing against a computer opponent that "cheats" by doing things a human player can't do, whether by operating under a different set of rules or by having inhuman characteristics such as perfect aim. It's also important to make sure that your AI doesn't have any major blind spots or flaws, as an otherwise competent AI will be fatally handicapped by obvious problems that turn off players.

Any other advice to give budding programmers who are coding AI for their first game? Polge says:

> Many developers make the mistake of putting AI implementation off until near the end of the project, because they're too busy getting the rendering and basic game elements in place. It's important to get the AI working early, because it's such a key part of gameplay and has a major impact on level design. With the AI working, it's easy to assess and refine gameplay as the game is developed—something that really helped improve the polish of *Unreal Tournament*. It's also important to have the time to balance AI features with their performance overhead. Often what's hard is not implementing a behavior, but implementing it with acceptable performance. It takes time to discover the right tradeoffs to get the best performance.

In light of action games such as 3D shooters, are there different kinds of AI to be concerned with? What's important with games like *Unreal Tournament*? Polge is encouraged to get technical, rather than theoretical:

> Navigation is one of the most basic and important elements of AI. Whether it's a 3D first-person shooter or a real-time strategy game, if the creatures or units can't get around their world intelligently, the AI looks dumb and is frustrating for the player. In addition, solid navigation AI is a key foundation for more complex behaviors you may want to implement. Without a solid navigation system, the bots in *Unreal Tournament* would have been unable to intelligently play games such as *Capture the Flag*, or run away effectively when injured. For *Unreal Tournament*, we used a *waypoint* system. Waypoints were laid down in advance by the level designers (primarily by hand, although we now have an automatic waypoint generator in the editor). A final pre-processing step "defines" the paths between these waypoints—connecting waypoints that can be directly reached, and specifying the parameters of the connection (what size creature can use this path, and what special abilities or physics modes are needed to use this path). During gameplay, bots first figure out which nearest waypoint they can reach by doing an imaginary walk to the waypoint (which is relatively expensive due to the physics/collision computations) and can move to any arbitrary location in the level by following the waypoint network to the nearest waypoint to the destination, and from there to the actual destination. Finding the best path is done by doing a weighted breadth-first search of the navigation network.

Polge maintains that object-oriented programming makes AI code design much simpler, and discusses how the AI in *Unreal Tournament* was coded:

> [*Unreal Tournament*] was written in UnrealScript, an object-oriented language Epic developed. It includes extensions such as states (and state-scoping of functions) and latent execution of functions, which facilitate clean and straightforward AI design. (*Note:* If you buy *Unreal Tournament*, you can browse through and modify the game and AI code using the Unreal Editor, which comes with the game.) Designing a solid AI framework really depends on defining the right set of objects and interfaces to objects. Distributing the functionality appropriately across several objects will make your AI code easier to maintain and easier to extend. A good example of this is how bots understand how to use weapons in *Unreal Tournament*. When they're assessing what inventory item to go after next, they query available items about their

usefulness to the bot by calling the items' BotDesireability() function. When entering combat, they choose which weapon to use by calling the RateSelf() function for all the weapons in their inventory. During combat, they call their chosen weapon's SuggestAttackStyle() function to request adjustments to their combat style (for example, charging versus strafing or backing off).

The following is a piece of code illustrating the implementation of these functions for *Unreal Tournament*'s rocket launcher. By putting this functionality into the weapons, it's easy to add new weapons and have the bots understand how to use them without making any changes to the bot code:

```
// tell the bot how much it wants this weapon
// called when the bot is trying to decide
// which inventory item to go after next
event float BotDesireability(Pawn Bot)
{
  local Weapon AlreadyHas;
  local float desire;
  // bots adjust their desire for their favorite weapons
  desire = MaxDesireability + Bot.AdjustDesireFor(self);
  // see if bot already has a weapon of this type
  AlreadyHas = Weapon(Bot.FindInventoryType(class));
  if ( AlreadyHas != None )
  {
    if ( (RespawnTime < 10)
      && ( bHidden || (AlreadyHas.AmmoType == None)
        || (AlreadyHas.AmmoType.AmmoAmount < AlreadyHas.AmmoType.MaxAmmo)) )
      return 0;
    // can't pick it up if weapon stay is on
    if ( (!bHeldItem || bTossedOut) && bWeaponStay )
      return 0;
    if ( AlreadyHas.AmmoType == None )
      return 0.25 * desire;
    // bot wants this weapon for the ammo it holds
    if ( AlreadyHas.AmmoType.AmmoAmount > 0 )
      return FMax( 0.25 * desire,
          AlreadyHas.AmmoType.MaxDesireability
          * FMin(1, 0.15 *
          ➥AlreadyHas.AmmoType.MaxAmmo/AlreadyHas.AmmoType.AmmoAmount) );
    else
      return 0.05;
  }

  // incentivize bot to get this weapon if
  // it doesn't have a good weapon already
  if ( (Bot.Weapon == None) || (Bot.Weapon.AIRating <= 0.4) )
    return 2*desire;
  return desire;
}
```

continues

continued

```
// return delta to combat style while using this weapon
function float SuggestAttackStyle()
{
  local float EnemyDist;
  // recommend backing off if target is too close
  EnemyDist = VSize(Pawn(Owner).Enemy.Location - Owner.Location);
  if ( EnemyDist < 600 )
  {
    if ( EnemyDist < 300 )
      return -1.5;
    else
      return -0.7;
  }
  else
    return -0.2;
}
// tell bot how valuable this weapon would be to use,
// based on the bot's combat situation
// also suggest whether to use regular or alternate fire mode
function float RateSelf( out int bUseAltMode )
{
  local float EnemyDist, Rating;
  local bool bRetreating;
  local vector EnemyDir;
  local Pawn P;
  // don't recommend self if out of ammo
  if ( AmmoType.AmmoAmount <=0 )
    return -2;
  // by default use regular mode (rockets)
  bUseAltMode = 0;
  P = Pawn(Owner);
  if ( P.Enemy == None )
    return AIRating;
  // if standing on a lift, make sure not about to go around a corner
  // and lose sight of target
  // (don't want to blow up a rocket in bot's face)
  if ( (P.Base != None) && (P.Base.Velocity != vect(0,0,0))
    && !P.CheckFutureSight(0.1) )
    return 0.1;
  EnemyDir = P.Enemy.Location - Owner.Location;
  EnemyDist = VSize(EnemyDir);
  Rating = AIRating;
  // don't pick rocket launcher if enemy is too close
  if ( EnemyDist < 360 )
  {
    if ( P.Weapon == self )
    {
```

```
      // don't switch away from rocket launcher unless
      // really bad tactical situation
      if ( (EnemyDist > 230) || ((P.Health < 50) &&
      ➡(P.Health < P.Enemy.Health - 30)) )
        return Rating;
    }
    return 0.05 + EnemyDist * 0.001;
  }
  // increase rating for situations for which rocket launcher is well suited
  if ( P.Enemy.IsA('StationaryPawn') )
    Rating += 0.4;
  // rockets are good if higher than target, bad if lower than target
  if ( Owner.Location.Z > P.Enemy.Location.Z + 120 )
    Rating += 0.25;
  else if ( P.Enemy.Location.Z > Owner.Location.Z + 160 )
    Rating -= 0.35;
  else if ( P.Enemy.Location.Z > Owner.Location.Z + 80 )
    Rating -= 0.05;
  // decide if should use alternate fire (grenades) instead
  if ( (Owner.Physics == PHYS_Falling) || Owner.Region.Zone.bWaterZone )
    bUseAltMode = 0;
  else if ( EnemyDist < -1.5 * EnemyDir.Z )
    bUseAltMode = int( FRand() < 0.5 );
  else
  {
    // grenades are good covering fire when retreating
    bRetreating = ( ((EnemyDir/EnemyDist) Dot Owner.Velocity) < -0.7 );
    bUseAltMode = 0;
    if ( bRetreating && (EnemyDist < 800) && (FRand() < 0.4) )
      bUseAltMode = 1;
  }
  return Rating;
}
```

Polge reminds newbie game programmers that there's more to AI than the above advice, but it should provide a clearer understanding of what goes into games such as *Unreal Tournament*, and how AI can be applied to other projects.

TOBY SIMPSON, CYBERLIFE TECHNOLOGIES

Toby Simpson is the creative director for all *Creatures* products at CyberLife Technologies, based in Cambridge, England. As producer of *Creatures 1, 2,* and *3,* he has worked on quite a different kind of AI than in other genres, since the whole emphasis of the *Creatures* series is on sustaining and teaching these virtual pets.

Ever wanted to know how those cute Norns in *Creatures* acted so lifelike, each with a different personality type and seemingly "human" emotions and desires?

The following is a short essay Simpson wrote for this book on artificial intelligence. In it, he discusses his four commandments for successfully giving life to inanimate objects:

> The most important aspect is to get out of the frame of mind that one "codes some AI." AI, implemented as a black-box add-on, is normally highly superficial and full of inconsistencies and faults. Building adaptive systems into entertainment products requires a whole new approach to the problem. However, if I were to distill this into things to remember, I'd probably come up with the following:

MODEL, NOT EMULATE

> A model and a simulation are both types of simulation, but have dramatically different approaches to the same problem. Emulations attempt merely to *appear* like something else, whereas models attempt to *be* that something. A model tries to capture the fundamental structure and mechanisms underlying a system. Both models and emulations have the same ultimate aim, but models have some distinct advantages:
>
> ■ There is little or no scope in emulated systems for intelligence or autonomy—as there is no logical relationship between the parameters of a system and the outward behavior.
>
> ■ Models provide "order for free," as they're not abstract representations of a system; i.e., models are built from the inside out. Emulations are built from the outside in, and will never be a faithful simulation.
>
> ■ Models are expandable, components can be exchanged, and they can be broken down and rebuilt in new ways—not true with an emulation.

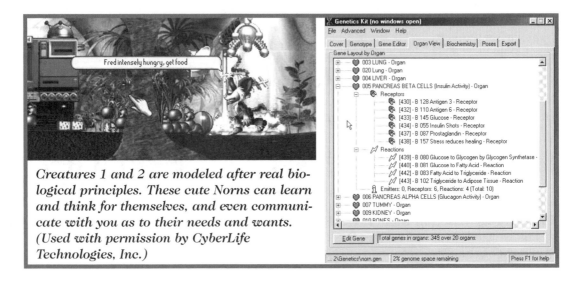

Creatures 1 and 2 are modeled after real biological principles. These cute Norns can learn and think for themselves, and even communicate with you as to their needs and wants. (Used with permission by CyberLife Technologies, Inc.)

THINK STRUCTURE, NOT BEHAVIOR

Try to get out of the mindset of looking at problems from the top down. Put in place a structure that allows the behaviors you require to *emerge*. You *do not* have to fully understand how a system works in order to get its functionality! By thinking of a computer as a container of machines rather than a data-processing device, you've already made a leap in the right direction. Many people are now constructing game engines that build in "autonomous agents" (although *agent* is a flaky word that's often misused) right from the start—an expansion of the object-oriented design paradigm—and therefore they're shifting focus away from code and onto data. This shift in thinking is taking place everywhere, as people realize that creating complex virtual worlds in which entertainment can take place is practically impossible without a change of approach.

NATURE IS A GREAT PLACE TO LOOK FOR HELP

By far the most incredible computing device on the face of this planet is a biological brain. Its ability to adapt to its own unique problem set (by making it up as it goes along), generalize, and learn directly the difference between positive and negative actions has never been reproduced inside a computer. Furthermore, when broken down, human systems are remarkably simple—10 trillion simple cells built from 100,000 genes. We understand the cells, and yet we don't understand why when they're arranged in a certain way we get a conscious, thinking human being. This is complexity management on scales never seen before—10 trillion simple "agents" that cooperate, allowing consciousness to *emerge*. There is no cell in charge. No "master program." There's a lot we can learn from this! Bear in mind that if we can model a bridge or a tank, we can model biological building blocks and then build artificial organisms from those building blocks. If you want plausible artificial actors inside self-consistent virtual worlds, then biological processes and structures may be the only way of managing that complexity. I don't have Mother Nature's 3.7 billion-year research and development program handy to reinvent a wheel that works fine already.

THINK, AND BE PROFESSIONAL

You *cannot* develop professional software without professional software development practices! No amount of neat and groovy technology is going to save your soul if your processes stink or are missing entirely. Be professional! If you aren't part of a defined QMS (quality management system), define your own. Think about planning, module testing, effective design, and proper documentation. *Stick to your processes, and don't cut corners—it will come back to haunt you!*

There is quite a bit more to read on Toby Simpson's cyberbiology and AI practices as they pertain to the *Creatures* line of products, so be sure to visit the following Web sites: www.cyberlife.co.uk, www.creatures.co.uk, and www.cyberbiology.org.

SCOTT ORR, EA SPORTS

As executive producer at EA Sports, Scott Orr not only helped the *Madden* football series come to fruition nine years ago, but he also oversaw the development of other well-known EA Sports franchises such as *NHL Hockey*, *Andretti Racing*, *NASCAR Racing*, *NCAA College Football*, *March Madness*, and *Knockout Kings*. In preparation for this chapter of the book, Orr's name was brought up many times as the "AI guru."

REALISM

"The first thing to consider is that the AI needs to be realistic," reminds Orr.

> By this I mean that computer players need to move and react as closely as possible to their real-life counterparts. That's why all the players in EA Sports games have ratings ranging from their field intelligence to their speed/quickness to their throwing/catching ability. We also work with pro players and coaches who help us capture reality. I can't tell you how many times John Madden has looked at a play we've implemented in our game and literally gone to the whiteboard to diagram how it should really look.

It's this level of detail that sets EA Sports games apart from the competition, believes Orr. Okay, well, what if a gamer doesn't have the money or connections to get hands-on advice from the likes of John Madden or today's pro football players? His next two points don't require any six-figure budgets.

REALISM VERSUS FUN

"The second point you need to keep in mind is that there needs to be a balance between making the game realistic and making it fun to play," says Orr.

> Computer AI has progressed to such a level that we could make the computer virtually unbeatable. Obviously, this would make the game challenging but not a lot of fun to play, and we would lose our customers. A lot of designers resort to little cheats to keep the computer competitive. This can range from knowing what play the human player has called to moving the computer's players faster than the human's players. An EA Sports game would never take that "cheat" approach, however.

SIMPLIFIED AI PROGRAMMING

The final thing to consider when you design computer AI is to keep it simple from a coding standpoint. Orr says, "The more calculations you use, the bigger stress you put on the processor." What kind of effect will that have on gameplay?

> This can slow down your frame rate and compromise gameplay. Use lookup tables to keep rule-based data and speed up your processing. You'll get more bang for the buck this way, and smarter AI as a result.

Is sports game AI any harder to code than other genres? Orr answers, "Sports games are both harder and easier than other games from an AI standpoint." Here's why:

> Since we're designing products based on known rules and player behaviors, in some ways it's easier to define what needs to be created. On the other hand, designing how the AI works is harder than in other types of games because customers' expectations are higher, since they know the real sport. You can't drop a computer player behavior simply because you can't get it to work correctly. If it's in the [real] game, it has to be in your game; otherwise, gamers will feel like something is missing. As we work with more powerful processors, the sophistication of the AI will improve. The things the computer players do now versus what they did just five years ago—from how smart they are about play calling to how well they work off of what their teammates are doing during a given play—is truly amazing. This is only going to get better as we design for more powerful hardware and build on the experience we get by the time we send another game to market.

Orr was reminded that this book is meant for budding game designers who may want to program AI in a shareware, freeware, or even retail title. When asked for any AI advice in light of C++, Orr offers the following:

> All I can say is that practice makes perfect. Try different approaches and then test them. Eventually you'll come up with something that works—or works better than what you started with. Try to develop a library of common routines. By building a library of routines (hopefully they're efficient, with low overhead), you can build on your past work more quickly. [And] don't forget the power of using lookup tables to reduce the number of calculations you need to make to keep the frame rate up and gameplay fast.

MARC AUBANEL, EA SPORTS

Also at EA Sports is Marc Aubanel, producer of the best-selling and internationally recognized *FIFA* series of soccer games (and the *World Cup* incarnations).

Aubanel says AI in team-based sports games can get quite tricky, since the program is dealing with a number of characters at the same time (a soccer game has 22 players on the field). "Humans have incredible natural intuition, a sense of how something should act," says Aubanel. "The computer has no intuition whatsoever, so it has to be taught how to simulate intuition." According to Aubanel, the hardest sports game to code AI for is baseball, for a few reasons.

> First, the user likely has a subconscious expectation of what the player should be doing, and if the AI differs from this expectation, the AI will be considered *bad*. For instance, if a ball is hit to left field by the player, the outfielder has to make a split decision on what to do with the ball, if caught. Throw to home? To second? To third? Not throw at all? The second issue is the programming required to make these kinds of split decisions. Many factors have to be taken into account, such as how many people are on bases, how many outs there are, and so forth.

"With soccer," says Aubanel, "it's all about form, space, and working toward a single goal." Although he admits that this game, too, has its own set of AI barriers, soccer intelligence is generally easier to model than that of baseball games.

In discussing how the AI is programmed in the *FIFA* series, such as *FIFA '99*, Aubanel says one practice during bug testing is to have the player take shots on an AI goalie, and report any scored balls that should have been saves, or saved balls that should have gone in the net. After careful deliberation, a realistic middle ground is nailed down.

Another practice is to try to teach the AI players in the game their sense of space on the field. According to Aubanel, this is quite a difficult task:

> It's not hard to position the soccer players in the ways they should be positioned on the field, but it's very hard for them to "recognize" why they are placed there, when to hold position, what tactical strategy to employ, and, generally speaking, how to give the players an understanding of "space."

Aubanel says in the event of a red card, where one team has a player off on a penalty, another AI challenge is to have the other players compensate. "They must scale their positions accordingly, to make up for the absence," says Aubanel.

The best way to create AI for a game is to do so in a testing environment:

> When we work on the AI in *FIFA*, we don't have any nice graphics or audio or anything. We want to strip it down to stick figures on a flat green field. This way, there's no confusion. Then we have multicolored arrows and lines coming out from players to illustrate their AI for everything—for passes, pathing, etc.—so it's all possible to debug. If we didn't do this, only the programmer would be able to know if there was a bug in the AI. This way, everyone on the design team can see and understand any potential issues. It's an effective test environment, so we can tune it and tune it a lot.

"Don't confuse reality with fun," says Aubanel.

> [The best AI looks real,] but it's not—all for the sake of the game. We break more rules about physical reality than adhere to them. For example, it takes roughly 18 seconds for a real soccer player to run across the length of a soccer field, but in *FIFA*, it's about half of that—because 18 seconds in a game is a long time.

Marc Aubanel also discusses user interfaces in sports games in Chapter 12.

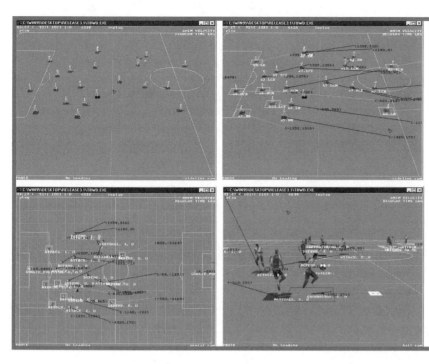

These four images illustrate how Aubanel and the rest of his team test the AI for the FIFA series. They take note of each of the player commands, such as seek ball, attack, defend, and pass, and use numbers to represent the player's position on the grid (field). (Used with permission by Electronic Arts, Inc.)

JAY WILSON, MONOLITH PRODUCTIONS

As lead level designer for *Blood* and *Blood: Plasma Pak* and project lead on *Blood 2: The Chosen*, Jay Wilson believes AI is one of the most important areas of 3D action game design.

He maintains that there are considerable advances in AI in the gaming industry—with games such as *Half-Life*, *Unreal*, and *Starcraft* as excellent examples—but agrees with the intro to this chapter that not everyone wants to play games online. He cites his father as an example of someone who plays games to relax and not compete (as found in most multiplayer games).

When it comes to creating AI for first-person perspective shooters, Wilson says the characters in the game aren't necessarily emulating real people, but rather multiplayer Deathmatch opponents. Explains Wilson:

> The shooters today with strong AI play like bots and not like real people. That isn't particularly hard to do. What I'd like to see when I'm playing these games is for the AI to act like humans do: run for cover, drop weapons, shoot and miss the target, and so on.

Web surfers should definitely check out this stellar site dedicated to computer game artificial intelligence: www.cris.com/~swoodcoc/ai.html. The Game AI Page contains a discussion of AI in light of a number of new and classic PC games, and contains a meaty links section directing the visitor to many related areas of interest on the Internet.

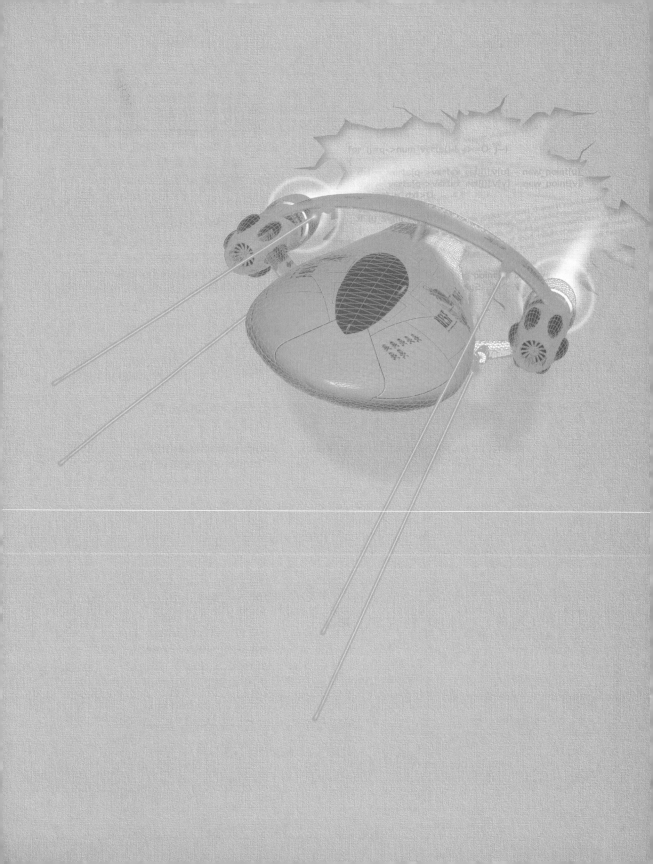

CHAPTER 10
GAME ART

Computer and console game graphics are among the most important facets of game design; they eat up the biggest piece of the game-budget pie, contribute more to a game's immersion factor, and, from a marketing standpoint, are crucial selling points (think of all the prerelease screen shots in magazines or on the Internet, and on the outside of the box at retail).

Generally speaking, there are two kinds of art in gaming: *concept* and *in-game*. In most cases, *concept artists* work with the game designers to help flesh out the graphical vision of the product by sketching characters and backgrounds, and perhaps do some 3D modeling as well. *In-game artists* may work on character art ("painting" textures on 2D sprites or 3D polygons, for example) and background art (game locations). Then there are *animators*, of course (covered in the next chapter), and in some companies *art technicians*, who work specifically on the programming side of placing the graphics in the game engine.

This chapter hosts a diverse collection of game artists who would like to share their advice and expertise with others on creating art for games, what tools to use, and the best ways to get into the industry as an artist. All genres are covered, but their order of appearance is purely random.

TETSUYA NOMURA, SQUARE, LTD.

As director and character designer on the celebrated *Final Fantasy* role-playing game series for the Sony PlayStation and PC, Tetsuya Nomura is internationally respected for his work on such memorable characters as Cloud and Aeris. Following the incredible success of *Final Fantasy VII*, Nomura went on to design characters for *Parasite Eve*, *Final Fantasy VIII*, and a number of the famous CG (computer graphics) sequences of *Final Fantasy VIII* as well.

Nomura was asked to highlight three of the most important pieces of advice he could give to a budding game artist or animator starting out. He responds as follows:

 First, the most important aspect is the communication between the staff on the game development team. Game design involves character design, 3D models, textures, motion, and other details, so it's necessary to understand the overall flow of development and to be aware of progress.

Final Fantasy VIII pushed the boundaries of the Sony PlayStation's capacity, as evidenced by this beautiful screen capture from 2000's Final Fantasy VIII. (Used with permission by SQUARE USA, Inc. and Electronic Arts, Inc.)

> Secondly, it's also necessary to have interests other than games. In my case, I watch many movies. I tend to like action movies, but I watch movies in all genres. I also watch a lot of TV. I have an interest in images overall. I also am interested in fashion. I go through fashion magazines and I like to shop.
>
> The third point is not to mistake yourself for an "artist." We are not "artists," but "creators." Our goal is to create newer and more fun games. Art is not our goal. There are those who say that games are a form of art within digital entertainment, but I believe that games are toys that are to be enjoyed.

What tools do artists use at Square to create the breathtaking images in the *Final Fantasy* series? Says Nomura:

> My work entails creating designs and storyboards that serve as blueprints in the process of creating images, so I use an HB mechanical pencil and size A4 copy paper. I use Photoshop for coloring and touching up the images. I have no special techniques; I draw and create images based on feeling and inspiration.

For some words of wisdom on game design given by Square's Hironobu Sakaguchi, see Chapter 3.

MAARTEN KRAAIJVANGER, NIHILISTIC SOFTWARE

The very talented Maarten Kraaijvanger started his career creating art for computer games back in 1994 at Cyclone Studios (later to be acquired by 3DO). He worked on a number of titles there, including *Captain Quazar* and *Requiem*, and then went to Novato, California's Nihilistic Software to begin work on the eagerly anticipated *Vampire: The Masquerade – Redemption*, where he served as lead artist.

According to Kraaijvanger, the following are a number of helpful tips for budding game artists who are looking to be hired by a development company:

- When applying for a job, don't include animated tunnels and Photoshop filters in your demo tape. Why? Every company can spot them, and since anyone can use them, they do not impress.

- Try to stay away from flying spaceships and walking mechs (unless you're applying for a job to make mechs or spaceships!).

- Only show your best work. If you have some work that's not finished or isn't as good as some of your other work, don't include it.

- Show creativity and work created on your own time rather then compulsory work completed in school.

And after you've been hired…

- Don't rush the pre-production. When I first starting working as an artist, we didn't think about doing much pre-production. I would do a sketch, model it, paint it, attach and animate it, and finally get it into the game. Without getting a full picture of the entire game, the quality might vary throughout the entire project. You might be spending too much time on one part rather than focusing on the "big picture." I found that all the time spent on pre-production can easily be made up during the project. Plan out what you're going to do before you start, and you'll find the final product will be much better.

- Know when to let your work go. The fact is that every piece of art is always incomplete. It can always be improved in some way. As an artist you can't keep working on the same thing, or you're going to miss deadlines or get fired. Complete your art as quickly as you can and move on. You can always touch it up later when you have made a first pass at all the art.

Kraaijvanger was asked to list some of the better software tools to use to create the stunning images found in *Vampire: The Masquerade—Redemption*. He answers, "The most import thing to remember is your work is not going to be judged by the tools you use."

The talent an artist has is much more important than the list of tools on the résumé. I can show someone how to use a program much easier than I can teach them how to do a good walk animation. Depending on which discipline the artist wants to pursue, he should use the best tools to help him show off his talent. Your mission on your portfolio should be to show how you can make an impact at a company. If you want to animate, use the best tools to animate.

Maya and SOFTIMAGE are two of the best tools in the industry. They're robust packages that are easy to use and give the animator a lot of freedom to animate. If you want to paint textures for characters or world textures, learn how to use Photoshop and Painter very well. Stay away from using filters. Anybody can use a filter, but not everybody can paint well. If you want to model, most 3D packages on the market should do the job. The modeling packages most often used are 3DStudio MAX, Power Animator, Maya, SOFT-IMAGE, Nichimen. They all provide roughly the same tools, and it should be easy to switch between packages once you learn the fundamentals.

All 120 characters in Nihilistic's Vampire: The Masquerade—Redemption were rendered using Alias|Wavefront's Maya. (Used with permission by Activision, Inc.)

When it comes to art/animation in today's games, is there anything that *disturbs* Kraaijvanger? He replies:

> What's wrong with some of the art in some of the games today is that [it doesn't] always measure up in all the various components that make the art feel complete. To make good art, you need a good concept. You need an excellent modeler who can accurately create a 3D model of the concept. A texture artist who paints convincing textures that make the characters look authentic. And finally, you need an animator to bring life to the character. Each one of these disciplines takes a very talented artist. On *Vampire* we have been extremely lucky in finding incredible talent that maintained a high quality level through the entire art process. The chain is only as strong as the weakest link; the same applies for the art in a game. Each one of the disciplines needs to maintain a high level of quality or the player's attention will be drawn to what's wrong with the art rather than focusing on the positives.

Be sure to flip to Chapter 11, where Kraaijvanger offers advice for budding animators.

MARK BERNAL, BUNGIE SOFTWARE

All the eye candy you see in games such as *Marathon 2*, *Myth: The Fallen Lords*, and *Myth II: Soulblighter* is due to Mark Bernal and his talented team of 12 artists at Bungie Software (including the West Coast office). Bernal currently serves as lead artist and art director for these award-winning PC and Mac titles.

Bernal starts off by discussing what he believes are the most important things to keep in mind as a new game artist.

KNOW YOUR BOUNDARIES

"Understand the restrictions of the game engine in respect to sprite and texture resolutions, color palettes, and their importance relative to other sprites and textures," explains Bernal. As examples, he offers the following:

> 3D FX cards cannot support textures larger than 256 × 256 pixel textures. Some games use one 256-color palette for the whole game; others use a 256-color palette for each individual character.
>
> Another example relates to time management; that is, deciding which of the game elements should be higher resolution than others, based on their importance and placement in the game world.

DON'T RELY ON SOFTWARE

Bernal insists you must have very good artistic skills and organizational skills, above all else:

> Knowing how to use different software applications such as Photoshop and 3D Studio MAX is not enough to become a computer game artist. Computer software plug-ins are not going to create the artwork for you. The numbers of resources (sprites, models, sounds, etc.) we have in our games has been growing larger and larger with every title, so you need to be able to organize the art you create and the way you manage your production time.

TEAMWORK

"There are several people working on a computer game, and each relies on the others," says Bernal, "so you can't work in a bubble." He expands:

> Good communication between all the members of a team will make game development progress much smoother. Level designers need artists to create environments that depict the layouts that they have designed. Programmers need artwork to be created a certain way, or else the artwork might make the game crash. And so on.

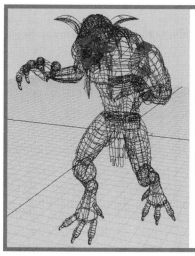 

On the left is the wireframe model of the Myrkridia monster in Myth II: Soulblighter. It was created in Alias' Power Animator. On the right is a rendered version of the same character. While in 3D now, it became a 2D sprite when it was placed into the game. (Used with permission by Bungie Software Products Corp.)

Bernal offers a short primer on the differences in painting 2D versus 3D objects:

> Currently, most games represent objects in two ways: 2D sprite objects or 3D polygon objects. *2D sprites* (characters, buildings, and so on) can be created either by painting them in a drawing program or by creating a 3D object in a 3D program and then rendering it (the rendered image is used as a 2D sprite). *3D polygon objects* (again, characters, buildings, etc.) are created in a 3D program, and then all the data that describes the object is exported out of the 3D program and imported into the game. The actual textures that are applied to the 3D polygon object are painted in Photoshop or some other painting application.
>
> When painting characters as sprites, you have to paint every view of every animation for the character. When creating 3D characters, you build and paint the character once, and then create its various animations. It's quicker to build a 3D model and animate it than to draw every frame of a 2D sprite. What often happens, though, is that the time saved with 3D models is used to test and tweak the model's animations, textures, and the overall structure of the model.

This in-game screen shot from Myth II: Soulblighter illustrates the amount of detail given to the environment. While not presented here in color, the grass and path each contain a mixture of textures to add additional realism. (Used with permission by Bungie Software Products Prod.)

How challenging is it to paint backgrounds in a 3D environment, such as in *Myth: The Fallen Lords* or *Myth II: Soulblighter*?

> Painting a texture is no problem if you have good artistic skills, though there's a tradeoff between detail and resolution. For example, often you might want to draw every rock of a paved road, but the resolution of the landscape texture isn't high enough to accommodate that type of detail (small rocks would be represented by a pixel or less, thus becoming blurred with the ground around them and possibly a waste of time).
>
> The landscape needs to convey information to the game player and at the same time maintain the same style as the rest of the game textures. Tops of cliffs need to look different from sides of cliffs, to convey impassable terrain. Paths and roads should guide players as to which way they should or could travel. Texture colors for all objects should complement each other and indicate the light source in the world.

To accomplish the stunning visuals seen in a Bungie game, Bernal lists the tools they use to create all the artwork in their PC and Mac games ("[…]along with our internal tools, 'Fear, Loathing, and Vegas'"):

- Photoshop (Adobe)

- Power Animator and StudioPaint (SGI)

- 3D Studio MAX 2.5 and Character Studio (Autodesk—Kinetix)

- MeshPaint 3D (a 3D Studio MAX plug-in from Positron Publishing)

While not required, Bernal says it also may help if an artist is familiar with any of these software applications:

- LightWave (NewTek)

- trueSpace (Caligari)

- StudioPro (Strata)

- Infini-D (MetaCreations)

- Maya (SGI)

- SOFTIMAGE (Softimage Inc.)

- Electric Image (Electric Image Inc.)

- form*Z (auto*des*sys, Inc.,)

- DeBabelizer (Equilibrium)

- Premiere, After Effects, and Illustrator (Adobe)

- Painter (created by Fractal Design, now owned by MetaCreations)

- FreeHand (Macromedia)

So what's next for Bernal and the art team at Bungie? While the West Coast studio is working on *Oni*, a futuristic, animé-inspired 3D action game, Bernal is secretly readying for another game scheduled for Fall 2000. Could it be *Myth III*?

JOSHUA STAUB, CYAN

Joshua Staub is the CG (computer graphics) art director at Cyan, the famous development studio responsible for the best-selling computer game of all time, *Myst*. Staub also worked on the follow-up product, *Riven: The Sequel to Myst*. According to Staub, new game artists should adhere to the following rules:

WORLD CONSISTENCY

" I suppose in the earliest stages of the artistic "design" process, the most important thing to remember is what you might call "world consistency." For example, after creating your environment, make sure your design for the characters fits the environment they live in. What types of clothes would they really wear in such an environment? What type of materials would be readily available in the environment for someone to make their homes with? Wood? Stone? Metal? Carry that through everything that gets designed. Expand the design to include a culture and history for your world.

CREATE YOUR OWN AMBIENT LIGHTING

As far as aesthetics go, the simplest thing that you can do in a scene to achieve realism is to turn ambient lighting off. I can't stress this enough. Basically, turning ambient light off makes your entire scene black, until you add lights to it. Most programs default to having ambient light set to a brightness of 5 or 10 (sometimes it's a scene preference, sometimes it's actually set on an object's material), so that nothing in the scene ever gets completely black. Even if an object is in complete darkness, it "glows" a bit, which detracts from the realism in a scene. [Turning ambient light off] allows you to have ultimate control over the lighting in a scene; all of your shadows will be black until you add light to "fill" them. It means creating your own ambient or bounce light, which is much better than letting the software do it for you. In fact, having a bit of complete darkness in the corners of a room generally isn't a bad thing; it's a way of adding contrast, intrigue, and mood.

TEXTURING

Finally, the most important thing to grasp is texturing. On virtually any model, for every minute I spend actually modeling I spend at least three creating its texture, for several reasons. For starters, using a texture to create the look of geometry is far more efficient than using actual geometry. If you can achieve the same beveled edge, bumpy feel, intricate pattern, etc. using a texture, you put a lot less stress on your computer when it tries to render it. This is vitally important for pre-rendered games (like *Myst* and *Riven*) but even more important for real-time games, where you have so much less geometry to work with. And it looks better! The best way to get a realistic-looking texture is to go and find one in the real world. Take your camera everywhere you go; take pictures of every interesting piece of wood, stone, rusted metal, architectural detail, etc., and use it for the basis of your textures. At Cyan, we have our coveted Raw Texture Library filled with hundreds of patterns and materials that we use to create textures every day, and it continues to grow.

After turning to this massive texture library, what does an artist at Cyan do from there? What tools are used?

There has never been a better time to enter the world of computer graphics, and 3D graphics in particular. Game companies, movie studios, ad agencies, etc. are looking to improve their content with realistic-looking (but computer-generated) scenes, creatures, etc., and best of all, creating it is now affordable. Just before production of *Riven* began, we tested various hardware/software packages and realized that (at the time) the only way to get the speed and quality we needed was to trade up from our trusty Macs to robust Silicon

Graphics workstations and the best 3D/animation/rendering package we could find: SOFTIMAGE. Frankly, the costs were staggering. Today, with personal computers approaching speeds up to 900 MHz and programs like Kinetix' 3D Studio MAX and Strata's StudioPro, you can "play with the big boys" for a reasonable investment of around $5,000. Add Photoshop (the industry standard for photo and texture manipulation) and perhaps Painter and you're well on your way to creating fantastic, realistic images.

The texture for the leather of this chair, left, was actually based on a picture of someone's hand, because they didn't have a good reference photo of real leather. Neat, huh? Right is an early version of the "Firemarble Press" as seen at the end of Riven. The gears didn't make it to the final version, but note the rustic detail to give the impression of the machine's age. (Used with permission by Cyan, Inc.)

 If you're short on cash as a budding game artist, rule out SOFT-IMAGE as a software tool. The latest version of SOFTIMAGE 3D (v.3.9) retails for roughly $10,000 to $15,000 U.S. It requires a Silicon Graphics workstation or a fast Pentium PC running Windows NT [Windows 2000 is also supported]. The SOFTIMAGE official Web site has an impressive gallery of images used with this software tool, plus an archive of techniques and a list of events to attend (www.softimage.com).

BRYCE COCHRANE, EA SPORTS

At the ripe old age of 29, Bryce Cochrane is lead artist for the award-winning *NHL* series (PC, PlayStation, and Nintendo 64 platforms) at Electronic Arts in Canada. Here are his two (Canadian) cents on starting as an artist at a game company:

YOU ARE NOT ALONE

"The most important thing to remember is that you're part of a team," says Cochrane, "and teams don't always get along." He continues:

> You'll be working with programmers, producers, managers, and a whole bunch of other people, and all these people have to do one thing—make a game. Be prepared to fight for the ideas that you think are good; and remember that you have to work with these people every day, so keep it professional.

KEEP YOUR CHOPS UP

Cochrane says to make sure your classical arts skills (drawing, painting, sculpting, etc.) don't fall behind:

> When I look at someone's portfolio, I'm most impressed with an artist who has drawing and painting skills—not just Photoshop touch-ups and 3D model tweaks. I feel I can teach any talented artist how to use a piece of software in just a couple of days, but it would take me years to train him or her to be an artist.

BE PREPARED FOR CRITICISM—FROM EVERYONE

When it comes to criticism, Cochrane says, people can be cruel, so take it constructively and move on:

> Be prepared for it at your workplace from fellow artists and programmers. But the really tough critics are the general public and video game reviewers—they don't care if you only had a day to do a player model, or if the computer kept crashing. They only care about the bottom line—does it look good? I've had reviewers say a game that I've done "didn't get released, it escaped," or this game "was as fun as beating a dead horse." Just learn from your mistakes.

EA Sports' Bryce Cochrane says not to waste time working in the highest resolution; detailed player jerseys like these are 600 pixels wide by 800 long, but when that texture makes it to the game, it's only going to be 120 wide by 160 pixels. (Used with permission by EA Sports)

Cochrane says he uses a number of standard art apps and proprietary software:

> EA has a lot of internal tools for getting the art from the computer and into the game, but most of the art is done in a few programs. For 3D, it's Maya/Alias, Power Animator, and 3D Studio MAX. These are some of the higher-end programs, but you have to remember that I'm only using 1,000–100 polys [polygons] to make player models; you don't need top-of-the-line software to do this. Any 3D package can handle 1,000 polys; just keep it simple, because you're making games and not a movie. For 2D art, Photoshop, Illustrator, After Effects, Painter; and the same stuff applies to 2D art as to 3D art. Keep it simple—and don't waste time working in the highest resolution, because in video games it's more important to have things look good with as little as possible.

EMMANUEL VALDEZ, MIDWAY ENTERTAINMENT

While his name may not be familiar—yet—his work certainly is. If you've ever laughed at the over-the-top animated faces of the fighters in Midway's *Ready 2 Rumble Boxing*, you've seen the work of the very talented Emmanuel Valdez. Currently, Valdez is the lead artist at Midway Home Entertainment Inc.; before creating virtual celebs such as "Afro Thunder," he worked on *ESPN Extreme Games* and *Bio F.r.e.a.k.s.* His future aspirations are to "be in the industry long enough to work on games that blur the line between the virtual world and the real world."

Valdez outlines three key rules for budding game artists to keep in mind:

COMMUNICATION

Valdez says that game art and graphics are the first things most consumers relate to when they purchase a video game. "It is the goal of a computer graphics artist to clearly communicate the overall look and feel of the game in every aspect of the graphics, including the interface, the animations, and the gameplay graphics."

ATTENTION TO DETAIL

According to Valdez, every game artist should set goals in establishing the look of the game. He explains: "Go the extra mile and apply visual stimulation into the art in elements such as color, design, texture, and animation…Computer graphics that scream to be looked at will draw praise from consumers and fellow game developers alike. The added details reflect the artist's and game developer's devotion to creating depth and show effort in making a game."

KNOW WHEN TO SAY WHEN

To balance out the level of detail, Valdez warns that it's important to know when to stop fiddling and fighting with the art. "An artist is never happy with the results and often spends a lot of time trying to experiment and rework the game graphics. Time to develop video games is getting shorter and shorter, and is the single most defining factor in game-art compromises."

Asked to supply examples for these three tips, Valdez replies:

> On the subject of communication, the interface of *Ready 2 Rumble Boxing* revolved around the use of a plain white background and "bouncing" cartoony fonts. Instead of cluttering the screen with "cool" and trendy graphics, we opted to concentrate on clearly defining your options while providing a "fun" and playful feeling, since the game focuses on a comical approach to boxing and less a simulation.

"The animation in Ready 2 Rumble Boxing reflects the attention to detail that goes into creating a video game character," says Valdez. Pictured here is the funkadelic Afro Thunder. Can you dig it? (Used with permission by Midway Games, Inc.)

> With motion-capture, we were able to show the intricacies in human motion that's apparent in our supporting animations to help establish personality and character. Every boxer has a set of introduction, victory, taunting, and fighting animations that establish emotion and distinct personalities.
>
> With *Ready 2 Rumble Boxing 2*, the advent of Sony PlayStation2 and the upcoming Microsoft X-Box are providing the opportunity to create highly detailed, cinema-quality computer graphics. We're creating characters that are more defined and can now have larger animation move sets and an abundance of texture memory, allowing texture map artists to create detail that was once deemed a luxury to pursue. Soon the video game industry will converge with the movie industry and create the next level in entertainment.

Valdez was asked how he achieved the look and feel of the *Ready 2 Rumble Boxing* series. And what tools should budding game artists use? Answers Valdez:

> Every art director or lead artist should always lay down the groundwork for the overall look that they want to base the graphics on. It may be just one idea on a character's costume or an elaborate level with complex lighting and geometry that dictates the flow and coherent quality of the entire game—a sort of "graphics bible." Any divergence from "the look" that is totally unrelated in quality or style (unless deliberately done) is game art that usually doesn't work. A good way to get started is to gather visual information on subjects related to the game or visuals that inspire and motivate the computer artist. Often you can draw from an assortment of influences that spark interesting and visually stimulating impressions, helping the artists convey a message that reflects their overall vision for a game.
>
> A variety of applications are available these days to aspiring computer graphics artists. Essentially, Photoshop for all your 2D needs and a well-rounded 3D application like Maya or 3D Studio MAX are included in an artist's arsenal. The industry is very interested in acquiring artists that have a broad range of talents in many subjects in art, including graphic design, animation, architecture, photography, illustration, and film. A background in one or many of these subjects is crucial in determining if an artist is to be hired in the video game industry.

Other tips on breaking into the video game industry can be found in Chapter 20.

RODNEY GREENBLAT, FREELANCE

Not only has this talented New York–based artist created paintings and sculpture exhibited in galleries and museums throughout the world, he is also an author and illustrator of children's books; director of the Center for Advanced Whimsy (an independent art, design, and music company); and the inventor of Sony's characters for the PlayStation hits *Parappa the Rapper* (1997) and *Um Jammer Lammy* (1999), among others.

Greenblat was asked to list the three most important principles of video game art. His response is as follows:

" ■ Think about the kind of art you really enjoy personally—and do that.

■ Create a personal style. Try to make your art distinguishable [from that of other artists].

■ And forget about reality; just because game machines have the capability to "simulate" real environments and motion, that [still] might not be very interesting. "

How did Greenblat come up with the unique 2D, paper-thin-looking characters in the Parappa and Um Jammer games? "We felt like preserving as much of my original art style as possible. My work is primarily 2D cartoon style, and converting them into full low-res 3D just didn't seem natural. When we tested them as 3D 'cutouts' it really worked." (Used with permission by Sony Computer Entertainment America (SCEA))

" Basically I like to draw. I can easily entertain myself for hours with just a pencil and paper. The computer lured me into a world of technical production, but even though I use common tools used by many designers, the grounding of my work is in drawing. Parappa and all of the *RodneyFun* characters reflect a hand-drawn quality. I think this creates a warmer, more personal look. I hope it's obvious that my creations are linked to me.

Humor is another subject I have always been interested in. I really like to laugh and smile at funny things. Offbeat craziness that makes you think is my favorite. It's the basic premise of projects I have done, like *Wonder Window* and *Dazzeloids*.

> The animation in Parappa is a combination of motion-capture and very clever synchronization. The game software designers created some great programs to make the characters bend and fold to the rhythm. It's the work of many people.

While we're on the subject, where does one look for inspiration? Greenblat says to look at your own personal experience, and make your art out of that.

Any advice on the necessary tools for a game artist in the 21st century? Says Greenblat, "It's best to think of animation as a collaborative art. If you feel you can write and animate, concentrate on one, and 'demo' the other." He provides an example:

> If you love to animate, create short pieces that directors and writers can hook into. If you love to write (create characters and stories), draw, and storyboard, people who love to animate can hook into that.
>
> As far as tools go for 2D, try Director, After Effects, or Flash. For 3D, get the best program you can afford. There are so many now I can't even make a suggestion. Get a flatbed scanner and scan your drawings. Use the computer to make them move.
>
> As far as I know, there are no consumer-priced tools for creating for PlayStation, Sega, or Nintendo games. If you're out to prove yourself on those systems, work it out on the PC first. If your idea is good, it will work on any system. You can tune it for set-top machines later.

For a comprehensive gallery of Rodney Greenblat's work, visit his official Web page at www.whimsyload.com.

GREG THOMAS, SEGA OF AMERICA

In Chapter 8, this veteran console game designer offers a number of programming tips for beginners. In the following passage, he outlines three excellent "rules" for game artists:

> First and foremost, artists are creative people. But they're working within a team, so one of the most important things is to leave your ego at the door, as there are many creative people on a team. What I mean by this is that an artist needs to be able to take criticism well. Often there are many "re-dos."
>
> Another thing that an artist must always remember is that we're creating an interactive experience, not a movie. So gameplay comes before visuals. Often this ends up in cutting frames of animation or slightly degrading elements of artwork, etc. This is very important, though, and artists [may not] fully understand this. If an artist wants to solely focus on visuals, the game industry is not the place for him or her.
>
> Finally, an artist needs to be somewhat technical in understanding what the machine is capable of doing. I've seen some awesome artists end up with work [more average than that of] an artist who has less basic art skills but understands technically what's going on. For example, an artist might be able to

> make a football player model that looks perfectly real but the hardware can't use it. What's better is to have an artist who will make the model simpler at first and then continue to add details until the limits are reached.

Thomas says the tools used to create such stunning games as Sega Sports' NFL2K and NBA2K were Alias Power Animator/Power Modeling, Adobe Photoshop, some motion-capture work (more on this in Chapter 11), and a few custom in-house tools. (Used with permission by Sega of America, Inc.)

NICK COREA, ELECTRONIC ARTS

Nick Corea is a computer graphic artist at Electronic Arts who has added his golden touch to many award-winning Jane's Combat Simulations titles, such as *US Navy Fighters '97* and *WWII Fighters*, where he served as lead artist on both. He joins us here to talk about game artistry, essential tools, and the best way to break into the industry.

EXPECT THE UNEXPECTED

> Computer art is usually produced for new technology. This means that although you think you know how to do something, and how long it will take, things will come up that you didn't expect. For example, say you have to make 6 sports cars for the next 3D racing game. You made 10 cars for the previous version and they took you 15 days each (5 days for the 3D model, 8 days for texture, and 2 days for integration and fixes). Your boss gives you more polygons, more articulation, and more texture. You really know what you're doing this time and you can make these new ones even better. You plan on taking 15 days for each of these.
>
> Later you find, surprisingly, that "more polygons" didn't make it easier to define the forms—it made perfecting the shapes more precise and less forgiving (4 additional days/car). "More articulation" added doors to the car. Getting the doors to sit in their frames correctly became a tedious integration task (8 days burned). Eventually, you added a "closed door" object that disappears as the door opens, and an "opening door" object that disappears when the door is closed (2 additional days/car). Also, the shocks compress on this new version. As they do, the coarse z-buffer of the in-game 3D system causes the tire and fender to flash and trade in an ugly way.

More work with the programmers, who suggest a new and very specific grouping hierarchy that has to be applied to all cars, including those completed (10 days burned). "More texture" meant that the car's textures had to be broken into two pages. A car is now 500 pixels long and 256×256 is max texture size. The "texture page *Tetris* game" (cutting up and reorganizing the texture bits to fit efficiently on the texture page) becomes more difficult (2 additional days/car). Also, your boss doesn't want both sides of the car to share the same texture. "It looks fine when the car's in good shape, but if both sides are damaged," he says, "they shouldn't look the same." There's no room on the texture page for this new extra side, so you have to shrink and re-*Tetris* the textures of three previously completed cars to make room (7 days burned). Then this extra side is added to the task list (1 additional day/car). You thank your boss for telling you so late.

In the above example, a 90-day task on the schedule became more than 150 days. That's three unplanned man-months! Believe it or not, this happens a lot. Some of these items could have been foreseen and some could not have been planned for. (Items like the "more polygons = more time" and "more texture = splitting pages" should have been known.)

When scheduling computer art, try to think about all of the possible problems. Create a detailed task list of every aspect you can think of. (Remember integration time). Then add 20–40% to cover the unexpected. The more unknown the task, the more percentage reserved for surprises.

IT'S OKAY TO COMPROMISE YOUR ARTISTIC VISION

Corea warns, "None of you want to hear this, but computer games are produced to make money." Okay, we know that, but what is he getting at exactly?

The game business is a lot like the film business. Art films don't usually make a lot of money. Game productions have deadlines and they have to sell well. Features and cost outweigh art and expression.

He offers the following scenarios to illustrate his point:

You are creating the enemies for a first-person shooter, to compete with *Quake XI*. The plan is for 20 different enemies to populate 10 levels. They're already designed and sketched out in color. The schedule shows you get one 256×256 texture page and 250 polygons at 10 days each. You break it down to 4 days for the 3D model, 5 days for the texture, and 1 day for integration. Your first beast becomes a masterpiece of flesh and scales, carrying a big iron club. Everyone in the group is totally impressed. The detail is awesome, right down to his sweaty brow. It took you 3 extra days, but man, it was worth it. The second villain is even more impressive. You can't wait to see the screenshots in CGW [*Computer Gaming World* magazine]. By now you're over a week behind plan, and your boss is "giving you the business." You promise to pull your production back on schedule. The third bandit on your list is a turtle with a missile launcher. Trying to make him look as good as the first two is tough. You're able to do him in 11 days, but you had to stay late twice. The programmers have the game running and they call everyone into a meeting to see how it's all looking. When your baddies are onscreen, they look great, but no one can see the amazing extra detail that you put into them. And the game is one enemy short.

GET THE WORK DONE AS FAST AS POSSIBLE WITHIN THE ALLOTTED TIME

In fact, try to get stuff done early. Everybody else on the team will appreciate it—your art director, programmer, producer, and game designer. You can always put more into the work if needed. Don't think of it as "selling out." The best game artists do amazing work in a short time. They know when and how to make compromises. Their artwork might not be perfect, but it's within the constraints of production and the medium. That becomes the challenge: How good can the piece be, given a limited amount of time and effort? It's a skill that will take you far. Any company can spend tons of money for the most beautiful art ever produced, but can they make that money back?

Chances are, many gamers who have launched Jane's *WWII Fighters* have stopped to admire the graphic detail at some point. Corea discusses the 2D and 3D tools he used to create the art for the game.

2D TOOLS

According to Corea, Adobe Photoshop is the industry standard image-creation tool for its power and versatility. Says Corea:

Get to know as much about its tool set as possible. The more used to the tools you are, the more you can be creative with them. (Don't spend too much time on effects filters; too many artists depend on them.) Photoshop was used in *WWII Fighters* to produce the textures and just about every other piece of art. Photoshop knowledge is a must for your résumé.

[Equilibrium's] DeBabelizer is a common image-processing tool. Game developers use it to process large numbers of images at a time. Its batch capabilities are unmatched. It includes alternate color-reduction methods and filters. A collection of images can be reduced to a "super palette" and then all of the images mapped to that palette. The list of useful features goes on and on. Also a good one to have on your résumé. In *WWII Fighters*, DeBab was used to process object and terrain textures.

[MetaCreations'] (Fractal Design) Painter is a wonderful painting tool. It mimics real-world paint, ink, watercolor, paper, chalk, light, etc. Fun to play with, and amaze your friends. Clever artists will find ways to make textures fast and with a very natural feel. Drawing tablet is a must. Many folks paint in FD Painter and then move the results to Photoshop for pixel cleanup and/or processing. Nice one to know.

Microsoft Paint (free with Windows 95/98) is a perfectly fine tool for getting to know pixel art. It has nowhere near the tool set of Photoshop, but it's fine if you want to get to know about painting with light. Try loading icon and game art, and modifying it. Many artists in the business started with DPaint or Mac Paint, similar in simplicity. If you're talented, it will show.

3D TOOLS

Corea believes 3D Studio MAX is a great tool for modeling, lighting, and animation:

> It isn't the best at any one thing, but it is very good at just about everything. 3D Studio MAX is currently used by many game companies for high-end cinematics, in-game 3D shapes, or pre-rendered sprite-style graphics. It's an expensive package, but if an older version of the tool can be "discovered," it would be perfect to learn 3D on. There are several third-party books on using the tool. 3D Studio MAX was used in *WWII Fighters* to build the in-game shapes.
>
> LightWave 3D is another terrific tool. A different "theory" of modeling, but very powerful, and versatile. Some artists swear by its abilities as a renderer and modeling tool. Used on *WWII Fighters* to produce the museum models and images.

LAUNCHING YOUR CAREER

In this final section, Corea gives us the skinny on how artists should break into the gaming industry. There's some shrewd advice here, so be sure to take heed:

> When learning to produce game art, select a subject matter that you really love. The processes that you learn might be *very* tedious, and you'll need that energy to help you complete the work. You'll also have a tendency to add more detail to the piece if you really care about it.
>
> If you're learning 3D modeling, natural forms are very difficult. You might want to stay away from the human form or animals, to start out. Imitating what you see on TV or film (a vehicle from *Star Trek*, for example) is a fine exercise, but don't focus on one subject for all of your work. Art directors see many demo reels and portfolios, and many young artists choose these same topics. Since many TV shows and films are made using computer graphics, however, they are a terrific place to get texture, modeling, effects, and lighting hints.
>
> Examples of computer art are not the only things art directors want to see. They'll want to see pencil sketches, photography, painting, sculpting—anything that shows artistic ability. Important things are lighting, composition, color, form, storytelling, sculpting, detail, wrist (rendering), problem solving, and confidence.
>
> Show an example or two of process. If you've painted a mural, for example, include sketches, color comps, and a picture of the final piece on the wall. On your reel, don't show the same animation over and over. If it's very short, show it twice, with a nice little pause in between. If the AD wants to see it again, he'll rewind. Also, show only your best work. If you have 20 pieces, and you aren't too proud of three of them, you're better off leaving them out. A few bad pieces can put a bad taste in an art director's mouth. And watch the length. If it's long, the AD will get bored, and that's the worst. Make it short and beautiful. Leave 'em hungry for more.

DANIEL THRON, LOOKING GLASS STUDIOS

Since 1995, Daniel Thron has worked at the celebrated Looking Glass Studios as creative director. His latest efforts include the mega-popular *Thief: The Dark Project* and *Thief 2*. Thron created the game's visual style and was responsible for its pre-rendered cut-scenes, as well as logos and box design.

Thron takes a few minutes out of his hectic schedule to share some words with game artists who may seek some direction. He narrows his advice to three pointers:

DON'T WORK IN A VACUUM

Get to know the folks you work with. Your first responsibility as a game artist is to the player's immersion—and the only way to achieve that is by making sure that the game feels like a whole and consistent piece. So get to know everyone on your project—the programmers, the designers, etc. Listen to them, and see what their vision is of the final product. Let these things be the source of your work.

DRAW ALL THE TIME

The second tip is to draw all the time. On paper. And don't just do spaceships. Don't let your skills become sedentary, purely technical ones. Keep a sketchbook, go to life-drawing sessions. Also, *Aliens*, the *X-Men*, and *Star Wars* are all cool, but don't rely solely upon these for your inspiration, or you will only have a derivative-looking product. Flip through art history, architecture, and photography books to get ideas, instead of copying the last issue of *WildCats*. This will keep you fresh, and prevent your game from looking like the next ten on the rack.

TAKE CARE OF HANDS AND HOME

This goes for everyone, but doubly for artists: If you can't move your hands because of carpal tunnel, voice command isn't an option for you. Get information on how to set up better physical work habits for yourself. Taking care of yourself seems like a common-sense issue, but the fact is that the games business is not a culture that promotes this idea; in fact, treating yourself poorly seems to be a "badge of honor" in many ways—working all night long, eating poorly, etc. Go home. Get sleep. Have a life. You will not be productive for long if you grind yourself into the ground, have wrecked wrists, have no friends, and eat from a snack machine.

Pretty straightforward, huh?

TED BACKMAN, VALVE SOFTWARE

Ted Backman is an artist and animator at Valve Software. For two years, he worked tirelessly on *Half-Life*, Valve's debut release. And what a "premier" title that was!

"As home PCs become more powerful, computer game art is becoming less archaic and process-oriented," says Backman. Fortunately, technological advancements in the industry are doing away with once-common constraints, such as having a limited amount of information to work with. Says Backman, "Frequently [artists] were held to a small color set or a very low-resolution image space (usually both)." On *Half-Life*, those things were not a concern. With the power and speed of Valve's graphics engine, Backman could concentrate on traditional problems in art, "without having to worry about painting with only 16 or 32 colors in an image."

So, as the medium comes into its own, the problems of old resurface, namely: a) using good reference material, b) incorporating valid criticism, and c) having the patience to see a piece of work through to its proper state of completion. Let Backman walk you through each of these three crucial areas and take note of examples from his own personal experiences while working on *Half-Life*.

GOOD REFERENCE MATERIAL

Using good reference material is something that many an artist forgets. I can look back on the creation of *Half-Life* and see times when I should have gone to the library instead of banging my head against an artistic problem for hours on end. A good artist knows that he or she cannot rely on invention and fantasy alone. You must continually draw upon real-world things. For example, when creating the skin for the bullsquid, I looked at many things for inspiration. I looked at the markings on sea slugs, the patterns on jungle cats, and many other unusual sources. When you create an image, you're communicating in a visual language; the vocabulary of that language is the shared set of images and experiences that all people know. So if you neglect to include pieces of our shared visual experience, you really aren't communicating at all. In the case of the bullsquid, the coloration should cue most people that this is a poisonous animal. Yellow and black markings are nature's way of saying "stay away."

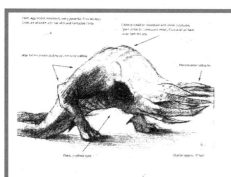

Backman decorated the back of this bullsquid with yellow and black markings to hint that this predatory animal is extremely dangerous—a common color association for most humans. The image on the left is a preliminary sketch of the creature. (Half-Life is a registered trademark of Sierra On-Line, Inc. Images used with permission. Copyright 1999-2000 Sierra On-Line, Inc. All Rights Reserved.)

ACCEPT CRITICISM

> Criticism is an inseparable part of traditional art. From time to time, you must let a trusted friend look at your unfinished work and help you to see problems that you may not have noticed. Very frequently a piece of work will have a handful of features or areas that are the focus of the piece. In developing these focal areas, an artist can lose perspective on the piece as a whole. The role of the critic, then, is to help the artist see what he or she has been neglecting. Use trusted criticism early and often in the creative process; you will have a better finished piece because of it.

PERSEVERANCE

> Finally, having the perseverance to work a given piece of art to its proper state of completion is the most important aspect of working on game art—or any kind of art. You must have the patience to keep working on something, not in a linear start-to-finish mentality, but in a free, explorative manner. When you begin to design a character, for instance, you must make many preliminary drawings so you can capture a range of good ideas. From these you must sort and rework, always keeping yourself open to a change in direction. Many people make the mistake of thinking of the final outcome when they first begin to draw. I can't say enough that you must keep yourself open to new ideas. Make many drawings, throw them away, keep working; you'll arrive at your inspiration when it's ready to come to you. Don't be heavy-handed.

Half-Life had rich, imaginative characters. How were these created? What tools were used in the process?

> To create a new monster or character in *Half-Life*, I would use a range of software, from a 2D package like Photoshop or Painter to the 3D editing environment (3D Studio MAX). The process in terms of the tools goes like this: scan pencil sketches into Painter and continue to work the image with surface quality and coloration in mind, with last-minute adjustments for form also taking place here. Use that color illustration as the basis for your model. Print it out if you can, and keep it close to your monitor.

> Next, you must begin to make the shapes that will eventually become your character. I start with a plug-in for [3D Studio] MAX called Clay Studio Pro [Digimation]. With this plug-in, I can create rough musculature for the parts of the character. I always build the character in pieces or subassemblies. For a human, I'll make a leg separately from the torso, mirror it for the other leg, then continue that kind of process for the arms. Make sure you're looking at external references at this point. Once all the pieces are formed, I'll begin to weld them together and adjust proportions. Usually at this point I have a higher resolution than I'd like, so I'll divide the model along any kind of symmetry it might have and begin to eliminate any unimportant faces.

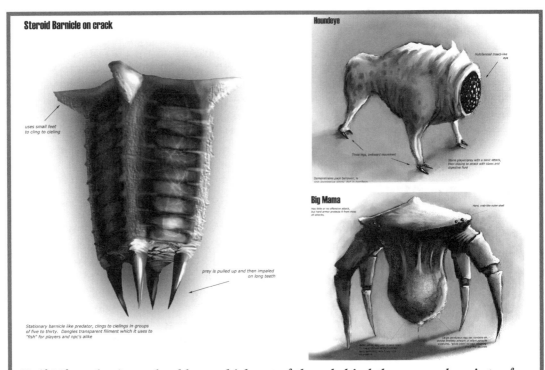

Half-Life enthusiasts should get a kick out of these behind-the-scenes drawings of a few memorable enemies: the barnicle, houndeye, and big mama. (Half-Life is a registered trademark of Sierra On-Line, Inc. Images used with permission. Copyright 1999-2000 Sierra On-Line, Inc. All Rights Reserved.)

> Once you have an efficient model, you can begin to paint the skin for it. I'll use the Windows Print Screen function quite a bit in this phase. I'll select a set of faces in [3D Studio] MAX, apply a mapping plane to them, and then essentially take a screenshot of that selection set and mapping plane and use that as a template in Painter.

Backman says in the future he hopes to be able to "create intriguing game worlds, compelling characters, and engaging scenarios in many game genres." If Half-Life is any indication, we should be seeing a lot more from Backman over the next few years.

MIKE NICHOLSON, DREAMFORGE INTERTAINMENT

We are privileged to have Dreamforge's senior artist and designer with us for this chapter on game art. And you can thank Mike Nicholson for your nightmares—he was one of the driving forces behind the beautiful (and disturbing) PC game *Sanitarium*. Nicholson directs his advice to game designers and how they should approach the subject of art.

FOCUS

> You *must* have a focused idea in your mind on how the game will look. It's *very* easy to see other styles in various media and become influenced by them throughout the development cycle of a game. If you don't have a definite vision and you switch art styles in the middle of the game, the game will become muddled, and conflicting styles will destroy the overall look you wanted in the first place.

TOUGH LOVE

> If you employ an art staff (which is almost mandatory nowadays), it can be difficult to reject artwork—no matter how well done—simply because it doesn't fit within the established look of the game. As you can well imagine, this can lead to heated discussions, and if diplomacy is not applied, to disaster! Very early on, it's *crucial* to get the art staff on the same page, and be willing to except rejection if their style conflicts with the game's look and feel. If, as a designer, you are not artistic, then bring in photos, movies, books, or anything that can convey to the art team what look or feel you want the game to have.

ORIGINALITY VERSUS EXECUTION

And a word to artists:

> Somewhere out there, your artistic vision has already been done before, is being done right now, and will be duplicated after *you* are done! As hard as that is to accept, it's sadly true. The reason I bring this up is merely to point out that this is not uncommon, and that you should stick to your guns. With so many games in development at one time, it's a fair guess that someone else is thinking up the same "brilliant" idea as you! It all boils down to execution. If you maintain a consistent look and feel to your game, then you'll succeed in your goal. We felt that, although 3D engines are the rage, we needed a more 2D, traditional approach to the game to pack in the detail level we wanted.

With Sanitarium, Nicholson and company's main goal in the look of the game was to convey a "Twilight Zone" type of atmosphere throughout the game, with stylized cinematics. (Used with permission by Dreamforge Intertainment, Inc.)

KNOW YOUR LIMITATIONS

"The best suggestion I can give is to know your limitations early on, and work within them," offers Nicholson.

> Careful planning will reduce headaches that can arise from poor palette choices. For example, if you know your main character has to be incorporated into a palette range of 256 colors that must also include background art, set aside a certain range just for the character (say 36) and then reduce the palette of your backgrounds separately. That way, if you find later on that changes need to be made to either the background or the character, they won't have a crippling domino effect on the rest of your artwork.
>
> *Sanitarium* was our best example of good, complex palette work. Luckily, I had the good fortune to work with two extremely talented individuals on the project: Keith Lash and Jason Alexander. Those two guys had the less-than-glamorous task of palettizing entire levels of *Sanitarium* into one 256-color range. That included Max (the main character), all NPCs for the level, their animations, inventory objects, and the sprawling background images. It was tough, but they tweaked the palette until all the individual components worked well with each other, with as little dithering as possible.

Along with most of the other artists that comprise this chapter, Nicholson maintains that Adobe's Photoshop is the best overall art program out there, and it was heavily used during *Sanitarium*'s development. Nicholson believes that the newest version of Photoshop "also has great palette abilities, but we prefer to use [Equilibrium's] DeBabelizer Pro for the bulk of our paletting work."

LOUIS CASTLE, WESTWOOD STUDIOS

For the past 14 years, Louis Castle has worked as a designer, executive producer, programmer, artist, and art director in the gaming industry. He is also one of the cofounders of Westwood Studios, one of the hottest PC development houses in the world. When asked what makes the artwork in *Blade Runner*, *Lands of Lore III*, and the *Command & Conquer* series stand out, Castle responds:

> At Westwood, the artists work with the game designers to make sure the art is appropriate for the game, but the overall look of the game really comes from the artists themselves. You want your artists to feel an ownership of the visual presentation, so try not to dictate things in too great detail. Try to keep lead artists and designer/artists from over-directing your talent. If they tell them *exactly* what to do, you'll never get those moments of raw creativity that every artist should be capable of.

But there must be some focused form to start, no? Don't a game's visuals require some consistency?

"We use concept drawings and storyboards a great deal. The art staff often want to create their own designs, but in general I have found that having specialists in design and storyboarding tends to work better. A concept artist can own the look of a product and maintain consistency, but things get a bit divergent when too many people are doing concept work. If you're doing a large production, you may have to separate out logical sections and have multiple concept artists.

[…]Once the concepts are done and edited, the execution takes place. Again, each artist is encouraged to put [his or her] own ideas into every moment. We have a very flat management structure, so the more competitive members of the staff really only have quality to compete over. I think that helps keep people focused on their work.

My best piece of advice would be to very clearly define your art pipeline and the scope of your product in advance. This includes any technical limitations. You can always choose to let an artist run with an idea once you have a plan, but don't expect someone else to do the hard work of deciding what your game is about, or the scope of the product."

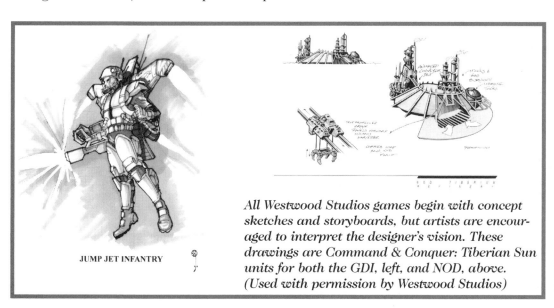

JUMP JET INFANTRY

All Westwood Studios games begin with concept sketches and storyboards, but artists are encouraged to interpret the designer's vision. These drawings are Command & Conquer: Tiberian Sun units for both the GDI, left, and NOD, above. (Used with permission by Westwood Studios)

JOEL THOMAS, RITUAL ENTERTAINMENT

Joel F. Thomas is the concept artist at Dallas' Ritual Studios, the savvy developers responsible for Activision's 3D shooter *Sin* and an official *Quake* add-on pack, *Scourge of Armagon*.

Learning software tools often takes precedence over raw art ability in the gaming industry. Thomas explains why this *shouldn't* be the case:

> One of the most important things for a new game artist to know is how to draw. The better the artist's drawing ability, the better the 3D model will be. It will also give the modeler a chance to spend his time making the model as good as it can be, as opposed to spending time deciphering an amateurish drawing.

Okay, assuming an individual has some genuine artistic talent, what should he or she concentrate on?

> They should also realize how important it is to *know* reality. The world around you is an excellent tool for creating fantastic creatures, weapons, or items. A lot of artists, especially first timers, are afraid to use a reference source, thinking it will make them look less creative. Of course, the exact opposite is true—the less you look at the world around you for reference, the less inspired your concept will be.
>
> Also, it's very important to have some understanding of basic human anatomy. Muscle placement, as well as proportion, is vital in pulling off a realistic character. In all bipedal creatures, regardless of size or sex, the muscles and their placement are unchanging. The artist's aesthetic treatment of them is what brings variety and flair.
>
> An awful lot of aspiring artists learn to draw from comic books. While this has some minor benefits, it can limit your visual effectiveness. Learn the anatomy first and then look to your references. That's how to do it properly.

Thomas discusses what he believes to be a good artist's ultimate downfall:

> THE most important thing to remember is this. Never, ever believe your own press. You may be good, but there is *always* someone better and faster. The way to hold your own in a progressive and often cutthroat field is by getting to know who's out there. Learn from the competition. […] Honor those you admire and help those coming up. Not only will you learn a great deal, but you'll also create some invaluable allies.

You might think that Thomas, as a concept artist, doesn't use a computer as much as a CG artist would. This isn't entirely true, though. He explains:

> Well, first I start with the basics. Sketches. I do all my sketch work in pen and ink. I don't like to use pencils because I feel it makes the mind sloppy. With a pencil, you can lay down lines and erase them over and over until you have a starting point. With a pen, you have to think about what you're doing. The line means more, and you have to think on the run. When I finish with the ink sketch, I'll use a whiteout pen and remove the excess lines to clean it up, or I'll scan it in and start to work toward a final version in Photoshop.
>
> The other way I'll start a drawing is right in Photoshop. I use a Wacom pad with a pen stylus and start drawing. I find that to be a little more liberating because I'm able to resize and move portions of the sketch on the fly. This adds to the spontaneity of the design. From there, I'll finish it up and send it off to the modeler. On *Heavy Metal: F.A.K.K. 2* [Ritual's next game], I'm doing more digital paintings and fully finished images. This is to help everyone involved feel the story and get to know the characters as I see them.

KEVIN CLOUD, ID SOFTWARE

Kevin Cloud is an artist and part owner at id Software, who started way back during the development of the classic *Wolfenstein 3D*. Since then, he has worked on such hit games as *Doom*, *Doom II*, *Quake*, *Quake II*, and *Quake III: Arena*. Cloud takes some time out of his busy schedule to offer his expertise on creating art for games. He starts with the following:

> What's been most difficult for me is following good advice. Because everyone is different, with different talents and different circumstances, each individual must find his or her own way. But if you want to make sure you're going in the right direction, watch what other successful artists have done. So I guess my first bit of advice is to be a student of life. Always maintain your interest in the world around you and be open to understanding and learning from the successes and failures of other artists.

The golden rule for being successful at anything is to do something you enjoy. I know it's a cliché, but that's because it's true. And this is a rule everyone tends to forget and relearn. Computer game artists need to like computer games, enjoy working with a team, and being part of a process. As a computer game artist, you'll be subject to creating things that other people design, making art that follows bizarre restrictions, and working under criticism from others. But if you love making worlds for people to play, you'll enjoy doing it all. Certainly tons of game artists are ambivalent about games. But from my experience these people are rarely happy doing their jobs. And trust me, you can't be successful unless you're happy. Happiness is a requirement for success.

The next stage, says Cloud, may sound fairly obvious, but it tends to be overlooked quite a bit in today's gaming industry. Cloud admits even *he* has learned this way:

> Next, learn to be an artist, not just a computer artist. I graduated with a degree in political science. And although I took several art classes, I wish I would have taken more. I'm proud of my ability to learn new tools and take advantage of what's available to make the best art I can in the quickest possible time. But I've had to pick up on many fundamental skills as I've gone along. If I started out today with the skills I had in '85 when I started at my first job, I probably wouldn't be hired. The day of the hacker/computer artist is over. Either by reading books or going to school, learning the fundamentals of art is imperative. Color theory, animation, the human form, painting, drawing techniques, composition, and so on aren't skills you pick up on your own.

So what's someone to do outside of school? What are the tools to learn first, and best?

> Get set up at home with your own system. You can't learn to be a computer artist unless you spend time on the computer. Buy an old system and find public domain or used software on the Internet. Take the bus or bike to the university, but get a computer. You don't need the best software or system to get started, but you do need something. There are many good programs out there, but you won't make a mistake by learning two programs—Photoshop

and 3D Studio. If you can't find an old copy of one of those, then get any 32-bit art program and polygon-modeling tool you can afford. Other alternatives to having a system at home are using a friend's system, using the school's, or getting a job (any job) at a place that has computers. Some suggestions are a copy/fax place, a service bureau, or a small computer store. Although I applied for the position of artist at my first computer company, Softdisk, they said they didn't need an artist. Instead I took the job of answering technical support calls. It took time to convince Softdisk they needed an artist, but in the meantime I got a chance to talk to their programmers and use their computers and software to learn.

Cloud says once you've got some schooling and real-world experience behind you, the next step is to focus on being a better artist. He expands:

Avoid the millions of distractions that come your way. This is a lesson I have to learn over and over again. Although I never stop doing art, I often get sidetracked on other projects, and about a year later my head explodes. I have to learn once again that I'm an artist because that's what I like doing. Throughout your career, remain focused on being a better artist. Seek out more art resources—books, good Web sites, art collections on disk. There are tons of biographies about artists featuring their art and stories about their lives. Every artist should spend some time following the lives of [his or her] favorite artists and emulating their styles. You'll learn so much just by trying to match the style of a great artist, and in the end you'll gain the flexibility to create your own style. Look for discussion groups on the Web, and don't be afraid to ask questions. And ask the advice and comments of your coworkers. Surround yourself with positive people who are interested in becoming better artists. Focus on improving your art skills, and opportunities will be out there for you.

Finally, the extra piece of advice is don't be afraid to move, take risks, and strive to be great. If possible, finish the project you're on—but if a better opportunity comes along, take it. Try to surround yourself with positive and talented people. Working with the best will always bring out the best in you. And keep in mind that your future is in your hands. Don't settle for being just one of the many. Do something different to set yourself apart. Develop a style or technique that is your own.

The last words from Cloud are to "try to make a difference on any project you're on, so that people will know that your hands have been on that game." Amen to that.

 For further reading, the Gamespot e-zine in the U.K. has published an excellent feature story on art and animation in today's computer games. Point your browser to www.gamespot.co.uk/pc.gamespot/features/atoa_uk.

BRAD CROW, ENSEMBLE STUDIOS

Our third Texan artist in a row (purely coincidental!) creates breathtaking images for a different genre altogether. Brad Crow is the lead artist at Ensemble Studios, a hot young design company currently creating strategy games for Microsoft. Past products include the best-selling and award-winning *Age of Empires*, *Age of Empires Expansion: The Rise of Rome* and *Age of Empires II: Age of Kings*.

Interestingly, almost all artists in this chapter are offering very similar pieces of advice for newcomer game artists, regardless of the game genre. Crow is no exception. He suggests artists adhere to the following principles:

> ■ **Have a clear vision for how you want your game to look.** This allows you to make a lot of progress in the early stages of production.
>
> ■ **Be flexible with your vision once production is underway.** Allow the look of the game to grow and evolve to something different from your original vision. Constantly reevaluate your vision and allow new techniques, technological advances, and, most importantly, the artistic strengths of individuals on your team to influence and improve your original vision.
>
> ■ **Look for and evaluate artistic criticism from anyone.** You want your game to be played by many people—no sense in limiting your market by following a style of artwork that only a small percentage of potential players like. If someone has a problem with how a part of your game looks, evaluate those concerns for any validity; many others may share the same view.

Currently Ensemble Studios is primarily a 3D Studio MAX house. On *Age of Empires*, most of the game was completed in 3D Studio, Release 4, before the very end of the project, when 3D Studio MAX was released. For *Age of Empires II: The Rise of Rome*, Crow and company used 3D Studio MAX for the art and animation.

JOE KOBERSTEIN, RAVEN SOFTWARE

Joe Koberstein has been in the industry for six years (eons, for the gaming biz!) and is currently employed at Raven Software as an artist. The last product shipped out of their Madison, Wisconsin, studios was the well-received *Soldier of Fortune*, published by Activision.

On advice for newbies, Koberstein is straight and to the point:

> ■ The computer is just a tool, like a pencil or brush.
>
> ■ Learn to draw—it's the foundation to great art (computer or not).
>
> ■ Don't take your work too personally; you're not a fine artist. Your vision may not coincide with the director's, but the people who are going to succeed in this industry are the people who are able to adapt. This industry changes on almost an hourly basis; this is very exciting, but can also be very intimidating. Just keep your ego in check and choose your battles carefully.

Koberstein agrees with most of the game artists in this chapter on what tools to use when creating a hit game:

> Photoshop and 3D Studio MAX have become the standard in paint programs and they're great tools to learn. The learning curves are a little high, but these programs are very powerful and offer a lot. Advice to anyone learning Photoshop: Use layers. They allow you to take chances you normally may not take in traditional art. Advice for 3D Studio MAX: Read the tutorial and start small. Don't attempt to make the *Star Wars* trilogy for your first project.
>
> Creating breathtaking images on the computer or on canvas, it all comes down to practice, and lots of it.

MIKE NICHOLS, SURREAL SOFTWARE

Psygnosis' *Drakan* was one of the most highly anticipated action/adventure hybrids of 1999. Mike Nichols is the VP, founder, and creative director at Surreal Software, the developers for the game. Nichols offers budding game designers and artists his views on the three most significant considerations of game art. He decrees:

COMPOSITION

> When it comes to painting the landscape, the designer, just as an artist, needs to be aware of the composition. Make sure all your tiles are placed correctly. You wouldn't want a solid dirt texture next to a solid grass texture without some sort of transition.

AESTHETICS

> It's important that a designer have some aesthetic sense. A mountain isn't just a textured, cone-shaped object. This is where you really need to be an observer of shape. Even before a single texture is painted, a shape should convey its meaning and emotion. In *Drakan*, the landscape is every bit as important as the characters. Some might even say it's the lead character.

SWEAT THE DETAILS

> Attention to detail. It makes all the difference in the world, and the player appreciates it. Personally I'm more interested in games that *involve* me in the world, not just put me in it.

As a reference point, Nichols discusses *Drakan* in light of the aforementioned points:

> *Drakan* includes some of the most expansive landscapes ever seen in a video game. When designers approach a level, they need to have a clear understanding of the flow. How does it start and carry the player through the level to the end? Make it "feel" correct. The shape of the level has everything to do with how the player will explore it.

In *Drakan*, the designer must shape the polygons to reflect a "natural" scene. An artist creates a set of tiles that the designer uses to paint on the landscape. These tiles are a series of pictures that, when put together, can create the illusion of an expansive landscape. *Tile* also refers to the method of how these bitmaps are created. They're drawn to tile or mesh with each other without a seam. We use this tile method because we don't have the memory to create the HUGE bitmaps it would require to texture our vast landscapes.

To achieve these detailed and expansive landscapes, a number of tools are used by the Surreal art team.

FOR 3D ART: 3D STUDIO MAX AND SOFTIMAGE

"MAX is a solid choice for creating games for several reasons," says Nichols.

It covers all the functions you need in a single package and it's cheap. Unfortunately, one of the drawbacks of a product like this is you get what you pay for, and not everything works the way you'd like—and that can get frustrating the more you use the program.

It's also an easy tool to learn on. For a beginning 3D student, it's a snap to get into and start learning your way around the world of 3D.

SOFTIMAGE, on the other hand, is a much more robust tool. It's our number one choice for character animation. It offers advanced animators the control they need to take their animations to the next level.

FOR 2D ART: PHOTOSHOP

"It's a standard," agrees Nichols, but "a good standard. Photoshop is one of those tools no 2D artist can do without. It has an easy interface and powerful tools to help you create beautiful textures." He continues:

By no means are [these programs] the end-all of computer artistic creation. There are many software packages that are worthy of note. It really comes down to what's familiar and has the ability to grow as you do. A tool that can't do what's in your head is worthless.

For anyone creating art—or wanting to create art—on the computer, it's important to stay true to your vision and not let the software dictate how your creations look. Take control of your software; don't let your software control you! It's always worth the extra investment in time it takes to really get on the screen what's inside your head. Many times I see artists let the program dictate what their artwork looks like, and it's a good explanation why a lot of artwork out there looks the same—and why many who are not artistic think they can be.

In the next segment, Nichols covers what he believes is "one of the most important skills you can have as an artist…the one you learn first and never master."

UNDERSTANDING SHAPES

> I don't mean having the ability to draw any shape in the world. I mean having the understanding and the observation skills required to create meaningful and expressive shapes. Master artists spend their lives trying to conquer just one aspect of shape—the human figure, still lifes, landscapes, etc.—and not one will ever tell you they have truly mastered it.
>
> So relax and enjoy what you create, and, as my art teacher used to say, "Always look around for inspiration, whether it be in a colleague's work, nature, or a bottle."

TONY LUPIDI, EA SPORTS

Tony Lupidi is the art director for Scoreboard Productions, an in-house division of Electronic Arts that concentrates on the *March Madness* basketball simulation series for EA Sports. Lupidi has worked on art and animation for a number of games, TV programs, and movies, so he has some lessons to share with newbies to the industry:

> Never become so enamored with the latest whizbang technology as to allow it to overwhelm the fundamentals of your craft. For example, just because the latest 3D cards can do real-time bump mapping with reflect maps doesn't mean all worlds must now be shiny and bumpy. The basics of design and composition apply to game art as much as any other genre of art.
>
> Use pencil-and-paper sketches to do your conceptual designs. Don't design directly on the computer. It's much faster and more efficient to do loose sketches for conceptual work. There's less of a tendency to become emotionally attached to a sketch, and this makes it easier to develop your design.
>
> Create the best art possible within the performance limits of your game engine. *People will never see your work if the game is too sluggish to be fun to play.* The art should enhance the player's experience, not hinder it. Game art is inevitably a compromise between quality and performance. Games ship all the time with this problem.

Lupidi comments on creating art for sports games, and how it may differ from other genres:

> Sports games are a type of simulation, and as such usually try to mimic the broadcast television experience. Everyone knows what a televised basketball game looks like, and [you] have a set of expectations as to how the game should look. Since no one has ever seen 16-armed purple aliens, as an artist you can have more "wiggle room" in your interpretation when making a non-sports title.
>
> I liken developing sports games to automobile design. Like cars, sports games usually come out annually, since they're tied to the sports season. Like cars, these games undergo incremental technical/artistic improvements each year. Like cars, people appreciate a continuity of design from year to year. Like cars, a nice, polished, clean design and great performance will satisfy your customer.

Does Lupidi use the same tools as other artists in the gaming industry? More or less, he confirms:

> Our current platform for developing games is Windows 98/NT 4.0, and our software tool set consists of 3D Studio MAX 2.5 for 3D modeling/animation/texturing; Character Studio 2.x with the Promotion plug-in, Photoshop 5.0, and [Adobe] Illustrator 8.0. And a whole bunch of internally developed tools.

And for people looking to break into the biz? Any secrets or strategies?

> For someone just getting into the [industry], the *Doom/Quake/Quake II* engines are very extensible and modifiable, and are an excellent way to get your feet wet. You can create/replace everything in the games—worlds, textures, models, sounds, etc. The tool sets to create whole new games based on these engines are available for free (or very little) on the Internet. The other nice thing about this is that there are many very helpful people willing to give advice to newcomers. Many people who work professionally in the industry got their start doing this. Some of the tools people use are Paint Shop Pro, Worldcraft [www.worldcraft.com], and QPed [planetquake.com/qped] to manipulate *Quake* archive files.

In closing, Lupidi predicts "we are right on the verge of the emergence of a new, interactive form of mass media." Some of the technologies driving this new media are real-time 3D display hardware as a consumer technology (à la Voodoo or TNT cards), broadband networks (cable modems for the masses), and continued development of faster and cheaper computers. Can you say, "There's never been a more exciting time to come aboard"?

TOBY SIMPSON, CYBERLIFE TECHNOLOGIES

As creative director for the Creatures life simulations, Simpson discusses his approach to computer game art and how it may differ from that of other disciplines:

> In order to achieve self-consistency, Creatures products are theme-based rather than story-based. We define history and geography first, so that it's possible to create self-consistent stories out of that theme. This makes it easier to be creative within the correct scope, as it's akin to having a style guide to stories. This is the sort of approach Tolkien used to create his Middle Earth stories—design the world first that you're going to set your stories in, as it saves a hell of a lot of time!
>
> Initially, we work out where any given product fits into the theme. This automatically defines the geography, and we then follow the Creatures style to sketch scenes within the new world. Eventually, we'll have designed the entire environment and its contents (both living and non-living) on good old-fashioned paper. This then gets scanned into the computer and placed in the product so that development can take place, while the artists gradually fill in the drawing with rendered or hand-retouched computer artwork.

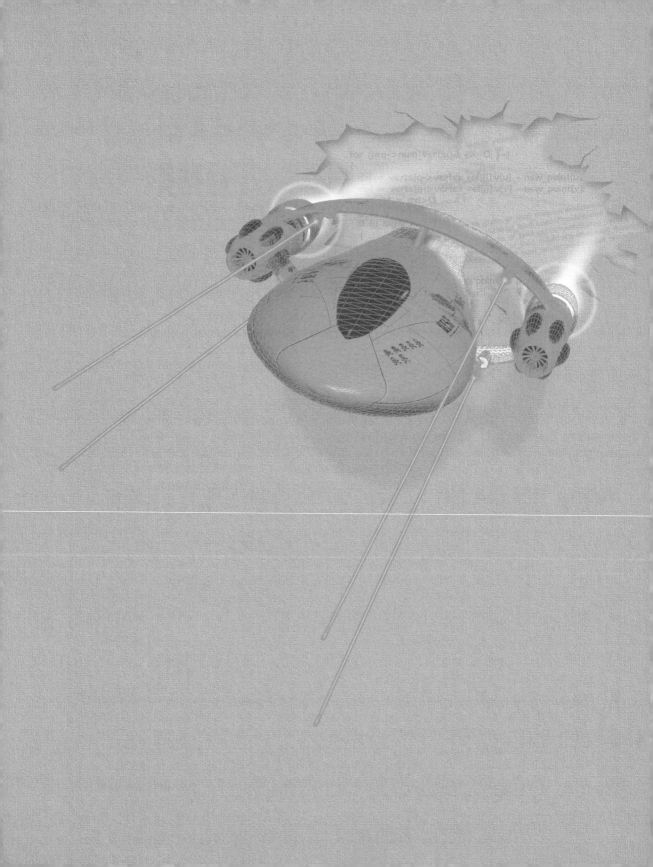

CHAPTER 11
ANIMATION

Working hand-in-hand with art is animation, since objects rarely remain static throughout a game. Quite simply, the purpose of animation in games, movies, or television programs is to simulate life through frames of movement. Animation in games is even more challenging, because it must synchronize with the program's artificial intelligence to mimic life (or machinery) and must be easily controlled by the player at the same time.

 There is also pre-rendered animation that's not interactive, such as the Silicon Graphics (SG) intro movies and cut-scenes that are popular in PC and console games today.

This chapter focuses on both classical *2D animation* (sprite-based) and *3D modeling* and *rendering*, using traditional key framing, motion-capture, and other proprietary and alternative animation techniques. We will hear from—and soak up some pointers from—a number of animators in the industry, representing companies such as Electronic Arts, Sierra, Valve Software, Treyarch Invention, Ubi Soft, and Ensemble Studios.

TED BACKMAN, VALVE SOFTWARE

Ted Backman, an artist and animator at Valve Software in Kirkland, Washington, offers his *savoir faire* on game animation and alludes to his work on the megasuccessful and critically celebrated game, *Half-Life*. (For Backman's views and advice on game art, see Chapter 10.)

Backman believes the three most important things a new game designer should pay attention to are how the animation affects behavior (artificial intelligence), using reference material, and being especially careful with timing. The following is an elaboration on these precepts.

ANIMATION AND AI

 Character animation in *Half-Life* is one portion of the character's outward expression of its artificial intelligence (AI); the character may also display its AI through sound cues and visual effects. What I mean by this is that the nature of the character animations can drastically change creature behavior—things like how fast they run, how often they attack, how quickly they recover from taking damage are all controlled by the length of the associated animation. You can do great harm to the behavior of the creature if you aren't careful in planning the relative speeds of the above-mentioned actions. It's very important to create an ongoing dialogue with the engineer responsible for creating the AI.

USE REFERENCE MATERIAL

Motion, especially human motion, is a familiar thing to all people. If you create an animation of a human and are not extraordinarily careful to re-create all the subtle gestures and weight shift, it will stand out. People can spot bad human motion very easily. The only way to make believable human motion is to look at how people move on video and in pictures.

Backman says one especially useful source is a book by Eadweard Muybridge, *The Human Figure in Motion* (1989, Dover Pub.).

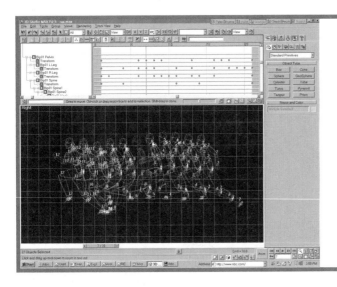

As seen here in 3D Studio MAX, Backman referred to a side view of a person running from an Eadweard Muybridge book to help create natural and believable human motion. (Used with permission by Valve Software)

WATCH YOUR TIMING

Another thing I see all too often is for someone to make an animation start to finish and then never go back over the motion to add subtlety and good timing. I spend more time working on timing and subtle motion than any other part of the animation process. Some general rules I like to follow: a) animate from the center of mass out; b) start with broad motions, then add smaller motions; c) slide keys around until the timing is correct.

But how does Backman achieve the fluid animation in games such as *Half-Life* and make it look so lifelike without using motion-capture technology? And what's the advantage to using a skeletal animation system? He answers:

> The main difference between *Half-Life* and its competitors was the amount of data available to the animation engine. In most cases, artists will set up a bone system in a character they want to animate. The difference with *Half-Life* is that the engine actually looks at the position of the bones every frame, instead of the position of all the points on the mesh every frame. Since there's much less data to describe each frame of animation, you can have more animation for the same memory cost. This means you can animate at 30 frames per second as opposed to the traditional 10 frames per second. This yields a smoother and more realistic final animation.

Backman offers a few tips for newbie game animators, and discusses what software tools he uses:

> There are really no tricks to creating good animation, though; you just have to be patient and observant. Don't settle for something that looks okay; keep working until you're absolutely satisfied. Having a solid process helps—this means having a clear idea of what you want when you start, acting out the motion in front of a mirror, looking at video. And keep working on something, even though your deadline is in one week. The only way to get good motion is to work very hard at it; there are no shortcuts.
>
> The only real tip I can offer is to look at whatever you wish to animate, figure out where its center of mass is, and map out where that center of mass will move in relation to the feet. This is really how all motion occurs.
>
> The tools I use to animate are fairly standard: 3D Studio MAX and Character Studio [an Autodesk/Kinetix plug-in for the 3D Studio MAX modeling package]. There is little out there in the way of plug-ins or great tools to simplify the process.

Backman is currently working on the art and animation for Valve Software's upcoming *Team Fortress 2*.

PETER AKEMANN, TREYARCH INVENTION

Peter T. Akemann, Ph.D., is a managing member of Treyarch Invention and project lead on the critically acclaimed *Die by the Sword* by Interplay. He created the VSIM system that drives most of the animation in *Die by the Sword* and *Limb from Limb*. The fluid and lifelike animation in these products garnered attention from the gaming community.

Is there a difference to working on game animation instead of television or movie animation? What's best remembered by a junior game animator? Akemann offers three pieces of advice in this area: Responsiveness (to control) is more important than smoothness; response (to action) is at least as important as the action itself; and 80% of the appreciation will be for 20% of your effort (most likely the easy 20%!), so accept this in advance and don't sweat it when it happens.

When asked how the VSIM technology works and why it's advantageous for games, Akemann responds:

> VSIM was a new take on the animation process, wherein we used a mathematical model to simulate the character motion, rather than pre-scripting it via a key framed or motion-captured sequence. It was something less than a full physical simulation, but at the same time it was better because it focused on the game it was created for (*Die by the Sword*) and was more amenable to artist tweaks than a complete simulation would have been.
>
> Most animators are familiar with IK (inverse kinematics) from animation tools such as 3D Studio MAX, etc. Here they use an algorithm to orient a jointed body in a natural way to achieve a desired end result (e.g., the foot on the ground, the hand on the object being reached for, and so on). VSIM takes this a step further by not only generating an end result, but the motion required to get there. It's largely a combination of IK targeting and a muscle/joint physical simulation underneath.
>
> It's the inevitable progress of every technology that automation always increases. However, far from putting animators out of work, these technologies should allow them to achieve even better results with greater ease than was previously possible.

According to Akemann, the animation was mostly created in their in-house Move Editor, a kind of virtual motion-capture studio for VSIM characters. "That and loads of text files with parameters. Not really the ideal path," admits Akemann. Traditional key framed animations (for the non-interactive movie segments) were created in 3D Studio (not MAX) by Interplay's Mike McCarthy. "I think [3D Studio] is a good tool for an intro-level animator, and you can probably get it *really* cheap, since it's old," suggests Akemann.

Akemann closes by saying, "The best piece of advice I can offer is, when you're thinking about animation, try to envision the mathematical structures implicit in the motion. That was definitely the root of the inspiration for VSIM and *Die by the Sword*."

 Rotoscoping is another form of 2D/3D animating, but it isn't often used in games. In this process, actors are filmed and then animated over top. *The Last Express* from Brøderbund was one such PC game to use this technique.

Midway's Emmanuel Valdez (*Ready 2 Rumble Boxing*) and Sony's Rodney Greenblat (*Parappa the Rapper*, *Um Jammer Lammy*), offer insight in Chapter 10 on how they animated characters in each of their hit games.

JEAN-FRANÇOIS MALOUIN, UBI SOFT

As art director at Ubi Soft's Canadian headquarters in Montreal, Jean-François Malouin has worked on the Playmobil lineup for kids. Similar to the response from Peter Akemann at Treyarch Invention, Malouin reminds readers about the key difference in creating animation for games, as opposed to other entertainment media such as TV and movies:

> In the video game industry, an animator has to be conscious of the fact that a player will control the character he's animating (if it's the main character) or at least interact with it (if it's a secondary character).

Since every game has its own pace, its own way of interacting with the environment, and its own character design, the animator doesn't really have a specific recipe to follow. Some games will allow animation with more frames for greater realism, but usually games need animations with very few frames that allow a better reaction time by the enemies in the game, or better control over the main character. Personally, I think that game developers—especially in 3D—are not paying enough attention to that.

FUN OVER REALISM

Nintendo's *Mario 64* is cited by Malouin as having good animation, yet not necessarily adhering to the rules of nature:

The appeal of *Mario 64* is largely due to the control of the main character. It's even fun just to run around without actually playing the game! If the basic principles of animation had always been followed to animate Mario, the game wouldn't have been as good. For example, Mario can bounce unrealistically far or jump extremely high. The animators did it so Mario would be a very lively and dynamic character, and we understand everything he does.

Malouin says that, although this doesn't necessarily hold true for all game styles, animators should aim for a drastic change in the pose of the character, for a dramatic effect.

wrong   good

A bad "receiving hit" animation, left, and a good one. The bad one is not extreme enough because it takes more time to understand it and the message is less clear. (Used with permission by Ubi Soft, Inc.)

UNDERSTAND THE CHARACTER'S ACTIONS

"Since he doesn't have a lot of frames to illustrate a certain movement, the animator has to concentrate on the message he wants to give," advises Malouin.

The player has to know what's happening to the main character because he *is* the main character. The player also has to know what people/creatures/objects around him are doing. If you hit a bad guy, it has to show right away; if there are questions about it, it's no good. If there are strong currents in the water, illustrate it—otherwise the player will expect to swim in a lake and will be frustrated to miss whatever move he wanted to do. Both these aspects are very important because the interaction between the player and the machine depends on them.

Once you're conscious that what you do as an animator will influence the player's mood, I guess the most important thing is to stay deeply interested in your game. Teams that love their game usually produce better products, because they're motivated.

What tools do Malouin and his team use to create animation in Ubi Soft games? Aside from some proprietary in-house software, they use the standard 3D Studio MAX and 3D Studio (www.autodesk.com). Malouin urges animators who are really serious about their work to practice lots of classical 2D animation as well, whether on paper or computer.

SCOTT EASLEY, ODDWORLD INHABITANTS

Scott Easley is the senior animator for Oddworld Inhabitants, and has been there since its inception as a world-class development studio. Outside of Oddworld Inhabitants, Easley won two Emmys for the animation and also writing of a television commercial in 1994, and he also did the first computer-rendered poster for Marvel Comics in 1995.

Easley believes gameplay takes precedence over everything—including animation. He explains:

The game designer should create the best game he can, without the bias of including animation or graphics because it looks cool. It should be the last thing on his mind, as opposed to the engaging gameplay. We make stuff look sexy, but it should be restricted to when useful, not gratuitous. Imagery is all about conveying a clear story, as in movies or commercials—or gameplay, in video games. If I see one more chrome gargoyle on a demo tape, I'm going to throw the TV out the window. Tell me a story with animated blocks—and no spinning camera.

Conveying the message is premier, and in most cases, people get drunk on the imagery possibilities.

When asked what makes the animation in *Oddworld: Abe's Oddysee* and *Oddworld: Abe's Exoddus* look so good, and whether he can share any tricks or techniques, Easley replies:

There's no secret pill or "Do It" button. It's simply studying motion as best you can with the same basics afforded the Disney folk or Max Fleischer. Look at the Eadweard Muybridge photographs and copy them, verbatim, into a skeleton you've made to have the same proportions in your software. Make the skin of your character out of boxes. Stay away from anything other than a boring block model so you can concentrate on motion alone. Study it from every angle, make it work from every angle. If you haven't spent an exhausting week on a 12-frame walk, you don't care as much as the guy who will get hired. Period.

> Study motion, as we all do, every day. Look at the silent body-language conversation between two people whom you see across the street or through a window. Are they in love, in hate, indifferent? Do extremes at first—the grasp of subtlety will come with time.

What are the tools Easley uses to create breathtaking animation? Is there any motion-capture in the *Abe*'s games?

> I can't stress enough that while motion-capture has its place for football or sports games, I believe it atrophies the natural abilities of the animator. It's a quick way to impress friends and family, but you really didn't animate it—you *maybe* modified existing data.

 Game animators on the Internet should get to know the Usenet newsgroups comp.graphics.animation and rec.arts.animation. Newsgroups serve as interactive bulletin boards for like-minded people.

MAARTEN KRAAIJVANGER, NIHILISTIC SOFTWARE

As lead artist on the popular *Vampire: The Masquerade – Redemption* (Activision, for the PC), Kraaijvanger offered quite a bit of advice on static art in Chapter 10. Here, he gives some pointers for budding animators:

> - I love working with [Alias|Wavefront's] Maya since it's flexible and gives great feedback.
>
> - Don't get caught up in how good your model looks. If you want to animate, create a low-polygon model, attach it to a simple model, and start animating it. Don't worry about rendering pretty images. Your focus should be on giving the characters life and making the viewer care about what they do.
>
> - Try to infuse a simple story into your animation. A simple gag or story will give your character a purpose and can really drive the animations of the character.
>
> - Buy Preston Blair animation books, cartoon animation, and film cartoons. These are the best and most-used animation teaching books in the industry. Every animator has them around for reference.
>
> - Don't create an epic for your demo reel. You will never finish it, and incomplete work doesn't look as good as something that's polished and finished. If you create an epic, odds are that the quality of the animation is not going to be high throughout the entire piece. Focus on something short and to the point, and really make it shine.

Kraaijvanger advises, "Study animated movies and break down what they're doing. Focus on timing, staging, movement. What actions makes the personality shine through?" Pictured here is a scene from Nihilistic/Activision's Vampire: The Masquerade – Redemption.
(Used with permission by Activision, Inc.)

VANCE COOK, SIERRA SPORTS

Having developed golf simulators for close to a decade, Vance Cook has not only witnessed the evolution of sports game animation, but has been a significant participant. In fact, Cook worked on the coveted *Links* golf series at Access Software before leaving to start his own company, Headgate, Inc. (later to be sold to Sierra, where Cook is today).

Right off the bat, Cook explains why character animation is a challenge to achieve:

> Human motion is one of the most difficult things to do because everyone knows exactly what normal movement looks like and they can pick out even the smallest problems. Our golfer characters can move in hundreds of different motions, but the golf swings were by far the most difficult. I believe that the golf swing is one of the most scrutinized motions in sports.

Vance Cook says he wouldn't recommend trying to mimic human motion without motion-capture. If cost is a factor, libraries of motion are becoming more cost-effective. Notice the female golfer's underlying polygon mesh and her appearance with texture skins, above. The image below is a rendering of the same character's swing from PGA Championship Golf: 1999 Edition. (PGA Championship Golf 1999 Edition is a registered trademark of Sierra On-Line, Inc. Images used with permission. Copyright 1999-2000 Sierra On-Line, Inc. All Rights Reserved. PGA Championship Golf is a trademark owned by The PGA of America.)

Therefore, Cook and company used motion-capture in *PGA Championship Golf*. But that's not an easy task in itself:

> We went into the studio with a couple of actors, talented motion-capture directors, and a script of several hundred motions. We left a week later worn out. After the studio session, the work was just beginning. Many weeks of editing were still ahead of us.
>
> We spent quite a bit of time heading down a non–motion-capture path before giving up. We attempted to mathematically represent a golf swing. We were able to basically put a body through its motions, but soon learned that basic motions are nowhere close to looking realistic without all of the numerous subtle motions one makes.

 Motion-capture (or *mo-cap*) is the process by which the movement of a real object (usually a person) is captured and mapped onto a computer-generated object. Unfortunately, many novice game animators don't have the opportunity (or budget) to learn how to use mo-cap because of the limited number of available studios and its enormous expense.

When it comes to striving for realism, is there such as thing as going too far? Cook responds:

> I think it's possible to make a game *too* realistic. Many games are attempting to simulate real-world challenges. I think you've become too realistic when you start modeling the bad aspects of a real-world challenge. In golf, when we start making you book tee times and find your lost ball in the woods, we may have gone too far. I think it's hard, though, to make a game too realistic-*looking*. There are certainly some stylistic reasons to not look realistic, but most of us are chasing the realism dream in our games.

 Acclaim's wrestling game, *WWF: Attitude*, featured a whopping 400 motion-captured moves! Acclaim has a motion-capture studio in their Glencove, New York, studios.

EVAN HIRSCH, EA SPORTS

Evan Hirsch is the mo-cap guru at Electronic Arts in Burnaby, British Columbia (outside of Vancouver). This location houses EA's only motion-capture studio.

"First of all," begins Hirsch, "motion-capture is just another medium; it's not a substitute for good animation, nor is it a substitute for a good game." Hirsch explains the two different kind of motion-capture:

> *Optical motion-capture* uses triangular calculations in the form of markers we place on a human body. Each marker becomes the third point.
>
> *Magnetic motion-capture* is easier to set up, but the subject must wear wires, a harness. Obviously, this isn't too safe for stunts.

Markers are taped on a character's joints and other key areas. With optical motion-capture, the points between the markers are inferred by the computer; with magnetic motion-capture, you get position and rotational information directly from the input device itself. "EA uses optical motion-capture because it gives us better data. Roughly 20 to 30 markers," says Hirsch. (Used with permission by EA Sports, Inc.)

So does Hirsch prefer motion-capture technology over more traditional animation for the same reasons as Vance Cook?

> The benefits are as follows. For one, it's an easier and quicker way to get animation into a Silicon Graphics machine (these workstations are used for all of EA's animation editing). Second is the human subtleties it picks up—the natural *warmth* of human motion and expression. It keeps this flavor in the game. For example, in games like *FIFA*, subtleties such as shaking or wincing.

Hirsch reminds gamers that mo-cap doesn't do it all for you:

> You have to be a good animator, too. Motion-capture is just a tool, and what you do with that data is everything. Because mo-cap is so expensive, you have to do your pre-production: have your move lists, directions, details, and lots of rehearsal.
>
> Gamers are the ultimate judge. Boot up a recent copy of *Triple Play Baseball*, *NHL Hockey*, *Madden NFL*, *FIFA*, or *NBA Live*, and notice how lifelike and fluid the animation is.

BRAD CROW, ENSEMBLE STUDIOS

We heard from this savvy lead artist in Chapter 10, where he offers techniques on game art. Here, Ensemble Studios' Brad Crow gives budding animators a piece of advice. According to Crow, the most important aspect of character animation is one's attention to detail—or lack of it:

It's the most subtle motions or gestures that bring character animation to life. We're all experts on how the human figure moves because we experience movement and study it every day of our lives. So it makes perfect sense when somebody looks at digital character animation and can determine that "something isn't right" with the movement. The hard part is figuring out what small detail we left out of the animation that gave it away.

Currently, Ensemble Studios uses 3D Studio MAX as [our] primary animation tool. In fact, *Age of Empires* was completed in 3D Studio, Release 4, and it wasn't until the very end of the game's development cycle that 3D Studio MAX was released.

Crow says he achieved the fluid movement of the humans, animals, and weapons in *Age of Empires* and *Age of Empires Expansion: The Rise of Rome* by studying movies and books, and he "actually acted out movements sometimes, in order to catch all the details."

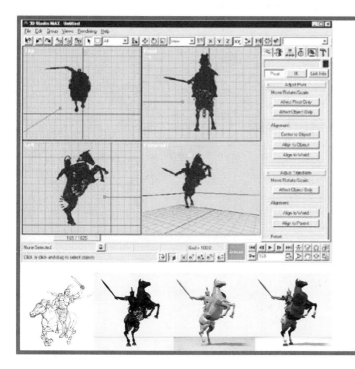

Ensemble Studios' Brad Crow offers these rare screens for Age of Empires fans. Above, a horse animated in 3D Studio MAX. Below, the same unit in transition from sketch to wireframe to final rendered image. (Used with permission by Ensemble Studios, Inc.)

NOTE *Stop-motion animation* is the cinematic process by which an object is brought to life by filming one frame of film per increment. This classic animation technique isn't found often in games, but a perfect example is DreamWorks Interactive's *The Neverhood Chronicles*.

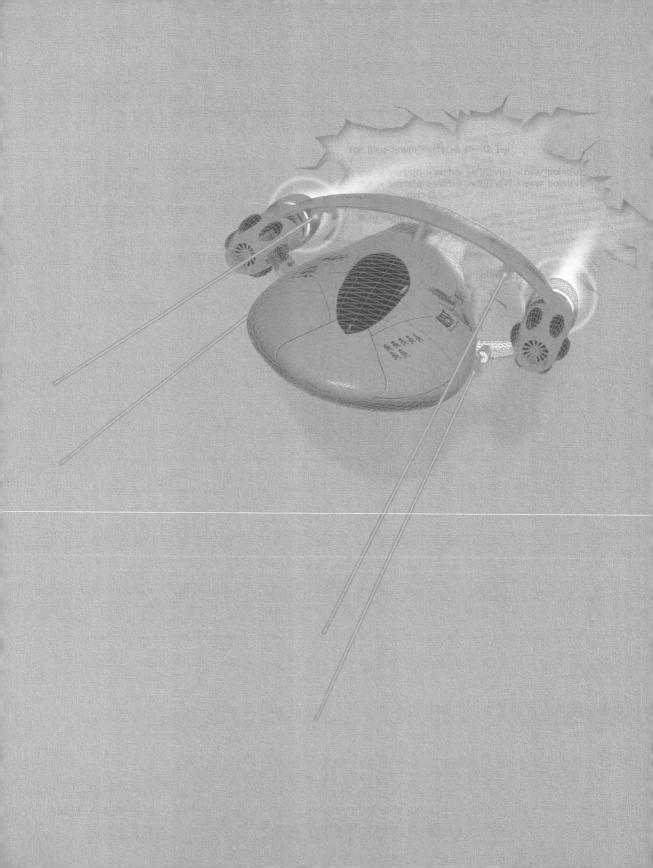

CHAPTER 12

THE ALL-IMPORTANT USER INTERFACE (UI) AND GAME CONTROL

While it's likely that you'll find some conflicting advice in areas of this book on art techniques, level design suggestions, or the best way to animate a character, it's universally recognized that a bad *user interface* (*UI*) in a game can be its own demise, regardless of how good the content is.

While compiling this book, a number of designers were asked if there was any truth to the gaming industry adage that a user interface can make or break a game. For the most part, the designers agreed that it can indeed *break* a game. They were also clear that if the game itself isn't good, the UI certainly can't save it. Nonetheless, it's one of the most significant areas of game design that's often over-looked.

Keep in mind that there are two distinct areas of a game's interface. The first is the menu screen, or *shell interface*, used mainly to set up video or sound options, configure controls, launch a multiplayer game, access saved games, exit to a desktop, and so on. The second is the *in-game user interface*—that is, what the player sees on the screen while playing.

Control is another important aspect to game design, and many lump this area into user interface because they're closely related. Far too often, the player pays $50 for a game and can't control the character or machine (or "camera" angle of the action, in some games). In other cases, the control layout is fine, but the objects onscreen don't respond quickly or smoothly enough.

Many gamers would agree that the sports game genre seems to have the most difficulty when it comes to a good in-game UI. With team-based sports games such as football, soccer, basketball, or hockey, part of the reason is that the gamer must have all the players accessible at all times, and must choose which player(s) to control. To complicate the issue even more, in some cases it's also necessary to give commands to other team members. I'll cover team-based sports games in a moment, but first let's look at sports games where there's only one character to control—such as in golf, skiing, or boxing. These sports games have their own sets of UI challenges.

VANCE COOK, SIERRA SPORTS

Vance Cook, lead designer on Sierra Sports' *PGA Championship Golf 1999 Edition*, answers the question, "How important is a good UI in a sports game such as golf?"

> A good user interface is important in all software products, not just games. A great game must achieve a high level of quality in all areas: shell interface, in-game interface, graphics, playability, game balancing, storyline, etc. If any one of the pieces is weak, the game will be weak. It's not very useful to discuss which is the most important. With that said, you definitely don't want to get your in-game interface wrong. That's where the rubber hits the road. That's where the customer connects to your game.

When discussing the different kinds of UI, Cook recommends adhering to the following guidelines.

SHELL INTERFACE

Cook suggests managing the choices for the customer in the menu or shell screens of the game (not gameplay). This is done to prevent the player from being overwhelmed with too many choices. "Present only the relevant information for a given context, and hide everything else. If making a certain choice removes the possibility of other choices, make it obvious that those choices are no longer available by graying them out or hiding them," says Cook.

All the pertinent information the golfer must know before taking a swing is accessible to the right of the player...nothing more, nothing less, and just the right size. (PGA Championship Golf 1999 Edition is a registered trademark of Sierra On-Line, Inc. Images used with permission. Copyright 1999-2000 Sierra On-Line, Inc. All Rights Reserved. PGA Championship Golf is a trademark owned by The PGA of America.)

IN-GAME INTERFACE

"Different games must use different philosophies, but many games are faced with the challenge of needing to maximize the viewing window while still allowing the user to perform many interface actions," believes Cook. When creating a new game, developers are often faced with the battle between hiding interface choices to keep the viewing screen clean, and making them easily accessible:

> It's easy to hide interface choices if you don't care about how many steps the customer must take to perform an action. It's also easy to make interface actions very accessible if you don't care about how much screen real estate you take up. Game developers are always coming up with creative ways to balance these two requirements. You first have to determine the proper balance between screen real estate and accessibility for your particular game. Categorize your interface actions into two groups: items that require frequent access, and items that require infrequent access. Items requiring frequent access must be only one or two steps away. (A step could be a mouse click, a mouse drag, or a keystroke.) Items requiring infrequent access can easily be hidden behind an Options button or icon.

PGA Championship Golf 1999 Edition is used as an example of how the in-game user interface can be split up for functionality versus aesthetics. According to Cook, there are four main areas to the UI:

> 1. The aiming and swinging interface is located right by the golfer and requires only one step.
>
> 2. The shot information is grouped together in the lower-right corner of the screen. The user can see all of the necessary information without taking any steps. The user also has the option to click on existing pieces of information for more detail if he or she wishes. For example, the most important distance is the distance between the ball and the hole. The distance readout is always displayed. Sometimes it's nice to know what the elevation difference is between the ball and the hole. This information is accessible by clicking on the distance readout.
>
> 3. Frequent interface actions are grouped together in the lower-left corner of the screen. These actions are things like selecting a club or setting up a creative shot. These actions are one or two steps and located close to the golfer for easy access.
>
> 4. Less frequent actions such as finding the flag are available by first selecting the Options button in the lower-left corner of the screen. Only choices that are currently available show up when you click Options. An extra step of clicking Options is required for all of these actions, but it's worth it because the Options button takes up very little real estate and these actions are not frequently needed.

GAME CONTROL INTERFACE

Cook says game control is unique to every product; therefore, it's difficult to give advice on it as general rules:

> But this is often where the real magic of a game is created. Depending on the game and game genre, there are currently a few choices available for game control: mouse, keyboard, joystick, gamepad, steering wheel. Others are available, but most developers stick with these basics in order to make the game playable by most people. You have to look at these choices and decide which device or combination of devices is most similar to the real-world challenge you're trying to create. In most games, these devices are not even close.

> In the case of golf, none of them are close, but we've chosen to go with a mouse swing because it has the most parallels to a real swing. Customers can control the path and speed of the golf club. This gives us the ability to simulate very soft and very hard shots. It also gives us the ability to introduce side spin (hooks and slices) when the mouse slides sideways out of the straight path. Finally, it allows us to simulate missed hits when they don't return the mouse to the place where it started.

One of the key points Cook makes is that game control is one of the most important aspects of the immersion factor:

> You must make your customers feel connected to the game. The control devices must become an extension of themselves, and with time become intuitive. Anything you do to remind them they're playing a game will detract from the enjoyment of the experience.

Golf games exemplify this statement, says Cook, and he offers his own game as a reference point:

> My competitors may not agree with me here, but I believe that a delay between when you've performed a swing action and when the golfer starts swinging greatly detracts from the experience. In *PGA Championship Golf*, the golfer moves at the same time you're swinging and he or she moves in the same path that you move your mouse. If you slide to the right or left, the golfer will move the club outside or inside of the swing plane.

As Cook touches on, UI and game control may be a personal thing, so many developers of PC and console games are now allowing players to customize these settings to their liking. For instance, in many 3D shooters and simulations, it's possible to select or de-select what information is given onscreen with the tap of a key or click/drag of a mouse. Similarly, most games, in all genres, allow players to remap keys/buttons to their liking, or assign hotkeys or macros. Give players the option to make the game their own.

In closing, Cook reminds readers that, above all else, "You must attempt to immerse customers into the experience—make them forget who they are and make them believe they're the character onscreen."

Vance Cook's advice on menu or shell UI is applicable to all other game genres as well. Note the simplistic design for the Options screen in Interplay's Baldur's Gate, an award-winning RPG developed by BioWare. (Used with permission by Interplay Productions)

SCOTT ORR, EA SPORTS

Having designed, produced, and executive produced at EA Sports for a number of years, Scott Orr understands the necessity of extremely good UI. Some of the award-winning titles and series under his belt include *Madden Football*, *NHL Hockey*, *Andretti Racing*, *NASCAR Racing*, and *NCAA College Football*.

According to Orr, the key word in interface design is *simplicity*. He elaborates:

> Gamers are notorious for not reading manuals. If they can't quickly and easily get into a game, they'll become frustrated and look to other games for satisfaction. If they can't immediately play a game and have some measure of success, they'll put it down and look elsewhere. As a result, designers should spend a considerable amount of time working on the menu interface as well as the game controller interface. This is not as easy as it seems, given the incredible number of options most sports games have on the 32-bit and PC systems.

It's one thing to say designers *should* spend time working on a simplified UI, and it's another thing to spend the time and effort to do it. Are there any examples at EA Sports? Orr responds:

> My goal in the *Madden 2000* product is to literally be able to pick a team and kick off with no more than two button presses in Arcade mode, and to greatly reduce the number of menus gamers need to navigate in Sim mode. Our designers have spent a lot of time trying to simplify the menu interface without sacrificing the number of options available to our customers. It's an ongoing process, and one that benefits from focus group testing and feedback from our customers and reviewers.

When it comes to controlling the game, Orr says the very same principles apply as with creating a good UI—it all boils down to player intuition and simplicity:

> Look at arcade games for inspiration, since they're usually the best examples of game interfaces [that are] easy to understand and play. Look at other products in the same sport to see if there are *de facto* standards to adhere to. For example, if the top-selling game in a particular sport uses the X button as the Action button, you should probably use it too, since gamers are already used to it that way. That familiarity makes it easier for them to play the game and get hooked by it sooner.

"Finally, create a controller interface that works with your AI," concludes Orr. Instead of using three different buttons to accomplish three different moves, Orr says to map them to one button and use the AI to trigger the right move based on the context of the action (which Orr and the folks at EA Sports refer to as *context-sensitive artificial intelligence*). "That way, you get all the benefits of the multiple moves while keeping your controller interface simple. Of course, this only works if your computer AI is topnotch—but when it works, it works great."

MARC AUBANEL, EA SPORTS

Marc Aubanel is the producer of the celebrated *FIFA* and World Cup soccer series for the PC, PlayStation, and Nintendo 64 platforms. He works at the beautiful Electronic Arts Canada studio in Burnaby, British Columbia.

Most of Aubanel's suggestions pertain to soccer games, because this is what he spends all of his time on, and he leans more toward the control aspect of UI. Keep in mind that in most cases his advice could be applied to other team-based sports games and the challenges faced when designing a good UI for them.

CAMERA VERSUS CHARACTER CONTROL

At EA Sports, Aubanel says, they have always opted for *camera-relative control*, as opposed to *character-relative*. That is, if the player presses on the down button on the controller, the player onscreen moves toward the bottom of the screen. If the game was created to move relative to the character, and the down button or arrow was pressed, the character onscreen would move downscreen according to the character's perspective.

According to Aubanel, the camera-relative option is much more intuitive to the player, unless the game opts for a first-person perspective view of the action, so it's as if the gamer is looking out of the character's eyes (as with many shooters). "In *FIFA* and other soccer games, you don't see the world through the player's eyes, so, in my opinion, it's a mistake to go with character-relative control in a third-person camera game." The only exception is when the player has the ball and is targeting the object (such as the net in soccer); then it switches to character-relative targeting so the player can aim where he or she wants the ball to go.

The players in EA Sports' FIFA 2000 are contextually sensitive, so they may act differently depending on the situation or context. However, the player doesn't have to learn additional controls. (Used with permission by Electronic Arts, Inc.)

KEEPING IT SIMPLE

Another challenge when working on UI for soccer games is allowing the player to have quite a bit of control while at the same time keeping the control method simple and intuitive. Aubanel explains:

> The goal here is to try to get the kind of complexity you want in a soccer game—like "deeking out" opponents or changing speeds on the fly as in real soccer games—while at the same time maintaining simplified control.
>
> The way we get around that is to *contextualize* what's happening onscreen; therefore, the program determines the desired or logical act in question. For instance, if you want to get the ball from someone and you choose to be a bit rough in getting it, you can push or elbow him if close enough; but if [you're] five feet away, the player may slide down to steal the ball. It's the same button command, but it's contextually sensitive. It's the same when you're scoring on the net. If you kick the ball toward an open net, it may look different than if you're farther away or if the goalie is in the net. This is to make it more realistic. Other examples are some of the special moves, such as the "air play" moves. The program will figure out which header or chest play move to perform. Instead of "diving headers" or "volleys," the player may "bicycle kick" the ball [backward] if he's 180 to the net. So this aids in the challenge to have many moves, but with few buttons.

Aubanel provides solid advice for game designers who may be working on UI and control:

FOLLOW YOUR ASSUMPTIONS, AND TEST THEM

"Focus on whatever your assumptions are when it comes to a user interface, and take into account other people's preferences," recommends Aubanel. "The only way to do this is to study other people playing them, with as many testers as possible. For the *FIFA* games, it's not unlikely that we'll get 60 testers to play the game and tell us what they prefer, and I remember I had to put my opinions aside in one instance because the majority had spoken. While I say 'go with your assumptions,' it's also important to remember the game isn't just for you, so ensure that you're testing."

EXPERIMENT WITH IDEAS, AND TEST THEM

"Here's another fine line," says Aubanel. "Don't feel like you have to stick with what others have done before you [in that type of sports game], but don't go crazy by adding too many new things, either." Aubanel says to experiment, but test out these changes with a large testing group. When it comes to game control and soccer games, Aubanel admits they have a long way to go in this area.

GIVING THE BEST OF BOTH WORLDS

The last piece of advice from Aubanel is very specific to soccer games and other team-based sports games. For non-control UI issues, Aubanel says that the farther the camera is from the gameplay, the easier it is to play, since you can see everyone on both teams. But with more players on the screen at the same time, it can be a frame-rate issue, so you have to find that balance.

Aubanel says that many players like to play the game with the close camera option to appreciate the art and animation, but it isn't the best way to play the game, since not all characters are in sight. Therefore, to give the game the best of both worlds, *FIFA* games and other EA Sports titles often show close-ups and other scripted segments up close for dramatic effect when the ball is out of play (after a goal is scored, penalties, and so forth).

Be sure to also flip to Chapter 9, where Marc Aubanel discusses artificial intelligence issues and solutions in sports games.

BRUCE C. SHELLEY, ENSEMBLE STUDIOS

Creating a well-oiled user interface for console and computer games is not just a priority for sports game designers. The venerable Mr. Bruce Shelley of Ensemble Studios offers plenty of words of wisdom in Chapter 2 on real-time strategy game design, but here he discusses at length the importance of a solid user interface:

> The user interface in a computer game is second in importance to gameplay, but still requires a lot of thought and planning because a poor interface can kill player interest and sabotage the product. No one plays a game because it has a cool interface, but people will quit a promising game because it's hard or confusing to play. The game designer's principal role is to create entertaining gameplay. The creative effort provides positive reasons for people to experience a game. The purpose of the interface is to make that entertainment accessible. Players must be able to get the information they need out of the game and then insert their play choices quickly. The ideal interface does this seamlessly, with minimum effort and frustration on the player's part. At a minimum, the interface should get out of the player's way.

In the following discussion, Shelley draws examples from the award-winning and best-selling *Age of Empires* series to support his advice.

AGE OF EMPIRES I

> Part of the reason this first game from Ensemble Studios was so successful was because it was relatively easy to get into and play. The entire game can be played using only the mouse. More experienced players can improve their play by mastering keyboard commands and hotkeys. We redesigned our interface several times, trying to improve the flow of information and commands back and forth. At Ensemble Studios, we believe that the first 15 minutes of play are crucial. If a new player is not engaged and having fun within that period, he or she may stop playing and never come back. The starting situation and mouse-driven interface of *Age of Empires I* minimized the risk of losing newcomers. Tony Goodman, Ensemble Studios CEO, came from a business software background and had learned the importance of a good interface. He stressed that continually during development.

AGE OF EMPIRES II

> [This game] won an award from *Computer Gaming World* magazine for best interface in 1999. We added a number of features that improved the interface for both casual and hardcore gamers. For example, more detailed unit commands

(patrol, guard) and stances (aggressive, hold ground) were things hardcore players wanted. Casual gamers never see them. The idle villager button (and keyboard command) was a welcome new interface feature for both groups. For this game, the designers at Ensemble Studios reexamined the entire game and how it was played, looking for ways to give the player more information and for ways that players could be more precise in their interactions with the game. These improvements had to be generally intuitive and not obscure. Such layers of interface mean that the basic game is accessible to newcomers and there are ways for experts to distinguish their play through great command of the interface.

How can a budding game designer aim to achieve a great user interface? What tips and/or techniques can he offer? Says Shelley:

1. Make some general plans and set goals for the interface. For *Age of Empires I*, for example, we wanted a mouse-driven interface, with optional keyboard commands. Being able to play a complete game while only using your mouse hand was an important goal.

2. Prototype early and adjust the interface through play. Be aware when aspects of play seem slow or frustrating, and find ways to smooth that confusion.

3. Continually get input from fresh players during development. People who have been on the game for a while become unaware of frustrating interface components. New players often spot a weakness right away.

4. Watch absolute newcomers try to play your game without any coaching or instruction. Note where they fail or have difficulty. Find ways to remove those problems. For *Age of Empires II*, Microsoft conducted extensive usability testing with absolute newcomers. Ensemble Studios designers watched those tests. One result was the creation of the learning campaign that leads newcomers through the play of the game step by step.

SHIGERU MIYAMOTO, NINTENDO

Nintendo's superstar game designer Shigeru Miyamoto was asked how important game control and the user interface are in relation to action/arcade game design. He responds:

I am always conscious that I should make games as entertainment commodities rather than as artistic works.[...]For players to enjoy themselves is taken for granted, so we [consider] the games from the players' point of view. The most understandable example of this consideration should be the *controllability*. When I am making games, I make them with my utmost care so that my own thoughts can be reflected in the games through the controller. Perhaps this is something that evokes players' emotional sympathy.

Read more of Miyamoto's approaches to game design in Chapters 2, 4, and 8.

RICHARD "LORD BRITISH" GARRIOTT

Lord British is one of the pioneers of the computer gaming industry, best known for his mega-successful *Ultima* role-playing game series, developed at Texas' Origin Systems. To date, there have been over a dozen sequels, plus countless other products including children's cartoons, comic books, novels, and songs. *Ultima: Ascension* is the ninth installment in the prestigious series (not including the second *Ultima VII* game), released in late 1999.

During the writing of this second edition of *Game Design: Secrets of the Sages*, Garriott announced that he was leaving Origin Systems, a company he cofounded nearly twenty years ago. He hasn't revealed where he is off to next, but the gaming industry is anxiously awaiting his return.

When asked his opinion on how a good UI should be implemented, Lord British declared that everyone has a different religion on this subject, but that he adheres to two main principles when creating games.

FAMILIARITY

"The more familiar the UI is to the player, the better," says Lord British. When elaborating on this "first hurdle," he says that this doesn't always mean it's the better interface, but the more familiar:

> Right now, the Windows 95/98 interface is familiar to many gamers, with the left and right mouse-click functionality. I'm not necessarily endorsing it, but more people can relate to it. If the game has a UI that resembles or borrows from Windows 95/98, the gamer will be better off because of its familiarity.

THE BACKHOE OPERATOR SYNDROME

The second principle stems from the familiarity factor and should be something every game designer strives for—making the UI so intuitive to the gamer that he or she becomes one with the onscreen avatar. Lord British calls this one "the backhoe operator syndrome." After familiarity, the key is to make the UI (from a dexterity standpoint) almost nonexistent, so the player no longer considers it an interface at all. Lord British elucidates:

> You know those backhoes on construction sites—those machines that dig dirt? After a period of time, the operator of the backhoe no longer thinks about how to tip the bucket and scoop up the dirt—he just does it.

Lord British explains that a good UI is the same thing. The player should *be* the avatar onscreen and not *control* it. Hey, after all, Origin Systems' motto is "We create worlds."

To achieve this level of immersion, Lord British insists that game designers should create as simple a UI as possible, without forfeiting the player's options. He explains that he learned this the hard way throughout the evolution of the *Ultima* series, and recalls how the simplicity factor has come full circle:

> With *Ultima I* on the Apple II, there were only a half dozen commands, such as north, south, east, and west movement, and hotkey letters that started with the first letter of that function, such as *s* for save and *l* for load. Then things

got more complicated as the series matured. By *Ultima VI*, every letter meant something—with no exception—so I had to stretch it. For instance, I had to use the *z* key to bring up stats because the *s* key was allocated for the save function. The problem was that I needed to add more commands, so I collapsed the keys into meta-commands, such as the word *use* to unlock a door or light a torch. Therefore, this noun/verb interface evolved, expanding into five graphical icons in *Ultima VII*, but it was still a two-step effort because you had to click on "talk to" and then click on a character, for example. Because the gamer had to do these two things, it was still difficult to get that "backhoe" effect. In *Ultima VIII* and *IX* [*Ascension*], it's one direct command and all mouse-driven. The program now determines what the player wants to do. For example, if there's an NPC [non-player character] on the screen and you want to talk to him, all you have to do is talk to him. If your sword is drawn, he'll fight. The UI is now contextually sensitive, with visual clues to confirm that this is indeed what the player wants to do before doing it.

Lord British has streamlined the UI in Ultima: Ascension to make the game more intuitive to the player. (Used with permission by Origin Systems, Inc.)

In Lord British's opinion, the UI we use today could have been done 20 years ago, but we needed to go through this stage of reorganization.

TOM HALL, ION STORM

Game designer and ION Storm cofounder and vice president Tom Hall has been preparing the PC gaming world for his ambitious 3D role-playing game, *Anachronox* (pronounced uh-NAH-kruh-nox). He has also worked on some of our industry's beloved classics, such as *Doom* and *Wolfenstein 3D*, at id Software.

It comes as no surprise when he points out—as do the other designers in this chapter—that a good UI is critical, and must be both easy to use and intuitive. "If you ship a demo and it's hard to control, people will get frustrated and go, '&#*@ this!' and never play it again, no matter how cool the content is," says Hall.

So how about some examples of games with good or bad UI?

Games I've worked on with great interfaces are *Commander Keen in "Goodbye, Galaxy!,"* *Wolfenstein 3D*, and *Doom*. They're simple and elegant. You don't have to search around for keys, or memorize the manual. You just go and do. I like all the LucasArts adventure interfaces. It's very clear how to do things.

> I don't want to go off on competitors' games, so two games that I've done that shipped with bad interfaces were *Keen Dreams*, whose menu was a horrible, non-intuitive nightmare, and *Rise of the Triad*, whose version 1.0 controls were unwieldy. By the time version 1.1 fixed them, we'd lost all those people who said, "&#*@ this!" You only get one chance at converting a player to your side; don't blow it. Have fans of your genre play it and be brutal.
>
> Your mom should be able to play the game intuitively, even if she doesn't like it.

BRAD MCQUAID, VERANT INTERACTIVE

We've heard about creating an effective user interface for single-player RPGs, but are there any differences for massively-multiplayer games? McQuaid is the producer for *EverQuest* and the *Ruins of Kunark* expansion pack; he agrees the UI is of critical importance, and touches on why *EverQuest* succeeds in this area:

> I think a good user interface is very important both short and long term as it relates to a player's experience and use of the game. Short term, a good interface doesn't overwhelm a new player with too much information or with operations and functions that aren't intuitive. Long term, a good interface is very user-customizable, allowing the player to configure the interface as it relates to his or her style of gameplay and what functions and commands he or she uses most often.
>
> I think *EverQuest* (*EQ*) did a decent job with our user interface, but there's much room for improvement in both areas. One aspect of *EQ*'s interface I'm most proud of are what we call "hot buttons," which is functionality that allows the player to set up a series of buttons representing commands and/or functionality that he or she uses most often. It's quite similar to customizable icon bars in popular spreadsheets and word processors. Credit goes out to Bill Trost, *EQ*'s lead game designer, for the idea and implementation.

RON GILBERT, HUMONGOUS ENTERTAINMENT

Tom Hall cites LucasArts adventure games as excellent examples of easy-to-use interfaces. Having conceived the idea for the *Monkey Island* series, one of LucasArts' most popular franchises, Ron Gilbert can take much of Hall's compliment, along with other adventure game designers at LucasArts, particularly Tim Schafer.

Gilbert left LucasArts to start Humongous Entertainment, a software company that quickly became one of the leading developers for kids' games.

In Gilbert's opinion, a good UI is critical: "Nothing gets me more frustrated than a game with a bad user interface." But a good interface design isn't as easy to create as one may think. Explains Gilbert, "There's a fine line here. The UI has to be simple and intuitive for the gamer, but at the same time you want to give the gamer a lot of choices, a lot of power. Very seldom these days is a UI so wrong, but there are a few games that have a poor user interface." As examples, he points to *Diablo* as having a very good interface, along with *Total Annihilation: Kingdoms*, a fantasy real-time strategy game Gilbert worked on.

ALEX GARDEN, RELIC ENTERTAINMENT

"Depending on how you look at it, every game ever made, every piece of it, is just a glorified UI," says Alex Garden, CEO of Relic Entertainment and lead designer of Sierra Studios' mega-popular PC hit, *Homeworld*. "The whole purpose of the game/UI is to help convey an idea to the player in the least obtrusive way possible." Since every game is essentially UI, what are some good or bad examples, and why? Garden responds:

> Take *Quake*, for example. Running through the world quickly becomes second nature to the player. The elements of the game don't take away from the game experience in any way, because each one is concise and easy to understand. There are a plethora of great ideas out there that fall short of the mark, because elements of the game/UI are too cumbersome to be "transparent" to the interactive experience. One poor example is *Star Wars: Rebellion*. *Rebellion* is a fantastic idea, but it's so buried under menus, screens, conflicting input systems, and information that it's almost impossible to play!
>
> The best UI is no UI. That's my motto. If you don't *have* to have a menu pop up, then don't. Wherever possible, use natural, real-life-based interaction to convey information. For instance, if you have a choice between popping up a window with some text on it or speaking the text out loud, it's always best to speak the text out loud, and provide a backup written transcript for the player to review.

For a great read, Garden recommends finding the chapter on UI in *Computer Graphics: Principles and Practice, Second Edition in C* by Foley, van Dam, Feiner, and Hughes (Addison-Wesley, 1996).

RANDY SMITH, LOOKING GLASS STUDIOS

In his three years at Looking Glass Studios, arguably one of the most sought-after and respected game design companies in the United States, Randy Smith's job responsibilities have included game design, mission building, and scripting for *Thief* and *Thief 2*.

Here, he discusses the role of a solid user interface and its place in the overall game-design process:

> The vast majority of work in video game development goes into the simulation and how the game communicates the state of the simulation to the users. In general, the only channels a video game uses for this communication are the pixels on the screen and the audio from the speakers. Developers toil endlessly to make sure the output of these channels is as rich and flawless as possible, and critics nit-pick the smallest inadequacies. This is all well understood and accepted.
>
> The user interface is the inverse of that communication. It's the sum of the users' channels to communicate to the game. With it, the users exert control over the simulation and express their intention. As the simulation's input bottleneck, the user interface inherently limits the users' ability to merge with the game, and therefore, just like the simulation's output, it should be as rich and flawless as possible.

> With a good user interface, the users can concentrate on their simulated presence in the game environment, which is (presumably) where the gameplay is centralized. As the quality of the user interface decreases, the users must spend more time thinking about their input channels to the simulation and less time enjoying the simulation itself. A poor user interface can limit the users' ability to express themselves to the point where they have a negative experience, even if the underlying simulation and its output are truly fantastic.

This book also features some discerning advice from other key Looking Glass Studios personnel, such as Tim Stellmach (Chapter 7), Marc LeBlanc (Chapter 9), and Daniel Thron (Chapter 10).

SID MEIER, FIRAXIS GAMES

When creating his latest game, *Alpha Centauri*, the UI was an important consideration to Sid Meier, and he tried to cater the UI design to both newbies and gaming veterans of the turn-based strategy genre:

> I wanted the game interface to be easy to use, with everything accessible with the mouse, but I also wanted keyboard shortcuts. In *Alpha Centauri*, we realized people wanted to learn more about the information onscreen—units, terrain, buildings—so if you right-click on a given area, it will tell you more information, in depth.

MATT HOUSEHOLDER, BLIZZARD NORTH

Following are a few quick UI pointers for new game designers from the producer of Blizzard's *Diablo II*:

> - Don't frustrate the player's desire for perfect control within the game world.
>
> - Any sense by the player of lack of control (however brief) can be fatal.
>
> - The user interface must be intuitive and consistent.
>
> This makes it easy for new players to learn and encourages experienced players to become experts.

JAY WILSON, MONOLITH PRODUCTIONS

Both the in-game UI and the interface during the menu screens are extremely important, according to Monolith's Jay Wilson. And customizability is also critical. Says Wilson:

> If I can't play a game the way I want, I just won't play. I'm not going to mention which game it was, but I waited a year and a half for it to come out because it looked incredible. And when it did, there was no mouse support at all. You have to make the way the game looks and controls familiar to the player.

Although most game companies don't do this, Wilson insists a menu screen should always have a Help box to click on that will explain all the options in the game.

CHAPTER 13
SOUND ENGINEERING

Not too long ago, sound effects in PC games meant the odd *bleep* or *chirp* from an internal speaker. Fast forward to 2000 when, during a heated game of *Thief 2*, you can literally hear a slimy enemy creep up from over your left shoulder…

As audio software and hardware continues to evolve for the PC, sound is becoming an incredibly significant part of the gaming experience. And consider for a moment the rate at which this new technology is not only accessible, but affordable. In less than two years, we've witnessed the emergence of Dolby Surround Sound, Dolby Digital (AC-3), Dolby Surround Pro Logic, Microsoft DirectSound and DirectSound 3D, Creative Lab's Environmental Audio, Aureal's A3D, surround-sound speakers, multiple-channel surround-sound speakers, DVD players, powerful subwoofers, USB connections for a cleaner channel, and digital inputs for all kinds of supported musical gear. Point made?

With this new technology comes a new breed of audio specialists, determined to breathe new life into the interactive entertainment industry. This chapter delivers advice from a number of well-known and respected sources in the gaming industry on getting into sound design as a profession, ways of achieving the effects heard in popular games, which archived sound packages are worth getting, and how sound design fits into the grand scheme of game design.

MATTHEW LEE JOHNSTON, MICROSOFT

Matthew Johnston, audio lead at Microsoft, has worked on a number of well-received and best-selling gaming and multimedia titles. Some of his most impressive works include *Flight Simulator 95* and *98*, *Microsoft Golf 2.0*, *3.0*, *98*, and *99*, and *Monster Truck Madness 1* and *2*. When asked what pieces of advice he could give budding sound engineers on succeeding in the gaming industry, he responds as follows:

UNDERSTAND THE WORLD OF THE DEVELOPER

According to Johnston, most sound designers currently working on games come from traditional post-production backgrounds, including many failed careers as live sound operators or recording bands down at the local rock star sweatshop. "I can't tell you how many times I've sat in a game developers conference discussion and listened to guys whine incessantly about how the developers never listen to them, don't understand them, or treat them like s---," says Johnston. He amplifies:

> This treatment, while it may not be entirely justified, is understandable. Waxing ecstatic about design concepts without being able to provide the developer with concrete examples of how it can be implemented is negligent, and can be offensive to someone who has spent the last year thinking about everything but the audio. Educate yourself on basic programming concepts, understand the relationship between the game engine and the sound engine, and be a diplomat when it comes to working with the development team; they're holding your design in their hands and can make or break your ideas.

MAKE YOURSELF USEFUL

"Rarely does anyone design game audio that has any use," Johnston believes. What does this mean, exactly? Surely he's not insulting the efforts made by fellow sound engineers? Of course not. He explains:

> Someone has brought you in at the last possible moment, and they hand you a list of individual sound effects that already map to some specific graphic element on the screen. This is a lot like scoring a film, and comes from a lack of awareness on how much of a part sound plays in the overall human experience. What people don't understand is that you're not making a movie; you are attempting to re-create an interactive environment that contains visual and aural elements that combine to create an "experience" that's totally defined by the player's actions. Think of your sound design as going way beyond "making sounds for the graphics," and come up with ways that the sound can be a critical element of gameplay. The gaming industry is way behind on this concept, and you will start to see games coming out that use sound as important parts of the gameplay more often. Get ahead of the game, and start thinking this way now.

Johnston cites an example of a game he's worked on where sound effects play a significant role in the player's actions. In Microsoft's *CART Precision Racing*, using engine sounds for other cars will warn the player of what's coming up behind, and using stereo panning localizes the predator to a particular side of the vehicle.

In Microsoft's CART Precision Racing, it's best to keep your eyes directly on the road and not on other cars. Spatialized audio cues are provided by Johnston so you know when another driver is sneaking up from behind, and on which side. (Used with permission by Microsoft Corp.)

BREAK THE MOLD

In the following passage, Johnston addresses respect, professionalism, and proving your competence:

> Nothing p---es me off more than being called a "musician" or "sound guy" after spending the last ten years of my life developing expertise in audio system design. Content creation is only part of the tune. Earning respect in this industry is already difficult because audio is such a subliminal partner in a multimedia presentation. Most people are not aware of how much effect the sound has on a person's perception, emotion, and immersion in a game product. If you couple this lack of awareness with a tight budget and the misperception that you're just a bong-smoking hipster with a guitar, you've got problems. Be a professional, cover your a-- by knowing all there is to know about the environment that your sounds will be such an integral part of, and [...] stop using the word "dude." Take on the role of the educator, and get used to having to prove yourself and your ideas to someone who thinks you are "a nice thing to have around, but not critical." You will eventually win them over with tight, thorough, and well-substantiated attempts to bring them out of the video coma and into a new aural enlightenment. Make the words "proof of concept" your new mantra.

Is it possible that audio can even influence visual perception? Indeed it can, says Johnston. He cites a classic example stemming from MIT research that proves the power of audio over the visual. In a nutshell, the MIT media lab showed two groups two video clips: one with bad audio content, and one with really great audio content. The overwhelming feedback received indicated the clip with the better audio track "looked better" to the subjects. Studies such as this one strongly suggest humans don't necessarily differentiate the sound content from the visual content. Because our visual senses are less subliminal and more conscious, all of the accolades go to the video.

In a related study at the University of Toronto, two groups of psychology students were shown the same video segment of a car accident. One video contained the original audio from the recorded fender bender. The second group was exposed to a "treated" audio track with an additional sound of tires screeching and a louder *slam* for the collision. Ninety percent of the second group felt the oncoming car was "speeding," compared to only twenty percent in the first group.

Matt Johnston recorded golf sounds for Microsoft Golf 1998 Edition on Rialto Beach on the Olympic Peninsula in Washington State, using a Neumann "Head" Binaural Microphone to capture nature noise as background sounds in the game. (Used with permission by Matthew Johnston)

MARTY O'DONNELL, TOTALAUDIO

This reputable Chicago-based sound solution company has worked on a hundred TV and radio commercials, but more and more TotalAudio is becoming involved in the interactive entertainment industry. Game credits include sound design, live-action video foley, and final mix for Cyan/Red Orb's *Riven: The Sequel to Myst*; all original music, sound design, and voices for Bungie's *Myth: The Fallen Lords* and *Myth II: Soulblighter*; plus others such as Monolith's *Septerra Core: Legacy of the Creator* and Bungie's *Oni* and *Halo*. Flip to the biography portion at the back of this book to read more on Marty O'Donnell's academic credentials and awards for game sound design.

Based on O'Donnell's lengthy and varied experience, he was asked to comment on the most important things to keep in mind for a sound designer looking to break into the gaming industry. His first answer is as follows:

> In commercial work, I've learned that one of the most important things to remember is that the actual sound of something is rarely exactly what people are expecting to hear. If you record the sound of a potato chip breaking, it might be accurate but also quite boring. Most likely adding the sound of a tree being felled in the forest will give the right dramatic impact to the slow-motion shot of a crispy chip. The same goes for game audio. The actual recording of a gunshot or an elevator is not enough to create the surreal mood of most game environments. Use the real sounds as starting points, and then add bigger and more exaggerated sounds to enhance and expand them. In one of the traps in *Riven* we added a woman's twisted scream to the sound of scraping metal, just to give the player the sense that something really bad was happening. I beat on a bundle of dried grapevines with a metal pipe to create some of the bone-crunching hits in *Myth*.

Next, O'Donnell says to get the best performers you can find. "Actors and musicians should be accomplished professionals. Equipment and software should be top notch, but more importantly be tools that you're comfortable working with."

O'Donnell suggests paying close attention to the actual final mix of all the audio elements in a game:

> You must know exactly how different game states will effect the differing types of audio you've created. In a linear medium, such as film, all of the audio, sound effects, dialogue, and music are brought together, mixed, and balanced precisely the way the designer wants the audience to experience it. In games, however, all these elements can be brought together in ways that might be impossible to anticipate—in effect, a real-time interactive final mix. An individual sound effect might be "cool" if it's played loud, but be totally inappropriate if a character is supposed to be whispering at the same time.

"Carefully balancing the audio will give the game the best chance at creating a sense of reality and the right mood for the player," says O'Donnell. "This is not unlike balancing character strengths for gameplay." (Used with permission by Bungie Software Products, Corp.)

The aforementioned advice is very handy if you're already working on a game, but what does O'Donnell believe is the best way for a budding sound engineer to break into the gaming industry? Here's his answer:

> At this point I believe that a young sound designer or composer should probably find an established sound and music production company and try to get hired as an intern. It also helps to be a fan of games and be extremely computer-savvy. Be a student of the use of audio in film, TV, and games. Produce some sound and music tracks for QuickTime videos and have them available to show to your potential employer. Find friends your own age who are doing a game or independent film project and work with them. Look for every opportunity and go for it.

Next, O'Donnell was asked to comment on why music and sound design are often overlooked when creating a game (i.e., usually the smallest portion of the budget goes to the audio). He responds:

> The only place that music *isn't* taken for granted is in the music industry. That's because music is recorded for the sake of music and not to enhance another product. In any other medium, music and sound are elements that are subservient to some larger work. Listening to a Beethoven symphony in a concert hall is quite different from listening to the same symphony underscoring a dramatic scene in a movie.
>
> In the game industry of the past, music was used to set a single mood (per level) and played constantly because it was hard to get enough variety in the sound effects to react interactively with the gameplay. Now we have the technology to have full-bandwidth music and audio, great actors, and some really great programming to get all this content to respond to the player's actions. But it will take some time for gamers and developers to desire that kind of content, because their expectations are still based on the past. The good news is that new gamers are expecting the kind of quality they're used to hearing on radio, TV, and film, and the developer who doesn't realize that will be beaten in the marketplace by those who do. In Japan, game soundtracks sell quite well to the general public, and I'm hoping that the same thing will happen soon in the West. Interactive sound design is quite different from sound design for linear mediums, and I think we're still working out some of the techniques that will help highlight the uniqueness of the art of interactive entertainment.

Finally, O'Donnell offers a comprehensive list of some (in)valuable sound design resources, recommended to sound engineers to better their craft:

> *Keyboard*, *Electronic Musician*, *Mix*, *Surround Sound*, and *Game Developer* are all good magazines for game audio folks. There are many good list servs I like—the best for me are the Interactive Audio Special Interest Group (IASIG), Video Games Musicians List, Game Audio Pro List, and the DAW-Mac (Digital Audio Workstation – Mac) list. By the way, I think it's important for any audio engineer to be fluent on both PCs and Macs, but there's no doubt that Macs are essential for anyone who wants to produce music and audio.

To learn more about Marty O'Donnell and the work produced by TotalAudio, drop into its official Web site on the Internet, at www.TotalAudio.com.

TIM LARKIN, CYAN

Speaking of *Riven: The Sequel to Myst*, one of the best-sounding computer games in the history of the interactive entertainment industry, another gentleman was also responsible for the game's award-winning audio. His name is Tim Larkin, and he's also part of the HUGESound Network (www.hugesound.com). Along with the other contributors to this chapter, Larkin believes game designers, generally speaking, don't realize the grave importance of sound in a game. "The tongue-in-cheek expression we use is that it's '50% of the experience, 10% of the bandwidth,'" jokes Larkin. In other words, he believes sound to be on par with the visual stimuli given during a game, but sound designers are usually not allotted more than a tenth of the CPU's power.

Larkin does believe this will change over time, and the ball has already started rolling. "Think about it—CD-ROM technology is only five years old, so multimedia is really only in its infancy. Compare that to the movie or TV industry, which has matured over time." Larkin says developers and publishers are starting to acknowledge the importance of audio in games, and even attributes the advancements in graphics: "Fortunately, graphic technology is getting better, so people will naturally want better sound, for balance."

There are two disciplines Larkin lives by as a sound engineer, and he passes on the following mandates to newcomers to the profession.

GET CREATIVE

Larkin says he's all for purchasing library CDs (and he particularly likes the *Hollywood Edge* ones) but the key is *not* to use the stock sounds as is. This is a big no-no, according to Larkin. "Sound designers ought to get in the habit of creating something unique, by using a sound and by editing, processing, and blending it together with others." He expands:

> For example, the trams in *Riven* (used to travel to the five islands) were created by a number of combined and edited sounds. First off, it started with a stock sound of the BART (Bay Area Rapid Transit), a fairly smooth-sounding electric train. After toying with the sound, a process wind effect was used over top, and then a rumble to simulate turbulence.

START OFF WITH A GOOD SOUND

Larkin points out it doesn't cost very much money to get your gear in order as an audio engineer, so there's very little excuse not to use high-quality sound in games—aside from dealing with bandwidth issues with the programmers! "Approach designing or editing sound for a game as if you were creating audio for a feature film," says Larkin. "You can buy a couple of stock CDs for $50 each to start, and the software is only a couple of hundred dollars now."

Macintosh software packages such as Macromedia's Deck II and Digidesign's Pro Tools were used for all the sounds heard in *Riven*. Macromedia's Deck II was bought by BIAS (Berkley Integrated Audio Software) and is now known as BIAS Deck 2.6. For info on this product, see www. bias-inc.com. For Pro Tools info, drop by www.digidesign.com.

Larkin admits he often creates music and sound in games not for the gamers themselves, but for his peers. "I do it for other sound designers—people who would critique my work."

CHRIS RIPPY, ENSEMBLE STUDIOS

Serving as sound director at Ensemble Studios, Chris Rippy has worked on the award-winning *Age of Empires*, *Age of Empires Expansion: The Rise of Rome*, and *Age of Empires II: The Age of Kings*. Much of his helpful advice for new sound designers circles around the basics: understanding you're part of a bigger picture, knowing the advantages and limitations of your software and hardware, and gathering plenty of hands-on experience.

> There are definitely a number of things to keep in mind when doing sound for games. I think the most important rule, and this goes for musicians, sound guys, artists, etc., is that the game is much more important than any one sound or "thing" that you're working on. In other words, if the sound gets in the way of the gaming experience, it's got to go. Secondly, it's very important to know your equipment inside and out. You'll make much better sounds, and make them much more efficiently, if you take the time to learn your software, your DAT, your mics, and anything else you might need. Finally, listen to everything. Listen to music, listen to water, listen to car doors, listen to feet, listen to cows breathing. The more you listen to the world around you, the better your sounds will be.

Rippy draws from his own experiences at Ensemble Studios to support his recommendations. First, there were several times where Rippy had to bite his lip and accept that the gameplay had priority over sounds he considered to be pretty cool.

> In *Age of Empires*, and in most games, we had to keep the size of the sound to a minimum (this is due to technical constraints, such as RAM availability and the speed at which the computer can play the sound). This immediately limits the length of the sounds that I can use, as well as the resolution of the sounds, so some of my ideas were quickly squashed. Other times, I've had sounds that I've liked a lot while developing them, only to have them annoy me (and my office pals) when placed in the game and played repetitively. Again, the game came first, and the sounds were pulled.

The second rule is contingent on how much time and effort is given to the sound engineer's tools. Recalls Rippy, "I know that when I first started using sound-editing tools like Sound Forge, I had a very narrow view of what they could do. But after spending many, many hours in them, I've learned my way around them, learned all of their tools, and learned their hotkeys. This just helps get things done faster, and your sounds will sound better."

The third and final piece of advice is more a way of life than a specific practice. For example, Rippy explains how the sound was achieved for the catapults in *Age of Empires*: "That sound is pieced together from several different sources, most of which I don't recall. The recoil sound of the catapult arm slapping the crossbar is something I do remember, though. I made that sound by bending a wooden ruler on the edge of my desk, then I released one end so it would slap the desk repeatedly. I then manipulated it in the computer, and *ta da*—a catapult. If I hadn't remembered making that sound in elementary school, we might have had a really quiet catapult!"

Now, every time you play Age of Empires, you'll remember that the catapult sound stemmed from Chris Rippy's delinquent class behavior! (Used with permission by Microsoft Corp.)

GEOFF KIRK, HUMONGOUS ENTERTAINMENT

As sound designer and sound effects programmer, Geoff Kirk has waxed his talents on all of Humongous Entertainment's mega-successful kids' lines, such as the *Pajama Sam* series, the *Putt-Putt* series, the *Freddi Fish* series, and more. Kirk's work focuses on cartoon adventure games, and, naturally, his advice on sound effects and music follows suit. "I would recommend watching cartoons," says Kirk. He elaborates:

The greatest preparation for what I'm doing today was the time spent when I was very young watching cartoons, especially the old Warner Brothers' Bugs Bunny. They used music as a sound effect in a way that's still rather revolutionary. The background music on those old cartoons is also very cool and ahead of its time.

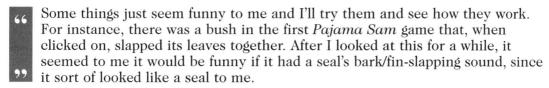

Pajama Sam was designed to be like an interactive cartoon, so the sound effects created by Geoff Kirk borrowed from good ol' Saturday morning inspiration. (Used with permission by Humongous Entertainment, Inc.)

If you're looking for TV cartoons' influence in some of Kirk's work, look no further than the first *Pajama Sam*, dubbed *Pajama Sam in There's No Need to Hide When It's Dark Outside*:

Some things just seem funny to me and I'll try them and see how they work. For instance, there was a bush in the first *Pajama Sam* game that, when clicked on, slapped its leaves together. After I looked at this for a while, it seemed to me it would be funny if it had a seal's bark/fin-slapping sound, since it sort of looked like a seal to me.

Kirk also attributes his wacky effects in Humongous titles as merely "messing around" with various sounds. That is, recording something and then changing the pitch by an extreme amount, and then mixing it with something else. "Animal growls and roars are quite commonly used in this fashion these days," says Kirk.

 Suggestions from Westwood Studios' sound designers also encourage experimentation and the use of unusual sounds. They claim it's often better to use something that doesn't sound "real," but rather sounds like an exaggeration of what's real. Real audio tracks tend to lack the impact of beefed-up sounds—a trend you can attribute to the movie and TV industry.

However, not all sounds are created out of this kind of experimentation:

 Some [effects] are based on the art that's drawn. For instance, if there's an elaborate background scene with many machines and so on, then we'll add a lot of background sound of printing presses or sorting machines mixed together. If they don't already have the room ambience of a large room or [manufacturing] plant, then [we'll try to simulate that] with the use of reverbs or delays.

Kirk recommends that sound engineers spend time learning the ins and outs of reputable sound-editing programs, such as Syntrillium Software's Cool Edit Pro (www.syntrillium.com) or Sonic Foundry's Sound Forge (www.sonicfoundry.com), and perhaps learning to program a synthesizer of some kind.

KELLY BAILEY, VALVE SOFTWARE

Half-Life was nominated for the "Best Sound in a Game" award in Gamespot's "Best of 1998" feature (www.gamespot.com/features/awards1998). The reason? For a development company's debut title, *Half-Life* enjoyed some of the best sound design and sound programming the business has seen (or heard, for that matter). This is all thanks to Kelly Bailey, who was also responsible for the music in the game. So what's the secret to creating such incredible sound?

WORK WITH THE OTHER ENGINEERS

According to Bailey, working very closely with the engineers who are placing the sounds in the game is critical:

> Working directly with the engineers who were adding the sound code to monsters, characters, and weapons turned out to be a very positive advantage. I was often able to construct a set of sounds, give it to the engineer (okay, who was sometimes me!) and hear the result directly in the game within a few minutes. This let me quickly determine whether or not the sounds were working for the weapon or monster, and provide quick feedback on volume levels, pitch, frequency of playback, etc. Having that fast turnaround time on hearing sounds in the game was a great benefit, and saved me a ton of time.

GET CREATIVE AND USE DIFFERENT SOURCES

The second pointer is using a creative mix of recorded and synthesized sounds, to bring sounds to life in the game environment. Says Bailey:

> I found that some recorded sounds, such as footsteps or bouncing shell casings, translated very well directly in the game. But often I found that I needed to augment certain sounds or portions of sounds to liven them up in the game environment. For instance, direct, cleanly recorded gunfire or explosions often translated as a quick sharp "pop" on anything but the most high-end playback system. In order to give the gunfire a more visceral quality, I would often mix in low-frequency synth information, or mix several attack transients together, or compress and distort to increase apparent loudness by broadening their frequency spectrums.
>
> Overall, I found I needed to do a lot of mixing and massaging of the original recordings to give them a more aggressive or exciting quality. Playing back sound effects on a wide variety of PC speaker systems, with and without subwoofers, was also very important to achieving equalization that translated well to a wide audience. Mixing and constructing sounds on just one set of speakers or headphones can lead to nasty surprises; you don't want the guy down the hall to start raging about his distorting subwoofer.

TEST THE SOUNDS—REPEATEDLY

The third piece of advice from Bailey is "letting sounds sit in the game for a period of play-testing time before calling them 'final.'" Here's an example:

> While playing a complete game for 20 or more hours, a player may listen to a particular sound effect thousands of times. It was really important to me to make sure we didn't include sounds that became accidentally grating or annoying after repeat listening. To help with this, many of our sounds are actually mixed and modified pseudo-randomly on playback. For instance, we may slightly change the pitch of a sound each time it's played, or swap in a slightly different version of the sound effect, or mix together two component sounds in different ways to come up with a single sound. Although a lot of this work is done with code, I reworked the effects for most of the frequently played sounds (such as gunfire) up to five times before settling on a final version. It helped to quickly get a sound into the game and have people live with it for a number of days. After a week of listening to a sound coming out of other offices down the hall, you develop a surprising awareness of what's working and what isn't.
>
> Also, try to pay attention to sounds that get people excited while they're playing the game. It's easy to get too used to your own sounds, so relying on the consensus of other people around you can really point out trouble sounds, and also help guide you toward the kinds of sounds people want to hear more of.

KEVIN SCHILDER, RAVEN SOFTWARE

Kevin Schilder is the manager of the audio department at Raven Software in Madison, Wisconsin. He is half of a team that concentrates solely on sound design, music composition, and audio production for their games. Past credits include *Heretic I* and *II*, *Hexen I* and *II*, and *Mageslayer*, to name a few.

With over 30 years experience under his belt, Schilder closes off this chapter with the following three commandments for becoming a successful sound designer at a game company:

THINK CREATIVELY

> When I first began using sampled sound effects, I realized the title on the CD often didn't correspond to the way I used it. If I need to make the sound of a large door closing, I may find that the recording of an actual door doesn't work as well as the sound of an explosion with some creative processing. You have to envision the sound you're looking for and then consider all possibilities for creating that sound.

EXAGGERATE FOR EFFECT

" In the action games I've worked on, the sound effects must be bigger than life. It isn't enough to make a flaming arrow sound like a real arrow firing with a campfire sound attached. That thing has to sound like a cruise missile and shake your speakers! "

WATCH YOUR PROCESSING

" Process sounds carefully. I have heard some people make nice sound effects but have them clip off too soon at the end. A little mistake takes away the realism. "

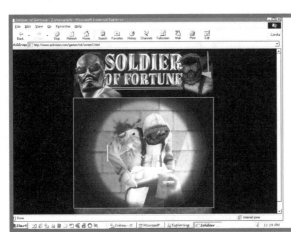

Schilder says, "It isn't enough to make a flaming arrow sound like a real arrow firing with a campfire sound attached. That thing has to sound like a cruise missile and shake your speakers!" Seen here is a "shot" from Soldier of Fortune. (Used with permission by Activision, Inc.)

CHAPTER 14
MUSIC AND GAMES

No other segment of the entertainment industry welcomes as many different talents and specialties as does the gaming industry. Where else can writers, programmers, artists, animators, sound engineers, and musicians all work together as a team for one single product? This is one of the key reasons why this young industry is so exciting. And the opportunities are virtually endless!

Fortunately, developers of PCs and console gaming titles are slowly recognizing the importance of a good musical soundtrack, and more effort and financial resources than ever before are being poured into music. Sure, it's still a tiny piece of the overall pie when compared to the money spent on graphics (and licensing, where applicable), but it's a growing field, and the top musicians in the gaming industry are able to make a good living. Sure beats playing seedy bars or giving it up for a day job, no?

Let's take a look at the top musicians in the business and what advice they can give to those looking to break into the gaming industry.

CHANCE THOMAS, HUGESOUND NETWORK

Before leaving to start his own production company less than a year ago, Chance Thomas was a senior music producer at Sierra's Yosemite Entertainment studio in Oakhurst, California, and chances are, you've heard his melodic and memorable scores on dozens of games. Along with creating orchestral tracks, rock singles, and independently released game music CDs, he spearheaded the fight for game music to be considered at the Grammy Awards. The ideal way to preface Thomas' advice is to read from the liner notes of Sierra's *Quest for Glory V* soundtrack. He writes:

> Music is mysterious, elusive, familiar, capricious....It's like a language we knew before our birth, its intimacy both surprising and obvious in turn. Writing music seems to be a tussled balance of discovery and ingenuity, of sheer will and catalyzed coincidence. The composer forages, struggles, demands, coaxes, curses, and finally relents. And often in the quiet humility of surrender, the muse comes out of her hiding place, satisfied that our best efforts have sufficiently softened the soul. She speaks to us from the inside out, triggering emotions so subtle and profound, as her voice finds an inevitable path to the surface.

First on Thomas' list for budding game musicians, and for new game designers who may be looking for musicians, is placing a priority on the *quality* of the game music. Says Thomas:

> Get the highest quality music you can. Our ears are trained to expect sonic excellence through our exposure to films, television shows, and our favorite albums. If the player ever has to make a mental downshift, "Oh well, this is just game music…" then an entire level of impact has just been obliterated. Music loses impact as it loses credibility.

Because we're used to hearing professionally recorded music with film and TV soundtracks, says Chance Thomas, if the music in a game is recorded in poor quality, its impact will be lessened considerably. (Used with permission by Chance Thomas)

If time permits and it's financially feasible, Thomas also recommends using real instruments, rather than synthesized ones:

> No amount of technology can ever overcome poor source material. There's no "emotion fader" on a mixing console. That's why more and more of us are proponents of hiring real, living, feeling, passionate professional musicians to play as much music as we can possibly afford. There's nothing like capturing a brilliant performance of red-hot musicians pouring their feelings into fine acoustic instruments to give you emotionally stirring source material to work with.

Thomas' recorded works are filled with this approach. As an example, he used a 36-piece orchestra and then a 32-piece orchestra for various sections of the *Quest for Glory V* soundtrack: "We recorded two passes on every track—recording multiple takes in each instance until we got the magic one—to create the sound of a 72- and 64-piece orchestra, respectively. I wish you could listen to the difference between the synthesized version and the live version of each. No comparison."

Quest for Glory V was Sierra's first live orchestral score. "Firsts" like this help to draw attention to a product; by the time this game was on retail shelves, there were over 40 different articles focusing on the music alone. (Used with permission by Chance Thomas)

Okay, so *most* game musicians don't have a full orchestra accessible to them. Understood. "The point is, if you want to make a BIG emotional impact, you'd better pay BIG attention to your music," asserts Thomas. "George Lucas said, 'Sound is half the movie-going experience.' Please keep that in mind as you consider the role of music in your games."

So when exactly should a game musician get involved in the development cycle? As early as possible, says Thomas:

> There is an amazing synergy that's only possible with early and ongoing involvement. I've written pieces of music early in development that inspired entirely new sections of a game. Having music in place can assist voice actors in delivering a more powerful and dynamic performance. Not to mention the raw enthusiasm that a great tune or score can generate with the creative people on a team.

Music is the language of emotion. It speaks to us in ways that words and images can never express. Thomas proposes to ask yourself, "'What do I want a player to *feel* in this game?' And if the composer is worth his salt, the score will induce that emotion."

GEORGE "THE FAT MAN" SANGER

George Alistair Sanger, a.k.a. The Fat Man, has been composing music for games since 1983. Along with Team Fat, his legendary team of three other cowboy composers, he is internationally recognized for having created music for more than 130 games, including *Wing Commander I* and *II*, *The 7th Guest I* and *II*, *NASCAR Racing*, *Putt-Putt Saves the Zoo*, *Tanarus*, and *ATF*.

Team Fat: Clockwise from top left are "Ramrod" Joe McDermott, David Govett, "Professor" K. Weston Phelan, and George "The Fat Man" Sanger. (Photo courtesy of Spanki Avallone, Avallone Media)

Throughout our lengthy telephone interview on creating game music for a living, the conversation continuously boils down to one factor: passion. To The Fat Man, whatever makes you get up in the middle of the night and say "Yes!" is what you should be doing for a living.

> If you don't like a lot of games and a lot of music, get out. In fact, you have to love games—not just *love* games, but LOVE games. You don't go to try to make it in Hollywood if you don't watch movies, do you? When something is really speaking to you, do it—whether it be making scads of money or making music for games. Love it even if you fail. Whenever you're making a game or music for a game, do it because you love it, not for someone else. Just forget whoever else may like it. Also, don't make decisions entirely on intellect. Balance that with info from your heart, and if it adds richness to your life, you're in the right business. You must follow your heart, your passion, your bliss.

Like Chance Thomas, The Fat Man recognizes that music is usually not a priority to larger developers, and believes the amount a company is willing to invest in the music is directly proportional to the quality and "wow" factor. "If you put 1% of your resources (i.e., money and time) in a game's music soundtrack, it will be good. At 3%, it's almost guaranteed…to get results where people will walk away and say the music is 'awesome,'" says The Fat Man.

But how should a game designer go about finding music for his/her game? The Fat Man urges you to work with people you know and trust at first, and be up-front about the project:

> If you are looking for people to create music for your game, be entirely honest with anyone you deal with, and give them whatever money you can afford—or a percentage of the game's revenue. Just give them something to start…even if it's just lunch. Go to your friends and find out if they are as motivated as you are.

Obviously, you can't have it all if you're just starting out. The Fat Man reminds new game designers that, "[…]as with most specialists in their respective fields, if they have no experience, it will be less money, but more hassle. On the flip side, the more experience they have, the more money it will cost you, but with less hassle."

Assuming you're the musician here, and not a game designer looking for a musician, what kind of equipment do you need? According to The Fat Man, whatever recording gear you have right now, and a good PC, is all you need to start off. "Just find a way of getting music into the PC via a [Sound Blaster] AWE 64 or Live! card or any other cards that have a good input, and a stereo one if possible. Then you'll need a CD burner or DAT [digital audio tape] to record WAV files." Once the music is recorded, it can be submitted to a game company for evaluation.

 The Fat Man hosts an annual Game Music Demo Marathon at the Game Developers Conference (GDC) in the early spring of each year. Ninety-second demos are accepted in the following formats (in order of preference):

- CD-ROM (PC format, 44.1 16-bit stereo .WAV)
- Audio CD
- DAT
- Standard audiocassette

If you want to get into the industry, this is a great way to start. The Fat Man's official Web site (www.fatman.com) has the complete rules, entry information, and CDs from past years.

The Fat Man also hosts an annual convention, known as "Project Bar-B-Q," dedicated to improving the production quality of music on computers and computer products. Information on attending can be found at his Web site.

In conclusion, The Fat Man reminds us that music is a contributing piece of the overall gaming experience, and as with many other art forms—poetry, music, visual arts—it's all about going beyond the power of words to express something in your heart. Yes, even if it's as simple as, "It's fun to kill stuff," The Fat Man concedes with a smile.

> Gaming is souls recognizing each other without relying on language. A relationship between the designer and the gamer. It's a deep connection that is beyond description.

TOMMY TALLARICO

Tommy Tallarico has worked on more than 150 games during his illustrious career. Some of the more well-known games (selling in excess of 25 million copies combined) include *Tomorrow Never Dies*, *Prince of Persia*, *The Terminator*, *Cool Spot*, *Aladdin*, *Earthworm Jim 1* and *2*, *MDK*, *Wild 9*, and *Test Drive 4* and *5*.

Tallarico comments on how important music is to the overall gaming experience:

> I truly believe music is 25% of the gaming experience. For the most part there are four parts of a game: *art*, which provides you with your graphics, visuals, animations, etc.; *programming*, which is the way the game moves, interfaces, acts, etc.; *design*, which is the level layout, fun factor, presentation, etc.; and *audio*, which can set a mood, accent a motion, and pretty much set the emotion for the scene/level. For example, you could have a scene where a character runs up to a huge cliff and slowly looks over it to reveal miles and miles of scenery. Depending on what the audio is doing is how the player is going to react to that circumstance. If the music is haunting or scary, it may seem like you're getting chased and you're trapped; if it's beautiful and epic, it will give you the sense of beauty and accomplishment. Oh yeah, and if it's country music, you'll want to turn the game off and shoot yourself in the head.

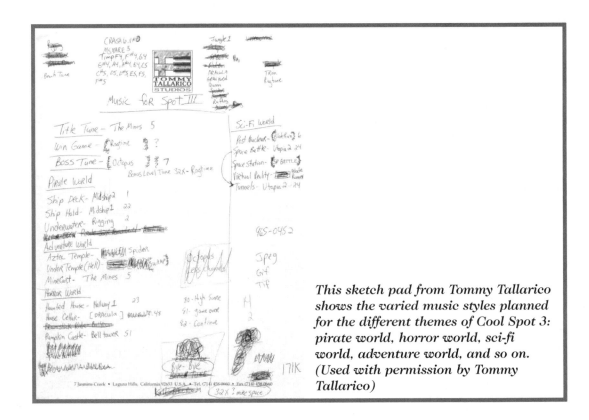

This sketch pad from Tommy Tallarico shows the varied music styles planned for the different themes of Cool Spot 3: pirate world, horror world, sci-fi world, adventure world, and so on. (Used with permission by Tommy Tallarico)

When asked the key to creating a successful video game soundtrack, Tallarico says what has worked for him is trying to create something different, and he provides a number of examples:

> All the soundtracks I've won awards on had one thing in common. It was the first time anyone had heard music like that in games. For example, in *Global Gladiators* I used samples triggered in the music (drums, guitar hits, orchestra hits, voice, etc.) to create a song. No one had really done that before to any extent on the Sega Genesis. They mostly used samples for speech. On *Terminator* for the Sega-CD, it was the first time anyone had heard live guitars and real rock music in a game. In *Skeleton Warriors*, it was huge 95-piece orchestral stuff. *Treasures of the Deep* had tons of acoustic guitars and things. In the *Wild 9* soundtrack, I took the beats and rhythms from techno and/or industrial music, but combined it with orchestras and guitars. The beats are great for flow, but the orchestra and guitars are perfect for power and melody. It's like creating a new style of music! Uniqueness is the key to writing great music for games, and I think the secret is to do something that no one has done yet—and probably the most fun part of what I do.

Chance Thomas mentioned that it can be quite helpful for both the musician and the game designer to get involved in creating music early on in the development cycle. But Tallarico says it's usually much later in the game's cycle before he plays the game (with no sound). Then he waits for the inspiration to hit him. He continues, "Then I go into my studio (upstairs) and figure out the notes on the keyboard that were dancing around in my head seconds before." If the game or level isn't complete, Tallarico may work off a storyboard.

As far as style of music is concerned, every company is different. There have been instances when developers have approached Tallarico with a clear vision (e.g. "Can we have the rhythm section of Prodigy, the sounds of The Chemical Brothers, the feel of Nine Inch Nails? Oh yeah, and the guitar sound of Waylon Jennings?"), but most of the time they leave it up to him to see what fits.

For example, in *Earthworm Jim*, Tallarico would play the game with no sound. In the first bonus level, Jim and Psycrow would be racing each other on rockets, and every time he played this portion of the game, it always looked like they were riding horses. "I kept hearing a country banjo-type thing, so I went with it," says Tallarico. In other levels, he would watch the way Jim moved or ran, and he would come up with rhythms based around that. And the environment itself plays a role, too: "For example, ambient or slower-type music always works well in darker areas."

The last portion of the interview focuses on what a budding game musician should be using for equipment and how exactly to break into the industry.

KEY GEAR

Any kind of sampler is good (Roland, Akai, etc.) because it provides the stand-alone musician with lots of diverse and acoustic sounds. With a CD-ROM hooked up to your sampler, you have an almost unlimited supply of hundreds of thousands of new and unique sounds. For a sound designer or sound effects guy, you should have a fast Mac with some good sound-editing software like Sound Edit Pro, Alchemy, Digital Performer, etc. For the PC diehard, Sound Forge is the way to go.

GETTING IN THE DOOR

The best thing to do is put together a demo tape with three or four of your best two- or three-minute tunes and send it to every publisher and developer in the industry. You can easily find lists of names and addresses on the Internet. The most effective way, however, is to go to either the Game Developers Conference or the Electronic Entertainment Exposition (E3). There is where you will personally meet designers, producers, VPs, and so forth. I've found it's always better to talk to someone in person than to just send out tapes.

Tommy "The King" Tallarico says it's key for musicians to make it to events such as E3 or GDC to strut your stuff. Thank you, thank you very much. (Used with permission by Tommy Tallarico)

Look for Tommy Tallarico's music on the *Tomorrow Never Dies*, *Messiah*, and *Pac-Man 3-D* game soundtracks.

BOBBY PRINCE

You may not have heard his name, but if you're a 3D shooter fanatic, chances are you've hummed his music in the shower many times. Bobby Prince is a composer and sound designer who has worked on such groundbreaking titles as *Wolfenstein 3D*, *Doom*, *Doom II*, and *Duke Nukem 3D*. He's best known for his melodic MIDI tunes. In fact, you can hear many of these instant classics at his Web site, www.bpmusic.com.

Prince usually gets involved early on in the development cycle. "In *Commander Keen*, my first game, the music was written long before the game was playable. I saw static artwork of the game's characters and had been told about what the game was expected to include. This was mostly true of all the games I have worked on up to *Duke Nukem 3D*."

Prince had the opportunity to plug in music and sound effects for the first time and try them out within a working game environment. "Even *Doom* required that I ask a programmer to recompile the game with prospective music/sound effects. This took a good bit of time and didn't allow quick-and-dirty tweaks," Prince recalls.

Prince believes it's possible to write appropriate music without seeing the game first if there's a good explanation of the characters and story of a game. Besides, it has been Prince's experience thus far that the story and characters will change several times before the project is finalized. "This is a great part of the fun and excitement in the game industry. It's a lot like early Hollywood—that is, tools of the trade are still being standardized and the middlemen still don't have a handle on things."

Bobby Prince is kind enough to share his top three pieces of advice for musicians looking to excel in the gaming industry:

1. **"Computer chops" on the part of the musician are at least a big plus.** For the most part, composing music for games is not a cut-and-dried, "deliver the music in *x* format and collect a check" business. This is especially true of MIDI music. Many times, I have had to debug code by writing sequences that tested the MIDI playback engine. On one occasion, the engine was removing note information and leaving less important data.

2. **Communication.** Be prepared to tutor non-musicians in all aspects of computer sound. Producers and programmers are generally a smart bunch, but, like the general public, they lack an understanding of the basics. There are those who will request digital music (audio CD or "Redbook") when the game leaves insufficient room on the game CD for it. It's also important to learn what non-musicians' music terminology actually means. I have had several occasions where I was requested to change the volume of the music, when it was actually the tone (equalization) that needed changing. I have also had cases where instrument names were confused.

3. **Don't wait for a gig to start writing music.** Luck is usually being ready for an opportunity when it hits. Before the opportunity hit me, I spent many, many nights writing music and learning the tools.

So what kind of tools are we looking at here? According to Prince, MIDI music players can successfully record music with the following equipment: a decent computer, basic sequencing software, a wavetable soundcard with the MIDI kit, a MIDI keyboard, speakers, and headphones. For digital audio, add digital recording/editing/effect software and some type of digital recording device for mastering (DAT, CD recorder, etc.). Any other equipment is nice and probably makes things easier, but it isn't required.

MICHAEL LAND, LUCASARTS

As sound department manager and a member of the music team at one of the hottest developers/publishers in the gaming business, Michael Land has composed music for a number of hit titles over the years: the *Monkey Island* series, *X-Wing*, *TIE Fighter*, *The Dig*, and *Day of the Tentacle*, to name a few. Asked what three most critical things a game musician should remember, the following words are Land's insightful response:

PLAY THE GAME

This one is fairly obvious, but it's easy to cut corners on it if you're in a hurry and you think of the "cue list" as your blueprint. Remember that whoever came up with that list was probably not a composer. While cue lists with descriptions are a great way to start, there's no substitute for actually playing the game yourself. Even looking over someone else's shoulder, while much better than not seeing the game at all, is not nearly as effective as actually getting in there and feeling the flow of the interactivity. Not only might you see ways to improve the cue list to better reflect the game's interactive structure, but more importantly, that experience of feeling the game yourself gives you an intangible edge in sensing what kind of music to write to enhance the player's experience. And as your music starts getting coded into the game, go back and play it again and see how it's working. You can often learn more about how to improve the music in that one moment than you could ever figure out by working on the music alone.

THE AUDIENCE IS A "PLAYER," NOT A "LISTENER" OR "VIEWER"

You're writing music to accompany an interactive experience, so no matter how good the music is, you have to make sure it translates well to the non-linear world of interactivity. Things like repetition, loop structures, transitions, and other issues unique to interactive music can either be seen as hassles or opportunities. Your music will end up working much better if you approach these "problems" as an artistic challenge, where the goal is not simply to deal with them, but to unlock their potential to leverage the unique power of interactivity. Start by diagramming out how every piece connects to every other piece. Then, as you write each piece, make sure to keep in mind how it will flow in and out of the neighboring pieces.

KNOW YOUR DELIVERY TECHNOLOGY

Make sure you have a good grasp of what the game's music and sound engine can and can't do, and find out what you'll be allowed to ship in terms of data format, resolution, disk space, etc. There are lots of variables in the technical domain, and most of them have some impact on your artistic options. Not all of these variables are cast in stone at the beginning of a project, so the sooner and deeper you get involved in the technical questions, the more influence you can have on how things turn out. The most obvious question is hard to miss (i.e., will the music be MIDI, Redbook, DLS, streamed audio, etc.?). But within each of these options is an entire tree of sub-questions that get increasingly more detailed (okay, maybe not for Redbook). The more you examine that tree, the more you'll be able to use the cool features and avoid the "gotchas" for whatever technology you'll be using.

Asked to discuss the inspiration behind some of his classic LucasArts soundtracks, and why LucasArts puts such an emphasis on music compared to many other game companies, Land responds:

The inspiration for the classic LucasArts soundtracks comes from several sources. Not in any particular order, these include the great stories and wonderful characters in the games, affinity for classic films and film music, the creative and thought-provoking insights of LucasArts game designers, deep love of many styles of music, and the collaborative and competitive aspects of three composers working closely together for almost 10 years.

KELLY BAILEY, VALVE SOFTWARE

Kelly Bailey was responsible for all the music and sound effects in the mega-hit *Half-Life*. He also wrote the code to allow characters to speak, and he implemented the software system that provides reverb and echo effects.

In the following paragraphs, Bailey takes some time to explain what he feels is critical for budding game musicians to remember, and draws from his own personal experiences while working on *Half-Life*.

WHAT'S THE MOOD?

The first rule, says Bailey, is to create the music to match the mood of the game design:

> One of the challenges I faced in constructing the *Half-Life* soundtrack was to make music that consistently reinforced the central mood of the game. *Half-Life* has a strong action/horror theme, and it was important to me to try to convey this in the music. I found that it was really important to continually keep in mind the kind of music I was trying to make, and be very intentional about musical choices. Limiting my choices to action and horror moods definitely helped me move forward in the studio, and not get too lost in the jungle of sound selection and construction. Sometimes, after letting a finished track sit for a week or so, I would return to it and discover that it just didn't quite fit with the mood of the game. I would either rework it or discard the track and move on to a new track. It's hard to decide to discard a track just because it doesn't quite fit with the mood [of the] game, but for me, trying to be my own best critic helped a great deal in keeping a consistent feel to the *Half-Life* tracks.
>
> I also found that composing for a game meant that, in our case, the tracks needed to stay between 30 seconds and 2 minutes in length due to space limitations on the CD. This was a constant challenge, and required a good deal of discipline and planning to accomplish.

A COMFORTABLE WORKPLACE

Number two on the list is to "have a great place to write, create, and experiment with soundscapes and ideas—and be able to return to the work after letting it sit for a while," says Bailey.

> It was important to me to be able to work on the soundtrack in a very comfortable environment. I updated my soundproof recording studio at home and populated it with a collection of analog and digital synths, samplers, a good-quality computer hard disk recorder, a very clean 8-bus mixer, some pro-level balanced outboard effects processors, and a number of "real" instruments such as guitar, drums, flute, and bass. Being able to work on music any hour of the day or night allowed me to stay productive in the studio, whether I was trying to construct an experimental soundscape late at night, or cleaning up and mixing down tracks earlier in the day. Later in the project, under fairly critical time pressure, having a studio at home that enabled me to keep flexible hours was a lifesaver.

WORKING UNDER PRESSURE

The third and final piece of advice from Bailey is to learn quickly how to produce under time and quality pressure:

> Being able to produce music under time pressure was surprisingly important. I had originally planned on having several months to finalize the last 10 tracks— but I was wrong! I ended up working up to 18 hours each day doing game design during the final five months of the project, and had to finish the music in my "off hours." By having a studio at home that I was very familiar with, and being disciplined about sticking to my creative process, I managed to get through it. Near the end of the project, I worked on many tracks simultaneously, which really helped keep my hours in the studio productive. If I was stuck, or just "too close" to a track, I could switch quickly to a different track and keep moving forward. It was also super important to be able to let tracks sit for several days before returning to work on them. This let me keep checking with fresh ears to make sure I was staying close to that action/horror theme.

Bailey is currently writing more music and creating new sound effects for Valve's *Team Fortress 2*.

ELLEN MEIJERS-GABRIEL, ODDWORLD INHABITANTS

As composer/sound designer at Oddworld Inhabitants, Ellen Meijers-Gabriel has written music and designed sound effects for both of the development studios' products: *Oddworld: Abe's Oddysee* and *Oddworld: Abe's Exoddus*. Meijers-Gabriel says there are a number of important rules to keep in mind for game musicians:

> First is to have a solid setup and to know how to use your equipment when starting out. Know your tools and the limits of the platforms you're dealing with, so you don't have to make major changes to your setup during projects. It's also good to be organized and to archive your work.
>
> Try to get as much information as possible about the game that you're about to work on. If you're working on the music while the game is being developed, you can start with storyboard images and watch videos of the game as it comes along. Eventually, when the game is close to finishing, you'll be able to play the game yourself, but by that time your work should be close to finishing as well. If you start writing the music after the game has been finished, you'll have the advantage of being able to see the complete product that you're writing the music for, but in this case it's likely that you'll have less time to work with. One of the advantages of working simultaneously with the development of the game is that you'll get the chance to try things out and sometimes even to change the outcome of the game.

In writing the music, try to be inventive, break boundaries. Instead of thinking about the individual pieces, I like to think of the game as an interactive piece of music rather than just a series of linear songs. The type of music you write for a game depends on the people behind the creation of the game, and on the game itself. After having spoken to the people who created the game, you should have a good idea of the style of music they're interested in for that specific game. After that, you'll write something in that style while trying to match the action in the game as much as possible. When the music you've created represents the feeling of each level and character in the game, and it enhances the experience of playing the game, you know you've done a good job.

ANDREW BARNABAS, VGM MAILING LIST

Andrew Barnabas runs a resourceful mailing list on the Internet. He says the following about this organization: "The VGM (Video Game Musician) mailing list is open to anyone who works professionally within the audio side of the games industry. Currently we're just over 100 members, covering the majority of the big software companies and a hefty wad of freelancers. The aim was to get musicians to communicate with each other (rather than being the hermits that I was used to). It was just a stupid idea I came up with because I was fed up with fielding questions from other musos (being the sociable type, I just phoned all these people up), and tried to get them all to talk to each other. We also have a Web-based FTP area on the free drive for musicians to upload music.

"The topics we cover vary from discussions concerning the upcoming developments in interactive audio [to] differing surround formats and musical styles to 'Why can't I link up two O2Rs, and tell me a PC audio card that can sync to a 44.1k word clock!' It has attracted a great deal of interest from hardware manufacturers and non-game software developers (Microsoft, Creative Labs, Cirrus Logic, Dolby) and has gotten the blessing and interest from various meetings at the CGDC and Fat Man's BBQ. I also know of people who have gotten work directly from the list!

"Currently it's based here where I work (Sony Computer Entertainment, Cambridge, UK—we just did *Medievil*, if you saw that). If anyone is interested in joining, they should send me a mail here at work at barney@scee.sony.co.uk, or, if that fails, try my home email address—bar.ney@dial.pipex.com. My only stipulation for joining is that members (assuming they meet the criteria) write a paragraph or two about themselves, covering what they do, what they do it with, and who they do it for."

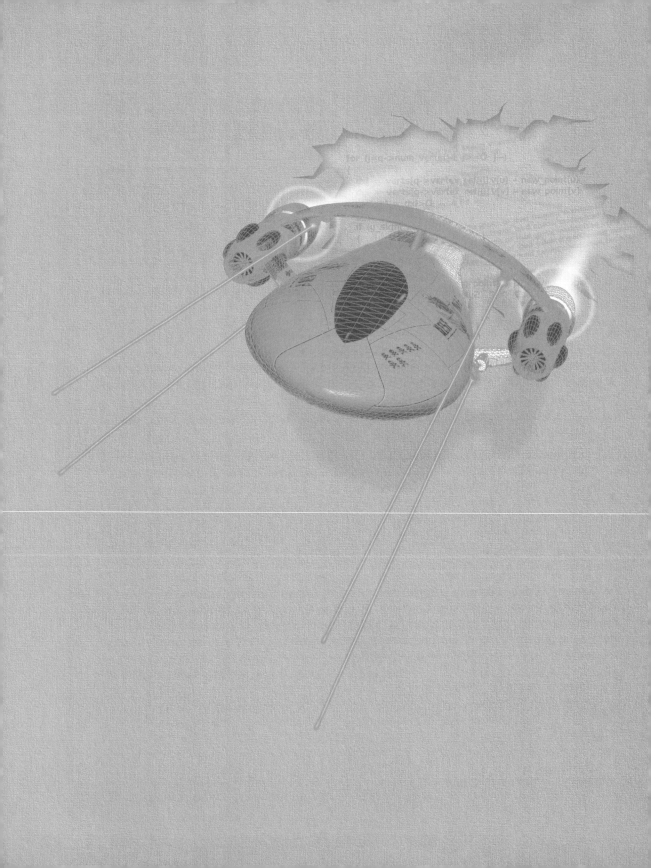

CHAPTER 15
TESTING

It has been mentioned innumerable times throughout this book that play testing a game is an extremely critical process that must be performed thoroughly before a product's release. So why then are there so many bugs in computer games? Why does it seem there are multiple patches for each game these days? Are designers getting lazy in this department, or are they taking advantage of the Internet as an effective distribution method for patches?

There are a number of reasons. First, developing a computer game is not like developing a game for a console platform, where the end user is playing the game on a fixed piece of hardware. That is, all the millions of PlayStations, Dreamcasts, and Nintendo 64s are built the same (though the software may vary for a geographic area, such as North America, Asia, or Europe).

With computers, very rarely do you find two gamers with the same setup. If you think about it for a moment, there are literally thousands of combinations of software and hardware, making it extremely difficult for a game to work smoothly on all systems. Thus, designing a game for a PC is like trying to hit a moving target.

Second, game companies are big business. If a product misses its shipment date, it loses money (especially during the profitable holiday season), and since many large game publishers are public, they must disclose quarterly fiscal results. One bad quarter may have an extremely adverse effect on the company's stock value. For this reason, on top of marketing commitments with various publications and distribution commitments with various retailers, many games are shipped out the door prematurely, with the attitude of "We'll have a patch up on the Internet within a couple of weeks." What game publishers are starting to understand, however, is that a gamer who is dissatisfied with a company's product may not purchase from that company again.

 According to *PC Data* video game report coordinator Matt Gravett, over 30% of console games and over 25% of computer games are sold during the month of December each year. The unfortunate reality is that many computer gaming publishers will ship their games prematurely to be on store shelves during this time.

It seems there are many ways for companies to test for bugs and compatibility issues for games, as we'll see in this chapter, but generally speaking there are two kinds of game testing:

■ Although it varies from company to company, *beta testing* is an incremental procedure handled internally at the development studio or publishing house, and in some cases distributed to volunteer consumers in the gaming community in exchange for feedback. It usually begins semi-formally when the game is in late alpha/early beta stage, hence the name.

■ *Quality assurance (QA) testing* is typically performed by outsiders in a proper testing environment and is usually administered toward the end of the game's development cycle. Bug reports and any other queries/beefs or comments are submitted for evaluation prior to the game's release. Then, after a game has shipped, technical support staff begins submitting user complaints (plus, developers read newsgroup postings and Web site forums), and a list of fixes will be collected and organized for the first patch. Keep in mind that in some cases the patches are fully justified, such as when a new 3D video or audio card is introduced after the game has been released.

This chapter concentrates on how to test your game properly throughout its development, with suggestions from a number of reputable companies: Acclaim Entertainment, Electronic Arts, Firaxis, Humongous Entertainment, and more.

CAROL CARACCIOLO, ACCLAIM ENTERTAINMENT

Carol Caracciolo is the quality assurance manager at Acclaim Entertainment in Glencove, New York. She has worked on many products, such as *Mortal Kombat II*, *Turok: Dinosaur Hunter*, *NFL Quarterback Club*, *All-Star Baseball*, *NBA Jam*, *WWF: Raw*, *WWF: Warzone*, *Alien Trilogy*, *Revolution X*, and many more. She is currently maintaining a staff of approximately 75 employees over two full-time shifts, seven days a week!

Caracciolo says the most important rules to live by when testing a game are as follows:

■ Never let anyone talk you out of writing up your bug.

■ Always research before reporting.

■ Verify, verify, verify.

How hard is it to find gamers to test your software? Says Caracciolo:

Finding testers is an easy process. You'll find that people who love games are driven in their passion; most times, they'll find you. The problem is sorting through the mountain of people who "love games" and finding the few who love them enough to spend 8 hours a day, 5 days a week for 4–6 months testing a game.

Caracciolo comments on how many people are needed during the quality assurance stage of a game, and how she ensures that her employees are reporting bugs properly:

> I find that a mixture of two temps to one full-timer is a good mix during crunch time. With a full-time staff of 20, I'll maintain up to 30 or 40 temps when the titles are coming in fast and furious.
>
> Ensuring quality testing with a group this large can be difficult; however, I have assembled a management staff of outstanding supervisors and lead analysts who guide them through the entire process and do some hand-holding for a probationary period. Over the years, we have culled all of the very best methods for approaching testing, with test plans and researching and reporting bugs. Spot checking bug sheets and databases always keeps everyone on target. We also require everyone to attend "re-training" classes periodically to keep fresh.

Are there any specific examples Caracciolo can pool from? She answers:

> One of the more recent products that changed our testing methodology was *Bust-A-Move*. This seems like a fairly innocuous title that could easily skate through the testing process. However, the amount of options in selecting a path seemed endless. This forced us to take a hard look at how we approached the testing process and committed us to extensive pre-planning in the form of a test plan. This is essential not only for tracking a project through test, but is invaluable for projecting testing needs in terms of personnel and equipment.

SEAN HOUSE, ELECTRONIC ARTS

Asked whether how they test games at EA Sports is any different from the "norm," Sean House, associate producer at Electronic Arts, responds that it is, and for good reason:

> The only real way to test the sports games is at the end (the last three months or so). This is because the schedule is generally accelerated (development to ship date is one year). The programming team is generally working their a--es off trying to get the features implemented that they signed up to implement; therefore, any bugs that testing may uncover during development will not get any attention. There isn't really any time to debug until the feature is nearly finished, or the programmer's list is nearly finished.

House recognizes that this isn't an ordinary situation and believes that, ideally, incremental testing is the way to go:

> This allows testers the ability to spend many months testing a product, even if this means constantly switching areas of the game to be tested. The testers usually are able to work on one area for a while, then move on to something else, then back to the original area. This reduces burnout and increases productivity among the test staff, because it keeps the tasks fresh. This also can make the debugging process much more efficient because usually many features are intertwined. A bug in one area can cause several in another; flushing out each feature as you go will lead to easier debugging down the road.

EA's Sean House says the testing process is a little different at EA because their development cycles are accelerated; they have only one year after the last version to get the new game out the door. This is a screen shot from Madden NFL '99. (Used with permission by Electronic Arts)

The differences between beta testing and quality assurance testing are explored by House as pertains to EA Sports:

> In my experience, QA is done by a group of people at the company that get the product after the regular product-testing guys. They're the last line of defense before the product hits the market. The game that comes to them should arrive "bug free." They are to take the attitude of an end user and give feedback on functionality of the game, as well as find any bugs that may have gotten through. They're also in charge of verifying legal issues with the product (legal screens, license info, etc.). These guys are generally the same people who will handle customer support on the product, so they have a definite stake in the quality of the product. The worse it is, the more work they have to do in supporting it.
>
> Beta testing is when you release a product that's in beta form (nearly complete, very few bugs remaining) to the public or select members of the public, and they play the game, giving feedback on issues or bugs that they find while playing the game. This is done to dramatically increase the number of eyes on the product in a short period of time, in an effort to quickly clear up any last-minute problems. We don't use beta testing on any of the products I've worked on here at EA. We do, however, use regular product testing, and this generally starts a month or so before the alpha stage (all major features are in the game, although buggy) and continues throughout the remaining development life of the product (ship).
>
> Both product testing and QA are important to the success of any software product, in my opinion. The two groups tend to balance each other out. Often, especially near the end of a project, many of the testers become fairly burned out (from working 16-hour days for too long), and it's easy to miss some obvious things. QA is there and fresh to find these issues. Also, their strength is in representing the end user, and because they're fresh and haven't been associated with the product until the end, they're able to give a good, objective view of the product.

House says he can recall a good example from his professional past on the importance of both kinds of testing. Here is the anecdote in its entirety:

> Five years ago, I was working as a product tester at Media Vision in Fremont, California. We were working on a few different multimedia titles. We had one product that was slated for release and needed to be final on the 26th of December. The product was almost done on the 23rd, and none of us wanted to work on the 25th, so we worked straight through from the 23rd through 6 a.m. Christmas day. Well, needless to say, we were all very burnt, and were getting pretty sloppy. The product was a floppy product. We got the last version of it at 3 a.m. on the 25th, and I was told to make copies and give them to everyone. There was one last bug that we needed to verify whether it was fixed or not, so I did it quickly once before distributing the disks to the others. It required that you enter your name and company info during installation. When prompted for the name/company during installation, I entered "coitus interruptus" (just a funny name). I got it all installed and the bug was fixed, so I then gave the other disks to the other testers. We all tested it for a while and then I gave my disks to our boss, who would take it to be mastered. We didn't have a QA department for software at this company, so he would just take it directly to the mastering people. We made it! We got it finished. We were all pretty happy.
>
> About three weeks later, after the product was in the store and everything, a few calls started coming in. People were unable to register their product for some reason. They said it kept coming up with the words "Coitus Interruptus." Well, needless to say, all the disks in circulation had to be recalled. It cost over $225,000. My boss took the brunt of the blame. Of course I felt really horrible, but I learned a valuable lesson: A last line of defense is a good thing. Had there been a QA department there, they would have caught our (my) slip-up in our extreme fatigue. A fresh crew of QA guys would have spotted it right away. Also, my boss probably should've given the product a once-over with the master disks, but that's another story.

House concludes by saying there have been numerous other instances in which the importance of testing and QA have been shown, and he can't imagine a development process without the two services.

BRAD MCQUAID, VERANT INTERACTIVE

EverQuest is one of the most successful online role-playing games in the history of PC gaming, and many of the kudos could be attributed to producer Brad McQuaid's emphasis on proper game testing. On how to test a massively-multiplayer online role-playing game (MMORPG), McQuaid offers the following:

> Testing is paramount to any game, massively-multiplayer or otherwise. Nobody wants bugs or broken game mechanics that lead to an unstable or unbalanced game. The challenge with testing as it relates to MMORPGs is that the size and nature of these games require long periods of testing involving a *lot* of people. Single-player games are typically tested internally with teams of perhaps 5–50 game testers for a period of time prior to the game's launch.

MMORPGs, on the other hand, typically employ both internal teams of testers as well as large armies of external testers (beta testers). *EverQuest*, for example, was in beta testing for approximately nine months. We began with approximately 50 external testers and brought that number up to 25,000 the month before release. And there are still bugs and problems we have had to address a year after release because 200,000 players will find problems that 25,000 didn't.

In game development, the terms *alpha* and *beta* are typically used to describe milestones prior to commercial launch. *Alpha* typically means "code and features complete" and *beta* that the game is stable enough to begin serious testing. With MMORPGs, or at least with *EverQuest*, *alpha* meant the game was playable and ready for internal testing. *Beta* meant opening the game to people outside Verant to help us debug and to offer suggestions and find problems with game mechanics. *Closed beta* typically means that the external people involved in the beta were hand-picked on an invite-only basis, whereas *open beta* means just about anybody from the public is welcome to participate.

MICHAEL BÜTTNER, X-AMPLE ARCHITECTURE

In Chapter 2, Michael Büttner outlines the advantages of developing on a PC verses a console platform and vice versa, and the pros and cons on working with a popular movie/TV franchise such as *Mission: Impossible*. Here he discusses how their small development team approaches game testing.

Asked about the importance of testing and how to go about it, Büttner answers as follows:

Testing is one of the essentials and has a great importance during a game's development. We start to test the game in-house right after reaching the alpha version. The quality assurance at the publisher side starts roughly one month before the beta version.

With *Mission: Impossible* for the Sony PlayStation, Büttner adds:

We also had two different teams doing the QA—one for the European version and one for the U.S. market. Our current project is again a license title. In-house we do a large QA session every month, which shows the current status of the project and brings up a new bug report for the designers and programmers. Testing at the publisher side this time will start two months before the first beta version, so there's enough time to react early and implement new ideas, features, and suggestions—which generally makes the game better.

For more information on Mission: Impossible—The Game, visit www.mi-thegame.com. The game is available on the Nintendo 64, Sony PlayStation, and Game Boy Color. (Used with permission from Infogrames North America, © 2000 PARAMOUNT PICTURES)

 For more on role-playing game testing, turn to Chapter 3 to read the comments of Blizzard Entertainment's Bill Roper, who discusses varied testing techniques while developing *Diablo* and *Diablo II*.

HARRY GOTTLIEB, JELLYVISION

Does the testing process differ for puzzle games, such as the coveted *You Don't Know Jack* series? To answer this question, Jellyvision's lead designer Harry Gottlieb begins by stressing, "Game testing isn't *important*. It's *essential*." He expands:

> Jellyvision doesn't release a program until we've confirmed that our audience thinks it's great *and* we as creators think it's great. I can't imagine releasing a program into the world that embarrassed me or that might flop creatively; a sip of hemlock is always preferable to a public stoning (and takes far less energy for all involved).
>
> We have a full-time Audience Information Services [A.I.S.] group at Jellyvision (and have had it in place from the time we were less than 30 people). All sorts of testing are fully integrated into Jellyvision's design process. Someone comes up with an idea. A designer fleshes it out on paper, getting feedback from colleagues. We simulate the play of the game in a "paper and pencil" format: We use index cards, overhead transparencies, bells, whistles, and whatnot. The designer or one of Jellyvision's many improv actors (who double as writers, editors, audio producers, programmers, or artists by day) acts as the host. First we test with our own staff. If the core idea (what we call "the interactive moment") is a complete flop, we drop the project. Otherwise, we shape it and bend it and keep testing it with our staff. This is surprisingly affordable.
>
> Once we think the program is brilliant, we then test it with outside folks—who often do us the favor of telling us otherwise. If the core idea is still engaging, we keep shaping. This is when things get exciting: Having your audience tell you that your "brilliant" ideas are merely "good" encourages a strong designer to come up with much better ideas—features to fix the problems are

so creative that, when the product is finished, you can't imagine it without them. When a good designer hears criticism, her imagination kicks into gear. Mediocre designers fix problems with obvious solutions (usually the ones subjects suggest in focus groups).

At Jellyvision, we are very clear about the role of the audience: their job is to tell us what's wrong. Our job is to come back with solutions that surprise them.

We never "explain" a product to a focus group. We always create a simulation, demo, or prototype that is adequately close to the real thing (given where we are in the process) so that we can get real feedback. Our A.I.S. staff helps us sort out the subject's biases created from the test instrument.

Before we start spending the big bucks to go into full production (adding teams of artists, writers, musicians, programmers, etc.), we do *prototype confirmation testing*. We create the full prototype with all the core gameplay features, including sample writing, music, performance, and well-honed timing, but without the pretty art. If that works, then we paint on all the fancy colors. (The original prototype for *You Don't Know Jack* was done in black and white in HyperCard. Except for the artwork, it plays almost identically to the game today.)

A key thing that studios and production houses need to remember: Hire great designers (or creative folks with great design potential), give them the training and support they need, require them to listen to feedback—but let them make the decisions. Testing is sometimes used by well-intentioned marketing folks to "backseat design" the program. That's why many creative development people hate focus groups, instead of loving them. (Jellyvision designers LOVE focus groups). A great program needs to be guided by someone with a clear, singular vision, who is smart enough to crave feedback and creative enough to respond to it in ways unexpected. But that someone needs the authority to run. Good designers in the right environment will know when to break out the hemlock on their own.

Gottlieb explains the term *interactive moment*:

The interactive moment: A key activity that makes the entire program psychologically engaging (e.g. trying to figure out the answer to a question, deciding whether to force your opponent to answer, deciding what cards to play in your hand, figuring out what route to take to dodge the ghosts and eat all the blue dots, etc.). The interactive moment doesn't happen on the screen; it happens in the player's head.

In Chapter 3, Harry Gottlieb covers a few of the game design "rules" they adhere to when developing these award-winning pop culture trivia diversions.

RICHARD "LORD BRITISH" GARRIOTT

The one and only Richard "Lord British" Garriott, formerely of Origin Systems and the conceiver of the legendary *Ultima* series at Origin, says a lot of effort is poured into game testing, especially for online games, as experienced with the popular

Ultima Online. Says Garriott, "A successful online game must have good engineering from the start; you have to have good code. And once you have good code, the QA testers can do their job well."

Unfortunately, there was no way to thoroughly test a breakthrough, massively-multiplayer game like *Ultima Online* early on in the process, as evidenced by a few unhappy players after the game's initial launch. But many more servers around the world have been added for less Internet congestion, while a handful of full-time engineers are handling the bandwidth issues back in Texas as well.

Garriott says when they tested games internally, they attempted to play the game as a player would, and went through a checklist procedure. This included all of the game's features and combinations of features, and could become quite the tedious task. He explains:

> For example, if a magic system has 50 spells, a tester must test each of the spells and the spell combinations, on all monster types, NPCs (non-player characters), and items, on every map. This is a huge matrix—in fact, they have binders full of these [checklists]. And you have to do this with every version of the game [every "build" throughout the game development process].

On top of all this, Garriott reminds us that this all has to be done on all machine types and configurations. Sounds like fun, huh?

SID MEIER, FIRAXIS GAMES

The honorable Mr. Sid Meier has appeared many times throughout this book to lend his thoughts on game design. When it comes to proper testing, he mirrors the sentiment offered by Richard Garriott.

> First is bug testing, which should be done by as many people [as possible] on many different machines. Also, it's important for the tester to use a method of reproducing and documenting the bug.

After all, finding a bug isn't worth its weight unless it can be captured and reported; therefore, Meier uses various techniques, such as an autosave feature in the game that will bookmark the game every 10 seconds or so. This way, a previous game can be loaded if a bug is found.

The second kind of testing done under Meier's supervision is to find out if the game is too hard or too easy:

> Designers have no way of telling because they're too close to the project to get an objective look at the game. The key is to give the game to people and watch what they're doing, and to see where they get stuck.

Meier also believes that the first half hour of gameplay is critical, and an important determinant of whether the gamer will keep playing the game.

RON GILBERT, HUMONGOUS ENTERTAINMENT

The omnipotent Ron Gilbert is responsible for many best-selling LucasArts, Humongous Entertainment, and Cavedog Entertainment games. When the topic of testing comes up, Gilbert reminds us that "adventure games are different." What does he mean by this?

> Adventure game testing is more just looking for bugs than anything else. You don't have balancing issues as in real-time strategy games, or the kind of testing needed in multiplayer games. In adventure games, there's a set path, set objects—not a whole lot of permutations.

Gilbert says when it comes to testing games like Cavedog Entertainment's *Total Annihilation: Kingdoms*, they spend days play testing it to make sure that all units are balanced properly. And after a multiplayer skirmish, they all get together to talk about the experience. Is this common? Says Gilbert:

> It's the only way to go for a game like this. For bugs, testers should fill out forms and documents, but when you're testing gameplay, it's best to talk about it.

Gilbert offers an example of a gameplay issue found while testing. "If archers are building up too quickly and you're able to swarm an enemy base, we adjust the building of those units by slowing it down, and then we play it again. We do this until everything is balanced out."

Gilbert says they do no outside testing at Humongous, as all QA testing is done internally by the respective teams.

CHAPTER 16
MARKETING AND PUBLIC RELATIONS

The unfortunate reality is that no matter how good a game is, if no one knows about it, it just won't sell. In this day and age, hype, exposure, and distribution muscle are needed to sell games—or at least one of the three. (Let's face it—the mega-successful *Deer Hunter* had no hype or magazine exposure, but it was found in every Wal-Mart, with a $19.99 price tag!)

Public relations representatives (reps) and marketing reps have the same goal—to get the product known—but how they go about it varies greatly. Loosely speaking, public relations (PR) reps work with the press to get media exposure, while marketing reps tend to deal more directly with the consumer through advertising, packaging, and promotions; and in some cases they deal with retailers regarding distribution channels and presentation issues.

Doug Lombardi, a marketing representative at Sierra Studios, elaborates on the job requirements for each of these two important positions:

> Two key areas that every game publisher must address in garnering critical mind share for a product are marketing and public relations.
>
> Generally speaking, *public relations* representatives handle all communications with the press, which subsequently gets the information to the end user via previews, features, news stories, etc. Specifically, the PR duties include setting up press tours, promotional events, and editorial visits to the studio or development house. Additionally, the PR reps manage the creation of releases about the product, developer, and company—while also responding to all inquiries from the press for interviews, artwork, etc.
>
> The *marketing* folks, on the other hand, manage the creation of more direct communications to the consumer, such as advertisements, packaging, and so on. In most cases, the marketing manager works very closely with a creative agency to produce the product's visual identity as well as the aforementioned promotional materials. And in some cases, the marketing manager pursues third-party (or *co-op*) promotions and agreements, in which a software publishing house, for example, partners with a technology company to co-promote both companies' products.

Many gaming developers and publishers opt to hire an outside PR agency or marketing firm to handle their business. There are pros and cons for hiring an agency, as discussed over the next few pages.

The goal of this chapter is to shed some light on these two roles by delivering helpful advice from seasoned industry professionals. They cover the best ways to conduct successful public relations and savvy marketing for your game.

PUBLIC RELATIONS

BILL LINN, LINN PR

Linn Public Relations, Inc. was founded by Bill Linn, a longtime game industry public relations veteran. His clients include well-known gaming companies such as THQ and the 3DO Company.

Linn maintains that game developers have greater pull in the media than publishers, and they should know this. Argues Linn:

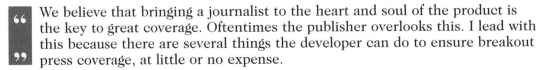

> We believe that bringing a journalist to the heart and soul of the product is the key to great coverage. Oftentimes the publisher overlooks this. I lead with this because there are several things the developer can do to ensure breakout press coverage, at little or no expense.

Following are but a few of Linn's golden rules on what separates the good PR reps from the inadequate.

RELATIONSHIPS

Linn believes that the best articles come from knowing the editors. Just how do you build that relationship?

> Developers who don't have PR people should go out of their way to give the "right" information to the "right" editor at the "right" time. I emphasize that because developers can over-communicate and irritate editors. For example, a developer reads in a magazine about another company doing a similar product. Find out who the editor is and shoot him an email. It might say, "I saw your article on (*game name goes here*) and wanted to let you know about our product. *Blah blah blah.*" End the *brief* email with an invitation to see the game in person. Don't panic if he or she doesn't reply. The next time you have a major milestone, send the editor a little note saying, "Hey, we just did x, y, or z; is this something you might be interested in seeing?" Casual, down to earth, and honest is the key. Editors hate arrogance, big claims, and pushy people.

SELL THE VISION

Although he admits it's a slightly different approach to what most PR reps do, Linn encourages developers to sell more than just the game's feature set. He explains:

> Early on, you must sell the vision of your game. What inspired you? What games influenced your design? How does your background play into the design? What team did you assemble to create it? Those are questions for

> which journalists want the answers. If you hit them with adjectives and unsubstantiated claims, you bore the crap out of them. A good way to [provide the details they want] is to create an outline—your game is the story. Make the outline chronological, from the time you began to the current date. Pick out the highlights that will be interesting to the journalist and then use them to map out a presentation.

TEAMPLAY

Along with selling the vision of the game, Linn recommends pitching your entire development team:

> Often we make sure that the journalist gets to meet the lead artists, the lead programmer, and even a tester. Everyone on the team contributes to selling the game. Make sure you use them. Before you do this, however, be sure to train them on working with the media, prepare an outline for a press visit, and practice a lot before anyone comes to your company.

To learn more about Bill Linn's philosophies, background, and services, visit www.linnpr.com.

GENEVIEVE OSTERGARD, SIERRA STUDIOS

As senior PR manager for Sierra Studios, Genevieve Ostergard works with both the gaming press and more consumer-based publications for the titles she represents. Before settling down with Sierra Studios, she worked at an outside agency and internally for some of the largest PC gaming publishers in the world, namely Microsoft and Interplay.

Ostergard confirms good relationships are key to a successful public relations career:

> Public relations is all about relationships. If you're doing your own PR, get to know the gaming editors by meeting them face to face. Good ways of doing that are at trade shows, industry gatherings, or meeting with the editors in their offices. Similarly, know their publications and which editors are assigned which beat.

Other than securing trusted bonds with journalists and editors, Ostergard offers a few random pointers to bear in mind as a new PR rep:

> - **Press releases:** Write well and to the point. Don't over-hype. Get a book on writing for the news or public-relations writing to get the gist of good writing techniques.
>
> - **Know your strategy.** Come up with a plan. Don't just throw information to the world and hope someone comes knocking on your door.
>
> - **Be responsive.** Call back or leave alternate ways of reaching you. This will help create a trusting relationship between you and the journalist.

- **Be creative.** Mailers, freebies, and giveaways are always good, but try an event and invite the press. Keep in mind that even though a party is fun, there's nothing newsworthy about it. But a party with a celebrity or special guest is sure to bring attention to your game and journalists in attendance.

- **Keep a very good database.** If you make a promise to follow up with someone, make sure you do it.

Scoring the front cover of a popular gaming publication for your product is as good as it gets. Of course, it helps to have a great game to pitch. Genevieve Ostergard arranged this Half-Life cover story with PC Accelerator magazine. (Used with permission by Sierra Studios and Imagine Media, Inc.)

Ostergard suggests that budding PR reps consider the following books as recommended reading: *The Associated Press Stylebook and Libel Manual*, Norm Goldstein, ed., et al (Perseus, 1998); *Writing Broadcast News: Shorter, Sharper, Stronger* by Mervin Block (Bonus Books, 1997); and the *Publicity Handbook* by David R. Yale (NTC, 1992).

JEANE WONG, ELECTRONIC ARTS

If there's one name incredibly familiar to the press covering the console or computer gaming industries, it's Jeane Wong. This hard-working public relations manager at the world's largest game software company, Electronic Arts, has been in the PR biz since 1996. Here, she shares her knowledge on getting your company's products reviewed.

According to Wong, the three most important requirements in public relations are to be creative, be organized, and be professional. She explains:

> The public relations field is definitely a fast-paced, exciting career. The industry you choose will somewhat depend on the way you work with others, namely the press. For example, the interactive gaming community is a much

younger audience when compared to that of mainstream press, business press, etc. A lot of the people are 30 and younger (some even in their teens). Because of the ages and nature of the industry in general, I think there's a good opportunity for everyone to branch out and be more creative than with a lot of the other "traditional" industries. Having a healthy PR/marketing budget definitely is helpful, but I firmly believe that it's much more beneficial to have a creative campaign than an expensive one…especially in the gaming industry, where there's a lot of money floating around.

In the following passage, Wong gives an example to support her advice, and discusses the PR representative's obligation to be truthful to the media:

Flying a press person around the world to wine and dine him/her isn't as beneficial to your PR efforts as implementing a creative PR angle and/or event that helps the journalist craft cool new story ideas, themes, etc. I've heard from many editorial friends that it isn't the money PR/companies spend on them, but the creative angles and opportunities they provide that can help sell an article to the editor. Quite honestly, I am glad to hear this, since it should never be about money, but quality of the product and PR pitch. The beauty of our job is that we're given a lot of creative freedom to position and publicize the projects in the best light. In addition, it's always good to be up front and honest about things…everyone always thinks that PR people lie, but I've always prided myself on being honest. There may be questions that I don't answer (avoid) and/or situations where I won't confirm things one way or the other, but that's different than boldface lying, which I find very offensive. You're only as good as your reputation, especially if you want to be successful at PR.

MICHAEL MEYERS, 3DO

Mike Meyers is the director of product public relations at 3DO. Before joining forces with this West Coast developer/publisher, Meyers was instrumental in the promotion of Acclaim Entertainment's console game products and worked on many campaigns such as *Turok: Dinosaur Hunter*, *Turok 2: Seeds of Evil*, *NFL Quarterback Club '98* and *'99*, *South Park*, *WWF: Warzone*, and many others. Meyers offers three crucial considerations for newbie PR reps:

KNOW YOUR MEDIA

Don't pitch any publication, television show, radio program, or Internet site unless you're very familiar with their style, editorial schedule, tendencies, etc. If you know a journalist's work, you'll have a better chance of the journalist wanting to become familiar with your product.

RELATIONSHIPS ARE ESSENTIAL

Game developers and gaming journalists have something in common—they're both passionate about games. One of the best things about my job is that I get to talk gaming with journalists who have the same passion about the subject. If journalists recognize your passion for gaming, they'll find you much more believable when you tell them your game is the best _____ for _____ platform.

DON'T OPERATE IN A VACUUM

> One of the biggest mistakes developers and/or PR representatives can make is presenting their product without thoroughly researching the competition.
>
> A journalist will want to know how your game differs from something else within the same genre. If you don't know how your game exceeds the competition, the journalist won't be able to tell his/her readers.

In the following anecdote, Meyers applies these three pieces of advice to a project he worked on recently:

> One of the largest PR efforts I've had the pleasure of being associated with was the launch of *Turok: Dinosaur Hunter* at Acclaim Entertainment. *Turok* was one of the first third-party titles available for the N64. More importantly, it was the first title of Acclaim's big turnaround effort—the survival of Acclaim was tied to its success.
>
> Everyone on the Acclaim PR team as well as at our agency (TSI) had a role in the *Turok* effort. I was in charge of what we deemed the "*Turok* Internet Assault." The Internet Assault was a grassroots PR effort to get every amateur and professional N64 site to dedicate a large portion of their front page to *Turok*. The Assault took place over an eight-week period leading up to the launch of the game. Every Monday we would distribute exclusive screenshots and QuickTime movies to the largest "professional" sites. Each of these large sites was given 3–4 days exclusivity, and then all materials were placed on a server where anyone could download them and use them on their site.
>
> Within weeks of the launch of this Internet effort, the Web was filled with images and buzz about Acclaim's upcoming game. Since consumers who read dedicated N64 Web sites are more likely to own an N64 (or plan on buying one soon), we provided our most valuable potential customers with all the information they needed to make an informed buying decision.

Keep in mind that many of Meyers' games were bestsellers in 1998: *South Park*, *Turok 2: Seeds of Evil*, and *WWF: Warzone* on the Nintendo 64 and Sony PlayStation.

The Public Relations Society of America (PRSA) is a great place to start for those interested in learning more about the trade. The URL is simply www.prsa.com.

ADAM KAHN, ACCLAIM ENTERTAINMENT

Just before moving to Acclaim's East Coast offices at the end of 1998, Kahn worked at Shandwick International, a PR firm, on the Microsoft games account. Over the next couple of pages, Kahn discusses his approach to gaming PR and what newcomers to the profession could gain from this advice.

> I think there are a few key things that game designers should know about PR in the games industry. First of all, they should know that it's not rocket science. PR for games is about being strategic, smart, and focused, but it's certainly nothing to get intimidated about. That being said, it's also important for them to understand that PR is best undertaken by someone who can be

strategic, smart, and focused. I've worked with a lot of small development companies, and seen a lot of people who think they're strategic, smart, and focused, but they're really not. There are a lot of examples out there that show it's very difficult to be a full-time game developer and a PR/marketing guru. They're wildly disparate job functions and probably cater to completely different personality styles. Developers would do well to leave the PR to someone who knows/enjoys PR and stay focused on developing a great game.

Here's what I mean by strategic, smart, and focused.

Being *strategic* means seeing PR from a very high altitude. It means looking at a PR campaign from beginning to end, very early on, and deciding when you want coverage, where you want coverage, and what types of coverage you want. I've seen a lot of developers get very tactical in their PR. They get whipped up on a title and start thinking that they need coverage *right now* in a certain magazine, or they see John Romero in *Rolling Stone* and think that should be them. It just can't work that way. If you're strategic, you've planned ahead and, barring any major shifts in the marketplace, you can sail right through those issues without worrying. Being strategic means making tough decisions very early on. Let's say you have two titles that are shipping within a few months of each other. Which one is your focus title? There are companies out there who say that every title they release gets the same marketing and PR budget, but that just can't work in the long run. Certain titles will benefit from bigger budgets, and others won't. Strategic thinkers look at these situations, step back from company politics, and make decisions.

Being *smart* means knowing who you're dealing with, specifically in the press. There are a lot of games out there, and editors and freelancers are under a lot of pressure to get their jobs done. Anything you can do to make their jobs easier will be rewarded in the long run. If writers call you and ask for screenshots, you get the screenshots to them as soon as possible. There are no ifs, ands, or buts about it. You just do it. Being smart also means that there isn't anyone small enough to ignore. Editors at the smallest gaming Web sites can become editor-in-chief at major gaming publications—it's happened before—and blowing someone off is the easiest way to kill a relationship. Pay attention to everyone.

Being *focused* is kind of the opposite of being strategic. You can't stay in the clouds all the time, so it pays to spend time focusing on tactical things like events, creative execution, and timing. Take pride in pulling off a great event that uses editors' time effectively. Be creative. But never waste writers' time. That goes back to being smart. You want editors to open your email every time you send them something. The fastest way to get into their "ignore" box is to waste their time.

Does someone need a lot of money to deal successfully with the press? Kahn talks about how someone with little or no budget can get their game exposure in the media:

It really doesn't cost that much to do PR, especially if you've been in the industry for a while and know the right people to contact. If you don't know the right people it's a lot harder, but you can do a lot of the grunt work just through research in magazines and on the Web. If you haven't been around very long, you're probably going to need to visit gaming publications and get in front of editors. This is the most efficient way to get noticed, and since the U.S. gaming press is mostly in San Francisco, it's easy to take a few days and see nearly everyone.

Of course, it's probably a good idea to hire a small PR agency that specializes in gaming. They've spent years developing relationships, and you can leverage those relationships financed by all the fees that other companies have paid them. Using an outside PR firm allows you to focus on game development, which is probably what you're best at since you're a developer.

And finally, Kahn says that, assuming you've spent some time getting to know the various editors at gaming magazines, getting reviews shouldn't be hard at all. Get them final code on time and they'll do a review.

When it comes to PR, should game developers or publishers do it themselves by bringing people in internally, or should they hire an outside agency? There are advantages and disadvantages to both scenarios. On one hand, internal PR has a chance to get closer to the development of the product—not to mention that they only work for that particular company, so their vision is arguably more focused. An agency, on the other hand, usually costs less than internal positions and likely has an experienced staff and a database full of great contacts in the media, and many of these PR reps already have a relationship with members of the press. However, an agency typically has multiple clients and may not give your account the attention it deserves.

MARKETING

BRANDON SMITH, HUMONGOUS ENTERTAINMENT

Having worked as communications manager on the breakthrough title *Total Annihilation* (and its expansion packs) while at Cavedog, you can bet Brandon Smith, now at sister company Humongous, played a role in the game's international success. Says Smith, "I think one of the most important things for any marketer to keep in mind as they develop strategies for marketing their products is to know their audience." He expands on this advice:

And I mean really *know* them. Know what they eat, where they hang out, what they do in their spare time (besides play games)—you name it, you should know it. I can't stress and/or express this enough. If you don't know these things, a marketer's life can become very difficult and a product's life can become very short.

However, with this knowledge firmly in place, what you need to do on the marketing front becomes much easier and more intuitive. You'll quickly discern what things incent your audience to make purchases and how best you can fit into that picture. For example, knowing that your particular audience has a preference for football over baseball could lead to an effective promotional campaign with the NFL. Or maybe your audience rents games from a retail chain at phenomenal rates; the result might be a special tie-in to offer dollars off a purchase of your game if they rent at least three titles from that retailer.

Asked how a company can market a product on a shoestring budget, Smith responds by saying this gets tougher and tougher each year, as our industry gets more and more competitive. "Truth be told, you really *must* partner with a strong publisher or distributor to do your title justice." So what's a small developer to do? Smith responds with a few ideas:

I think there are a few things that companies can do to help themselves out when they don't have an EA or GT Interactive providing the retail muscle most products need these days (and FYI, these points are true of all companies, regardless of stature):

You have to make a good product! There are no ifs, ands, or buts about it. No amount of marketing power will save a poor software title. I'm sure there are exceptions to the rule, but I would never want to bet money on that horse.

Focus your limited marketing funds on press relations. It's tremendously more efficient, with the potential of a much greater return. It's one thing to say that you have the hottest new game technology in an advertisement, but if an editor at Next Generation says the same thing it will have a much larger impact—guaranteed. Marketing and advertising are key to a well-rounded campaign, but can be extremely expensive (and if you have to shave dollars, I'd do it here). Positive press coverage of your title can create tremendous word-of-mouth and eventually demand for your title. It will also help accomplish the last point.

Build up grassroots support for the game with consumers early. This will help on a number of fronts. One of the most important (and expensive) aspects of marketing is convincing the retail channel to carry the game (hence the need for a strong publisher or distributor)—if they don't carry it, you can't sell it. This usually involves demonstrating to retail that the game will be supported with a MASSIVE marketing campaign. Unfortunately, this is quite expensive, and if you don't have the money the odds are already stacking up against you. This is effectively a traditional *push* strategy, where you're telling the retailer they must carry it because of what you're doing to support the title.

Smith elaborates on this last point, the grassroots aspect of a marketing campaign:

[This] can help (keyword *help*, since it's no guarantee) accomplish the same goal, but by using a different means. Rather than you convincing the retailer to carry the product, you allow the consumer to do so. By incenting and evangelizing consumers about the product, you can effectively get them to work to your goal of securing shelf space and selling units. With a combination of fans contacting their local software retailers and you informing them of the already huge consumer demand for the title (using press clippings, etc.) you can engage in a *pull* strategy, where retailers feel that they'll lose out on sales if they don't carry the title. You can end up at the same place, but just use a different route to get there. Of course, the best route would involve a solid combination of push and pull.

These are all simplistically detailed points, but still cover some key areas. How exactly individual companies go about doing these things is what will separate those that succeed from those that don't.

Can he offer any direct examples of faultless game marketing?

I really respected Sony's campaign to launch the PlayStation some years ago. They did everything right (of course they had a virtually bottomless budget). They knew the audience so well that they "out-cooled" the coolest company at the time—Sega—and stole their user base. They had a great piece of hardware.

At the same time it suddenly became okay for a 20+ year old to own the system, thanks to a clever ad campaign. This meant older consumers with larger disposable incomes were purchasing a traditionally younger platform. The product's ads were so effective that potential consumers were recording those on television and tearing them out of magazines because the company had hidden codes for the upcoming games in them. Thus ads were being viewed again and again, and being heavily discussed at work, home, and online. Great grassroots stuff.

They launched the PlayStation Underground—a club where consumers could get demos of the latest games—again, very grassroots focused.

I believe it to be one of the most effective consumer product launches of all time (not just in the game industry—*all* consumer products).

DOUG LOMBARDI, SIERRA STUDIOS

Along with giving us a more thorough explanation earlier in this chapter on the differences between public relations and marketing, Sierra Studios' Doug Lombardi is here to discuss the necessity and timeliness of Internet gaming demos.

From a purely marketing perspective, a public demo is one of the most powerful weapons for promoting a new product. This is especially true if said product has not captured a considerable amount of the gaming community's attention.

Sometimes a great title just isn't picked up by the gaming media, for whatever reason. In this case, releasing a killer demo—a few weeks before the product is published—gives gamers a chance to check it out, and the game can achieve critical mind share via word of mouth, the most effective form of advertising known to man. Any research done on the subject shows that most gamers prefer to try before they buy, and many gamers simply will not buy a game unless they have a chance to play it first. Given the short lifecycle of a software title in this day and age, it's now critical that some sort of compelling public sampling is made available in a timely fashion. A compelling demo gives players a look at the game's strongest features, and when done right can leave players thinking, "Wow, this is as good as they said it was. I must have it."

But is it possible a demo could backfire? Lombardi says it depends:

The other side of the coin is when demos were simply not ready for prime time, and there are dozens of examples of those—*or* those that gave away the farm, leaving the players feeling like they'd gotten their fill.

With reference to timing, releasing the demo before the full title hits store shelves can be effective, but also dangerous. Certainly, in the case of several classics, the demo helped make them—and arguably *made* them—a smash. But there are several examples of publishers/developers that released their demos way too soon, sometimes months before the full product's feature set was finally complete.

More and more these days, we're seeing the demo released just after the product is released. A risky option with a title that has received only limited buzz. But if the title has the hype, releasing a solid sampling within 90 days of the product's release can certainly help give the title a boost at retail. That is, so long as the demo rocks and leaves you wanting more.

LIZ BELL, THQ

THQ's Liz Bell comments on the option of free demos for PC games as an effective marketing strategy:

Demos should only be released on high-quality games that the publisher expects to be reviewed positively. They should be a clear representation of a piece of the final product, but should only include enough of the game to get the consumer excited. Withhold levels, weapons, characters, and the multiplayer option so the consumer longs for the complete experience. The ideal schedule would include a covermount [typically, the cardboard artwork on a magazine's demo disc] exclusive with a magazine eight weeks before ship, hitting online, and the rest of the covermounts four weeks out, and educating your smaller retail chain managers with the demo at ship. If the lead time on the demo is only four weeks, online exclusives are also very effective.

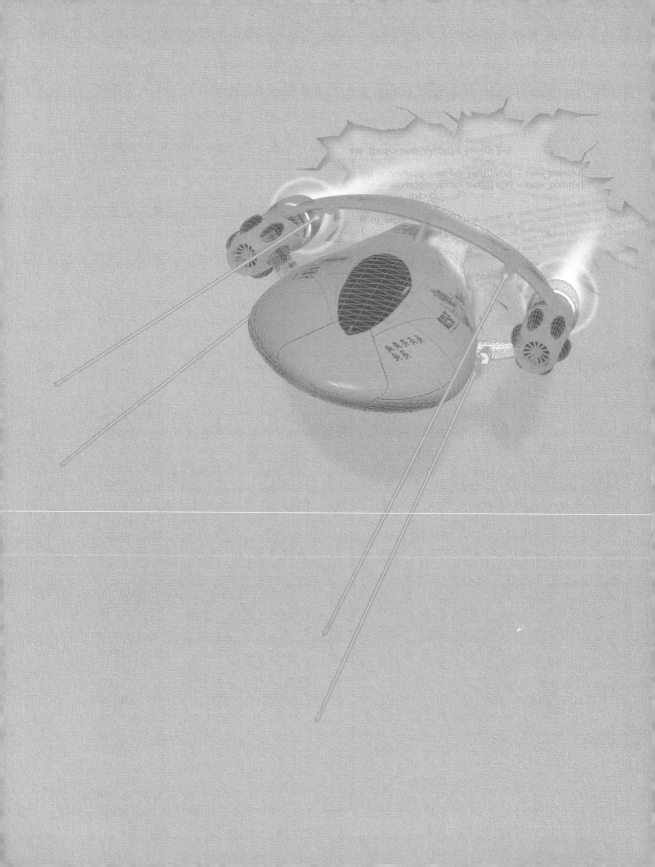

CHAPTER 17
GAMING WEB SITE DESIGN

In less than five years, the Internet evolved from being a virtually unheard-of medium to one of the most exciting innovations of the 20th century, from a couple thousand university students and government officials to over 50 million surfers, and growing exponentially.

The birth of the World Wide Web, in particular, was an integral component to the commercialization of the Internet in the mid-1990s. With the graphical and easy-to-use interfaces of Mosaic and Netscape, it was now easier than ever to navigate around this information highway to access the millions of documents and databases, not to mention that it added multimedia—pictures, sound, music, animation, and video—to all this text.

The Web is also one of the most important inventions for the gaming industry. People can play their favorite games against one another (or many others) from anywhere in the world. No longer do gamers have to wait a couple of weeks for a patch to arrive on a floppy disk. Gamers can "try before you buy" with an endless number of commercial game demos. Budding programmers, artists, game designers, and musicians can showcase their own creations internationally, from the comfort and convenience of home. Electronic magazines (e-zines) cater to the gaming community by the dozens. Game developers and publishers offer free, downloadable add-ins to their existing titles (or the opportunity for gamers to make their own modifications). Fan sites give dedicated gamers their own soapbox to millions of other like-minded individuals. Gamers can purchase games online and have them delivered right to their door. Free cheat codes, strategy guides, and walkthroughs make it harder to justify spending $15 on a hint book (plus all the interactive chat groups and bulletin boards gamers can partake in). Gaming journalists can work anywhere in the world for any magazine, newspaper, or Web site, since stories and images can be submitted electronically. And the list goes on and on (and on).

This chapter looks at the necessity of creating and maintaining an excellent Web site to accompany the release of a game, whether this is for your own shareware or freeware title or you want to work for a developer or publisher to help promote their games. Throughout the following pages, we'll hear from Webmasters as well as marketing representatives on using this new medium to your advantage—what's best to include on a Web site in this day and age, and a handful of tips on what separates great Web sites from lackluster ones.

DANIEL BRAY, CUBIK MEDIA AND MARKETING

Daniel Bray is a creative director at Cubik Media and Marketing, a company dedicated to designing and building Web sites. One of their biggest clients is Eidos Interactive, Inc. Bray was asked why a computer game publisher (or developer, for that matter) should create a Web site to correspond with the release of a game. What should be offered there? How important is the use of multimedia (plug-ins, etc.) versus load time? He responds:

> Cool Web sites go hand in hand with cool games. Gamers are very tech-savvy. They're on the Web; they use the Web as their first point for getting info on new games. Downloading demos is the number one reason why gamers come to gaming sites. A demo should always immediately precede the release of a game. Also, screenshots are crucial. They give the gamer an idea of how the game looks.
>
> Multimedia is very important. It brings the site to life, it makes it exciting. Yes, load time is an issue, but it will decrease in importance as technology races forward.

In short, Bray admits, "We love plug-ins!"

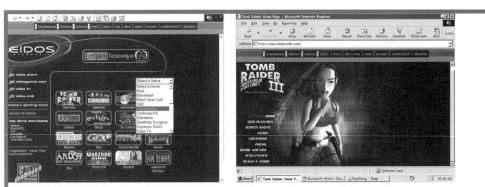

Bray predicts that gaming Web sites will soon become the number one way gamers get information on games. With that in mind, he says to add as much multimedia as possible to create a "buzz" about it. (Used with permission by Eidos Interactive, Inc.)

SACHA FERNANDES, EIDOS INTERACTIVE

While Cubik's Daniel Bray and company create the Web site layout for Eidos Interactive, Sacha Fernandes is the in-house online marketing manager, in charge of managing the interactive marketing and the Web site itself. Here's what she has to say about the importance of a good gaming Web site:

> With emerging trends in technology and the huge Internet revolution, the World Wide Web is a valuable tool that most businesses are not taking for granted. In the short history of online marketing, the Web has become a marketing vehicle of enormous proportions. Gamers are a tech-savvy audience, and they spend quite a substantial number of hours—long hours—surfing the Web for hints, tips, chat sessions, etc.
>
> More and more people are turning to the Web for information, travel arrangements, shopping needs, and entertainment, including online gaming networks. It's important to have a site up live corresponding to a product launch; in fact, gamers are looking for information months before a game is scheduled to launch. Having a Web site enables the publisher/developer to communicate with its consumer and therefore becomes an effective marketing tool. Often in this industry, products slip, and the Web becomes a viable source of the latest information. The goal is to keep people coming back and have your site become a community of sorts, gaining valuable cross-sell opportunities [corporate branding, building equity in other product brands, etc.].

On what should be included on game-related Web sites, Fernandes offers the following:

> Product information, including storyline and cool features. Remember, this is a marketing tool. Therefore, [include] all information pertinent to selling the game to the consumer within an aesthetically pleasing layout.
>
> With the slew of Web sites out there, you're competing for attention and need to have compelling stuff on your site to be able to stand out. In order to first sustain that traffic base and then increase it through word of mouth, you have to go above and beyond in terms of the quality of your Web site and the programming tools used. Dynamic [Shockwave] Flash, Java-enabled sites, etc. capture attention—more so than a basic Web site.
>
> Generally, we find our traffic base to own fairly good systems, browsers, and modems (more often than not, they have T1, ISDN, or DSL), so file size is not a big issue. We find that it's the content rather than load time that determines the download numbers. Demos can be as large as 50MB and the download numbers are huge. That's directly related to the hype revolved around that title. If it's a great game, people are going to find a way to get the demo or plug-in.
>
> Regarding downloads, installation instructions and approximate download times given various modem speeds are an optional courtesy.

We've covered content, but how important is good navigation? Fernandes responds by asserting that "navigation is key." She continues, "This comes into play more with e-commerce sites, but even otherwise, fluid, efficient navigation is a must. If it's too complicated or someone's spending a lot of time and getting nowhere, chances of them returning are slim—you failed to make it a pleasant experience."

While wrapping up, Fernandes discusses an extra bonus Eidos Interactive has added to their site for their consumers—Eidos TV.

> We launched Eidos TV (eTV) in April 1998, using Flash technology. In addition to just having product information on our wealth of Eidos games, we host fan clubs, newsletters, our strategy War Room, etc. All of this serves as an added value to our consumer and makes it all a pleasing, interactive, and fun environment for them to hang out in—and, more importantly, come back to.

Be sure to drop by and check out Eidos Interactive and Eidos TV at www.eidos.com.

MATTHEW D'ANDRIA, CYBERNATION

CyberNation creates Web sites for some of the more popular gaming destinations on the Internet, including Capcom, Activision, Konami, and Cendant Software. Chief creative officer Matthew D'Andria joins us here to discuss the importance of a stellar Web site and what makes it stand out among the online crowd:

> The Web provides a powerful platform from which to build brand recognition for any new game title. The gaming audience is one of the largest and most Internet-savvy groups online, and they tend to take full advantage of whatever the Web has to offer, including chat, online gameplay, multimedia content, and online commerce.
>
> A good game site will offer cool, exclusive content at its site as a value-add beyond what's available in the manual or other media. This way, game companies can count on a steady stream of return traffic from the game's most dedicated followers (and its best market for tie-ins and merchandise). Online commerce has extremely low overhead and offers worldwide distribution. CyberNation has built a number of successful online stores, including those for Capcom and Activision. It's always great to build an online community through chat, bulletin boards, or mailing lists for large game series such as *Resident Evil*.

But what about multimedia? What about those who have slow Internet connections? D'Andria says they've seen that most gamers have powerful computers, lots of memory, and fairly fast Internet connections. He continues:

> Therefore, we can create sites that require a little more bandwidth than we do for most of our other non-gaming clients. Wherever possible, we try to implement multimedia and an enhanced user experience without the use of plug-ins. We have built several online games without the use of plug-ins, including the first playable demo of a console game, *Super Puzzle Fighter*.

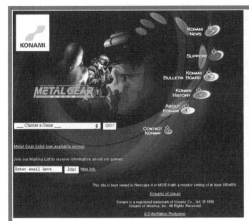

As illustrated here with three separate clients, game Web sites may feature key game information (Konami, above left), the option to purchase products online (Activision, above right), or online games (Capcom, right). (Used with permission by CyberNation)

Many game designers who are just starting out can't afford to hire CyberNation, so D'Andria offers some advice on creating content for the Web and getting the word out:

> You don't necessarily need a lot of money to design a good site—just good people. The best way to make a site successful is to offer something that can't be found anywhere else. Content is key. With very little money you can build a small site. Be sure to get the site listed on all the major search engines and portals—which is usually free. Also, start emailing and calling the people in charge of other successful game sites, and try to work out deals to exchange links. Word of mouth is always the best advertising for a Web site, no matter what your budget is.

All of CyberNation's work for their gaming clients can be accessed at their home page, www.cnation.com.

CHRIS SIVERTSEN, EA SPORTS

Chris Sivertsen, an Internet marketing specialist at EA Sports, says a Web site is an ideal medium to promote and market a video/PC game for numerous reasons:

> **Budget.** A site can scale to a wide spectrum of budgets. Whether you have a startup or *Star Wars* title to push, you can find an equitable way to present the information. Games are full of many wonderful digital assets (text, art, sounds, and so on) that you can feature within different levels of packaging. More budget, more sophisticated packaging.
>
> **Choices.** Gamers are online and they're accustomed to having numerous sources of info at their fingertips. You can provide much deeper info than any other medium allows. You can also update this information frequently and add new features to encourage consumers to return again and again. Where else will consumers learn about your game? You can also leverage proprietary content like "making of" stories, where you can share and educate consumers as to the painstaking efforts that went into the environments you created, or how 1,500 different sounds bring things to life on your screen.
>
> **Call to action.** A dynamic Web site can offer numerous actionable next steps for your consumers. On your site you can sell your game, sell related merchandise, register consumers to receive updates on your products via email, publicize tournament or other fan sites, run contests, ask for user submissions such as replays or screen shots, etc. This is your chance to make contact with your consumers and tell them you want them to become more involved with your product/company.

Sivertsen addresses what newbie designers should consider when creating a Web site for their game, in terms of content and navigation:

> A downloadable game demo is almost mandatory for a credible PC game launch. Research consistently rates product trial as the top factor in motivating game purchases. Consumers want to try before they buy, and you must respect that. Your competition is probably doing it.
>
> I'm a big fan of keeping site navigation simple. You should group related content and not make people work to find what's important or new on the site. You should spoon feed that info to them.

BARRY DORF, EA SPORTS

As assistant producer at Electronic Arts, Barry Dorf has worked on the *Madden Football* series and was responsible for running the popular *Fantasy Football* game on the EA Sports Web site. Dorf was asked why a game publisher should ponder creating new pages for each new game that's released, what should be offered there, and whether load times are ever a consideration at EA Sports:

> " Free advertising, baby! We have this huge Web site for EA. We're one of the top 100 sites on the Internet. It would be stupid for us not to put out a Web site that corresponds to the release of a new game. To take it a step further, there should be a Web site up at least six months before [the game's] release. "

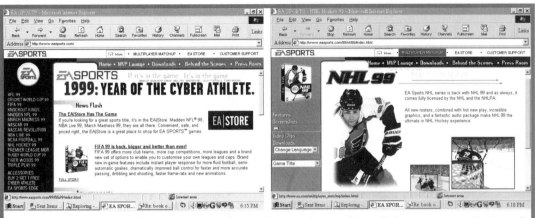

"We try to keep all of the critical info on the site just a few clicks away at all times," says Sivertsen. Left, check out the official EA Sports Web site. Right, the NHL Hockey page. (Used with permission by Electronic Arts, Inc.)

> " The site should have all the marketing hype you can fit on one page. The site should be updated often, and it should try to drive interest. When I worked on *Madden Football*, we never had the chance to get a demo ready before we shipped. A retail product differs from a Web-based product. It was important to us, but not more important then shipping a quality game. So as soon as we shipped, it was the first priority to get that demo up and show off our game. When we worked on the EA Sports Edge *Fantasy Football Analyzer*, we were able to put the whole product up for free. We gave it away for a few weeks and generated interest. The site had walkthroughs, sports content, and the analyzer. It was a new medium for EA and we were not sure how to sell it.
>
> Plug-ins, load times, and browser compatibility were all new questions. We didn't want to require plug-ins, but we had strict browser requirements. We thought that people would be willing to download a 4.0 version of Netscape or Explorer, because it's free. We were wrong. We also required a long initial load of all the stats. Once the load was done, people would be able to move around the site and get all the info they needed with no load times. If you had a 56K modem, this turned out to be about a 2–3 minute download. I thought it was worth it; there was so much info there, a one-time download was great. We figured it would be the longest load time the product would see. With the improving technology and modem speeds, if that was our biggest problem, we were in good shape. "

Dorf comments on the necessity of easy navigation:

> Navigation and interface is the key to any Web site. People like to surf but they want to be able to find the things they want fast. If you're on a football Web site, you want to be able to find the standings, stats, and transactions with one click. If you have too many submenus, people will get bored or sick of the load times between screens.

MICHAEL MCCART, ENSEMBLE STUDIOS

In this chapter, we've talked with people who either work at large publishing houses such as Eidos Interactive or Electronic Arts, or Web site design companies such as Cubik Media or CyberNation. However, this last entry will be from the development studio side of the industry.

Michael "Archangel" McCart is the Webmaster at Ensemble Studios, and he offers some insight on gaming Web site design. *Note:* His story is particularly inspiring since he was hired by Ensemble Studios because of his work on an *Age of Empires* fan site!

McCart discusses the indispensability of a good gaming Web site:

> We believe a developer should have a Web site as soon as possible, to state the company vision and its people. As early game development starts, some of the initial graphics for the game and a small fact sheet should be published on your Web site. The reason for these initial graphics and fact sheets is that they act like a teaser for the press, and help you on the road to a strong Internet fan base.
>
> As the game develops screenshots, more detailed information and designer comments should be added to your Web site. This practice develops a strong fan base and also gives the press somewhere to go for prerelease information.
>
> With the release of the game, more updated press, screenshots, files, etc., should be added to the game the site is covering. All this should be possible without the game part of your company Web site getting larger than 8–12 pages.

Should a gaming Web site be flashy and full of bells and whistles?

> As for multimedia (plug-ins, etc.), we shy away from those. At most, just a simple MIDI song from the game will be added to the main page on the different gaming Web sites we publish. The number one reason for this is that the number of images and screenshots we display on our gaming Web pages—for people to enjoy and get a visual feel for the game—increases load time.

What if you've spent all your money developing your game and have very little left to promote it online?

> If you have very little budget for this, your best bet is to get hosted by one of the larger gaming news sites. [McCart's *Age of Empires* Heaven page was hosted by GameStats (www.gamestats.com).] Most of the time, this type of site will offer you unlimited bandwidth (bandwidth usage = big $$$), which

your shareware or freeware program would eat up with a fair amount of downloads off the Internet.

Some of your other choices could be some of the large ISP networks that offer free home pages.

If you're just offering a shareware/freeware program on your Web site, include detailed program information (installing, what it is, etc.) and something about the company and its people. Most people who download shareware and freeware programs don't read the included *readme* file, so try to include as much as possible on your Web site.

On good versus bad navigation, McCart proposes the following:

For the most part, that's in the eye of the user, but I [prefer] a simple top (header), and a main menu with major topics listed, with a sidebar dividing up the subtopics. Trim down the use of Java applets and scripts; these sometimes have trouble with the older browsers.

McCart has published a long list of do's and don'ts for people who want to create and maintain their own gaming fan sites. He invites all those who are interested to read these suggestions at his home page, www.electrosonic.net/resources/angel.html. And be sure to see his work on the official Ensemble Studios Web site at www.ensemblestudios.com.

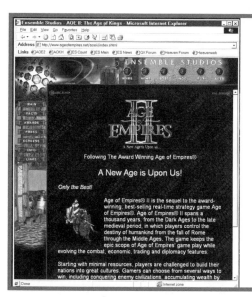

Ensemble Studios' McCart says to keep the information easily accessible, with a main header and a sidebar to divide up the subtopics. (Used with permission by Ensemble Studios, Inc.)

MARK DICKENSON, TEAM .366/3DO

The executive producer on the mega-popular *High Heat Baseball* series published by 3DO discusses whether or not a playable game demo is important today:

Well, if you have something compelling, it can be very important. Just make sure your demo can show it! For *High Heat Baseball 1999*, we made a mistake. We released a home run challenge demo. All it did for us was show that the game had an ugly batter animation. Now, when we were working on *High Heat Baseball 2000*, the team realized our mistake. Our strength was in the field gameplay, and the demo showed this. However, if you don't have the gameplay, a demo can't do anything but hurt you. Realistically, unless you can offer the very best gameplay in your given sport, it doesn't make sense to do a demo. In that case, you would only lose some sales you might gain from customers that would give a taste-test purchase. But if you have it, flaunt it!

Team .366's Mark Dickenson says, "[If you] time it right just before it ships, a demo will help build awareness, excitement, and sales." Seen here is Sammy Sosa High Heat Baseball 2001. (Used with permission by 3DO, Inc.)

CHAPTER 18
TECHNICAL SUPPORT AND CUSTOMER SERVICE

Once a game is released via traditional retail channels or over the Internet, it's then the company's responsibility to support the title for consumers. All this work done *after* the product ships is an essential part of the game's cycle. Furthermore, if and how the consumer's needs are met becomes a critical determinant in whether he or she will deal with the company again in the future.

There are two main areas of support in the gaming industry. *Technical support* provides troubleshooting help for installing, setting up, and running software or hardware. Common issues for the PC gaming industry are driver conflicts, setup for 3D accelerator support, multiplayer gaming, joystick configurations, and more general DirectX problems. *Customer service*, on the other hand, focuses on help with orders (purchases or returns), warranty issues, billing inquiries, account information (if it's an online game or network), and other non-technical problems. Both tech support and customer service provide consumers with avenues for satisfaction with their purchase.

Most gaming companies prefer to handle technical support and customer service internally, but in some cases they hire outside agencies to control the traffic. And it's a common practice for publishers to take care of the technical support and customer service issues, instead of the development studio. For example, Interplay will deal with any technical support calls, emails, and faxes relating to *Baldur's Gate*, rather than BioWare, the developers of the game.

This short chapter looks at the recommended ways of running a smooth technical support or customer service operation, whether this is to be done for your own shareware or freeware title or for those who want to get into this side of the gaming industry at a publishing company.

MICHAEL KELLY, EIDOS INTERACTIVE

Eidos Interactive's customer support manager, Michael Kelly, was asked how important this part of a game's cycle is, and why. Do game companies pay enough attention to it? Kelly responds:

> This is something that cannot be quantified. While customer service and technical support can and do lead to the overall happiness that the customer feels toward the company and the product that they've acquired, it doesn't express itself in any measurable manner. You rarely hear stories of how wonderful someone's experience with either of these departments has been. On the contrary, all I've ever read are bad experiences. Especially in the U.S., customers expect a high level of service for their dollar. Even if this level is not a reasonable expectation. I feel that the industry (computer game publishing) doesn't put high importance on either customer service or tech support, but the consumer seems to.

Asked what key points to consider if you're going to run your own customer service department—that is, the do's and don'ts of this field—Kelly responds:

> **Access.** The customer must have some sort of access to support.
>
> **Timeliness.** The customer should have some reply within a reasonable amount of time.
>
> **Accuracy.** The customer deserves and expects that the information given is accurate and useful to [solving] the problem.

Kelly insists that the end user *must* be given an answer to his or her query, and by useful means. He expands:

> I firmly believe that fax and email are very poor tools to use for technical support. There are just too many variables in computers for these media to be useful or productive in solving a customer's problem. However, it's quite satisfactory for providing user information that doesn't require a reply [from the consumer]—for example, where to send their disk for replacement.

In wrapping up, Kelly reminds companies to release patches as soon as they're available to ensure consumer satisfaction with the product.

MARK LINN, INTERPLAY

Mark Linn is the lead technician at Interplay's Irvine, California, headquarters, and has been part of the technical support team for close to three years. He explains that at Interplay his technicians are trained to handle customer service calls, so they can resolve issues on the spot. "One-call resolution is best for the consumer and for us," explains Linn. He admits that phone calls are more effective than email or faxed queries, and it's also faster for both parties—therefore less expensive for Interplay and more timely for consumers.

Because this book caters to budding game designers who may want to start their own company or who aim to get a job at an existing developer or publisher, we asked Linn for the best advice he can give on running a smooth technical support operation. His answers are as follows:

322

A GOOD DATABASE

According to Linn, setting up a database and good call-tracking is the most important first step. For larger companies, all technicians should be networked together in case customers don't get the same person on the phone each time. At Interplay, all calls are logged on a Microsoft Access database that records information about the user, his or her system, what happened during the last call, if the game in question has any known bugs (and how to get around them), and so forth. Linn admits that they tend to get calls from the same people repeatedly, so they call up the file by the customer's phone number. "Most of the people who call technical support are new computer users who are unfamiliar with the computer or older operating systems such as DOS," explains Linn.

Because they maintain a clean and organized database, they can often get to the root of the problem faster; therefore, it also reduces the hold time for customers calling in. "It's on their dime, so we try to make it quick and painless for them."

PROPER TRAINING

Linn emphasizes *proper* training, since most of their applicants are familiar with computers, but it must be on operating systems that are relevant to gaming and the games themselves. Says Linn:

> We won't even give them an interview before they pass a test to make sure they understand computers the way we need them to (for example, operating systems such as Windows 95/98 and DOS). Then, for the first few days of training, we sit them down and make them play the games. The more familiar they are with the games, the more they'll be able to assist the callers.

BE A GOOD LISTENER

Linn says it's crucial that his staff be good listeners and possess good customer service skills. Moreover, they must not take things personally. "Callers may be irate—and they don't think of it as 'something is wrong with *their* computer,' but more like 'something is wrong with *your* product.'"

If these three rules are adhered to, any technical support operation should run smoothly and efficiently, says Linn.

TOM BAZZANO, 3DO

Customer support supervisor Tom Bazzano takes some time out on his day off from 3DO to offer his expertise on the proper way to handle technical support and customer service. First off, how important are these two areas at a game company, and why?

> Tech support should hold a much more important role in the development cycle of a game, although for the majority of titles/publishers in the industry today, it's usually an afterthought. If your customer support group is allowed to work with a development and test team during the alpha and beta phases of a product's development, they can provide valuable feedback to the development team on issues that could incur serious support costs. The reality of the situation is that many support groups don't get a copy of a game that they'll need to support until after the game ships to stores!
>
> Some of the most frustrating things for a customer support group are the small annoyances in a game's install or interface that consistently generate customer calls. These types of contacts are *usually* quick phone/email contacts, but they're also completely avoidable by getting your support group involved during the development phase. The CS [customer service] reps can tell QA [quality assurance testers] or development exactly how the customers are going to react to a questionable feature or situation that is occurring in a game that's in development. They'll also be able to pinpoint features in a product that will cause customer frustration.
>
> Our support organization is involved with nearly every aspect of product development. Our CS reps review all of the printed materials that are packaged with every product we make. They scrutinize the box, manual, artwork, system requirements, Web pages, strategy guides, keyboard overlays, quick reference cards, installation instructions—as well as the actual software itself. There isn't another group in our company that will be as diligent as the support reps in finding problems or inconsistencies in these types of materials. It's always going to be in their best interest to find problems during the development cycle, because when typos or errors slip by the production groups and product development, it's Customer Support that will have to answer the calls about it.

With this in mind, Bazzano says if tech support and customer service employees/departments adhere to the following rules, they should be able to satisfy their customers:

GOOD FOLLOW-THROUGH

> Your support group has to have good follow-through on all customer issues. You need solid tools to make this happen, and you need to think hard about department policies. Without consistency and the proper tools to do the job, you'll have poor follow-through. The absolute last comment you want to hear from a customer is that they have been promised a callback the last *x* times they have called, and have never heard from anyone in your group.

SHARE INFORMATION

> It's critical that your customer support staff share information with each other in order to provide the best support possible. It's also critical for a CS group to get this information out to customers in as many ways as possible. For example, during the launch of *Might and Magic 6*, our CS group was holding meetings at noon and at the end of the day to discuss new customer issues and to

see if any of the reps had found workarounds. When one was found and confirmed, we would immediately publish it to all members of the group via email, and post on our FAQ on the *Might and Magic 6* Web site. This ensured that at least some customers could get their problems solved outside of normal business hours, and noticeably reduced the number of calls on those topics.

TREAT YOUR CUSTOMERS WELL

When dealing with customers, don't make it seem like an effort. Try to be upbeat and happy when talking to them on the phone. Use their first name and build up a rapport with them. Don't intentionally lie or deceive your customers; tell them the truth. A customer can deal with the fact that there is a problem with a product they purchased, as long as they are dealt with fairly and they have faith that the company will do right by them and patch it or remedy the situation. Forcing your employees to intentionally lie, deceive, or "state the company line" in order to save face will only frustrate your customers and demoralize your support reps!

Some busy technical support and customer services offices rely on automated phone systems (for example, "press one for game *x*, two for game *y*," and so on); others rely strictly on Web feedback (email queries and discussion forums); and a handful of publishers still depend on the old-fashioned telephone and snail mail. What does 3DO use, and prefer? Answers Bazzano:

You should make an attempt to have your tech support group reachable by any and all mediums. Give your customers as many options as possible. Following are some thoughts, both pro and con, for each of the methods of reaching a tech support group.

The phone is the fastest way to resolve tech support issues. When a phone rep is on a call, he or she is in a one-on-one situation with the customer. Because of this, the phone will also have higher CPT (cost per touch), as there is little opportunity to practice the concept of "one to many."

Email, fax, or a tech support message board are the second-best methods. They have reasonably fast turnaround times, and you can employ the use of FAQs or scripts to increase efficiency. The downside to email and message boards is that a single issue can drag on for weeks, whereas the same issue on a phone call, with the customer at the computer, could be resolved in under 20 minutes.

Snail mail should really be a last resort for tech support issues. If someone is trying to resolve an actual technical problem via snail mail, your best bet is to get them on the phone or some other more expedient medium.

But what if the publisher or small developer has very few resources (time and employees) to set aside for support? Can a game company survive with little or poor support? Bazzano replies:

No, this is just not a sane way to do business. Smaller companies need to scale their level of service accordingly. They should start by handling customer contacts via email, normal postal mail, or even fax. This will allow you to answer a large number of customer questions using scripts.

Once again, this is where the one-to-many philosophy will come into play. You should look at ways to get the largest amount of information to your customers with the least amount of labor. The most obvious is via the World Wide Web; posting a support site for your game should take minimal time, and could easily incorporate FAQs (frequently asked questions) and basic troubleshooting, as well as links to things such as Microsoft's DirectX page, or driver pages for various sound and video card manufacturers.

Another concept for the World Wide Web is that of a message board, where your customers can post questions and your designated support person (you did say they had no money) can post the answers. This will allow other customers to browse the board and find posts of people with similar problems. With this type of setup, you'll also find that many customers will help each other with workarounds that they've found on their own.

Speaking of Web sites, Bazzano comments on the timeliness of patches to repair/update games:

The issue of when to release a patch should really be taken on a case-by-case basis. You NEVER want to prematurely rush a patch out the door. If you find that you have a problem with a title that's going to require a patch, and it's within the first week or two of a title's release, WAIT! Chances are there are other unanticipated problems that can be combined into a larger patch.

You can find yourself in a situation that demands that you release an immediate patch, where you don't have the luxury of waiting to include other fixes. If there's a bug or issue with a game that prevents people from being able to play or install the product, you're going to need to fix it ASAP.

Public demand can easily drive a company to release multiple patches in short order, but remember that this is an undesirable position to be in; you should seek creative solutions that appease your customer base and allow development to implement fixes for all known problems, rather than rushing out a patch every two weeks.

One of the best ideas to handle such situations is getting your customer base involved in "testing" your patches for you by starting a "beta" program where the customers test early versions of the patch and return feedback about its performance and what hardware they tested it on. This will a) buy your development team time to address all the bugs they would like to fix, rather than just the ones people are most vocal about; and b) give your customers an active role in the patch's development and show them that the company is responding directly to their feedback.

RODNEY HODGE, INTERACTIVE ENTERTAINMENT NETWORK (IEN)

As a game producer at the Interactive Entertainment Network, or iEN, Rodney "Hatch" Hodge adds some different flavor to this chapter on support, since he works primarily with online games, such as the mega-popular *WarBirds*. Do the same standards apply? Is technical support as important for online games as for a boxed game? Hatch says even more so for multiplayer games.

> In our business model, customer service is very important. Unlike the retail side of the business, where you make a product, ship it, support it for a time, then move on to the next product, we develop an ongoing relationship with our customers. We have an ever-increasing customer base that has been growing steadily since we opened our doors four years ago, including accountholders that have been with us since day one. Our yearly release schedule averages three releases and/or upgrades per game, as we're continually improving each with new graphics, features, and the like. This means that we have to satisfy new accountholders when they're just getting started, and also keep our long-time customers up and running with the problems that they invariably encounter with new releases, installing other software, hard drive crashes, and the like.

Hatch was asked if they handle their technical support queries by phone, email, and/or fax, and what works the best for them and their customers:

> I'm kind of old-fashioned in this area, and think a quick connection to a calm, instructive human voice is the best way to go. In most cases, in my experience, when a consumer calls you, he has already beaten his brains out trying to figure out the problem, and is usually at the end of his rope.

> The last thing I like doing when I'm in this state is sitting on hold waiting, or finding my way through a maze of pushbutton menu choices, when all I want is to tell someone about the problem I'm having and have them tell me what to do. Second best case is a quick email reply.

> We have our tech support Web pages split into help areas for each game. In each respective help area, you'll find a phone number and staffing information, FAQs and newsgroup support areas, and last but not least an email form to fill out and submit.

> One of the newest forms of help that I particularly like is the support newsgroup. The support newsgroup is very nice when you have an established player base, because it takes the least amount of input for the benefits it provides. This is an area where the customer can go to look for and/or post about the problem he's having. More times than not, another customer has already run into this problem and has posted about it, or will answer a post, explaining a fix to the problem. On top of that, a developer can go through this support newsgroup answering problems that have yet to be resolved by another player, and address a larger number of people with one post than he can effectively reach with one-on-one phone or email support. The developer can also use the support group as a good place to see what kinds of bugs or problems his customers are experiencing, and use this information to help find bugs or make design changes that improve the usability of his product.

iEN can also boast one additional technical support angle not found in most gaming companies. Hatch divulges this unique practice:

> Another aspect of customer support, which I haven't even touched on, is the method of drawing from your customer base to help train the newcomers on the finer aspects of your products.
>
> These pages were all put together by players, for players, costing nothing more than free connect time for the people involved. They also staff a training arena five nights a week for 2½ hours.

Hatch agrees it may be best to consider only email and FAQ files if money is tight, since it can get costly to run a support line and employ technicians to receive the call. "In that case," says Hatch, "just be sure to be prompt and professional." He continues, "The main objective here is to promote the image to your consumers that you care and want to help them, and will do so to the best of your ability."

CHAPTER 19

DOING IT YOURSELF AND THE SHAREWARE REVOLUTION

Not all success stories in this book involve getting a job at a well-known development house or publishing company and climbing the ranks from within. Sure, it's probably beneficial to work around the likes of Sid Meier or Warren Spector, but, similar to what's happening in the music industry with the emergence of many popular independent bands, some designers have chosen to simply sell their own creations over the Internet, and, in many cases, work from home.

You can create your own company, corporation, or other legal entity to manufacture, market, and distribute your game, but this chapter focuses on those game producers who distribute and sell their games over the World Wide Web as *shareware*. For the uninitiated, shareware games are free to download, but a small payment from the user is required to continue playing. This "try before you buy" software may be limited in time (for example, two hours of play) or in features (perhaps three out of ten levels are available), or the entire game can be given up front in good faith.

Is it really worth releasing your beloved game this way? What are the pros and cons for selling shareware, as opposed to working toward a packaged retail product? The following entries are from folks who made the decision to do it alone, and have succeeded. If this is the road you choose, take heed to this advice.

JEFF VOGEL, SPIDERWEB SOFTWARE

Jeff Vogel is the president of Spiderweb Software, Inc., a small two-person operation in Seattle, Washington. With the help of a few freelancers, they produce and sell shareware fantasy games for the Macintosh and Windows, and likely are best known for their *Exile* role-playing game series. In fact, *Exile III: Ruined World* won the 1998 Shareware Game of the Year award from *Computer Gaming World*.

For Vogel, shareware is the best way to go:

> Someone just getting started in game development would be doing themselves a grotesque disservice to not consider shareware. Research the computer game industry, and you'll find a very bloody, competitive, corporate place. If you develop a game, you almost always have to make it recognizably part of an

established genre, with the graphics done in just such a way, with all the buzz-words covered (polygons, Internet play, etc.), and even then you have to scramble like mad to get your game in the stores. With shareware, you can do your game exactly the way you want, how you want, keeping the hours you want.

But can you make a lot of money going the shareware route? "Well, no," says Vogel. "You won't get rich...but you can make a very, very good living." As with any part of the gaming industry, shareware is not a get-rich-quick scheme. As Vogel puts it, "You must first program a game good enough for people to give you money for it." Admittedly, this is no easy task in itself, and then Web surfers must notice the game, download it, and play it. "But if you can get these things, shareware is a terrific way to make a living in the computer game industry."

Shareware games don't need to feature the latest and greatest in graphic or sound technology, or have multiplayer support, says Vogel. (Used with permission by Spiderweb Software)

Just how much money can a shareware game yield? According to Vogel, his games that "look crude, have no Internet play, and have rough sounds" are making six figures a year. He explains why this is:

> Because, first, for all the graphical lack, they're extremely well-designed games. Second, I have worked hard at making sure that they get properly marketed and people hear about them. I send out a lot of press releases. I don't use magic spells to get people to buy my games. I work hard to develop them, and I work hard on our Web site and on Usenet to find and communicate with gaming magazines (online and otherwise).
>
> Your game has to be fun. Not just "kind of fun." *Really* fun. Fun enough to get a person to pull a credit card out of his/her wallet and give you the number. This is shareware. People get to play the demo. You have nowhere to hide. Your game has to be very fun. It can look rough. It can have lame sounds. It can even have a few bugs. But if it doesn't grab people and shake the change out of their pockets, it will fail. Again, to succeed, you have to write a game that's good, no matter what.

Vogel has experienced over 100,000 downloads of Spiderweb Software games, and has received a number of calls to put his games on shareware CD compilations. However, he hasn't been approached by any major game publishers to re-release his games in retail. Not that he's interested anyway, but he qualifies it as follows:

> I just don't do anything they're interested in. I write old-school iconic games, like *Ultima IV* or *VI*. For one player. I have no interest in multiplayer, fancy cut-scenes, or the like. This is something no publisher will touch, and I can't blame them. If my games don't have these qualities, the stores won't put them on the shelves.

Along with many of the larger shareware repositories on the Web (see the following list), Spiderweb Software games can be downloaded from their official Web site at www.spidweb.com. In addition, their Web site contains game news, screen shots, downloadable plug-in modules, contact information, and registration forms.

Make some room on your hard drive, because the following Web sites contain thousands upon thousands of PC and Mac shareware games, freeware, and commercial game demos:

- shareware.com
  www.shareware.com

- DOWNLOADS.COM
  www.downloads.com

- Happy Puppy
  www.happypuppy.com

- Games Domain
  www.gamesdomain.com

- Filez
  www.filez.com

- File Mine
  www.filemine.com

- File Pile
  www.filepile.com

- Jumbo
  www.jumbo.com

- TuCows
  www.tucows.com

- ZDNet Software Library
  www.hotfiles.com

- WinSite
  www.winsite.com

- 32bit.com
  www.32bit.com

- Softsite
  www.softsite.com

- Beyond.com
  www.beyond.com

SETH ROBINSON, ROBINSON TECHNOLOGIES

At 25, Seth Robinson is the CEO of Robinson Technologies, Inc. (www.rtsoft.com). You may have heard of this small Oregonian gaming company because his latest freeware game, *Dink Smallwood*, has been featured in a number of international publications. The game was originally shareware, but they eventually decided to give it away free while working on other shareware titles. Much of their success is due to the Internet as an effective distribution medium, according to Robinson.

> Today, self-distributing through the shareware route makes much more sense than it did a number of years ago when there wasn't the [commercialization of the] Internet. With the Web, you can instantly put a demo of your product in 50,000 people's hands, and if you provide an easy way to buy the product that's quicker than driving down to the store, people will do it. Especially if the product is niche—it might not even exist in the stores.
>
> The best part is the cost! Generally the only investment is time and a small fee for Web access (which by now I'm sure *everybody* has). If your product sells badly, so what? Update it or start a new one.

Seth Robinson serves as lead designer/programmer at RT Soft, Greg Smith does "a little of everything," and they generally hire artists on a project-by-project basis. Here's a shot from the celebrated Dink Smallwood. (Used with permission by Robinsoft Technologies, Inc.)

Robinson has covered *why* a game designer should take the shareware approach, but more important is *how* to go about doing it. When asked to supply some do's and don'ts for gamers looking to selling their goods online, Robinson gives us a number of pointers to bear in mind:

> ■ Start saving email addresses of game-site editors. They don't always see your game—and then magically they'll announce it and put it up for download the first day it's out. It's up to you to have a "press" list to keep informed. This list will grow as you make friends in the industry and will prove invaluable later.
>
> ■ We didn't make a fortune off *Dink Smallwood*, but it did open many doors for us. Being able to take a jewel case with a game you wrote to an interview proves many things to your possible future employer, not to mention the fact that you have "finished" something. A rare breed!
>
> ■ People always say how hard the gaming industry is to break into and that you need experience to get in. The solution is simple: Work for free. Find a local gaming company and see if they offer internship. Greg [Smith] started here that way; now he has a salaried position.
>
> ■ Don't even *think* about taking preorders for an unfinished game—especially if this is your first game—as we did, and I regretted it. The two months we were late were hellish…

- Don't be discouraged by low sales. The first year *LORD* was available, I sold only 7 copies. Over the next 7 years, I sold 30,000 more. The point is if your product is high quality, word of mouth will do its thing. Just don't forget to update it regularly, especially your support Web page. Constant updating (at least monthly) tells the consumer that you still care about the product and won't leave them high and dry if there's a problem.

- Start small. Rate your project's difficulty from 1 to 10 and *never* start on a project that is more than 2 rating points higher than the last one you completed. Your first project? Pick a 1 or 2. That would be something like a random-quote generator or a simple screensaver.

- Use Microsoft Visual C++ and DirectX.

- Ask a friend to try your game, and watch him play it. Notice which parts he gets confused by and which keys he instinctively hits to abort menus, etc.

Wrapping up, Robinson comments on the ways to remind gamers to register their shareware product. There are many different schools of thought in this area, and Robinson believes it depends on the shareware type:

> For a utility that's used over a long period of time (macro program, paint program, etc.), showing the days left at each startup and disabling it after 30 days or so is a great way. For games, the 30-day or limited time is a bad idea. You want to provide them with the "not too hard" beginning of the game—and remember, if they don't finish the shareware portion, why would they buy the full version? So keep the shareware easy and fun and end it right about when things seem the most interesting. Think about what products you personally have registered; most likely they used a great registration scheme.

Robinson's words on shareware may be fitting for adventure/role-playing games such as *Dink Smallwood*, but what about classic card games? Do the same principles apply? What about the ways to remind gamers to register? Let's take a look at two other companies that make a living from creating and selling package-less *Solitaire* card games.

JONAS STEWART, SILVER CREEK ENTERTAINMENT

"Well, let's start out with the fact that when you're a small fish in a big pond, you better give them your lunch money or get a shark cage," quips Jonas Stewart, vice president and "lead creative guy" at Silver Creek Entertainment (www.silvercrk.com). Hardwood *Solitaire* and *Hardwood Solitaire II* for the PC and Mac are their flagship products. Stewart is commenting on how difficult it is to get your product out in the stores, and how little the people who actually make the game take home at the end of the day. He expands:

If you want to sell in a store, you have to find a publisher (who takes their cut) and distributor (who then takes their cut), and hopefully they find you some shelf space at a superstore. You'll be lucky to get a couple dollars a game—and more than likely, even less than that. Now, if you aren't well known or your game isn't mainstream, you'll probably be lucky to get in the valueware $5 CDs. And after all those cuts...well, you do the math.

So what's a little game company to do? "Pull up a seat to the Web, my friend," says Stewart. "If you think you have a great game and know the world's gonna love it, and the publishers are not biting, the Web is the place to be."

In his opinion, the shareware model works great on the Internet because it allows game designers like Silver Creek to pop up a site and sell games just like anyone else. As Stewart puts it, "Basically, all you need to do is make your game, build your site, promote it, and if you have a game that people like...watch the orders come in."

Stewart believes that with shareware, everyone wins. "The gamers get a good feel for what the full version of the game is like, and the designers benefit from greater consumer satisfaction. Since you have to deal with all of the customers directly by selling games yourself, it will be less hassle, and there should be fewer dissatisfied gamers because they had an opportunity to see what the game is all about before reaching for their credit card."

"With shareware," continues Stewart, "you can make as many or as few improvements as you like, and you decide if at some certain point you feel that you've added enough to warrant selling a new version of your game." He recalls the decision to sell *Hardwood Solitaire II*: "We had spent a lot of time, and more importantly had made enough improvements, to call it a new version of the game to sell."

Getting gamers to reach into their pockets and spring for the full version is not an easy thing, warns Stewart. "They don't give it to you without a fight, so what seems to work best is to use the ⅓ rule. That is, give them a third of the game for free, and if they want more fun and excitement they need to pay."

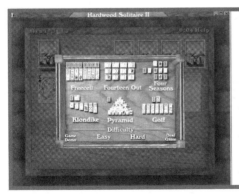

In Hardwood Solitaire II, Klondike is free, but the other games and additional features are unlocked once the registration fee is collected. (Used with permission by Silver Creek Entertainment)

To collect the money sold from your games, Stewart says there are roughly three ways to do this: Get a merchant account and take orders on your Web site; use a service that collects them for you, and they'll take care of the processing and credit card orders (but will likely take around a 25% fee); or use "ad-ware," where the full game is given away to the consumer for free but you must sell advertisement space in your game. This last option is commonly found on Internet-only games.

To learn more about shareware marketing and other handy advice, be sure to drop by and visit with the Association of Shareware Professionals (ASP). Their mission statement, FAQ, and membership information are available at www.asp-shareware.org.

BRYAN HORLING, FREEVERSE SOFTWARE

Some shareware developers take a slightly more aggressive approach to reminding the user that the program needs to be paid for to continue playing. Such is the case with Freeverse Software (www.freeverse.com). If you've never heard of *Burning Monkey Solitaire*, chances are that you're not visiting the shareware archives regularly enough. Bryan Horling is an associate programmer on this popular PC and Mac game that adds animation, a whole host of options, and most importantly humor, to a collection of *Solitaire* card games.

In *Burning Monkey Solitaire*, if the gamer doesn't register the program after 15 plays per game, it will be unavailable the 16th time the game is booted up. For instance, if you play *Klondike* the most, it will be deleted from the list of options. Then, after another 15 plays of, say, *Strict Klondike* or *Pyramid Solitaire*, they'll become unavailable as well. This continues until all of the games are inaccessible, unless a registration code is given. So why this approach? Horling says:

> Make sure you have something in the program that either cuts off some features or annoys [users] if they haven't paid their shareware fee. Given the opportunity, many users will use your software forever without paying, either through deliberate choice or ignorance. If you're just writing for the experience and knowledge that people like your stuff, this isn't a big deal, but if you hope to finance your next computer upgrade, it's more of an issue.

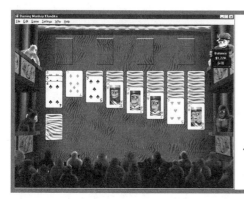

The latest version of Burning Monkey Solitaire for the PC garnered more than 30,000 downloads in its first two weeks from one site. (Used with permission by Freeverse Software)

This method still beats selling the game up front through regular retail channels, believes Horling, and it boils down to "simplicity and control." Says Horling, "Shareware is a very simple model—you basically write it and release it. You control the distribution and collect all the profits." But how can a company that makes classic card games make any money? Freeverse's *Burning Monkey Solitaire* and Silver Creek Entertainment's *Hardwood Solitaire II* are both good examples of simply improving on a good thing. In other words, shareware game designers need not feel they must reinvent the wheel. It's possible to create a product—and demand for that product—by borrowing from the classics. Does Horling believe this to be true?

> Yes, absolutely. But check out your competition. Download all the relevant competitors and make sure you have more features, lower price, or a better implementation. On the whole, though, I do think it's a good idea. Improving lets you start with a presumably successful base and just work on making it better. This is much easier than starting from scratch and then trying to both teach users a new game and convince them that it's a good idea in the same breath.

SEUMAS MCNALLY, LONGBOW DIGITAL ARTS

Sadly, at the time of writing this book, 21-year-old Seumas McNally passed away after an arduous three-year battle with Hodgkins' disease. McNally was the founder and lead programmer at Longbow Digital Arts (www.longbowdigitalarts.com), responsible for such shareware hits as *Tread Marks* (2000), *DX-Ball 2* (1999), and *Particle Fire* (1998). The fact that Seumas (along with the other three McNallys in the family software business) lived in central Ontario, Canada, and not Silicon Valley did not matter.

 At the request of Seumas' father and coworker Jim, the following is the original interview with Seumas conducted in early 1999 for the first edition of this book.

Asked to comment on how the Internet has helped shareware designers, Seumas responds as follows:

> Right now the World Wide Web is becoming a very viable medium for independent software sales and advertising. We're just starting to see computers and the Internet become almost ubiquitous in the middle-class home, and the large credit card companies are finally opening up to Internet transactions with prime-time TV commercials extolling the benefits of shopping with a point and a click. Unfounded consumer fear regarding online transactions is diminishing, as more and more people realize how easy it is to shop on the Internet.

McNally recognizes that the Internet is an exciting and practical tool for shareware developers, but this technology isn't worth much if the game isn't up to par:

> What it all boils down to, of course, is having a kickass product. It's easy to be blinded by your own love for a game, especially if it's your first project. You have to look at a game objectively, taking into account all the other products in the genre, to get a good feel for how it will do. I've seen a lot of shareware games for Windows that perhaps shouldn't have even been released as freeware. But don't be discouraged, learn from your mistakes, and your next products will be better.

McNally insists that once you have a good product, a lot of the marketing will take care of itself, with player word of mouth and online editorial coverage. After all, the overhead is minimal to run the operation yourself. Says McNally, "Two key things are having your own Web site with a domain name (only $100 a year or so, plus perhaps $20/month for Web storage and a few email accounts), and getting your software's demo or free version as widely known as possible."

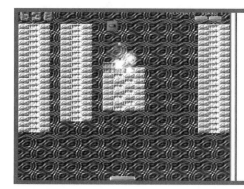

McNally says if a game is really not catching on, no matter how hard it's pushed and promoted, that probably means it's just not that good, or at least the learning curve is too steep for people to get into it. (Used with permission by Longbow Digital Arts)

TIP To increase the awareness of your shareware product, it may be worth investing in AddWeb (www.cyberspacehq.com), a program that automatically submits your web site to hundreds of search engines and directories. A free demo is also offered.

We've looked at how role-playing games and card games typically "request" payment from the gamer. Where does an arcade game like *DX-Ball 2* fit in? "Giving people the whole product and asking them to pay if they use it, the most classic and altruistic form of shareware, doesn't work worth beans," says McNally. "You need to give them a little, just enough to get them hooked, and then gently suggest that they can instantly purchase even more of this fun goodness for only *xx* dollars online at _____." For *DX-Ball 2*, that "little bit of goodness" is 24 free levels out of a total of 150 in the full version.

In closing, McNally also suggests that it helps to include an offline ordering method (send a check or money order for *xx* dollars to the company address) to give people confidence that you're not just some fly-by-night Internet operation, and for the odd person who doesn't have a credit card.

STEVE MORAFF, MORAFFWARE

Steve Moraff was one of the first independent game developers to release "shareware" in the early 1980s, though he was not aware of the term *shareware* until a few years later. Some of his best-selling work includes *MoreJongg*, *SphereJongg*, and *RingJongg*, three variations of the classic Asian tile game *Mahjongg* available from his Florida company, MoraffWare (www.moraff.com).

When asked why a game developer would prefer to go the shareware route, as opposed to working at a development house, Moraff offers this straightforward guidance:

> The bottom line is that authors have to decide what kind of lifestyle they want. If they self-publish shareware, they have a real relationship with their users and they're their own boss, but they have to handle a lot of non-programming work to support their business. If they go with a publisher, they have to do what the publisher wants, and they're at the mercy of the random winds of the corrupt retail distribution system, but they don't have to deal with non-programming tasks as much.

Moraff and company offer full games up front to the user, but with fewer background images, music, and tile sets to choose from. The following are Moraff's opinions on finding the right way to encourage gamers to pay money:

> Shareware reminders generally have to be somewhat obnoxious to work. Making games stop functioning after a 30-day trial may be the most effective way, but it really annoys users and cuts down on distribution. Annoying nag screens that have to be clicked off at the end of the game are what I use, and I find them to be the best balance between the need to get registrations and the need to maintain a desirable shareware game.

He concedes, though, "I do have a particularly annoying second nag screen that appears after about eight hours of use."

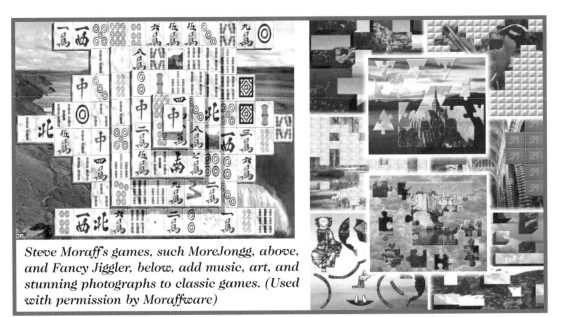

Steve Moraff's games, such MoreJongg, above, and Fancy Jiggler, below, add music, art, and stunning photographs to classic games. (Used with permission by Moraffware)

CHAPTER 20
BREAKING INTO THE INDUSTRY

As evidenced by the interviews published in this book, there are many ways to break into the gaming industry. The two most common ways, however, are to get a job at an existing development studio or publishing company, or to create the game on your own terms and approach a publisher and/or distributor to pick up the title. Exactly what kind of company you launch on your own is another consideration altogether, and there many varied ways to do so.

The gaming industry is full of success stories from people who have chosen either of these two popular avenues. The first half of this chapter focuses on the best ways to present your idea for a game (or the game itself) to a publisher, and the second half concentrates on getting a job at a game company—and the best ways to get in the door. Keep in mind that other chapters, such as those on art, animation, programming, and music, offer advice specific for those fields.

Before diving into this chapter, here are a few inspiring and valuable words from Jim Charne, president and executive director of the Academy of Interactive Arts and Sciences (AIAS). He reminds budding game designers that PC and console gaming has gone from a hobby to a thriving industry over the last 10 years, and it's an exciting time to jump in:

> This means there are long-term career opportunities for people who are serious, hardworking, and prepared. Like any career, it takes talent, hard work, perseverance, and luck to rise to the top. But there's no doubt the opportunities are there.

Charne also offers tips on ensuring your success:

> Get as much education as you can. As systems become more complex, training at the university level and even postgraduate work will serve you well. This is especially important in technical areas (advanced math is critical), but also applies to music, art, and design.

> Keep current in the literature of the field. Read the magazines, know the products. Don't just play the products—study them. Know what works and what doesn't. Form opinions and be able to express them intelligently. People respect that.

And finally, Charne encourages you to learn what's going on the world:

> Read the *New York Times* every day. Be able to discuss politics, religion, history, literature, music, current events. Your game must find an audience in the real world. Don't isolate yourself from it.

And on with the chapter we go...

PITCHING YOUR GAME TO A PUBLISHER

This is the preferred path, but it's hard to pull off. This strategy is the most ideal to a designer because the chances of getting your own game on store shelves are much greater, and of course faster, than working your way up internally at another company. Assuming this is the way you want to go, the following talented advisory board offers do's and don'ts of how, when, and why a game should be pitched to a publisher.

As a full-time headhunter in the gaming industry, Melanie Cambron has learned a thing or two about what a publisher wants to see when someone is pitching a game. To read Cambron's article on ways to impress a publisher, turn to Chapter 21, "Game Agents and Headhunters."

MITZI MCGILVRAY, ELECTRONIC ARTS

Mitzi McGilvray is a supervising producer at Electronic Arts. Some of the well-known franchises she's worked on include *NCAA Football*, *March Madness*, and *NHL Hockey*. McGilvray admits she has received quite a few pitches on EA's behalf from budding game designers, so she's eager to discuss how a game or game idea should be presented for consideration to a publishing company.

Before we get into the content of the package, McGilvray urges game designers to protect themselves and their ideas:

> I don't recommend sending anything unsolicited without making some contact within a company. Some companies require that nondisclosure agreements be signed in advance; others may wait. Remember, you may think you have the most innovative, creative idea ever, but there's a high likelihood that it's been done before, is being done, or has been rejected. *Great ideas are easy to come by; great executions take hard work, talent, timing, and luck!*

McGilvray admits she's witnessed some pretty sloppy pitches from game designers, so she wants to set the record straight on the best way to impress a publisher. She insists a well-presented "package" is very important because "if you can't clearly communicate your ideas and present them in a way that the publisher gets excited about it, how do you think the consumer is going to like your work?"

DESIGN DOCUMENTS

A *design document* should be included with the package, and according to McGilvray, it should contain a way for production and marketing to understand

and plan for what the game is intended to be, and a blueprint for programmers to create the code for the game. Most important of all, the design document should be a "living" document that can evolve as the game comes to life.

McGilvray indicates what she believes to be critical when writing a design document:

- **Details, details, details.** As you're creating the design document, imagine that you won't be around when the game is being programmed. Be sure to cover all of the details.

- **Plan for flexibility.** It's very likely that once you complete the design document you'll need to go back and modify it on a regular basis. Keep the design modular so updates can be made without impacting large portions of the game. Examples would be to allow the addition (or subtraction) of game features without blowing up the entire game. Also, have a few sacrificial features that you can eliminate if you run out of time.

- **Listen, listen, listen.** Get lots of feedback on your design by a good variety of skill sets before you start coding. You'll learn that you've probably left a lot of holes in the design and that there may be more effective ways of communicating your ideas.

- **Be graphic!** This may sound goofy, but pictures, flow charts, and diagrams really help out the artists and programmers when they're trying to figure it out.

PERSISTENCE VERSUS ANNOYANCE

McGilvray says if you're ready to pitch your game—or even after you've made your presentation—*do* follow up, but *don't* annoy:

This is a very fine line. Publishers are usually very busy, so it's important that you "stay above the noise" by sending occasional emails or phone messages to see what's up. Don't be a pain, however.

And don't try to snow the publisher! Most publishers have been burned too many times and get very nervous when someone comes in and says that they can do the impossible.

THE IDEAL PITCH

Want to know what to do to maximize your chances? McGilvray lays out what she believes to be a solid package from a game designer:

Ideally a finished, polished product. But since this is the real world, publishers understand that most people don't have the funding to do this on their own.

Next best thing to a finished product is to get a prototype. This should be working code and graphics that captures a small portion of the look and feel of the product. In addition to the prototype, include a one-pager that describes what the product is to be and how it will play. Also, a great thing to include would be a sample "back of the box." This would include a few mocked-up screens as well as the top selling points and competitive features of the game.

> Can't do a prototype? Then just send off the one-pager and the sample back of the box. Also, include a few paragraphs on what the game might be like to play. Include info on what the buttons will do and what will be fun.
>
> Be prepared once you pitch a product to supply additional information, such as a more complete design document. If you're planning on developing the product yourself (with artists, programmers, audio technicians, etc.), many publishers will request budgets, timelines, documentation on ownership of the design, as well as information on the financial status of your company.

Mitzi McGilvray says she'd like to start a line of sports products at EA geared toward the "girl gamer." Have any ideas? Now you know how to pitch 'em.

JOSH RESNICK, PANDEMIC STUDIOS

At Activision, Josh Resnick served as producer for *Mechwarrior 2* and director for *Dark Reign*, and oversaw the production of *Battlezone*. In 1998, he left Activision to form and preside over Pandemic Studios, a new development house affiliate for Activision. Resnick says there are five key pointers on pitching a game idea to a publisher. But shouldn't gamers first try to make the game on their own and then try to sell it? Didn't EA's McGilvray says it's ideal if the game is already finished? While Resnick agrees it may be easier to get it picked up if it's already done or near-done, he urges gamers to "start getting experience on someone else's dime first," and comments that someone "would be absolutely crazy to do it all on their own." At the very least, there should be a working demo of the game engine, says Resnick. With that in mind, let's get right to his five commandments:

GET A TEAM

"It's getting more difficult for one guy with a concept to go to a publisher these days," admits Resnick. "Publishers are interested in *teams*, and everyone on the team should have a background." At the same time, Resnick understands the catch-22 here about publishers preferring designers with backgrounds. As with most (if not all) of the entertainment industries, such as film, music, or television, production companies/labels expect you to have experience, but it's often hard to get experience unless a company hires you! "Teams are absolutely critical in my opinion," repeats Resnick. "You won't get the best development deal in the world if it's just you cranking away on a game in your basement."

BE REALISTIC AND PROFESSIONAL

"Don't walk into a publisher's office and pitch them on an idea that isn't realistic, such as expensive full-motion video or 100+ missions," warns Resnick. "Look at what others can do with a certain amount of money within a timeframe, because you have to look like you know what you're doing. It's critical to prove yourself realistic and professional." Show an accessible interface; show that the engine can compete against what's out there.

For instance, a *Battlezone* or *Dark Reign* style of game will cost roughly $1 million to $1.5 million. Says Resnick, "If that's the case, show you're willing to eat

Cup-a-Noodles for a year! Publishers want to see commitment, and that you're willing to make it work—maybe even not take salary for a year."

WHAT ABOUT A LICENSED PROPERTY?

"One of the best bets is to ask yourself, 'How can I attach this to an licensed property?'" says Resnick. Publishers are focused on a licensed property because the consumer is already familiar with the game's universe, rules, and characters. Only franchises allow publishers to have stability in their portfolio and budget planning. Once they know that a particular title will be able to sell at least *x* number of units, they can then be much more accurate in their spending against that title and their revenue projections. "That's one of the differences between a game like *Dark Reign* and *GoldenEye 007*," comments Resnick. "But as luck and talent would have it, *Dark Reign* has now become a franchise, with its own consumer recognition."

Another reason why publishers are drawn to a popular franchise, says Resnick, is because they can own it outright—for a price, but it will likely be worth it. (Chapters 2 and 3 discuss the pros and cons of working with a well-known franchise. Content in those chapters is contributed by folks who have worked on *Star Trek*, *Star Wars*, and *Dungeons & Dragons* PC games.)

Depending on the franchise rights, publishers may also have to pay roughly 10% of the revenues to the owners.

But sometimes licensed properties don't work out. Explains Resnick:

In hindsight, we shouldn't have spent the money to license the *Battlezone* property; as it turned out, we didn't need it and [the game] wasn't anywhere close to the original. It probably worked against us. This was because the gameplay was totally new, cutting edge, and not like the original arcade game. It caused confusion.

Battlezone was one of the first games to mix real-time strategy and a first-person perspective view of the action. Other games that melded these genres include 3DO's *Uprising* and Microsoft's *Urban Assault*.

PROTECT YOURSELF

As a rule, Resnick advises, "You can never protect yourself enough," but fortunately, "publishers are not out to steal ideas." In fact, a mutual NDA (nondisclosure agreement) may be insisted upon by the publisher to say that it's the designer's game and/or game idea, says Resnick. These NDA forms can likely be picked up in a stationery or office supply store.

Before even approaching publishers, game designers with little cash can mail the game (or design document for the game) to themselves in an envelope—and then don't open it. Why, you ask? The stamp will be dated, proving when the idea was originally documented or programmed. Of course, this is a temporary measure.

Resnick suggests that game designers who are worried about someone stealing their idea have a lawyer witness the idea during a meeting, with the lawyer taking notes to record the idea. "This may cost a couple hundred dollars," says Resnick, "but it may be worth it."

As a side note, Resnick advises that if game designers are lucky enough to sign on with a publisher, they should watch what they're signing:

Don't sign your life away. [Contracts] can be very one-sided. Publishers will naturally try to grab everything they can. A *one-off* deal [an agreement with the company to publish just one game at a time] is great because you're not obligated to the publisher for 10 years or anything. And besides, if the game is successful, they will surely come back for more, or other publishers will.

GET IN THE DOOR

Resnick recommends that game designers take advantage of the fact that the PC and console gaming industries are still relatively young. He explains:

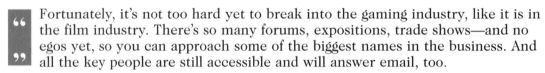

Fortunately, it's not too hard yet to break into the gaming industry, like it is in the film industry. There's so many forums, expositions, trade shows—and no egos yet, so you can approach some of the biggest names in the business. And all the key people are still accessible and will answer email, too.

Perhaps the last of Resnick's advice is the most pointed—thousands of people out there are capable of making a great game, but only a few have the desire and *chutzpah* to sell themselves, their team, and/or their game to a well-known publisher. Just remember, the worst case scenario (if you protect your idea) is that they won't be interested. With nothing to lose and so much to gain, the only ones who lose out are the ones who don't do anything with their idea at all...

"Dave" from the popular "Dave's Video Game Classics" Web site says downloading emulator source code is a good way to test out your game-programming skills. Says Dave: "Open source code allows anyone interested in working on the project to get involved, and thus allows the project to develop more rapidly (assuming it gets popular enough, like MAME [Multiple Arcade Machine Emulator] did)." According to Dave, a few authors who started by resurrecting arcade games via emulators such as MAME have gone on to large development companies. "Dave's Video Game Classics" is at www.davesclassics.com.

MICHAEL RUBINELLI, THQ

As vice president of development at THQ, Inc., Michael Rubinelli manages the people who manage the game developers. Who better to ask about the best ways to approach a publishing company?

Rubinelli says there are three pieces to the puzzle, and, while you don't need all three to spark interest with a publisher, the more you have, the better:

First on the list is a compelling design document. To reiterate, this is a comprehensive outline of all the game's features and story, with information for all members of the design team.

 Second, a 2D, colorized storyboard or character model collection is recommended. Rubinelli says it's important to have an artist give the publisher an idea of the visual tone or flavor of the game by submitting sketches, rendered characters, or background drawings.

 Third on the list is some form of demo technology—that is, a working prototype of the game's engine.

Rubinelli says it sure helps if you have a talented team already chosen to work on the game.

The last piece of advice from Rubinelli is to know the platform on which the game is going to be published. In other words, understand the strengths and limitations of the platform (for example, Sony PlayStation or Nintendo 64), and be sure the publishers know you're aware of the platform.

 Rubinelli says it can cost anywhere from $20,000 to $25,000 for a console development kit. This is something the publishers would likely have to purchase for the developers. Yes, this is on top of paying salaries for the developers.

When asked what kinds of games he looks to scoop up at THQ, Rubinelli admits that his answer would sound trite, but couldn't be closer to the truth:

> I'm looking for a *hit* game. That is, I want to know what kind of game a designer has a real passion for. If the developers are working on something they really want to work on, it comes through in the game, and everyone wins, regardless of the game genre.

Rubinelli admits he thinks sports games are a little limited in scope, while action games have more flexibility to them, with more variations of gameplay.

FRANZ LANZINGER, ACTUAL ENTERTAINMENT

After independently developing games such as *Gubble 1* and *2* for about 10 years, Actual Entertainment's Franz Lanzinger has a few words of wisdom he'd be happy to share with others. Though it may be more sobering than one would wish to hear, it's the truth, according to Lanzinger:

> My general advice to aspiring game developers is this: Don't quit your day job. It's about as tough to make money in the game business as it is to break into the movie business. Most people start by taking a job at a game company first, and then breaking away once they know something about the business.
>
> If you love games and simply have to work on games because anything else would [stink] in comparison, then yes, give it a try, but don't expect to get rich right away—if ever.

> Marketing and distributing your game on your own isn't for the faint of heart, or poor of pocket. Be prepared to lose whatever money and time you might be inclined to invest. Sometimes it's the only option to get your game out there, and it can be fun to try. Be aware, though, that most of these attempts, including ours at Actual Entertainment, turn into labors of love rather than big, successful companies.

PAUL O'CONNOR, ODDWORLD INHABITANTS

We heard from this veteran game and level designer in Chapter 6, but he offers a few words here on breaking into the business:

> My answer is to seek a well-rounded education. For every game you play, read three books. Take writing courses in college.
>
> Develop an ability to critically analyze all forms of entertainment—learn to break things down and determine what makes them tick. Game design is a collaborative art, so if you can't get along with others, seek other work.
>
> This task involves meetings and continual compromise. If you want to work alone in a garret, you're better off writing novels. As far as breaking in is concerned, most game designers seem to start as testers—it's a low-wage job with impossible hours, but it's your best opportunity to impress a company with your grasp of games and move up into a design position.

GETTING A JOB AT A GAMING COMPANY

Getting a job at a game developer or publishing company may be the most educational and advantageous plan in the long run. Consider the time spent with a hand-picked team of talented artists, animators, programmers, level designers, musicians, and so forth, where each member is responsible for his or her own part of the overall picture. Moreover, development tools are provided, so it costs much less to work at a development company rather than starting your own right away. And finally, this scenario allows the individual to understand the codependent relationship between a developer and publisher.

The following is a collection of advice on getting into your favorite development studio or publishing company.

PAUL JAQUAYS, ID SOFTWARE

id Software's Paul Jaquays reminds game designers that it's not that easy to become a respected "pro" in this field.

> For every 10,000 kids who dream of working as a professional game maker, only a relative few will actually make it as a pro within the industry. And of those who do make it, even fewer will become "household names," even inside the industry.

So how do you know you're fit for the part? Jaquays begins as follows:

> Evaluate yourself and answer the following questions *honestly*:
>
> ■ Do you have a driving urge to make things?
>
> ■ Do you prefer making games to playing them?
>
> ■ Do you like the challenge of solving problems on a daily basis?
>
> ■ Are you willing to commit yourself to a career in which your working hours will be longer—sometimes *far* longer—than those of the average working guy or gal?
>
> ■ Do you have creative ability in more than a single area?
>
> ■ If you're already in a relationship with someone, does he or she understand how much of your life will be consumed by your job (and is he or she willing to accept that)?
>
> Needless to say, the correct answer really needs to be "yes" to all questions.

As someone who works at one of the most prestigious gaming development houses in the world, Jaquays has often been asked what kind of background it takes to make it in the biz. The answer? "A varied one," says Jaquays. He expands:

> A successful candidate needs to develop multiple talents and skill packages. Examples of talent areas include but are not limited to story creation, 2D texture art, 3D modeling, model skins, level design, game scenario script writing, dialogue writing, music, sound effects, programming, project management, and business. Focus on one skill in particular, but try to be a polymath with as many other useful skills as you can manage. The most valuable team members are those who can wear many hats and perform several functions on a project.

Raw skill is all fine and dandy, but Jaquays encourages schooling, where possible, to get training in your talent areas:

> Employers really want creativity, but they really *need* people with the technical skills to put those talents to use. If you want to write, obviously you should take a creative writing class, but just as important, take a typing class. If you want to do game art, take all the art classes you can get—even if they have nothing to do with computers. If you want to build 3D game levels, take computer assisted drafting (CAD) classes. Want to make music? Join the band.

Going back to the point on "wearing many hats," Jaquays insists that even if you don't have skill in all aspects of game product creation, you should learn as much as you can about the areas that are not your forte. "You will need to understand your future teammates and what it is that they do."

If you can get an interview, Jaquays reminds you to be prepared: "Always have a printed résumé and a presentation package of your best work available to send out at a moment's notice." He also suggests having additional résumés handy, and mentions that it may be worthwhile to set up an account with a next-day delivery service so that you have shipping supplies on hand at all times.

Assuming someone has some raw talent and schooling to help sharpen their skills, when should they begin knocking down doors? Jaquays offers the following:

> " Don't expect a potential employer to immediately recognize your raw talents. Get experience first. Generally this means nonprofessional experience participating in noncommercial conversions or modifications of existing games. Treat the project like it's a commercial endeavor. Show that you can do work of professional caliber, and, most important, finish your contribution to the project on schedule. "

Once you've made up your mind that this is what you'd like to do for a living, is it best to jump in feet first? Is your meal ticket written? Jaquays says it's not likely:

> " Don't quit your day job. This is important. Chances are you'll spend a long time before getting your foot in the door. Even if you're living rent-free in your parents' home, you'll need to keep yourself in relatively up-to-date computer hardware.
>
> Everyone dreams of being a star. The truth is, most folks working in the business don't get their pictures in *Newsweek* or their pithy thoughts quoted in *Rolling Stone*. They don't drive expensive foreign sports cars or vacation frequently on tropical islands. You can dream, but don't expect to start at the top, or even somewhere in the middle. There are a lot of "overnight success stories" out there, but most of them paid their dues to get there, starting off at the bottom of the food chain. Now, just because I've said that, it doesn't mean that you shouldn't set your goals high. It doesn't hurt to apply to high-profile game development companies, but recognize that most of them are as successful as they are because they have already hired experienced people. "

Instead, Jaquays recommends you consider temporary employment situations, since it's a chance to show someone what you really can do. Talented temporary staff often find their way into full-time situations with their employer, or even a recommendation to another development company. Need an example? Here's one right from the horse's mouth:

> " My first job in the computer game business started with a nine-week contract at Coleco, trying to design a fantasy role-playing game that would work with a primitive bar code reader. By the time it ended, I was a creative director in charge of a staff of designers making games for the ColecoVision, Atari 2600, Intellivision, and ADAM computer.
>
> And don't limit your job choices to a single geographic area. Be prepared to move around as needed. Make sure that your spouse (or future spouse) understands this. Companies come and go in this business. Don't plan on being anyplace for long. "

Many people are overwhelmed by the size of the growing gaming industry and feel they can't penetrate its borders. How can someone from the outside get in? Keep your eyes and ears open, says Jaquays, and get out to gaming events:

> " There's a great deal of truth in the old saw, "It's not what you know, but who you know." Quite often, industry jobs are gained by someone referring someone they know as a friend or acquaintance, or have met in person at least

once before. I know that as an art director, I was usually more willing to assign illustration projects to people I had met than to unknowns who just sent me portfolios. Given this, you should try to go places where industry professionals get together. National or even regional LAN parties, professional game tournaments, and design seminars are all excellent places to meet people already working in the industry. Make an effort to introduce yourself, and if possible have them look over samples of your work.

And once you're in the door? What happens now? Jaquays says to "be nice to each other." Isn't that obvious?

I shouldn't have to explain that, but I will. The Internet has rapidly replaced the fan magazines and amateur press associations that were prevalent when I started my career. Fans of old used those venues to express their opinions on their hallowed topics, "flaming" any who disagreed with them. Interchanges of ideas took place over periods of months. Now, fans who have interests in things can communicate with each other instantly in chat rooms, message boards, and online forums. The relative anonymity of the Net often lulls people into thinking that they can be rude to others whenever they feel like it. However, being disrespectful can catch up with a person. Trashing the comments, beliefs, or skills of someone online may feel good for the moment, but this is a small industry we work in (or hope to work in). Folks working in it tend to know lots of other folks working at other companies. And they talk to each other. Word gets around. It should go without saying that you ought to treat everyone working in the industry like they might possibly be your boss someday. That is to say, give them respect. Treat other would-be professionals with respect also. You never know when you might be on a development team together. Or even find yourself working for them.

When you finally get that job in the game industry, continue to treat everyone working in the industry like they may be your boss someday (two guys I hired to work at Coleco had previously hired me to do freelance work for the game companies they worked for). And remember to extend a helping hand to tomorrow's professionals.

But how do you really know if you're good enough to give it a shot? Who can you trust for honest advice?

Be wary of the flattery of your friends. Appreciate it, but recognize that your friends probably aren't qualified to give you the insight you need to grow and develop your skills (and friends often find it difficult to criticize). Seek out legitimate criticism of your work by people you recognize to be better at the task than you are. Accept criticism gracefully. Be especially appreciative if it's constructive criticism.

Finally, are there any downsides to making games for a living? There couldn't be, right? Jaquays warns:

Be prepared to lose your game-playing hobby. This has been true for me, but it may not be true for you. When I started creating games professionally, the type of game I worked on no longer became fun to play for pure recreation. It started when I was first doing role-playing adventures. The more I wrote game scenarios for pay, the less I wanted to do it for fun. When I started making arcade game conversions for Coleco, I quickly lost interest in popping quarters into machines in arcades. (However, due to the kind of designers I was able to hire, we put together an incredible role-playing game group after hours.) When I went back to designing role-playing adventures once more, I stopped doing it for fun again. Now I really like making 3D FPS [first-person shooter] games, but I have a hard time playing them for fun. It's not that I don't like them; it's that I can't play without turning on my professional eye. Essentially, when playing I don't see the game, I see how it's made.

KEVIN CLOUD, ID SOFTWARE

Artist and part owner of id Software Kevin Cloud believes that you should get into the industry at any position to start. Says Cloud:

A game designer shouldn't break into the business. Out of all of the positions in a game company, a designer requires the most experience. It isn't enough to have a good idea. Designers need to understand the process of creating a game. They need to understand what can be achieved, how many people are needed to get it done, and how long it will take. A game designer needs to break into the business as a writer, project manager, artist, programmer, level designer, or beta tester.

Concludes Cloud, "A designer needs to be anything but a designer when he starts."

CHRIS SAWYER, FREELANCE

The creator of *RollerCoaster Tycoon*, the best-selling PC game of 1999, offers a few words on the best ways to break into the gaming industry. Says Sawyer:

From my own perspective, you need a broad mixture of skills to create computer games, including programming, mathematics, graphic design, psychology, game design, organizational skills, management, and even financial skills. However, most people who work in the games industry specialize in just some of these skills—for example, programming and mathematics, or graphic design, or game design. Personally, I think you need a good understanding of most of these things to be successful in the games industry.

A game designer should have a basic understanding of programming, and a programmer should have an understanding of graphic design, for example. I did a degree course in computer science and microprocessor systems, but that taught me little more than the fundamentals of programming and 3D graphics—I've learned much more about game development while actually working on games. I don't think you can be taught how to create something unique game-wise, but you can be taught how to program, run your business well, manage your time, and develop any ideas or concepts you have.

GREG ZESCHUK, BIOWARE

Cofounder and CEO of Canada's hot development team responsible for the *Baldur's Gate* series and *MDK2*, Greg Zeschuk talks about what kind of design/tech training will get budding game developers into the industry.

Asked how much is education, how much is pure talent, and how much is *chutzpah*, Zeschuk answers as follows:

> I'd say that you must have a lot of *chutzpah* to make video games—it's a challenging and rewarding career, but it's also quite draining when it comes to the feared crunch time. Making games is like a marathon—the team that can go the distance will usually win. It's also very hard to always be creatively "on." Projects have stringent deadlines that can chew people up if they aren't ready for them. The people I work with have a variety of backgrounds; some are very educated (some with advanced degrees) while others are purely self-taught. I would say that training is an asset, and that no one truly has enough pure talent to carry them through creating a game. Teamwork is the key to the "new game development" landscape. It's impossible for a single person to make a complete game in today's market. Our smallest game development has 15 full time members and is supported by another 10 people.

PETER MOLYNEUX, LIONHEAD STUDIOS

The genius behind such beloved PC classics as *Populous*, *Syndicate*, *Dungeon Keeper*, and *Magic Carpet* offers the following advice on breaking into the gaming industry, and touches on a few do's and don'ts as well.

> There are three main ways into the game industry. The first is education—get a related degree such as math, programming, or philosophy if you want to be a programmer, or a branch of the visual arts if you intend to work as an artist. To take this route in the U.K., you would need a very good degree from a very good university.
>
> The second way would be to start at the bottom, say as a games tester or assistant, and work your way up.
>
> The third way, and the hardest way these days, is to get together with some like-minded game freaks and start your own company.
>
> My do's would be as follows—if you want to be successful at anything, you must be willing to make it the most important thing in your life. It's no good expecting to be a success if you want a 9-to-5 job. If you're sending stuff out to prospective employers, make it brief but exciting. This covers everything from CVs [curriculum vitae] to games design—detail can be long-winded and off-putting.

Finally, Molyneux urges you to "believe in yourself, because if you don't, no one else will."

ALEX GARDEN, RELIC ENTERTAINMENT

This 25-year-old successful game designer from Vancouver, British Columbia, explains what it takes to make it as a developer in the competitive gaming industry.

Says Garden: "Game creators come from every imaginable background. As far as production staff goes, there are four main areas: design, art, programming, and sound." Garden explains that most designers tend to come from the most diverse background because the only real design prerequisite is creativity and you really can't teach that in school. For the other three, Garden expands:

> Artists tend to have a ton of intrinsic artistic talent and come from a classical background with some degree of technical training. Programmers are the most technical, and therefore (in general) the most educated of the bunch. Sound designers are a totally random wildcard and may be über-educated or totally raw. In every case, successful people have to have a) a ton of pure talent, b) a ton of *chutzpah*. This is a very competitive industry.
>
> A great way to get in the industry is to critique existing products; play the entire game, write a design document, point out how to improve the game, and send it to the people who made the game—someone will take you seriously, and even if they don't hire you, you will get great practice.

PHIL STEINMEYER, POPTOP SOFTWARE

President, lead designer, and lead programmer at the newly formed PopTop Software (responsible for the award-winning *Railroad Tycoon II*), Phil Steinmeyer offers some words of wisdom on breaking into the industry.

DON'T OVERSHOOT ON YOUR FIRST GAME

> The Internet is littered with abandoned projects by three or four guys with no game-development experience who were going to create a better *Quake*, or the ultimate first-person RPG. If you're working in your spare time, with no prior experience, don't expect to outdo experienced, professional, large, well-financed teams. Shoot for something achievable. If you like level design, do a series of levels for your favorite first-person shooter or strategy game. If you're a programmer, do a clone of your favorite early 80s arcade game (*Pac-Man*, *Space Invaders*, etc.). If you're an artist, do skins for *Quake*, or 3D character animations based on your favorite game. Above all else—*complete it!* That's the main reason for choosing something of modest size and scope—it's achievable. I'd rather see a finished *Pac-Man* variant than a *Quake* killer that's 10% done, consisting of a few polygons slapped on the screen.

WHEN APPLYING FOR A JOB, HAVE SAMPLES

> With everyone hooked up to the Web these days, there's no excuse for not having electronic samples of your work available for any prospective employer—either attached to your application, or accessible at your Web site (include the URL with your application). For a level designer, this should be

levels, well made, preferably to two or more different games (the more games you do levels for, the more likely the person you're applying to will be familiar with at least one of them and be able to fire it up and take a quick look at your level). For an artist, include as wide a variety of art types as possible— 2D, 3D, hand drawn, animation, characters, mechanical objects, etc. For a programmer, a playable demo, with at least some art (you may have to hook up with a friend for the art).

BE VERSATILE

PopTop Software is a six-person company. We don't have separate full-time positions for every type of job we've got. One artist does sound as well. Another does video and art. Our chief scenario designer got the job in part because he's also a talented artist and a good writer—so for the long stretches of projects when the game is too rough to start level design, he can do other things.

CHOOSING A GAME THEME

The first time you're in a position to design a real commercial game, be original (remember, newbies, I recommend something simple for your first effort— now I'm talking about *after* you've got that under your belt). Most likely this first game will have a modest budget, and your own skills as well as those of your team may still be a bit rough. Don't try to outgun the 50-person, $3 million budget AAA titles that overcrowd the first-person shooter and real-time strategy genres. Pick a niche where there's little competition, or where the existing competition is similarly modest in budget. Some examples are war games, puzzle games, retro 2D action games.

In conclusion, Steinmeyer reminds us that "it's far easier to shine with little competition, then move up to more ambitious projects."

MIKE RUBINELLI, THQ

In the first half of this chapter, Mike Rubinelli spoke to game designers who want to pitch games or game ideas directly to publishers. Now he offers some advice on getting a job within an existing company:

Instead of trying to get into a company as a game designer or producer, it's best to start at an entry-level position, since these titles [game designer or producer] are usually given to those who have been in the industry for a while. The people who get those positions have a history, so if you're just starting out it's best to start off in the testing department or perhaps customer service. The good news is that when a large company starts hiring, they often look internally first; they look to promote from within.

Rubinelli says many employers turn to the testing group when looking to promote an employee.

JOSH RESNICK, PANDEMIC STUDIOS

Resnick, whom we also heard from in the first half of this chapter, says a great way to get in the door to a company is to submit levels or maps. In fact, Activision has even paid a few *Dark Reign* map designers when their content was used in some way. Says Resnick on using game editors, for all professions:

> It's one of the best ways to get hired for a development team, period. A level designer can make a level using free utilities for action or strategy games, programmers can submit a MOD, artists can make skins. It's never been easier. And it also kisses the a--es of publishers because these designers liked their games enough to take the time to create these add-ons.

In closing, Resnick reminds those who are looking for a job to get online. "Game developers and publishers are always looking for good people on the Internet."

SID MEIER, FIRAXIS GAMES

"Get involved as a play tester, and over time, demonstrate your knowledge, be active, and offer suggestions," says Meier, outlining the best traditional way to climb the ladder. "Another way is to write manuals for a company, says Meier. "That is, do something related to game design, and if you have talent, it will be recognized."

But what about doing it yourself instead of this traditional way of getting in the industry? Says Meier:

> The second route is the quickest but requires luck and a lot of talent. If this is what you want to do, and you're a programmer or are working with one, put together a playable demo of your game and shop it around. We all know of the story with *SimCity*. Will Wright took it to eight publishers who all turned it down, except Maxis. Now publishers are a lot more sensitive, but you must put together a good prototype. And it doesn't need FMV [full-motion video] or polished graphics.

Be sure to read Sid Meier's advice on general game design in Chapter 2.

RICHARD "LORD BRITISH" GARRIOTT

As one of the most-recognized and longest-running game designers in the industry, recently-departed Origin Systems cofounder Lord British has given quite a bit of advice over the years on how to get into the industry. He offers the following:

> Find a way into the building of a game company. Get a job in customer service or quality assurance testing, because it's very hard to be a game designer right off the bat. Maybe 20 years ago, but not now...But, on the flip side, our industry is very young, and it may only take you three to five years to get to the top; there are huge opportunities.
>
> Twenty years ago they didn't care if you had a degree, but now it's very important. Their fear is that you're a hacker and not an engineer. Hackers are good

too, because they're good at finding problems, but the industry needs and wants more quality engineers. You're also going to need more than classical education. You're going to need demonstrable capabilities, example pieces of code. Good practice is to write D & D (*Dungeons & Dragons*) modules or interactive novels.

Everyone believes they're competent designers five years before they are.

 Looking for a job in the gaming industry? In Chapter 24, "Game Design Resources on the Internet," GameJobs.com's Rick Vandervoorn talks about their free service and how the Internet has changed the way game developers can seek employment.

TOBY GARD, CONFOUNDING FACTOR

The gentleman who created the luscious Lara Croft for Core Design's *Tomb Raider* explains here how a game designer can get into this highly competitive industry. To Gard, the best way is to do an apprenticeship at a big company. He explains:

> Reading books is one thing, but it's no substitute for the sheer weight of knowledge and understanding you get from actually working on a game. Besides, you probably don't want to leap into one of your own games as your first project, because you'll have to learn so much that you'll end up making a bit of a mess. Better to be part of a team and get your experience that way. Also, if you've seen a game through to completion, people will take your game designs more seriously. So I wouldn't bother sending designs to people if you're just starting out; just get together a good art portfolio and start out that way. Resign yourself to learning the trade for a couple of years and then you'll have the experience to pull off one of your own designs afterwards.

JANE JENSEN, SIERRA ON-LINE

Jane Jensen is an award-winning writer and game designer at Sierra, where she conceived and directed the first three *Gabriel Knight* interactive mysteries: *Sins of the Fathers*; *The Beast Within*; and *Blood of the Sacred, Blood of the Damned*.

So what does this highly respected game designer have to say about breaking into the biz?

> It's quite difficult, so I usually recommend that they study some ancillary skill such as programming or art, and come into the business through that avenue. Very few companies will hire an inexperienced "game designer" off the street. Either they hire experienced people or they promote from within. Remember, most every programmer or artist working for a game company wants to be a game designer, and they, at least, have a chance to prove their creativity and motivation in-house. The other way in is to start your own little company with some friends and actually put together a prototype. If it's good enough you might be able to get hired into a company, or have a larger company fund

> your project to completion. But it does take a lot of work and time to make a great prototype—including fantastic art, etc.—and it's not easy putting together these resources on your own.

Notice a trend here?

MATT PRITCHARD, ENSEMBLE STUDIOS

Ensemble Studios' programmer Matt Pritchard shares his thoughts on the best ways to prepare for and get into the gaming industry. Before he breaks it into individual positions, Pritchard covers the basics first. In a nutshell? You need to a) love games, and b) be interested in more than just playing them. According to Pritchard, there are roughly four major categories of people involved in the direct creation of a game.

PROGRAMMERS

> These people are proficient in computer programming languages such as C++ and assembly. They usually have studied hard about such topics as software design, algorithms, data structures, and math.

ARTISTS

> These people are proficient in drawing the 2D and 3D images used in games. They have studied art and honed their artistic skills, which include texture and composition skills, as well as know how to use software such as Photoshop, 3D Studio MAX, and others.

SOUND ENGINEERS AND MUSICIANS

> These people usually are musicians in their own right, and are responsible for creating the sound effects and musical soundtracks for games. They are both musically inclined and sophisticated users of the latest in sound editing and music composition software and equipment.

GAME DESIGNERS

> These people understand the underlying game mechanics and theory. They usually have played a huge variety of games, including board games, war games, and pen-and-paper role-playing games. They're responsible for the myriad of statistics, properties, and rules that go into a game, and have to balance the details to make a game "fun." No specific course of study for designers, other than that they study everything: history, science, and the inner workings of hundred of games. Designers spend a great deal of their time creating the content that goes into a game—the levels, the puzzles, the scenarios, and so on.

SINJIN BAIN, PYROTECHNIX

Sinjin Bain is cofounder and studio manager at PyroTechnix, a wholly owned subsidiary of Sierra On-Line. Much of 1998 was spent completing the RPG sequel *Return to Krondor*, based on the work of author Raymond E. Feist.

In the following passage, Bain offers some advice on getting into the gaming industry:

> This is a rapidly maturing business and there are many areas of computer gaming that the designer must understand. Perhaps the greatest challenge for the game designer of today is to develop an innate understanding of how technology and art integrate. The challenge to develop a compelling game has been and always will be the objective, but as we all know, technology is changing at an ever-increasing pace. This really adds to the challenge of the designer in many ways. I can't emphasize enough the benefits of understanding the specifics of the hardware and software for whatever platform the game will be delivered on. The impact this area has on actual gameplay techniques, development cycle, budgets, and other areas is incalculable.

As an example, Bain refers to *Return to Krondor*, where their goal was to build and develop from the success of the popular *Betrayal at Krondor*. Recalls Bain:

> Our intent was to develop a "franchise" of games that complement Ray Feist's literary franchise. *Return to Krondor* was developed in a totally different style than the first game, *Betrayal at Krondor*. We did this for two specific reasons: First, we wanted to broaden the market for the franchise past a pure RPG market, so this impacted the design process. Second, we wanted to elevate the look and feel of the game to present a game in the RPG/adventure genre that hadn't been seen yet. We accomplished this by taking advantage of the art talent at our disposal and using our True3D real-time technologies. We adopted some design decisions and chose to use 2D pre-rendered backgrounds combined with real-time 3D characters with motion-capture animation and RGB color lighting, thereby producing a truly unique look and feel for the game. While it's important to innovate and advance, it also must be acknowledged that good gameplay is timeless, and *Betrayal at Krondor* had many elements of great gameplay, especially the turn-based combat system, so we were intent on maintaining this aspect of the game. In essence, what we focused on was producing an innovative and accessible RPG/adventure game that took advantage of all the new technology of today, while maintaining the great gameplay elements of the first game. I think we succeeded on many levels, but as with all things there is always room for improvement. One of the areas we will focus on in the future is more attention to interface elements, for example.

Be sure to read Sinjin Bain's bio in the appendix to this book.

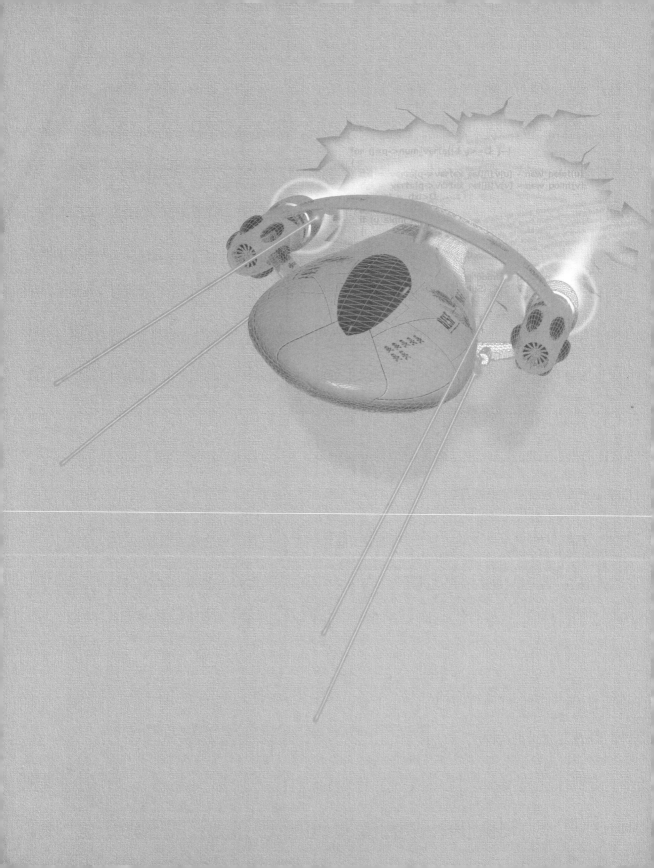

CHAPTER 21
GAME AGENTS
AND HEADHUNTERS

Let's face it—not all game designers have the know-how or courage to successfully sell themselves or their games to a reputable publisher. And in many cases, game designers *prefer* to concentrate only on the game itself, and leave the number-crunching to others.

Following suit with other entertainment industries, such as film and music, agents and headhunters represent designers and publishers, respectively. While they work differently, their goal is one and the same—to unite talented game designers and their products with publishers and/or distributors.

This chapter is dedicated to both of these third parties by covering how they work—and more importantly, how you as a game designer can take advantage of the services they offer.

SUSAN LEWIS, THINKBIG

Susan Lewis is the founder and president of ThinkBIG, can agency created to represent and promote the interests of game developers and publishing companies. In particular, their focus is to aid game developers who are seeking worldwide publishing deals, as well as publishers who may want to expand their distribution into foreign territories.

Lewis comments on why a game designer should opt to sign on with an agent, as opposed to pitching a publisher directly, and what they should do to prepare for the relationship:

> A game studio tends to hire an agent, not a game designer. So the first advice is for the game designer to get a team together before approaching an agent. That said, the group needs a game design document—or at least a precursor to a full design doc—as well as a functional prototype of the game. This is not to say that, given a particularly intriguing group, exceptions aren't made. One recent client of mine was made up of two guys who were leads on one of the biggest PC games of the previous year. All I had was a two-page game design and two guys, and a bunch of commitments from their friends to join the team if I got them a deal. It was a laborious process with so little to go on.

> However, based on the résumés of these two guys, we landed a deal with a top publisher. This was an unusual situation, however, and the exception to the rule as far as I'm concerned. If you don't have a fleshed-out concept and a prototype, you need a very impressive track record to get the attention of most agents.

How exactly does the process work? And how is the agency compensated?

> The process is somewhat similar to submitting to a publisher. I get solicited and unsolicited game designs and prototypes regularly. If my company is interested, I'll begin a dialogue with that developer and gain an understanding of the game design, the prototype, [and] get a feel for the staff and their capabilities and weaknesses. I was a recruiter for the game industry before becoming an agent, so I can be very helpful in filling in gaps in a team. If I like what I see, and feel it's *sellable*, I'll sign a contract with the developer, which appoints ThinkBIG as their exclusive worldwide agent. There is often a big difference between games I personally like and games I know I can sell. For instance, I love sprite-based real-time strategy games like *Warcraft* and *Command & Conquer*, but I will rarely if ever agree to represent one. The reason is that unless it's in one of these big brands, it's lucky to sell 20,000 units, and most of the publishers wouldn't even bother to look at it.
>
> After the contract is signed, I contact the appropriate publishers and arrange to meet with the executives, show them the prototype, and pitch the concept. When it gets to the contract stage, I work with the developer's attorney and the publisher's legal department to negotiate the deal terms and contract. Following the signing of the contract, I stay peripherally involved in the project, checking up on the developer's progress, checking in with the producer, following up on late milestones or payments, and interfacing with the publisher if there's a problem.
>
> I get paid based on what the developer receives from the publisher; that is, 10% of all up-front development advances and 10% of all back-end royalties and bonuses.

Lewis mentions in her bio that she has a working relationship with a number of publishers, such as Electronic Arts, Acclaim, Fox Interactive, Atari Games, and BMG Interactive. Naturally, readers will be curious about any success stories she can share.

> I'm quite proud of the work I did for BMG Interactive with their N64 basketball game. BMG retained me to sell off U.S. or worldwide rights to some of their titles when they closed their U.S. division. The basketball game, developed by Z-Axis, was an NBA game with a nontransferable license. Well, NBA is one of the most difficult licenses to acquire, and virtually all of the publishers who have one have their own basketball game. Exhausting the options we had as an NBA game (plenty of publishers wanted the game but none could secure a license), it was decided that Z-Axis would do a quick conversion to college basketball. The new problem was that we were precariously close to "March madness," and Nintendo has a lengthy final approval process before a game

> can manufacture and ship. In the end, I contacted Fox Interactive, who had just announced their entry into sports products; they picked up the game, which released in the fall of 1998 at the start of the new season as *Fox Sports College Hoops*.

For more information on ThinkBIG, visit their Web site at www.thinkbigco.com, or for answers to general queries, go directly to their FAQ (frequently asked questions) page at www.thinkbigco.com/faq.html.

MELANIE CAMBRON, VIRTUAL SEARCH

As a self-proclaimed "game recruiting goddess" at Virtual Search, Melanie Cambron serves as a full-time headhunter for a number of such well-known clients as Electronic Arts, Microprose, Hasbro, Mattel, Accolade, and many more. Cambron outlines the best way for a game designer to begin a relationship with a recruiter:

> Send a well-written, proofread résumé to one reputable recruiter. When you work with several, oftentimes efforts are duplicated and folks get annoyed. Be selective when choosing a recruiter. Showing up at a GDC [Game Developers Conference] or IGDN [International Game Developers Network] doesn't hurt either.
>
> Programmers need to have clean, well-commented code samples ready to show. Artists need to have a mind-blowing demo reel complete with music. Game designers should have design documentation to show—obviously, check on status of NDAs [non-disclosure agreements] before sending it around. After receiving your résumé, hiring managers will frequently request code samples/demo reel before ever chatting with a candidate.

So how does a headhunter get paid? Cambron responds as follows:

> My fees are paid by the hiring company [i.e., the developer/publisher]. Some clients retain my services, while others choose to pay on a contingency basis, meaning that the employer pays me a percentage of the new hire's first-year annual salary.

Other than the fact that it's free for game designers, Cambron comments on other benefits game designers have by working with a recruiter:

> Often brilliant people have no idea how to market themselves. I've seen so many résumés with atrocious mistakes! That old adage about first impressions is painfully true. Also, good recruiters have a wealth of contacts within well-established game companies and can often get your résumé to the hiring manager, who will actually sit up and take notice.

Cambron has provided us with a short article on breaking into the gaming industry. It was originally written for programmers, but can be applied to general game design as well:

THE RÉSUMÉ

Without omitting important information, try to be concise. Résumés should be no more than two pages—ideally, just one page. Translation: Don't list every grunt job you've ever had. Focus on what you've done that's applicable to the desired position in the game industry. If you have done some *gratis* game design/programming, by all means, list this on your résumé. ANY, repeat ANY computer skills that are not from the Land That Time Forgot should be one of the first things on the page. Those of you who actually received your degree, you should place your education info at the beginning of your résumé; therefore taking the spotlight off of your lack of experience. Most importantly, proofread your résumé before you send it in. It's amazing how many résumés are submitted with basic spelling and grammar mistakes, as well as seriously incorrect dates of employment and education. Your résumé is usually the first impression you make on a company or an agent. Yes, you may be a programmer, and you may feel your spelling ability simply isn't important to writing code, but companies are looking for well-rounded, intelligent people who care about everything they produce.

Résumés can be very personal things, but if you can, have a friend, family member, or trusted game agent read over your résumé before you send it out. You may have looked at it a thousand times, but many times a "fresh eye" will catch mistakes your tired brain simply missed. Finally, chill on the funky fonts and colors. Today, many companies scan résumés, so use a basic font (in black) on white paper. Furthermore, hiring managers want to find the important information easily, rather than meandering through a maze of wacky fonts and graphics. In addition to your résumé, it's *imperative* that you have code samples ready to send to potential employers upon request. These samples should be about three pages of very clean, well-commented code. Once again, have this proofread by a knowledgeable *amigo*.

THE GAME DEMO

Game companies want to know not only that you can cut code, but that you have a passion for games. So dedicated are you to the making of games that you would program your own game just out of sheer love for the industry. It doesn't matter if the game is a pixelated mess, just show that you made the effort and you have the passion. This goes a long way. Ask around. You'll find that most folks in this biz are not here for the money.

COMMON MISTAKES/SIMPLE TIPS

Oftentimes, extremely zealous individuals will spam their résumés to companies repeatedly. All this does is annoy. You end up looking "desperate or just plain stupid," to quote the hiring manager of a very large game developer.

Be sure to keep an accurate record of where and when you have sent your résumé to avoid [duplication]. The other résumé turnoff is telling hiring managers or recruiters to "check out" your résumé on the Web. These folks receive such a voluminous amount of résumés that they don't have time to hunt down your info on the Net. Make it easy on them; you'll get a much better response.

Moreover, only send your résumés to companies for whom you really want to work. If you have no intention of moving to Florida, don't send your résumé to Gainesville Games. Also, when working with an agent, be sure to share this information so they don't get rejected due to your previous résumé submission, or having to reject the company's interest due to your location requirements. No one likes rejection.

Be prepared for that big interview. Regardless of whether it's a phone screen or you're actually sitting on the other side of the desk of the Vice President/Chief Technical Director of Everything, do your homework. Make sure you have thoroughly researched the company and are prepared to answer questions about your skills as well as your favorite games. With regard to fashion, being overdressed is always better than appearing as if you sauntered in for a sandwich. Pants/khakis and a button-down shirt are usually appropriate for game industry interviews. When in doubt, don the suit.

Most importantly, even if you think you have a brilliant idea for a game, get experience first. The game biz is much like the film industry—it's who you know. Each year, hundreds of companies come and go without ever getting a game on the shelf. Save yourself some heartache, time, and expense by starting your career with an established company. Learn from those who have been there, done that. Then, if you still feel a burning desire to do your own *thang*, good luck to you.

To learn more about Virtual Search, drop into www.vsearch.com or call 1-800-779-3334.

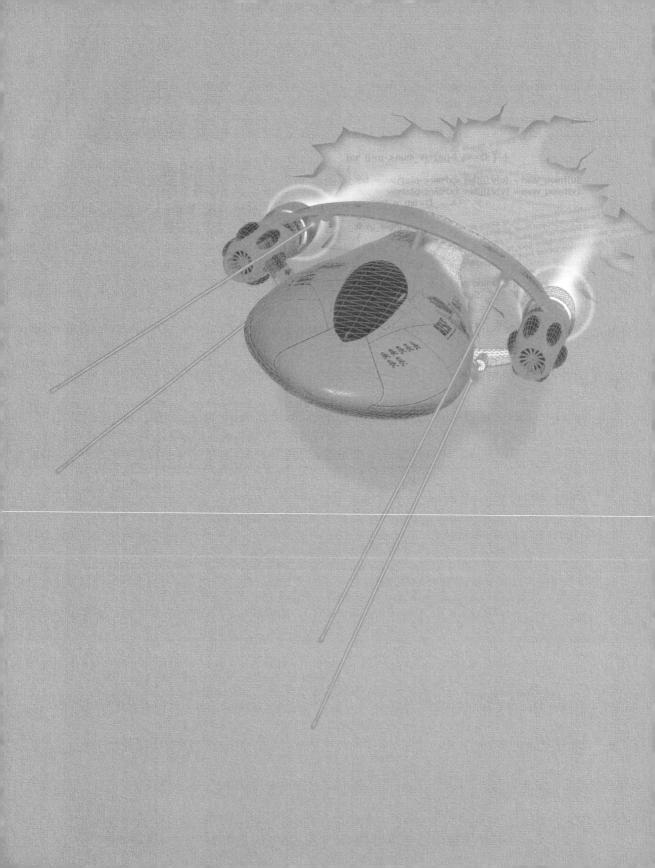

CHAPTER 22
DIVINE INTERVENTION— G.O.D.'S WAY

As we've covered elsewhere in this book, there are many different kinds of development companies to form and varied deals to sign with publishers and/or distributors. There is another option, however. A new company, and a new *kind* of company, formed in mid-1998, known as Gathering of Developers, or simply G.O.D. In a nutshell, G.O.D. was built upon a different philosophical business model, designed to treat game developers in a more *just* way. In particular, this means paying higher royalties, more creative freedom, and less rigid contracts.

This chapter highlights G.O.D.'s roots, their clients and goals, and how they aim to revolutionize the gaming industry well into the 21st century. At the end of this chapter, CEO Mike Wilson talks about game design and innovation, working with popular franchises, and what the future holds for the interactive entertainment industry.

ROOTS

Mike Wilson came up with the idea to start Gathering of Developers when he was still the official "biz guy" at id Software, then and now one of the top independent game developers in North America. Unless you've been living under a rock for the past five years, you probably know that this talented team of programmers and artists was responsible for the first-person perspective 3D shooter revolution with *Wolfenstein 3D* and the mega-successful *Doom* and *Quake* action series.

At that time, their publisher was GT Interactive, a then-small company whose products were a Fabio screen saver and a Richard Simmons "Deal a Meal" CD-ROM! Then id Software's *Doom II* became one of the first real PC gaming breakthrough titles, selling over two million units (even before Cyan's *Myst* was released). This title, plus other blockbusters from this southern studio, turned GT Interactive into a billion-dollar initial public offering, the largest IPO of 1995, in fact. According to Wilson, they were paid what were considered fair royalties at the time, but in retrospect, they were "horribly low" if you consider that *Doom II* generated over $80 million in revenues.

And thus, the idea for G.O.D. was born...

MISSION

G.O.D.'s goal is to become the premier publisher and worldwide leader in the delivery of commercially successful game software, designed for both the computer and console platforms. Just how do they plan on accomplishing this? CEO Mike Wilson answers, "By securing long-term relationships with the industry's top independent development talent."

With this approach, G.O.D. aims to establish a new status quo for developer/publisher relations based on a number of mandates: fair treatment of developers; royalties based on title sell-through; a title approval process that incorporates the judgment of development experts in the computer gaming industry; and management's successful experience in providing marketing, operational, and financial expertise.

THE G.O.D. DIFFERENCE

Wilson believes that the most critical functions of the publisher are to identify development talent and secure long term relationships with these "hit-makers." Ironically, says Wilson, "these are also the most difficult functions for publishers, even (and sometimes especially) for the largest publishers. The reason for this stems from two things: distrust of the developers for traditional business people, and a poor understanding of developers and their needs." He expands:

> G.O.D. takes advantage of its management's unique understanding of these problems, as well as the management's close relationships to the industry's top talent. Unlike other publishers, the company launched with a lineup of long-term development deals that are truly unparalleled in the industry.

Wilson says he wants G.O.D. to be recognized as the leader in developer relations and gamer relations, and hopes others will follow suit in doing so successfully:

> We have no desire to publish games for non-gamers. We want to publish the ones that those who live and breathe games will recognize as brilliant artistry from professional game developers. Now if, in doing this, we prove our point that a publisher can be successful by maintaining mutually beneficial relationships with respected artists, rather than by taking over their companies or robbing them of their intellectual property, or keeping them so broke that they can't negotiate, then we hope the industry will take note. If we're left alone to work under this model, so be it, but I think it's more likely that we signal the start of a very important trend for all publisher/developer relations. At the least, we will ensure that developers are informed about what they're worth and what they can expect to be able to negotiate based on that worth.

Are business relationships really that one-sided between developers and publishers? President and director of new business development Harry A. Miller answers:

> [Developers] are currently strong-armed by publishers, misinformed as to industry standards, misled due to their lack of business savvy in some instances, due to their ideals about partnership in others. The strategy has been to pay very meager advances and royalties, keeping developers "barefoot and pregnant," unable to negotiate or to shop around because of the uncertainty that comes from being economically dependent on that next milestone payment. Only a healthy, independent developer with proper business representation and good information to work with can strike a deal properly. Our strategy is to keep those developers informed so that, when they do reach that point, they know that they can turn to us for a relationship that will ensure that their work reaches their fans with minimum hassle and maximum integrity.

G.O.D. announced in January of 1999 that they would co-present the first annual Game Developers Conference (GDC) "Independent Games Festival" along with Miller Freeman, Inc. This festival is designed to promote interactive entertainment as an art form, and provide a forum for independent game developers from around the world to showcase their work, receive recognition, and meet potential publishers. Read more about this in Chapter 25.

GAMES AND DISTRIBUTION

Many other publishing companies believe G.O.D.'s mission statement sounds fine on paper, but there are enormous distribution and marketing costs they must factor into their budget. G.O.D. insists this has all been accounted for. For one, Take 2 Interactive is distributing the first 10 G.O.D. titles through its BMG subsidiary in Europe, the U.S., and Canada, and they use the same retail channels as everyone else. This includes CompUSA, Wal-Mart, Best Buy, Electronics Boutique, Babbages/Software Etc., Computer City (now owned by CompUSA), FRYs, etc. Wilson says about 10 accounts make up 90% of sales in our industry, plus G.O.D. has smaller distributors that specialize in "mom and pop" operations to handle the rest, and another arrangement for direct sales over the Internet (although this is still a small fraction of total sales).

G.O.D. launched with six red-hot development studios under their belt. These are, in no particular order: 3D Realms (responsible for the popular *Duke Nukem* series); Ritual Entertainment (*Sin* and *Quake: Scourge of Armagon*); PopTop Software (headed by industry veteran Phil Steinmeyer), Terminal Reality (*Monster Truck Madness* series for Microsoft, and many others); Epic Games (creators of the smash 3D shooter *Unreal*); and newcomers Edge of Reality (currently porting *Monster Truck Madness II* for the Nintendo 64). Heading Edge of Reality is Rob Cohen, who left Iguana after serving as lead programmer on the 1.5 million-selling *Turok: Dinosaur Hunter*.

G.O.D.'s first two releases were Epic Games' *Jazz Jackrabbit 2* and PopTop Software's *Railroad Tycoon II*, with both titles receiving critical acclaim.

For more information about G.O.D., their board of directors, and their impressive lineup of 2000 and 2001 titles, drop into www.godgames.com. Who knows—maybe you and your development team may be touched by the hand of G.O.D. one day!

AN INTERVIEW WITH MIKE WILSON

The well-known CEO and cofounder of Gathering of Developers sat down to discuss the direction G.O.D. is going, working with popular franchises, and a few of his beefs on the gaming industry as a whole.

Where does a game designer look for inspiration and innovation? What's *missing* with most of today's games?

> Unfortunately, game designers are most often inspired by games they have already played and other sci-fi influences: comics, action figures, sci-fi movies and television, etc. Other than that, pen-and-paper strategy and role-playing games. Mostly geeky sci-fi technophile stuff. This is the reason that our industry is by-and-large still a closet culture, even at $8 billion a year (or whatever that last number was). The games are being written by a very targeted group of designers—white males, for the most part, with an almost universal interest in science fiction, technology, and gaming. Almost no women, almost no minorities, almost no influences from outside our little group. When the demographics of the creators change, that's when we'll see true inspiration and innovation geared for the rest of the world. It's as if we're Hollywood and the only genres that exist right now are horror, sci fi, and "action." Oh, and sports. But only men's sports.

Why is it so important for Gathering to work with popular licenses such as the *Blair Witch Project*, heavy metal, or KISS? Does it hurt or help the game?

> What buying a license that has its own following does for a developer, in my mind at least, is give them a head start on the game being a commercially viable project. This can actually enable the teams to take more chances and to make more design decisions without always worrying about whether these decisions will make the game a commercial flop. These days, most games don't make enough money to recoup the sizable development costs. This is because there is so much competition, and so much access to technology—unlike even as recently as *Quake*'s launch, in 1996, it's no longer enough to have a screaming 3D engine—that the small pie that is the "hardcore gaming audience" is being sliced much thinner than before. Only a few games each year, mostly sequels to already strong franchises (which is like a license in itself) and other licensed properties, break out into a market that's broad enough to make money.
>
> I really don't think that an "original" property makes a game's storyline inherently "cooler." Game designers have come up with some of the most lame characters, universes, and storylines in the history of creative content. Taking a rich world from another medium gives game developers an excellent base to work from, as well as a built-in audience outside the core gamer crowd that can help ensure its success, or at least give it a head start, as I said. In the end, you still have to make a great game. Well...actually, sometimes you don't (see the success of the *Barbie* games, *Frogger*, *Monopoly*, and most recently, *Who Wants to Be a Millionaire?*). But from our standpoint, we're going to make sure any licenses we pick up are attached to top talent (developers) and a healthy budget to make a quality game.

What kind of design/tech training will get developers work in the video gaming industry? How much of it is education, how much is pure talent, and how much is *chutzpah*?

> Most of it is talent. The Internet has made "making the connection" *so* much easier. You don't have to know anybody, you don't have to have the right agent, you don't need a degree or even a high school diploma. If you have the skills, however you attained them, and you can show something brilliant, there is a job waiting for you in this business. Unfortunately, colleges are ill-suited to keep up with the breakneck speed of change in our industry. With our industry growth and fun factor, you can be assured that anyone with any real skills or talent to offer won't be working at a high school or university teaching these things. They'll be making games. Almost all great game developers that I've encountered are self-taught or peer-taught.

Can you think of any recent technology and design innovations in the gaming industry, and why? For example, EA Sports' "Play Against the Pros" technology (allowing gamers to play "against" real pro golfers) could be considered a recent technological innovation.

> I don't know of a lot of technology or design innovations in the past year or two…that sounds crazy, I know. But most "innovation" has been derivative at best. The real breakthrough story of 1999 was definitely *RollerCoaster Tycoon*. Its "innovation" was getting back to the basics…forget the temptations and limitations of high end 3D graphics and "sophisticated" interfaces. Those guys made a really fun game that anyone could play. That doesn't sound like innovation, but it's the kind of "thinking outside the box" that makes for the real breakthrough hits (i.e., *Deer Hunter*, *Who Wants to Be a Millionaire?*, *Myst*, etc.). The rest of the big hits for the year were nearly all high-end sequels to existing franchises.

What does the future hold? How about for online games (broadband, etc.)?

> The future holds "the rest of the world." Interactive entertainment for all levels of bandwidth, processor power, and interests. All the other genres of interest and entertainment have yet to be explored, really. Love stories, comedy, music, etc., etc. We're just getting started. Just glad to be here for the ride!

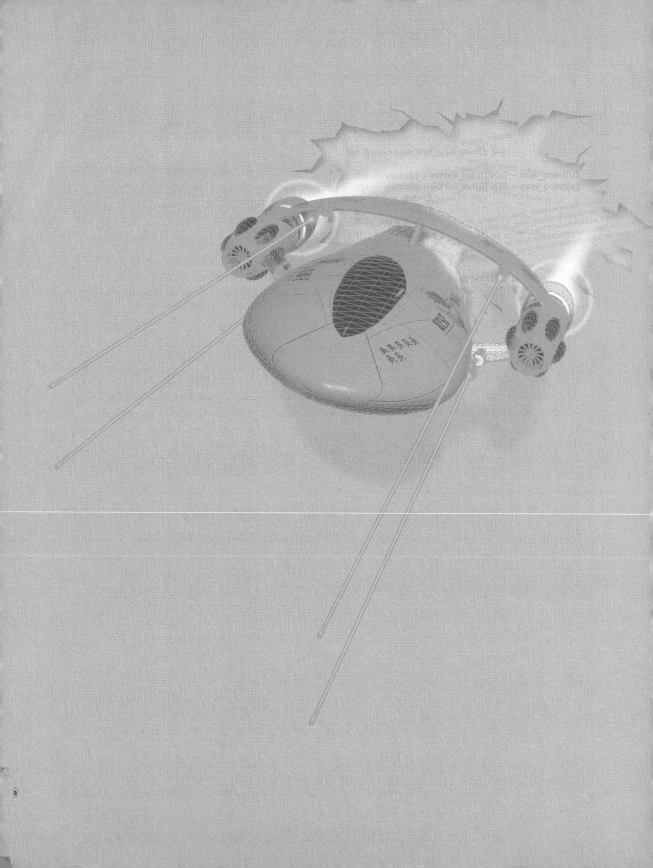

CHAPTER 23
DESIGN SCHOOLS

As evident by their entries in this book, dozens of successful game designers, programmers, and artists believe some level of advanced schooling is an important asset, and serves as a solid foundation on which to build a career in the interactive entertainment industry. In fact, many project leaders and producers will not employ someone unless they have a degree related to their specialty (such as a university/college computer science diploma for programmers). There are hundreds of such courses for programmers, artists, animators, musicians, and sound engineers, but very few that focus specifically on how these disciplines relate to computer or console *gaming*. And it comes as no surprise that there's even less that's strictly on game *design*.

This chapter takes a look at a few schools and courses that cater to individuals who want to make a living as a developer in the computer or console gaming industry.

DIGIPEN INSTITUTE OF TECHNOLOGY (WWW.DIGIPEN.EDU)

Jason Chu, registrar of DigiPen Institute of Technology, takes some time out of his schedule to chat with us about what this unique school has to offer.

First, a bit of history. DigiPen Corporation was founded by Claude Comair in Vancouver, British Columbia, Canada in 1988. Its beginnings were as a company that provided services in 3D computer animation and special effects to the entertainment industry. Comair and company recognized that there was a tremendous shortage of 3D computer animators, and decided to do something about it. DigiPen started to offer educational programs for artists to become 3D animators.

In 1991, they had a meeting with Nintendo of America (NOA) and discussed the possibility for DigiPen to offer educational programs in video game programming. This idea became reality in September of 1994, when they started the computer game programming program, supported by NOA. According to Chu, they realized that this program was the only one of its kind in Canada or the U.S. It was a two-year program; however, games were becoming more complex to program when the trend shifted to 3D. Therefore, DigiPen expanded the course to a four-year bachelors degree program. In February, 1998, DigiPen opened a larger campus in Redmond, Washington.

Chu explains that video games are essentially interactive simulation programs in real time, hence the name they chose for the discipline: Bachelor of Science Degree in Real-Time Interactive Simulation.

This curriculum currently consists of 9 levels of mathematics, 2 levels of physics, 4 levels of computer animation, 23 levels of computer science, and 4 complete projects in game implementation. The degree, in total, consists of 154 credits. DigiPen also offers a two-year associate degree program and a high school summer course.

In the fall of 1999, DigiPen debuted a new program for animators: an Associate of Applied Arts Degree in 3D Computer Animation. And there are talks of offering a masters and Ph.D. degree in the near future as well.

The photo at left was taken during the ribbon-cutting ceremony for the official open house of the Redmond, Washington, campus on Feb. 18, 1998. Left to right: Washington State Governor Gary Locke; Chairman and President of Nintendo Howard Lincoln; and the founder of DigiPen, Claude Comair. Above, a classroom of students working on a project. (Used with permission by Jason Chu)

Asked why someone who wants to learn about game programming or 3D animation would attend DigiPen, Chu answers in light of the current curriculum on programming:

> This is a highly specialized educational program in the area of game programming. As far as we're aware, we are currently the only degree-granting institution in the world dedicated to video game programming. If one is committed to becoming a game programmer as a career, this is the right school for the training.

For more information, such as course overviews, full descriptions, prerequisites, student lists, galleries, and tuition/financial assistance info, visit www.digipen.edu on the World Wide Web.

FULL SAIL (WWW.FULLSAIL.COM)

Another high-tech college with a program dedicated to game design is Full Sail in Winterpark, Florida. Their motto is "real world education," and game design is but one of the digital media programs offered. The Game Design Degree Program was established to teach students the skills necessary to design and create single and multiplayer computer games for networks, PCs, and dedicated gaming consoles.

The course starts at an introductory level, beginning with basic mathematical and programming techniques and a sweeping chronological perspective of the computer gaming industry, in order to study and identify market trends that determine successful gaming hardware and software. This preface provides the foundation needed for the heart of the course: math and physics, programming in C++, artificial intelligence techniques in modeling opponent behavior, coding multiplayer games, and ultimately a game project and significant clock hours on the PC.

Full Sail has a career placement assistance department to arrange post-graduate internships in game development companies.

For a free catalog or a more thorough description of each of the 14 modules in the 58-week game design program, drop into Full Sail's home page at www.fullsail.com.

NBCC MIRAMICHI (WWW.MIRAMICHI.NBCC.NB.CA)

This Canadian school, on the eastern side of the country, offers a program in "electronic game design technology." This branch of New Brunswick Community College (NBCC) teaches apprentice game designers how to design, script, and develop various categories of electronic games.

According to the course calendar, the focus of this 80-week (six semesters) program is to prepare students to develop interactive entertainment and educational software products (also known as "edutainment"). Modules within semesters include computer programming, game mechanics, game design, graphics and animation, software testing, marketing, and a handful of related electives. Considerable emphasis is placed on learning by doing. In fact, an essential requirement for the completion of the course is for students to develop a product "deemed marketable by the industry and the college."

For more information, visit the following address on the Web:

www.miramichi.nbcc.nb.ca/nbccmira/our_programs/frames/elec_game_des.html

OTHER SCHOOLS TO CONSIDER

The following is a list of additional schools and links to consider for amateur game designers, programmers, and animators alike:

- Art Institutes International (AII)
  www.aii.edu

- The Bell Centre for Creative
  Communications at Centennial College
  www.bccc.com

- The Center for Advanced Digital
  Applications at New York University
  www.sce.nyu.edu/cada

- The Center for Digital Imaging
  and Sound
  www.artschool.com

- Centre National d'animation et de Design
  www.nad.qc.ca

- Cogswell Polytechnical College
  www.cogswell.edu

- DeVry Institute of Technology
  www.devry.edu

- Eastern Business Computer Institute, College of Applied Arts and Technology
  www.ebci.ca

- Herzing Institute
  www.herzing.edu

- L'Institut d'informatique de Québec
  www.iiq.qc.ca

- Marycrest International University
  www.mcrest.edu

- MIT Artificial Intelligence Laboratory
  www.ai.mit.edu/

- National Centre for Computer Animation at Bournemouth University
  http://ncca.bournemouth.ac.uk/

- Pratt Institute
  www.pratt.edu/ad/cgim

- Rochester Institute of Technology
  www.rit.edu

- San Francisco State University
  www.cel.sfsu.edu/MSP/msp.html

- School of Com.munication Arts
  www.ncsca.com

- School of Computer Science and Cognitive Science Research Centre
  www.cs.bham.ac.uk/~axs

- School of Computing at Middlesex University
  www.cs.mdx.ac.uk/cg/

- University of Abertay Dundee
  www.tay.ac.uk

- University of California, Los Angeles
  www.ucla.edu

- University of Michigan
  http://ai.eecs.umich.edu/ugclasses.html

- University of North Texas
  www.cs.unt.edu

- University of Southern California
  www.usc.edu/dept/cs/degree_programs/

- ViaGrafix
  www.viagrafix.com

 The University of California at Irvine has recently announced the addition of Interdisciplinary Gaming Studies to its Fall 2000 curriculum. Other universities, such as the Massachusetts Institute of Technology and New York University, offer courses in gaming, but this curriculum is the first to create a specific interdisciplinary program. For more information, visit www.uci.edu.

 A special thanks goes to Alex Dunne, editorial director of Gamasutra (www.gamasutra.com) for assistance in compiling this list.

And remember to check the listings in your town. The 21st century is just around the corner, so you can expect many more schools to pop up around the world devoted to game design, programming, computer graphics, and interactive sound engineering.

CHAPTER 24
GAME DESIGN RESOURCES ON THE INTERNET

This book may cover a lot of ground in a number of areas, but by no means is it the final word on game design and how to break into this bustling industry. The Internet is an outstanding medium for both novice and seasoned designers and other game developers to learn, interact, and contribute as members of the thriving gaming community. The purpose of this chapter is to present a number of enlightening stopovers while surfing the information highway.

 Throughout this entire book, dozens of URLs and handy Usenet newsgroups have been offered for further and future reference, but this chapter is dedicated to more general game design.

The following Web sites and Usenet newsgroups are listed alphabetically.

COMPUTER GAME DESIGN

www.neversoft.com/christer/GR/design

A bit outdated but informative nonetheless, this e-zine, maintained by Christer Ericson, contains a collection of essays and links to a number of members of the interactive entertainment industry. Example features include "A Crash Course in Game Design and Production," "Designing Online Puzzle Games," "Project AI," and "Elements of Videogame Style." This page contains no graphics, so it will load remarkably fast.

DEVGAMES.COM

www.devgames.com

As the name suggests, DevGames.com is a Web e-zine devoted to the development of computer games. And what a resourceful site it is! Sections include news, feature articles, editorials, Q&A, helpful books, and other resources. Some good reads include

"The DirectX Programmer's Q&A," "The Basics of Game AI," "2D vs. 3D," the many development diaries for some of today's and tomorrow's hit games, and Microsoft articles on tackling Windows and Direct3D programming. Don't pass this one up.

GAMASUTRA

www.gamasutra.com

Gamasutra is simply one of the best game design Web sites, covering a wealth of topics from programming to graphic design, sound engineering to music, even areas dedicated to the production, legal, and business angles of the gaming industry. Each section includes regularly updated news, editorials, interviews, columns from experts in the industry, job classifieds, free utilities and source code, and much, much more. In short, make this your startup page on the Web.

Alex Dunne, the editor-in-chief of *Game Developer* magazine, is also the editorial director for Gamasutra.com, also a Miller-Freeman publication.

GAME DESIGN NEWSGROUP

rec.games.design

To keep abreast on all the latest happenings, to exchange ideas or ask queries yourself, the rec.games.design newsgroup on Usenet is a must for game designers to visit at least a few times a week.

Common posts include "An idea for a new multiplayer game," "Any game musicians out there?" and "Need help in creating rules for…"

The rec.games.design FAQ is available at the following address:

www.qucis.queensu.ca/home/dalamb/Games/design/design.html

GAME DESIGN @ GAMESLICE

www.gameslice.com/vgd/index.shtml

Formerly known as Video Games Design at www.videogamesdesign.com, this informative Web site is separated into four areas: game design, code (programming), graphics, and sound. Each section provides handfuls of interviews with famous game designers and developers, and a number of well-written and inspiring feature articles on the industry. At the end of this chapter, the editor of Game Design has a few words to share about this e-zine and the Web as a game designer's haven.

GAME DEVELOPER MAGAZINE

www.gdmag.com

Game Developer magazine is undisputedly the ultimate monthly bible devoted to game designers and developers. Edited by the creative force behind Gamasutra, Alex Dunne, *Game Developer* magazine and its online counterpart are a comprehensive look at the entire game development spectrum. At the Web site, users can subscribe to the magazine, search for back issues, or link to sister site Gamasutra for exclusive content.

GAME DEVELOPMENT SEARCH ENGINE

www.game-developer.com

Think of this Web site as the definitive search engine and directory to many of the game developer sites on the Internet. This includes news sites, articles, interviews, source code, graphic utilities, and much more. Visitors can either use the query box to type in a keyword or select a directory of interest and browse the links from there. Awesome!

GAMESLICE

www.gameslice.com

Simply one of the best "behind the scenes" Web sites for those who want to know what's happening in the computer gaming industry. Editor Geoff Keighley has his finger on the pulse of the biz and delivers news, reviews, hard-hitting editorials, and feature interviews and company profiles to his many readers.

GARAGEGAMES.COM

www.GarageGames.com

garageGames.com is the first Web-based publishing label for independent games and game makers. It provides independent game designers with everything they need to both make and sell high-quality games. Be sure to drop in to read all about this site's services and how this may be exactly what you're looking for.

HAPPY PUPPY: THE BIZ

http://happypuppy.com/biz/index.html

The mega-popular Happy Puppy Web site runs an exceptional page dedicated to the gaming industry. Sections include Developer Den, Game Companies, Job Listings, Classified, and more. The bulk of this page contains hundreds of hand-picked links to other game design, programming, art, and sound design resources.

I HAVE NO WORDS AND I MUST DESIGN

www.crossover.com/~costik/nowords.html

This well-written and thought-provoking article was originally published in 1994 in *Interactive Fantasy*, a British role-playing game journal. The lengthy essay analyzes games and game design in varied components and covers topics such as goals, resource management, game tokens, decision making, and a handful of suggestions to increase a game's strength. The article is available in English, Japanese, or Korean.

LOONY GAMES

www.loonygames.com

One of the newest Web sites on game design and development to emerge over the past couple of years is Loony Games, presented by Next Generation Online (www.next-generation.com) and published/hosted by Blue's News (www.bluesnews.com), the most popular action game Web hub on the net.

Loony Games houses many feature stories and regular columns written by some of the industry's finest game designers, programmers, and artists. Examples include "The History of Shareware," "What It's *Really* Like to Program for a Next-Generation Console," and hand-drawn texture tutorials, to name a few.

 The popular Gamecenter e-zine (listed at the end of this chapter) has published a seven-chapter feature story titled " Game Design 101: Designing a Game from the Polygons Up." Grab yourself a coffee or soda and head on over to www.gamecenter.com/Features/Exclusives/Design.

MURPHY'S RULES

http://kovalic.com/Murphys/Murphys.html

Call it the "Funniest Home Videos" for the gaming industry, but Murphy's rules are ones that don't make sense, or "holes" found in computer games. Visitors can read the history of this site, jump right in and read the lengthy list (and their significance), or can submit their own. There's also a humorous cartoon devoted to some of the larger holes found.

SO, YOU WANT TO BE A COMPUTER GAME DEVELOPER?

www.makegames.com

Diana Gruber's well-written and wonderfully laid-out step-by-step guide to breaking into the business covers everything from self-promotion to working with other people to the nature of the industry. A large area is devoted to writing your first and second games, plus a list of helpful books to ease the programming pain.

ULTIMATE GAMING RESOURCE—COMPANY DIRECTORY

www.ugr.net/listings/listings.htm

Hundreds of computer and console game developers and publishers are listed here in alphabetical format. All entries contain the link to their official home page, plus many of them have their phone number, address, and email contact information for those looking to send in a résumé or work sample. This is definitely a page to bookmark.

ESSENTIAL GAMING E-ZINES

The following is an alphabetical list of some of the top PC and console gaming e-zines on the World Wide Web:

- Adrenaline Vault
  www.avault.com
- All Games Network
  www.allgames.com
- Computer Games Online
  www.cdmag.com
- Computer Gaming World
  www.gamespot.com/cgw

- Console Domain
  www.consoledomain.com
- Daily Radar
  www.dailyradar.com
- Electric Playground
  www.elecplay.com
- Fastest Gaming News Online
  www.fgnonline.com
- Future Games Network
  www.futuregames.net

- Game Daily
  www.gamedaily.com
- Game Revolution
  www.game-revolution.com
- Gamecenter
  www.gamecenter.com
- GamePen
  www.gamepen.com
- GamePower
  www.gamepower.com
- GamePro
  www.gamepro.com
- Games Domain
  www.gamesdomain.com
- Gamesmania
  www.gamesmania.com
- Gamespot U.K.
  www.gamespot.co.uk
- Gamespot
  www.gamespot.com
- Gamestats
  www.gamestats.com
- Get in the Game News
  www.gignews.com
- Happy Puppy
  www.happypuppy.com
- Imagine Games Network
  www.imaginegames.com
- MCV
  www.mcvnow.com
- Meccaworld
  www.meccaworld.com
- Next Generation
  www.next-generation.com
- Online Gaming Review
  www.ogr.com
- PC Gamer
  www.pcgamer.com
- PC Games
  www.pcgames.com
- PC Multimedia & Entertainment
  www.pcme.com
- Sharky Extreme
  www.sharkyextreme.com
- UGO Alliance
  www.ugo.com
- Videogames.com
  www.videogames.com

ROBIN WARD, GAMESLICE'S GAME DESIGN

Robin Ward is the editor for the Game Design Page at GameSlice and is a freelance writer for other sites, including Gamasutra. He joins us here to chat about what GameSlice's Game Design page has to offer, and to provide his thoughts on the Web as a medium for budding game designers.

> Once upon a time I started up a site dedicated to game design, called videogamedesign.com—despite the word "video" being in the title, it really focused on all aspects of computer game creation. The specialty was interviews with top game designers, programmers, and artists, with questions that weren't like "What's your favorite food?"—they were about balance, design, and how to get into the industry.

Needless to say, there was quite a demand for that kind of thing, and the site got a decent amount of traffic. Later on, after updates became a little slow due to personal difficulties, Geoff Keighley of GameSlice offered to let me set up the site as a section of GameSlice.com. So now it resides at www.gameslice.com/vgd, and has all of our old interviews and articles, along with a few new ones that we post from time to time. We also have a FAQ that answers some commonly asked questions about game creation—specialty schools, how to get an idea created, etc.

The game industry attracts many people, but few people actually know how games are made. So when we interviewed designers, programmers, musicians and artists, we asked them specifically the types of questions that people ask us. Such as "How can I work at your company?" or "Is game design art?" So instead of features about whether the latest game features light-sourcing or *x* players at once, we have creation-related questions. And people really find that useful.

Also, we try and reply to every single email received. I can't claim to have replied to them all (some eventually get lost), but I'd say almost all of the people who send mail will get a reply. And not a one-liner, either. It will answer their question to the best of our ability.

I remember when I wanted to learn stuff about games a few years back, and all the sites I emailed didn't bother replying, even if I said "PLEASE REPLY." That really annoyed me. So I try to do it better.

What exactly can readers get from the site?

Readers will probably find the answers they're looking for when it comes to game development. A lot of people in the world want to develop games, but it's hard to find out how people actually go from regular Mr. John Doe to a high-profile developer.

In closing, Ward says "We can tell you how some of the best game designers did it, what the best path into game design is, and how to get there."

RICK VANDERVOORN, GAMEJOBS.COM

Rick Vandervoorn is an associate publisher at the CyberActive Media Group. He has these words to say about GameJobs.com and the purpose of the site:

GameJobs.com is a comprehensive listing of companies involved with the video games industry, with a direct link to the appropriate human resources page for each company. GameJobs.com came as an online extension of the print version housed in *GameWEEK* magazine. The vision for GameJobs.com is for it to become a full-function searchable interactive database for games-related and other high-tech job openings.

Vandervoorn says the Internet has changed the industry for budding game designers in several ways. He explains:

> First, it makes it easier for aspiring game designers to get hired. With services like GameJobs.com, the Internet helps to bridge the communications gap between successful game developers/publishers and budding game designers. Aspiring designers can unobtrusively make contact with game developers, plus the Internet (or, more accurately, the World Wide Web) can act as a forum to display the aspiring developer's work, which in the long run contributes to making it easier for the budding developer to get noticed and hired by a developer/publisher.
>
> Second, the Internet/Web makes it easier for the budding game designer who can't get hired by a developer/publisher or who wants to strike out on his/her own to market his/her creation. The Internet/Web provides a storefront for the aspiring developer who wants to market a game to gamers around the world. With the advent of selling and distributing games on the Web, a presence at retail is no longer necessary.

Be sure to visit GameJobs.com at, you guessed it, www.gamejobs.com.

CHAPTER 25
KEY CONVENTIONS, ORGANIZATIONS, AND AWARDS

In today's information age, it's possible for members of the gaming industry to work virtually anywhere in the world. With electronic file transfer via the Internet and relatively cheap overnight deliveries from courier services, there's no reason why game programmers, artists, and musicians need to work in the same room together, although there are obvious advantages in doing so.

However, if you're trying to get a job at a development company or attempting to get your game picked up by a publisher, or you want to keep an eye on what your competitors are up to, it's highly recommended that you get out there to meet and greet the gaming community in the flesh. In fact, in this book, many game designers recommend getting out there to talk face to face, because this makes a much better impression than dealing with someone via email or over the telephone. Therefore, the first half of this chapter deals with all the gaming industry's top conventions, trade shows, and conferences around the world. Each listing explains what the show is all about and who it's best suited for, and provides a link to the official World Wide Web site for that show. The second part of this chapter lists a number of essential organizations in the industry you may want to belong to, including various academies and associations that cater to different facets of the gaming industry.

CONVENTIONS AND TRADE SHOWS
ELECTRONIC ENTERTAINMENT EXPO (E3)

The Electronic Entertainment Expo (E3) is the largest and most extravagant event in the gaming industry. Period. In 1999, the fifth year of this annual mega-event, over 60,000 members of the international computer gaming, video gaming, and edutainment industry flocked to see—or display—the hottest products of the year. E3 is not only a gathering for exhibitors to showcase their upcoming gaming software and hardware to the media and retailers, but also a place for enlightening conferences and workshops hosted by the top names in the business. E3 is strictly a trade event; therefore, only professionals from the industry are allowed to attend.

And what a party it is! Techno music blasts through the booths, multiplayer games take place over 40-foot video screens, celebrities are present to rub elbows, larger-than-life mechanical creations of favorite video and computer game characters appear, and concerts at night feature famous bands sponsored by the likes of Sony, Nintendo, and Eidos Interactive (to name a few).

The event usually takes place at the end of May each year. It spent its first two years in Los Angeles, then moved to Atlanta for two years and went back to L.A. for 1999. For more information, visit www.e3expo.com, but also be sure to check out www.e3.net or www.e3daily.com.

GAME DEVELOPERS CONFERENCE (GDC)

Another extremely important conference for game designers to attend is the Game Developers Conference (GDC). This annual show takes place in the late winter/early spring and has something to offer for all roles of the industry: programming, visual arts, sound and music, production, general game design, and even the business and legal side of the gaming industry.

The four-day event is loaded with keynote speakers, tutorials/workshops, seminars, contests in each field, awards, and exhibitors. Be sure to check out past and future keynote topics and speakers at the organization's official Web site, www.gdconf.com.

In 1999, the Game Developers Conference added a new special sideshow and festival. Read on...

GAMEXECUTIVE

The first ever GAMEXecutive trade conference took place at the 1999 Game Developers Conference, and has been a staple ever since. This is a two-day trade event for CEOs; strategists; executives in marketing, sales, distribution, retail, and finance; venture capitalists; and others involved in the business side of the billion-dollar interactive entertainment industry. At GAMEXecutive, industry experts discuss and analyze statistics and a wide variety of business trends for both software and hardware for the PC and console systems. A full list of speakers and their topics for the 2001 show can be seen at www.gamexecutive.com.

INDEPENDENT GAMES FESTIVAL

The second new addition to the annual GDC is the Indie Games Festival, sponsored by the Gathering of Developers (G.O.D.). This event is intended to promote interactive entertainment as an art form and provide a forum for independent game developers from around the globe to show their work, receive recognition, and meet with potential publishers and/or distributors.

Indie designers can compete for prizes and the opportunity for their games to be submitted to the G.O.D. review board for publishing consideration. Categories are based on platform: PC, Macintosh, Sony PlayStation, Nintendo, or online games;

plus awards are also presented for technical excellence, art, audio, game design, and audience choice. For festival info, rules, and application procedures, interested developers should go to www.indiegames.com.

Is this the gaming industry's answer to the Sundance Film Festival?

ELECTRONIC CONSUMER TRADE SHOW (ECTS)

The ECTS is Europe's premier gaming conference, held every fall in London, England. Game developers and publishers from Europe and around the world display their top interactive products (software and hardware) for the fourth quarter and the following year. Like E3, ECTS is a glitzy trade show, but for members of the industry only. And it's on a much smaller scale, too—less than 2,000 attendees. Every year ECTS also hosts an awards ceremony for the top interactive entertainment products of the year. For more information, punch in www.ects.com while surfing the Web.

MILIA GAMES

Held in Cannes, France, is a spectacular annual event: Milia, the International Content Market for Interactive Media. In 1999, Milia began a separate entity exclusively reserved for the gaming industry, dubbed Milia Games. New game showcases, title announcements, keynote speeches and conferences, and the Milia Games awards ceremony are but a few of the festivities here. There's also a developer's day, with hundreds of freelance programmers, graphic and sound designers, and scriptwriters invited from around the world. In short, this event caters to the entire gaming industry, including designers, publishers, and distributors. Access more information on this event at www.milia.com.

SIGGRAPH

For computer graphic artists and animators, SIGGRAPH is one of the most important conventions of the year. Its main purpose is to promote "theory, design, implementation, and application of computer-generated graphics and interactive techniques to facilitate communication and understanding." The three-day event includes dozens of conferences and workshops, exhibits by software and hardware companies, and a career resource center for aspiring computer graphics specialists. To learn more about SIGGRAPH as an organization and/or the annual conference, visit www.siggraph.org.

GENCON

Held in Milwaukee each year, GenCon is a gaming convention for role-playing game (RPG) enthusiasts. Although I couldn't locate an official Web site for this annual show, Webcasts from previous years are available at this address:

www.evilgeniuses.org/gaming/archive/index.html

COMDEX, CES, MACWORLD EXPO, TOY FAIR

While wrapping up this half of the chapter, it should be noted that Comdex (www.comdex.com), the Consumer Electronics Show (www.cesweb.org), MacWorld Expo, and the various international toy fairs may also be good places to attend throughout the year as a game designer. They're not nearly as crucial as E3, GDC, or ECTS, but you may find inspiration or make good contacts with other members of the gaming industry.

The Flights of Fantasy Awards have been recognizing outstanding console and computer game talent since 1995. Awards are given for areas of excellence such as art direction, lighting/texturing, story, innovation, character design, character animation, best promotional campaign, music, sound, and so on. Be sure to visit www.flightsoffantasy.com for the complete list of nominees and winners over the past few years.

ORGANIZATIONS

ACADEMY OF INTERACTIVE ARTS AND SCIENCES (AIAS)

The Academy of Interactive Arts and Sciences (AIAS) was founded in 1996 as a not-for-profit organization dedicated to the advancement and recognition of the interactive arts and sciences. As stated in its bylaws and published on the Web site, this is the formal mission of the academy:

■ Promote and advance common interests in the worldwide interactive community.

■ Recognize outstanding achievement in the creation of interactive content.

■ Conduct an annual awards show and enhance the image and awareness of the interactive arts and sciences.

The annual awards show mentioned above takes place during the annual Electronic Entertainment Expo (E3). For membership information, news, events, and award winners, visit the AIAS at www.interactive.org.

INTERNATIONAL GAME DEVELOPERS ASSOCIATION (IGDN)

The International Game Developers Network (IGDN) is a grassroots not-for-profit membership association for the game developer community. Its primary focus is to serve members by providing and sharing resources that are not easily accessible anywhere else. This includes finding people, finances, publishers, attorneys, software, or hardware. This association also publishes a newsletter and hosts conventions for developers to congregate. The official Web site is at www.igdn.org.

SOFTWARE & INFORMATION INDUSTRY ASSOCIATION (SIIA)

The Software Publishers Association (SPA) and the Information Industry Association (IIA) merged on January 1, 1999, to form a new trade association representing the software and information industry: the Software & Information Industry Association (SIIA). Their mission statement, in part, is as follows:

 [...]unite the software code and information content industries into a powerful global consortium. This union of code and content in the digital age delivers unmatched industry advocacy, business development, research, and education to the nearly 1,500 SIIA member companies.

Some of the SIIA's efforts go toward anti-piracy, government affairs, and many other programs, publications, conferences/symposiums, and awards. Two of their popular awards events are highlighted in the following sections. (Tap into www.siia.net for more information about the SIIA.)

CODIE AWARDS

One of the oldest annual awards ceremonies held for the software industry is the Codies. There are 39 categories under different award groupings: general, online, enterprise, business/home office, consumer, games, and software for schools. Awards within the games category go to the best new adventure/role-playing game, best new arcade/action game, best new sports game, best new strategy and simulation game, and best new multiplayer online game. For a list of rules and past winners, visit www.siia.net/conf/codieawards/.

MARKETING ACHIEVEMENT AWARDS

There are two events under this heading, including the best software packaging award and the "Immy" awards for the industry's finest in marketing achievement. For details, see www.siia.net/conf/marketawards.htm.

COMPUTER GAME ARTISTS ASSOCIATION

This membership association exists to form a community of computer game artists that interact with (share, learn, teach, and influence) each other and their industry. Find out more about what they are and how they work at www.vectorg.com/cga.

INTERACTIVE DIGITAL SOFTWARE ASSOCIATION (IDSA)

Formed in 1994, the Interactive Digital Software Association (IDSA) is the only U.S. association exclusively dedicated to serving the business and public affairs interests of companies that publish console and computer games for video game consoles, PCs, and the Internet. Today, their members account for more than 85 percent of the billion-dollar interactive entertainment software sold in the United

States. In short, the IDSA offers services to gaming publishers, such as a robust anti-piracy program, government relations, business and consumer research, and First Amendment and intellectual property protection efforts. The official IDSA Web site can be accessed at www.idsa.com.

COMPUTER GAMES DEVELOPERS ASSOCIATION (CGDA)

The CGDA is dedicated to serving the interests of the worldwide computer game development community by offering a number of benefits and services. Find out about benefits and joining this membership association at www.cgda.org.

AMERICAN ASSOCIATION FOR ARTIFICIAL INTELLIGENCE (AAAI)

Founded 20 years ago, the American Association for Artificial Intelligence (AAAI) is a not-for-profit society devoted to advancing the scientific understanding of the mechanisms underlying thought and intelligent behavior and their embodiment in machines. Their aims include increasing public understanding of artificial intelligence (AI), improving the teaching and training of AI practitioners, and seeking funding for important developments. As outlined at their official Web site (www.aaai.org), there are many benefits for members, including conferences, symposia and workshops, magazines, and more.

ENTERTAINMENT SOFTWARE RATING BOARD (ESRB)

You may have seen a sticker in the corner of most computer game boxes that says "ESRB" accompanied by an age rating. The Entertainment Software Rating Board is an independent group that, with the support of the industry, has developed a standardized rating system for interactive entertainment software products, and now Web sites as well. The ESRB ratings are designed to give consumers information about the content of an interactive video or computer entertainment title and the ages for which it's appropriate. For more info and the various age ratings, visit www.esrb.com.

INTERACTIVE ENTERTAINMENT MERCHANTS ASSOCIATION (IEMA)

The IEMA is a not-for-profit organization serving the business and public affairs needs of interactive entertainment product retailers. Their mandate? To assist retail and distributor members of the IEMA by increasing their current and future effectiveness, longevity, and profitability. IEMA holds a convention as well; the official Web site for both the association and convention is at www.theiema.org.

RECREATIONAL SOFTWARE ADVISORY COUNCIL ON THE INTERNET (RSACI)

This not-for-profit organization aims to inform the public about adult content in electronic media, "by means of an open, objective content advisory system." The RSACi system provides consumers, especially concerned parents, with information about the level of sex, violence, and offensive language (vulgar or hate-motivated) in software games and Web sites. Find out more about the RSACi at www.rsac.org.

EUROPEAN LEISURE SOFTWARE PUBLISHERS ASSOCIATION (ELSPA)

This organization was founded in 1989 to establish a collective identity for the European computer and video games industry. ELSPA is concerned with the publishing and distribution of interactive leisure and entertainment software, working to promote the interests of all its members, as well as addressing issues that affect the industry as a whole. Point your browser to www.elspa.com to learn more.

PROJECT BAR-B-Q

Hosted by George "The Fat Man" Sanger and sponsored by Cirrus Logic, this annual conference is meant to serve as a think tank for computer musicians and sound engineers to solidify their opinions and put those opinions to work for the good of the manufacturers, developers, and primarily the consumers of computer/audio products. The Web address is www.fatman.com/bbq.htm.

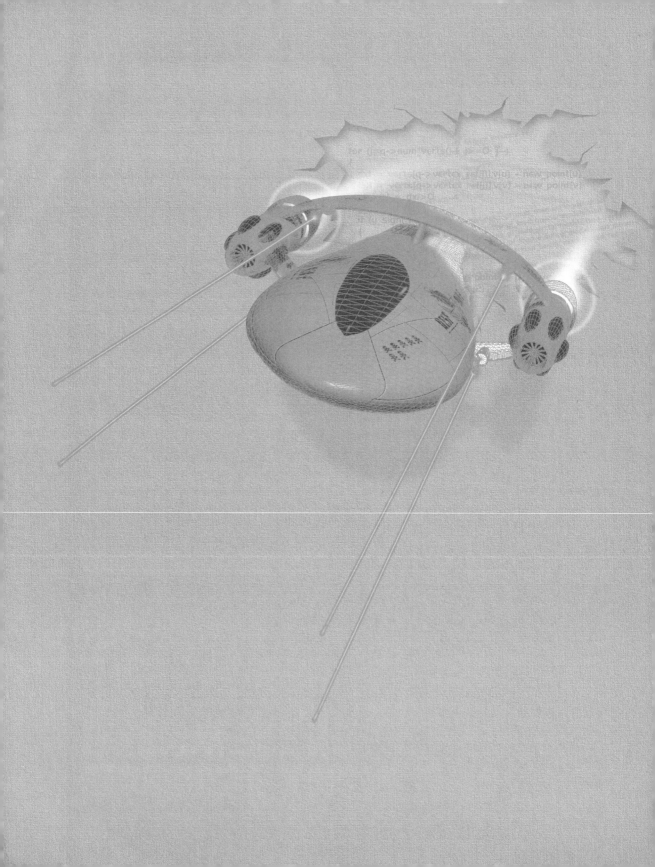

APPENDIX
BIOGRAPHIES

Alas, we have come to the end of the book. It's time now to learn a little more about the fine folks who have offered their discerning words of wisdom.

Though a few of our sages in the gaming industry were unable to supply a bio, most are listed here, in alphabetical order for easy reference. And perhaps one day you too will be listed in a book like this.

AKEMANN, PETER—TREYARCH INVENTION

Peter T. Akemann, Ph.D., is a managing member of Treyarch Invention and project lead on *Die by the Sword* (*DBTS*). He created the VSIM animation system that drives most of the animation in *DBTS*. The key framed sequences in the game (mostly in the movies) were done by several contract animators (mostly Mike McCarthy of Interplay); Treyarch has no animators on staff.

ARNLUND, KURT—ACCOLADE

As a programmer at Accolade, Arnlund worked on the action title *Slave Zero* for Infogrames, but prior to this project he programmed a number of hit games, including *Mechwarrior 2: NetMech*, *Interstate '76*, *The Interstate '76 Arsenal*, *The Interstate '76 Nitro Pack*, and *Heavy Gear 2*.

His future aspirations are many, but he says he'd like to continue to work on creative projects that don't just push the technological limits of the available hardware, but also give game players new experiences that are different from anything they've seen before. Says Arnlund, "I love the challenge of taking something that's been done in every game before it and thinking up a way to make it more spectacular than anything that has ever been seen." He'd also like to get more involved in game design and would like to pitch and start a project where he's more of a contributor toward the design.

BACKMAN, TED—VALVE SOFTWARE

As an artist and animator at Valve Software in Kirkland, Washington, Ted Backman worked on their first title, *Half-Life*. Now that *Half-Life* is done, he's busy poring over possible artistic reference material. "It's a hard thing to try to clear your mind of two years' worth of work and start fresh on a new project." Every night, he finds himself drawing and looking at a wide range of material, just to try to infuse some new ideas into his creative process. In the future, he hopes to be able to create intriguing game worlds, compelling characters, and engaging scenarios in many game genres.

BAILEY, KELLY—VALVE SOFTWARE

Kelly Bailey is a senior game designer and music and sound effects engineer at Valve Software. Kelly did all of the music and sound effects for *Half-Life*, and spent the 1998 summer and fall working on *Half-Life* game design. Earlier in the development of *Half-Life*, he wrote the code to allow characters to speak, and implemented the software DSP system that provides reverb and echo effects. Kelly's most recent musical background includes several years of singing, song writing, and playing guitar in local bands in the Seattle area. Although his initial work at Valve was full time on engineering, early in the project he presented a five-song demo CD to the company and found himself happily responsible for the game's full soundtrack.

BAIN, SINJIN—PYROTECHNIX

Sinjin Bain is the studio manager at PyroTechnix, a wholly owned subsidiary of Sierra On-Line. He cofounded PyroTechnix (originally named Computer Presentations, Inc./CPI) over 10 years ago as a computer graphics and disk-based marketing and animation company. Although PyroTechnix' primary thrust was business software, they pioneered a 3D authoring environment called True3D, and have been involved in a number of game-related projects with various licensors. Since being acquired by Sierra in 1998, they have released the very successful game *Return to Krondor*.

BATES, BOB—LEGEND ENTERTAINMENT

Bob Bates is Legend Entertainment's studio head, and he shares the duties of running the organization with Mike Verdu, who has been his partner at Legend since they founded the company in 1989. Bates' game-writing career started at Infocom in 1986, where he wrote two text adventures: *Sherlock! The Riddle of the Crown Jewels* and *Arthur: The Quest for Excalibur*. Since starting Legend, he has also written *TIMEQUEST*, *Eric The Unready*, and, most recently, *John Saul's Blackstone Chronicles*.

Altogether, he has written, co-designed, or produced over 20 games that have won more than 30 industry awards, most notably the 1992 Adventure Game of the Year award for *Eric The Unready*.

BERNAL, MARK—BUNGIE SOFTWARE

As lead artist and art director at Bungie Software, Bernal has worked on *Myth II: Soulblighter*, *Myth: The Fallen Lords*, and *Marathon 2*. His future aspirations are to continue to create entertaining, top-of-the-line "A list" games and to explore and develop the technical and creative aspects of computer games.

BIESSMAN, ERIC—RAVEN SOFTWARE

As project coordinator and lead designer for Raven Software, Eric Biessman has worked on *Heretic: Shadows of the Serpent Riders*, *Hexen*, *Hexen: Death Kings of the Dark Citadel*, *CyClones*, *Hexen II*, *Heretic II*, and *Soldier of Fortune*. During his tour of duty with Raven, the team that he has worked with has won numerous awards, including Most Valuable Product and Best Shareware for *Heretic*, and several industry awards, such as the Spotlight Award (Spotty) from the Computer Games Developers Association. These games have also always done well in the eyes of the reviewers and the public, which is the highest award that anyone can ask for.

The only thing that he can see in his future, says Biessman, is that he will continue to work on great games: "If this means that I continue with my current position, great! If it means that I continue in a different capacity, like producer, that would be fine too. Regardless, I have chosen this field for a career and I hope to have a long and prosperous one."

BLESZINSKI, CLIFF—EPIC GAMES

Cliff Bleszinski is a 25-year-old game designer who has been working in the industry since the age of 17. He originally began developing adventure games for Epic Games, and later found his calling in the realm of action-adventure titles. In 1993, Cliff designed *Jazz Jackrabbit*, commonly referred to as "the *Sonic the Hedgehog* of the PC," which went on to become a huge hit. Not one to rest on his laurels, Cliff immediately began working on a *Jazz* sequel and a little 3D shooter called *Unreal*. One of the original four developers for *Unreal*, it was Cliff's responsibility to oversee and assist with all level design on the game, as well as to contribute to the game's overall design and direction. He's probably most well-known for the infamous "Skaarj Introduction" and the terrifying first level "Vortex Rikers" in *Unreal*, which set a new standard for cinematic immersiveness; both were hailed as some of the most memorable moments in gaming history.

Cliff last worked on *Unreal Tournament*, an action title that takes place in the *Unreal* universe, pitting the player against the hardest (and most devious) criminals in all the galaxy in the ultimate test of Deathmatch skills.

BROUSSARD, GEORGE—3D REALMS

George Broussard is a partner and president of 3D Realms. Their past products include *Terminal Velocity* (developed by Terminal Reality), *Duke Nukem 3D*, and *Shadow Warrior*. They're currently working on *Duke Nukem Forever*, and have a small hand in *Max Payne* (being developed by Remedy Entertainment in Finland). Duke has been ported to every platform imaginable, and now they're starting to license original Duke games, such as *Duke Nukem: Time to Kill* (PSX) and *Duke Nukem: Zero Hour* (N64), while they continue to focus on PC games. Their future goals are to stay lean and mean and focused on a couple of quality 3D titles at a time, and continue to grow the company and their franchises.

BÜTTNER, MICHAEL—X-AMPLE ARCHITECTURE

Michael Büttner is director and cofounder of X-ample Architecture Productions, an independent game developer based in Darmstadt, Germany. Best known for the development of the recent smash hit *Mission: Impossible* for the Nintendo 64 and PlayStation consoles, they also developed a 3D shooter called *Viper* in 1998.

Prior to the formation of X-ample, Mr. Büttner founded Neon Software Group, where he led the programming and design elements of several hit games including *Vanished Powers* in 1996 for the PC; *Tunnel B1* in 1997 for PlayStation, Sega Saturn, and the PC; and *Mr. Nutz* in 1995 for the Amiga and Sega Megadrive.

CAGE, DAVID—QUANTIC DREAM

David Cage, 30 years old, is the founder and CEO of Quantic Dream. He is also the game designer of *Omikron: The Nomad Soul* and *Quark*. *Nomad Soul* was his first game (he comes from the music industry). His aspirations at Quantic are to produce ambitious products and link video games to the other media industries, the movie industry, the music industry, or comics.

CAIN, TIM—TROIKA GAMES

Best known as the producer, lead programmer, and designer of *Fallout* (recipient of many different "RPG of the Year" awards in 1997), Tim Cain has worked in the game industry since 1982. He started as a programmer on *Grand Slam Bridge*, published by Electronic Arts in 1985. After attending college and receiving a B.S. and M.S. in computer science, he worked at Interplay Productions from 1992 to 1998. In addition to *Fallout*, he was lead programmer on *Bard's Tale Construction Set* and *Rags to Riches*, and he also designed and programmed *GNW*, a user interface and OS-abstraction library, which supports *Fallout*, *Star Fleet Academy*, *M.A.X.*, *Atomic Bomberman*, and several other Interplay titles. He also wrote critical error-handling code for *Stonekeep* and digital sound-mixing code for *Star Trek 25th Anniversary CD-ROM Edition*. Tim is currently joint CEO of Troika Games LLC, a developer of computer game software.

CARACCIOLO, CAROL—ACCLAIM ENTERTAINMENT

Carol Caracciolo is the quality assurance manager at Acclaim, whose past products include *Mortal Kombat II*, *Turok*, *Quarterback Club*, *All-Star Baseball*, *NBA Jam*, *WWF: Raw*, *WWF: Warzone*, *Alien Trilogy*, *Revolution X*, and more. She founded Quality Assurance at Acclaim five and a half years ago with a staff of only three testers. She is currently maintaining a staff of approximately 75 over two full-time shifts, 7 days a week.

CASTLE, LOUIS—WESTWOOD STUDIOS

Louis Castle is the executive vice president and cofounder of Westwood Studios. For the past 13 years, he has worked as designer, executive producer, programmer, artist, and art director. In 1994, Castle brought *The Lion King* to Super Nintendo, and in 1995, he brought free parking to the Internet with the *Monopoly* CD-ROM. In 1997, Castle unleashed *Lands of Lore: Guardians of Destiny* and *Blade Runner*. His background in fine arts and computer science has helped him maintain an artistic vision for Westwood's products throughout the turbulent and explosive growth of the software industry.

CHAN, TREVOR—ENLIGHT SOFTWARE

Trevor Chan founded Enlight Software in 1993. Under his leadership, the company has received numerous accolades from the industry and become one of the world's leading developers of strategy and simulation games.

Trevor's first game, *Capitalism*, published by Interactive Magic in 1995, has won industry awards and been widely regarded as the best business-simulation game ever created. "*Capitalism* is the most realistic, detailed business sim on the market today, and one of the best economic games of all time," says *PC Gamer*.

With its remarkably high degree of realism, *Capitalism* has made the leap from playground to classroom. Harvard University and Stanford University pioneered the use of this award-winning business simulation in instructional purposes shortly after its release. Professor Tom Kosnik said, "*Capitalism* is a world-class, hands-on learning experience I've used at Stanford School of Engineering and Harvard Business School. Gamers not only learn the subtleties of growing an entrepreneurial business but also learn about leadership and team building necessary in any business situation." Additionally, the game has made its appearance on Business Week, The Discovery Channel, and CNBC-TV Cable.

Trevor then went on to produce *Capitalism Plus*, the eagerly anticipated follow-up to the original. Together with the original, over 150,000 copies of the *Capitalism* series have been sold worldwide.

Following the success of the *Capitalism* series, Trevor and Enlight scored another runaway success with the *Seven Kingdoms* series of real-time strategy games. "There hasn't been an empire builder this good since *Civilization II...Seven Kingdoms* is an outstanding game in every way," says GameSpot. Along with nominations for Strategy Game of the Year from GameSpot and *Online Gaming Review*, it won the Best Overall Strategy Game from *Gaming Nexus* and Strategy Game of the Year Award from *PowerPlay*, a leading gaming magazine in Germany. The series has sold over 200,000 copies worldwide.

Trevor Chan is now directing his teams at Enlight to produce *Capitalism II* and *Virtual U*. *Capitalism II* will take the award-winning business-simulation game to the next level with breathtaking graphics and increased realism. *Virtual U* is a simulation game of university co-developed with Jackson Hole Higher Education Group, which is headed by higher-education management guru William Massy, who was formerly the vice president of business development at Stanford University. The game's aim is to simulate the operation of a university with painstaking realism and serve as an educational tool to university management and students studying higher education courses.

CHARDOT, HUBERT—GAMESQUAD

Born in November, 1957, in Lyon, France, Hubert Chardot is the creative director at Gamesquad, a development company he founded with three friends (Laurent Salmeron, Laurent Paret, and Christophe Nazaret) in September, 1997.

Chardot began to write games eight years ago at Infogrames. He first wrote the script of *Shadow of the Comet*, and then the coveted H.P. Lovecraft–inspired *Alone in the Dark*.

Chardot later became a director and a producer, while writing scripts for even more games: *Alone in the Dark 2* and *3*, *Prisoner of Ice*, *Voodoo Kid*, *Time Gate*, and *Mission: Impossible*. Of late, he has served as a consultant for *Alone in the Dark 4*, *Asterix & Obelix Against Cesar*, *The Ring*, *Faust*, and *Devil Inside*.

Chardot is currently working with Frederick Raynal and Didier Quentin on *Agartha*, a future Dreamcast game to be released in 2001. Chardot says that if *Devil Inside* sells well, he plans to write a sequel (or two, since he envisioned the game to be a trilogy).

CHARNE, JIM—ACADEMY OF INTERACTIVE ARTS AND SCIENCES

Jim Charne is president and executive director of the Academy of Interactive Arts and Sciences (www.interactive.org). Before joining the Academy, Jim maintained an interactive entertainment and music industry law practice in Santa Monica, California. He has also served as vice president of legal and business affairs and general counsel for a large East Coast–based console software studio, produced entertainment and personal productivity software for Activision, served on the corporate staff of the Technology Acquisitions Group of Merrill Lynch & Co., Inc. in New York, and worked in the music industry as a national marketing department head for CBS Records (now Sony Music) and as in-house counsel for Arista Records. Jim is admitted to practice law in California, New York, and New Jersey, and has spoken at industry conferences presented by E3 Expo, Computer Game Developers Conference, California Lawyers for the Arts, and Digital Hollywood.

CLOUD, KEVIN W.—ID SOFTWARE

Kevin Cloud is an artist for id Software, plus part owner of id along with Adrian Carmack and John Carmack. He started with id during the development of *Wolfenstein 3D*. Prior to id, Cloud worked as a computer artist and editor at Softdisk, a small monthly on-disk magazine that provided users with five to seven programs per month along with regular columns, editorials on the industry, etc. As id has grown and developed, Cloud has spent the last few years wearing a number of different hats and involving himself in the day-to-day operations of the company. Lately, he's tried to put those duties aside and focus more of his attention on improving as an artist.

COALLIER, STEVEN—ELECTRONIC ARTS

Steven Coallier is currently the software development manager for an in-house development group (Scoreboard Productions) at Electronic Arts' Redwood Shores location, which is also the corporate headquarters.

He began in the industry as a tester for Sierra On-Line, but became a programmer for them fairly soon afterward and ended up porting more than 20 of their graphic adventure games to the Amiga computer. His time at EA has had a lot of variety to it—he's shipped a PC first-person shooter, *Shadowcaster*, which was actually the first game to ship using the *Doom* engine; a PlayStation port of *Wing Commander III*; and two versions of *NCAA March Madness*, a college basketball game for the PlayStation. Coallier's latest work can be found in the sequel to EA Sports' boxing game, *Knockout Kings*.

COCHRANE, BRYCE—ELECTRONIC ARTS

At 29, Bryce Cochrane is the lead artist for the *NHL* series (PC/PSX/N64) at Electronic Arts (Canada). Serving in capacities ranging from testing and map design to lead artist, modeling, and animation, Cochrane has also produced work for all sorts of platforms—NES, Saturn, 3DO, Genesis, PC, N64, and others. Past games include *James Bond Junior*, *Terminator*, *Bob*, *Wayne's World*, *Crash Test Dummies*, *Ren and Stimpy's Videots*, *NHL All-Star Hockey*, *MTV Sports*, *Foes of Ali*, *Phoenix 3*, *Perfect Weapon*, *Triple Play 99*, *NHL 98*, *NHL 99*, and *NHL 2000*.

COOK, VANCE—SIERRA ON-LINE

Vance Cook has been developing golf simulators for about 11 out of the last 13 years. It has consumed a significant portion of his life so far. He worked at Access Software for about six years with many other talented developers on several projects, most notably *Links* and *Links386 Pro*. He left Access Software about six years ago to fulfill his lifelong goal of starting his own company, and founded Headgate, Inc. After dabbling in business productivity products for a few years, Cook came back to golf simulators again and ended up selling the company to Sierra On-Line, where he has been happily employed for the last four years.

COREA, NICHOLAS J.—ELECTRONIC ARTS

Nick Corea is a computer graphic artist at Electronic Arts. His impressive résumé includes *Virtual Pinball* (all art), *US Navy Fighters* (terrain, cockpits, 3D shapes, some user interface), *Marine Fighters* (lead artist, terrain, 3D shapes, cockpits), *US Navy Fighters 97* (lead artist, some 3D shapes), and *WWII Fighters* (lead artist).

Corea wanted to design video games as a young teenager and made several pinball games with Bill Budge's *Pinball Construction Set* on the Atari 800. In 1983, he sent them to EA with a letter saying he wanted to design games for them. He soon discovered "girls, skateboarding, and an Amiga 2000." A "surfboard-shaper-friend's-brother" was the art director for video games at Disney, so Corea started working as a freelance artist in 1991 for Disney (Buena Vista Software) in Burbank, California, on a product called *Un-Natural Selection*. The work included a lot of user interface work and claymation. The producer left Disney for EA and offered a contracting job with Bill Budge on a new pinball project for the Sega Genesis (ten years after his letter!). He then came to work for EA a year later, on a permanent basis. USNF had room for a 3D artist, and luckily he had a chance to touch every type of art on the project. When the sequel started, he was chosen as lead artist.

On the *WWII Fighters* project, it was an opportunity to push the art. The hope now, says Corea, would be to someday become an art director of several projects.

DICKENSON, MARK—TEAM .366/3DO COMPANY

Mark Dickenson is the Executive Director at The 3DO Company, responsible for a number of PC and console titles. The last two projects were *Sammy Sosa High Heat Baseball 2001* and *Sammy Sosa Softball Slam*.

Before heading over to 3DO's Team .366 division to work on baseball games, Dickenson worked on a science fiction *Colonization* simulation named *Alien Legacy* (published by Sierra), two online fantasy role-playing games (*The Fates of Twinion* and *The Shadow of Yserbius*, both for the Imagination Network), *SpellCraft* (published by ASCII Entertainment), and *Hard Nova* (published by Electronic Arts).

High Heat Baseball 2000 won many awards, including PC Sports Game of the Year from the following: *Computer Gaming World*, *PC Gamer*, *PC Accelerator*, *Computer Games*, and GameSpot.

His future aspirations are simple: to work with the development of *Sammy Sosa High Heat Baseball* and *Sammy Sosa Softball Slam* until they're undeniably the number one sports products.

DORF, BARRY—ELECTRONIC ARTS

Barry Dorf was an assistant producer for the *Madden* series since 1998, and moved over to do online projects. He helped designed *The Edge* and is now in the process of designing several of EA Sports' new *Fantasy Football* and *Madden Football Interactive* Web sites. He came from working in TV in Los Angeles, and EA is the first video game company he worked for. Pretty good first call.

GOTTLIEB, HARRY—JELLYVISION

As founder and principle designer at Jellyvision, Harry Gottlieb has spearheaded *You Don't Know Jack* (volumes *1–4*, movies, TV, sports, question pack, offline, the netshow—all in partnership with Berkeley systems as distributor and publisher); a *You Don't Know Jack* tabletop game (with Tiger Electronics); and *That's A Fact, Jack!* (with Tom Snyder Productions).

Jellyvision also created, wrote, designed, and produced the *Who Wants to Be a Millionaire?* CD-ROM, in partnership with Disney Interactive, though it was based on the existing game show. Jellyvision has a new entertainment product (for which Hasbro Interactive is their partner) that's planned to launch soon, another entertainment product also has a launch set for this year, and a services product with a yet-to-be-disclosed partner is also planned for launch this year.

GREENBLAT, RODNEY ALAN—FREELANCE

Rodney Greenblat is a creator of intriguing and whimsical art. His paintings and sculpture have been exhibited in galleries and museums around the world. He is an author and illustrator of children's books, and director of the Center for Advanced Whimsy, an independent creative company that makes artwork, design, and music for children and adults.

"RodneyFun" is a group of original characters designed for Sony Creative Products, a Japanese licensing division of Sony Music. The characters have been used by Sony Computer for two hit PlayStation games, *Parappa the Rapper* (1997) and *Um Jammer Lammy* (1999), as well as for consumer products distributed in over 800 stores in Japan.

The mission of the Center for Advanced Whimsy is to create artwork and products that revel in imagination, push the boundaries of design, and remind the world how valuable fun, wonder, and play really are.

GRIMANI, MARIO—ENSEMBLE STUDIOS

Mario Grimani is an AI specialist at Ensemble Studios. Some of his past products include *Monty Python and the Quest for the Holy Grail*, developed by 7th Level, and *Dominion: Storm Over Gift 3*, developed by ION Storm. He last worked on computer player AI for *Age of Empires II: The Age of Kings*. Grimani expects to continue working on AI for real-time strategy games for a while.

HALL, TOM—ION STORM

Tom Hall is a game designer and president of ION Storm. He was also a cofounder of id Software, and then later ION Storm. Hall is originally from New Berlin, Wisconsin. After getting a programming degree from the University of Wisconsin, he turned his game-making hobby into a dream job. His history includes the *Commander Keen* series, *Wolfenstein 3D*, *Spear of Destiny*, *Doom*, *Duke Nukem II*, *Rise of the Triad*, *Terminal Velocity*, and now the 3D sci-fi RPG *Anachronox* (pronounced uh-NAH-kruh-nox).

HORLING, BRYAN C.—FREEVERSE SOFTWARE

Bryan C. Horling is a shareware programmer for Freeverse Software and a computer science graduate student who studied multi-agent systems. He has written *Burning Monkey Solitaire* for the Mac and PC, *Jared* and *Virtual Viagra* for Freeverse, and is in the process of finishing *Mr. Relaxer*. In the future, he plans on updating the Mac version of *Burning Monkey Solitaire* for Freeverse, and possibly incorporating Internet play into it. He may also write another "toy" program for them, involving a monkey that sits onscreen and says/does random things throughout the day.

HOUSE, SEAN—ELECTRONIC ARTS

Sean House is an associate producer at Electronic Arts for the *Madden NFL Football* series on the PC. His aspirations include "moving up the proverbial ladder, taking on more responsibility, and developing new and innovative entertainment software."

HOUSEHOLDER, MATT—BLIZZARD NORTH

Matt Householder has learned a lot over the years about game design and the production process on nearly any type of platform: coin-op (he witnessed the creation of *Q-Bert*), consoles (going back to the ColecoVision and including NES, Game Boy, SNES, Genesis, 3DO Multiplayer, and PSX), and home computers (Apple II, C64, DOS—going all the way back to CGA graphics, Amiga, Atari ST).

Householder started out programming coin-op games in 1981 and finished his first game, *Krull*, an action/RPG, in 1983. In 1984, he converted *Moon Patrol* to the ColecoVision (including doing most of the art and sound effects himself), and produced many original computer games for Epyx during 1985-88, including *Winter Games*, *World Games*, and *California Games* (which he created, designed, and directed). Since then, he has produced games with varying (mostly little) success for Activision, Epyx (again), DTMC (defunct), and 3DO. He joined Blizzard North to produce *Diablo II* and recruit game developer employees—programmers, artists, and sound/music artists.

JAQUAYS, PAUL—ID SOFTWARE

Paul Jaquays is a game designer at id Software, Inc., also serving as a level designer for *Quake II*. His last project was game and level design for *Quake III: Arena*. Previous computer/electronic game projects include script and map layouts for Interplay's *Lord of the Rings, Volume 1*, design for Expx's *4x4 Off Road Racing*, "script doctor" for *Bard's Tale IV* from EA, concept and co-design (with Joe Angiolillo) for *WarGames* for the ColecoVision and ADAM computer, the *Pac-Man* tabletop arcade from Coleco, and the *Donkey Kong* tabletop arcade from Coleco.

His previous jobs are an interesting mix, including staff cover artist and then director of graphics for TSR, Inc. (publisher of *Dungeons & Dragons*); freelance illustrator, game designer and editor; director of product development for Penguin Products; director of game design for Coleco Industries, Inc., and game designer and illustrator for Judges Guild.

Jaquays' other projects worth noting are role-playing game adventures: *Dark Tower*, *Caverns of Thracia*, *Book of Treasure Maps I*, *Hellpits of Nightfang*, *Griffin Mountain* (with Rudy Kraft and Greg Stafford), *The Savage Frontier*, and *The Shattered Statue*. He designed the concept for and wrote the first three books in the *Central Casting* character development book series and produced *City Books 4–6* for Flying Buffalo, Inc. Jaquays is on the development credits for *Marvel Super Heroes* dice game from TSR (he also did all the dice icon artwork), and illustrated numerous adventure game products and created the art look for the *Dragon Dice* game. He also directed the design and development of all Coleco's non-educational video games.

Future aspirations? "Keep having fun making games."

JENSEN, JANE—SIERRA ON-LINE

Jane Jensen is an award-winning game designer at Sierra On-Line whose past products include *EcoQuest: Search for Cetus* (co-designer), *King's Quest VI* (co-designer), *Gabriel Knight: Sins of the Fathers* (designer and series creator), *Gabriel Knight: The Beast Within*, and most recently, *Gabriel Knight III: Blood of the Sacred, Blood of the Damned*. She has also written and published two novels: *Gabriel Knight: Sins of the Fathers* and *Gabriel Knight: The Beast Within*, which are obviously based on the plot of the games. She has an original novel (i.e., not game-based) called *Millennium Rising*, and another original book due to be published by the end of 2000.

Her future aspirations are to continue to do books and games, although she will probably continue to move into a more independent role with the games, where she writes the design and perhaps the major dialogue scenes but doesn't participate as much during the development process. She finds the day-to-day production process more managerial and "grunt-workish" than she really cares for, and prefers to focus on writing.

JOHNSTON, MATTHEW LEE—MICROSOFT

Matt Johnston is the audio lead at Microsoft. As a youth, he was always into music and sound. A common afternoon would find him on the floor with headphones listening to the production subtleties of Pink Floyd's "The Wall," or sitting in a tree listening to the different Hawaiian bird species share their stories. Countless hours were also spent playing his Atari 2600 and riding his bike down to the "Fun Factory" to play *Crazy Climber*, *Cliffhanger*, *Astro Fighter*, or whatever was new, with stolen money from his parents' "money jar." In eighth grade, he became obsessed with computers after seeing the movie *WarGames*. Performing on his Apple IIe, he managed to orchestrate worldwide notoriety through moments of video game software piracy, more than a few phone system phreaking opuses, and a cacophony of bulletin board operation.

His parents had always explained the "hardships" of being a musician, and insisted he find something like his computer interests to fall back on. In college, he discovered a place called the "computer music lab," where two of his three obsessions seemed to exist in harmony. He spent the entirety of his interdisciplinary education either working with the Buchla Modular synth or Sound Designer 1.0 in the lab, or acting as music director at the college radio station, KAOS. Back in the "house of doom," his roommates and he were "blowing smoke, drinking malt liquor, and trying hard to kick each other's nads on the Genesis, NES, or the 2600." All of this activity became the ideal preparation for his current position as resident juvenile delinquent at Microsoft.

Projects Johnston has worked on at Microsoft include *Flight Simulator 95* and *98*; *Microsoft Golf 2.0, 3.0, 98*, and *99*; *3D Movie Maker*; *Cinemania 96*; *Reader's Digest Complete Do-It-Yourself Guide*; *Monster Truck Madness 1* and *2*; *CART Precision Racing*; *Combat Flight Simulator 1.0*; and *MS Digital Phone*.

His future aspirations include working on more hardware projects, preserving quiet places, and collaborating with Lauryn Hill on some interactive music.

KAHN, ADAM—ACCLAIM ENTERTAINMENT

Adam Kahn is a PR manager at Acclaim Entertainment. Before he joined Acclaim in the winter of 1998, he worked at Shandwick International, a PR firm, on the Microsoft Games account.

KIRK, GEOFF—HUMONGOUS ENTERTAINMENT

Humongous Entertainment's sound designer and sound effects programmer, Geoff Kirk, has worked on many titles, including *Pajama Sam*, *Putt-Putt Travels Through Time*, *Spy Fox*, *Freddi Fish 3*, *Pajama Sam 2*, *Putt Putt Enters the Race*, and *Freddi Fish 4*. He has also contributed background music for a couple of bonus levels in *Pajama Sam's Lost and Found* and the background music for the "Happy Fun Sub" in *Spy Fox*. Kirk is also a musician, but says, "I don't think this is necessary to become a good sound effects programmer."

In college, he studied a number of topics that helped him in his work at Humongous. He learned "classic" analog synth programming on instruments like the Arp 2600, and also basic recording techniques. He also learned tape editing, which in those ancient days was done with a razor, and experimented with such things as making long loops of tape with drums or other sounds on them and using them in various compositions. Later on, he worked for Muzak splicing tapes together, and while he was there used to make small tape loops with various silly things on them, which also helped develop some of the skills he uses today editing sounds together. During this time, he began building a small personal studio at home and learning about MIDI, the various types of digital synthesizers, and sampling. The greatest preparation for what he's doing today, says Kirk, was the time spent when he was very young watching cartoons, especially the old Warner Brother's Bugs Bunny. "They used music as a sound effect in a way that is still rather revolutionary. The background music on those old cartoons is also very cool and ahead of its time."

His future aspirations are to contribute more background music to games and to work on games that aren't just for young children.

KIRSCH, DAVE "ZOID"— THREEWAVE SOFTWARE

Past work of this Vancouver, British Columbia resident includes *ThreeWave Capture the Flag* (CTF) for *Quake*, Linux and other UNIX versions of *Quake*, *QuakeWorld* upgrades, *ThreeWave CTF for Quake II*, Linux and other UNIX versions of *Quake II*, *ThreeWave CTF for Quake III*, and Linux and other UNIX versions of *Quake III*.

For the future, Zoid hopes to design and build some of the most advanced, complete multiplayer games around with fast-action gameplay with acceptable treatment of Internet lag.

KOBERSTEIN, JOE—RAVEN SOFTWARE

Joe Koberstein is an artist at Raven Software and has been in the game industry about five years, working in California, Japan, and Wisconsin. He's currently in game development, but has also worked in publishing, advertising, and marketing of video games. Past employers include *GameFan* magazine, subsidiaries of Activision (Raven Software), marketing groups for Disney and Sony PlayStation (ASCII Entertainment), as well as his own freelance agency, Kdesign.

KRAAIJVANGER, MAARTEN—NIHILISTIC SOFTWARE

After graduating from Boston College with a minor in fine arts and a degree in philosophy and economics, Maarten started his career at Cyclone Studios in 1994. At Cyclone, he was responsible for creating sprites and textures for the game *Captain Quazar*. In early 1995 he became lead artist and designer on the acclaimed game *Battlesport* for the 3DO platform. After the 3DO purchase of the company, Cyclone Studios changed its focus from the 3DO console to PC development. As lead artist for *Requiem*, a much anticipated shooter, Maarten refined his animation and character-creation skills and had the freedom to create more exotic creatures. With Nihilistic, his main responsibilities, in addition to managing an extremely talented art team, are modeling, animating game characters, and incorporating the latest 3D technology. In his free time, Maarten has tried to limit his *Quake* gameplay, and likes to read science-fiction novels. In early 2000, Maarten began writing a regular artist column for *Game Developer* magazine, and has hosted rountable lectures and the annual Game Developer's Conference.

LAIDLAW, MARC—VALVE SOFTWARE

Marc Laidlaw is a writer/level team coordinator for *Half-Life* and a game designer at Valve Software. His published novels include *The 37th Mandala* (winner of the International Horror Guild Award for Best Novel of 1996), *Kalifornia*, *The Orchid Eater*, *Dad's Nuke*, *Neon Lotus*, and *The Third Force: A Novel of Gadget*. Future aspirations are to continue to hone the cutting edge where game design meets storytelling.

LAND, MICHAEL—LUCASARTS

Michael Land is the sound department manager and a member of the music team at LucasArts Entertainment and has contributed to many award-winning and best-selling products through the years: the entire *Monkey Island* series, *The Dig*, *X-Wing*, *TIE Fighter*, *Indiana Jones and the Fate of Atlantis*, and *Day of the Tentacle*. His future aspiration is simply to continue writing music.

LANZINGER, FRANZ—ACTUAL ENTERTAINMENT

Franz Lanzinger is the chairman of Actual Entertainment. Franz worked as a programmer and game designer at Atari Games Inc. and Tengen. He left in 1990 to cofound Bitmasters, where he was president until April of 1995. He then founded Actual Entertainment with Mark Robichek and Eric Ginner.

A terrific video game player, he held the world record for the arcade version of *Centipede* for six months in 1981. On September 19, 1997, Franz achieved further fame when Gamasutra selected him as their Geek of the Week! He is a bridge life master and broke 90 at Sunnyvale Municipal Golf Course on one of his better days. On top of all that, Franz programmed and designed a few games you might have heard of: *Crystal Castles* (coin-op, original), *Toobin* (NES, conversion), *Ms. Pac-Man* (NES, conversion), *Krazy Kreatures* (NES, original), *Rampart* (NES, SNES, conversion), *Championship Pool* (SNES, original), and *NCAA Final Four Basketball* (SNES, original). He also designed *Ms. Pac-Man* (Genesis, conversion), *Championship Pool* (Genesis, NES, Game Boy, original), and *NCAA Final Four Basketball* (Genesis, original).

LARKIN, TIM—CYAN AND THE HUGESOUND NETWORK

Tim Larkin is a senior sound designer at Cyan, the developers of the hit games *Myst* and *Riven*. He has also scored sound for the opening movie and cut-scenes for *Quest for Glory V* (Sierra On-Line, Inc.). Larkin served as lead sound designer and composer at Brøderbund, where he was the lead sound designer for *Riven: The Sequel to Myst*. This included creation of sound effects for over 900 individually rendered movies and animations, and close to an hour of interactive ambience. Also at Brøderbund, Larkin composed and produced music and/or sound design for the *Carmen Sandiego* series, *Rugrats*, *Warbreeds*, and more. Before that, Larkin produced and engineered sound and music for numerous TV themes, industrial videos, commercials, multimedia, and album projects.

LEBLANC, MARK—LOOKING GLASS STUDIOS

Marc "MAHK" LeBlanc has been making games at Looking Glass since 1992. His design and programming credits include *Ultima Underworld II*, *System Shock 1* and *2*, *Flight Unlimited*, and *Thief: The Dark Project*. As a game designer and a game technologist, he strives to expand the set of abstract tools and formalisms available to game designers. Currently, he is the lead engineer on Looking Glass' RPG Engine Team. In 1999, he gave game design lectures at the GDC and at NYU. He went to "that nerd school down the river from Harvard," where he earned a masters' degree in computer science.

LEVELORD, THE (RICHARD BAILEY GRAY)— RITUAL ENTERTAINMENT

According to his published bio, The Levelord is originally from New Haven, Connecticut. He has served a tour of duty in the U.S. Navy and attended several institutions of higher learning, from which he earned a technical degree in business-oriented programming and a degree in computer engineering. He has been doing level design since 1994.

The Levelord designed half of the levels for *Duke Nukem 3D* (The Abyss, Incubator, Warp Factor, Spin Cycle, Lunatic Fringe, Raw Meat, Bank Roll, Flood Zone, L.A. Rumble, The Movie Set, Rabid Transit, Fahrenheit, Hotel Hell, and Tier Drops). The latest release of *Scourge of Armagon* includes his levels The Lost Mine, Research Facility, The Crypt, Tur Torment, and The Edge of Oblivion.

This is where the Levelord's bio ends, but he then went to Ritual Entertainment and was lead level designer for Activision's *Sin*.

LEVESQUE, ADAM—BLUE FANG GAMES

Adam Levesque is currently the president of Blue Fang Games. He formerly worked at Papyrus, where he served as a 3D artist on *IndyCar Racing*, a producer/designer on *NASCAR Racing 1* and *2*, an executive producer on all Papyrus products, and general manager of the Papyrus division. He started Blue Fang Games last year to branch out into other game genres. He's currently working on *Dragon Hoard*, a strategy/RPG in which the player takes on the role of a dragon.

LEWIS, SUSAN—THINKBIG

Susan Lewis is the president of ThinkBIG, a company dedicated to representing and promoting the interests of client development and publishing companies. Publishers she has "closed deals" with include Electronic Arts, Acclaim, Fox Interactive, Atari Games, and BMG Interactive. Lewis deals with virtually every publisher out there, and her company has been featured in *Wired*, *Game Developer*, *SF Chronicle*, *Gamecenter*, *Salon*, and *Screen Magazine* (Germany) and on the television program TV.Com/CNET. She was invited to speak at E3 1997 ("The Art of the Pitch," with Bryan Neider, VP of Electronic Arts) and at GDC 1998 ("The Art of the Pitch," with Ed Zono, President of Zono Games).

LINN, BILL—LINN PUBLIC RELATIONS, INC.

Bill Linn is a longtime game industry public relations veteran. Before starting his agency in mid-1997, Linn spent seven years as the senior in-house public relations counsel for Sierra, The Imagination Network, and Accolade. He has worked on many of the game industry's best-known and best-selling products, including *King's Quest*, *Leisure Suit Larry*, *Daryl Gates' Police Quest*, *Hardball*, *Jack Nicklaus Golf*, *Prince of Persia*, *Riven*, *Uprising*, *Warlords*, and *Test Drive*. In all, he has launched more than 100 PC multimedia, console, and Internet games. Before joining the game industry, Linn spent several years promoting everything from politicians to concerts and worked as a journalist for several major newspapers.

A gamer at heart, Linn approaches product public relations by integrating his passion for interactive entertainment with his professional training and experience. He grew up playing everything from *Pong* and *Coleco Football* to *M.U.L.E.* and *Leisure Suit Larry*. Today, he devotes many hours to playing games on the PC, PlayStation, Nintendo 64, and at video arcades.

Linn's client roster includes some of the industry's leading companies: Sierra, THQ, Brøderbund, The 3DO Company, and ASCII Entertainment.

LUPIDI, TONY—ELECTRONIC ARTS

Tony Lupidi is an art director for Scoreboard Productions, an in-house development company at Electronic Arts. He has shipped two games—*March Madness '98* and *March Madness '99*—college basketball simulations on the PlayStation game platform.

Lupidi comments, "From my viewpoint, we are right on the verge of the emergence of a new, more interactive form of mass media. Some of the technologies driving this new media are 1) real-time 3D display hardware as a consumer technology (à la Voodoo, TNT); 2) broadband networks (cable modems for the masses); and 3) continued development of faster and cheaper computers. "The film industry has over 100 years of history and a successful formula for making money, and thus has neither the incentive nor imagination to develop interactive media. That is the reason I have switched careers from doing TV and film animation to working in the video game industry. If you look at the history of the development of new media, there is always a period at the beginning of intense experimentation, innovation, and risk taking before successful formulas are derived. As a creative type, this is the most exciting time since you have the fewest constraints placed on you. I want to participate in this next step in media."

MCCART, MICHAEL—ENSEMBLE STUDIOS

The way Michael McCart got his job at Ensemble Studios as their Webmaster is inspiring to anyone with a fan site. McCart ran the popular *Age of Empires* Heaven Web site, hosted by Gamestats, and was snagged from Ensemble Studios because they were pleased with his talent and dedication. That's the short answer. The longer one is available at Michael McCart's home page at www.electrosonic.net/resources/angel.html.

MCGRATH, MICHAEL D.—DYNAMIX

Michael McGrath is an engineer/programmer at Dynamix/Sierra. His past products include *Netrek* (public domain), *Extreme Warfare* (Trilobyte), and *Red Baron 3D* (Dynamix). Future plans include a rewrite of *Netrek*, plus sci-fi flight/combat sims and conquest titles.

MCQUAID, BRAD—VERANT INTERACTIVE

Brad McQuaid serves as vice president of California's Verant Interactive, Inc., developers of the smash hit massively-multiplayer online role-playing game (MMORPG) *EverQuest*. McQuaid was the producer on *EverQuest* and for the first official expansion pack, *The Ruins of Kunark*. Before becoming producer, McQuaid was lead programmer on *EverQuest* for a brief period of time. Before that he was co-owner of a company called MicroGenesis and was programmer/producer on a shareware title called *WarWizard* and a demo called *WarWizard 2*. His aspiration is to eventually create virtual 3D worlds with as much depth and detail as some of the paper-and-pencil RPG worlds that have evolved over the years. He plans on being involved in the development of MMORPGs for some time and feels we've only touched the tip of the iceberg in terms of where this genre will go in the future.

MECHNER, JORDAN—FREELANCE GAME DESIGNER

Jordan Mechner earned a reputation as one of the world's premier computer game designers by bringing cinematic techniques to the small screen in games like *Karateka*, *Prince of Persia*, and *The Last Express*. Mechner's passion for visual storytelling has now led him to a new career as a screenwriter and filmmaker.

In 1979, a 15-year-old Mechner bought his first Apple II computer. Fascinated by the new machine, he taught himself to program, first in BASIC, then in 6502 machine language, devoting his after-school hours to creating increasingly ambitious games. This five-year apprenticeship paid off when Brøderbund Software published Mechner's *Karateka* (1984), a labor of love that had occupied his first two years at Yale University. Drawing inspiration from his film studies classes, Mechner used cinematic devices such as cross-cutting, a moving camera, and a dramatic storyline for the first time in a computer game. The result was a software landmark that "took the gaming community by storm, introducing players to an epic experience never before achieved in a video game" (*Next Generation*). Acclaimed for its fluid animation and movie-like feel, *Karateka* became a #1 bestseller, with over 500,000 copies sold.

Following *Karateka*'s success, Mechner took a hiatus from software design to finish college, graduating with a degree in psychology. His next game, *Prince of Persia* (1989), a swashbuckling Arabian Nights action-adventure, revitalized the platform-game genre by blending fast-paced arcade action with dramatic visual storytelling in a way never seen before. It has been described as "the *Star Wars* of its field" (*Computer Gaming World*), "the standard by which all animated action-adventure games are judged" (*Electronic Games*), and "an ever-present in any compiled list of classic PC games of all time" (*PC Review*). Winner of numerous awards, *Prince of Persia* has sold over 2 million copies and has been translated into 12 languages and 20 computer and video game formats worldwide. More than ten years after its initial release, it is still being sold on formats as diverse as Windows, Macintosh, and the Nintendo Game Boy—a true mark of longevity in an industry known for rapid technological obsolescence. In 1997, *Prince of Persia* was named "Game of the Decade" by the French TV network Canal+.

With two hits under his belt, Mechner again returned to student life, first taking an intensive film production course at NYU, next moving to Salamanca to study Spanish, and finally to Paris. In the summer of 1992, Mechner produced and directed his first film, *Waiting for Dark*. A visual "poem without words" that traces a day in the life of Havana, Cuba, the film won prizes at prestigious international festivals including the Bilbao International Short Film Concourse, Philadelphia International Film Festival, and Jornada da Bahia of Brazil.

Mechner's two years abroad were punctuated by trips back to San Rafael, California, to supply creative guidance to Brøderbund Software's team of artists and programmers at work on *Prince of Persia 2: The Shadow and the Flame* (1993), designed and directed by Mechner. The sequel enjoyed strong sales and critical acclaim, selling 750,000 copies and winning awards including *Computer Gaming World*'s "Best Action Game of 1993." Mechner's new role as designer/director reflected an industry-wide shift in the way games were being made. No longer the work of solo programmers, games in the 1990s had become collaborative efforts employing teams of professional creative talent, often with six- and seven-figure development and marketing budgets.

Mechner's next title, *The Last Express*, was his most ambitious project yet. To create this epic adventure, set aboard the Orient Express crossing Europe on the eve of World War I, Mechner formed his own development company, Smoking Car Productions. The $5 million production included a team of 40 artists, animators, and programmers, and a live-action film shoot with an international cast of 60 actors, directed by Mechner. Four years in the making, the game was hailed by *Next Generation* as "a giant creative leap for Mechner, combining his love of film and game design into one masterpiece." One of 1997's most highly acclaimed titles, *The Last Express* was named "Best Adventure Game of the Year" by *Games*, *Family PC*, and *Macworld* magazines, among many other awards. Although sales were only respectable (100,000 copies), *The Last Express* gained a passionate cult following and continues to be cited as a game ahead of its time.

Following *The Last Express*, Mechner turned his attention to feature film screenwriting. His recent screenplays include an adaptation of *The Last Express*, entitled *The Firebird*, and *Follow Me*, a contemporary thriller. Mechner also acted as a design consultant on one of this year's most high-profile action game releases, *Prince of Persia 3D*, developed and published by Red Orb/Mindscape Entertainment. He is at work on a new screenplay.

MEIER, SID—FIRAXIS GAMES

Sid Meier is the chairman and director of creative development at Firaxis Games. Called the "father of the computer gaming industry," his career is a story of "firsts." He created the first combat flight simulator, *F15 Strike Eagle*, in the early 80s, which has sold well over a million copies and inaugurated the flight simulation industry. His *Silent Service* was the first submarine simulation. The innovative *Pirates!*, a unique blend of historical sim, arcade action, strategy, and role-playing, opened the doors to a plethora of genres. *F19 Stealth Fighter* was the first flight sim to incorporate an infinite mission-generation system, a mainstay of recent flight sims, and an element of strategy that made it one of the most popular flight games ever. Sid's recent titles, such as *Railroad Tycoon* and *Civilization*, ushered in the new era of "god games" that started yet another new genre in computer gaming. Having won every major award in the industry, Sid continues to be on the leading edge of entertainment software.

MEIJERS-GABRIEL, ELLEN—ODDWORLD INHABITANTS

As composer/sound designer at Oddworld Inhabitants, Ellen Meijers-Gabriel has written music and designed sound effects for both of the development studios' products, *Oddworld: Abe's Oddysee* and *Oddworld: Abe's Exoddus*.

Her first interaction with music was when she was about six years old and living in Holland. She studied piano for about 12 years before/until she developed a problem with her shoulders that prevented continuing her normal practice routine. This inability to practice meant that she could no longer pursue her goal to become a pianist and was now faced with what to do with her life. Wanting to stay in music, she chose to pursue other less physically-intense aspects of music. As soon as she accepted this decision, she enrolled in a masters program in musicology. Even before finishing the program, she was drawn to the technical side of music, so she concurrently started a music technology program at a different school. She enjoyed the technical side so much that she then began a master of arts program in interactive multimedia at The Royal College of Art in England. Immediately after graduating, Meijers-Gabriel was offered the opportunity to start working on games for a company in America.

Future aspirations include doing sound design and music for feature films; she would also like to further explore morphing techniques and synthesizing sounds from scratch, as opposed to changing existing sounds. To do this, she hopes to use tools like Kyma, Software DSP languages like MSP, and physical modeling synthesis, among others.

MEYERS, MICHAEL—3DO

Michael Meyers is the director of product public relations at 3DO, and prior to that, Acclaim Entertainment. He was involved in or in charge of the PR launches for *Turok: Dinosaur Hunter*, *Turok 2: Seeds of Evil*, *NFL Quarterback Club '98* and *'99*, *All-Star Baseball*, *Extreme-G*, *NBA Jam '99*, *WWF: Warzone*, *Jeremy McGrath Supercross*, and many others.

MIYAMOTO, SHIGERU—NINTENDO

Shigeru Miyamoto is the general manager of entertainment analysis and development at Nintendo Co. Ltd., Kyoto, Japan. The following is a list of all 50+ games he's worked on, from 1981 to the present. He served as producer on most of these, but in a few cases, as director or supervisor. In chronological order, they are *Donkey Kong*, *Donkey Kong Jr.*, *Mario Bros.*, *Popeye*, *Super Mario Bros.*, *Wild Gunman*, *Duck Hunt*, *Hogan's Alley*, *Excite Bike*, *The Legend of Zelda*, *Volley Ball*, *Super Mario Bros. 2*, *Zelda II: The Adventure of Link*, *Ice Hockey*, *Super Mario Bros. 3*, *Kirby's Adventure*, *Super Mario World*, *Pilot Wings*, *F-Zero*, *Sim City*, *The Legend of Zelda: A Link to the Past*, *Super MarioKart*, *Star Fox*, *Super Mario All Stars*, *Stunt Race FX*, *Super Donkey Kong*, *Earth Bound*, *Kirby's Dream Course*, *Super Mario World 2*, *Yoshi's Island*, *Super Mario RPG*, *Kirby Super Star*, *Radar Mission*, *Kirby's Dream Land*, *Wave Race*, *The Legend of Zelda: Link's Awaking*, *Kirby's Pinball Land*, *Donkey Kong*, *Mario's Picross*, *Kirby's Dream Land 2*, *Kirby's Blockball*, *Mole Mania*, *Super Mario 64*, *Pilot Wings 64*, *Wave Race 64*, *MarioKart 64*, *Star Fox 64*, *Yoshi's Story*, *1080 Snowboarding*, *F-Zero X*, and *The Legend of Zelda: Ocarina of Time*.

At the 1998 Electronic Entertainment Exposition, Miyamoto was honored as the first inductee into the Academy of Interactive Arts and Sciences Hall of Fame. His future aspirations are to continue to assist in the creation of new and exciting gameplay experiences for Nintendo.

MOE, RICHARD—HUMONGOUS ENTERTAINMENT

Richard Moe is a project lead for Humongous Entertainment, "a confusing title which means basically that I design, produce, and implement games from the ground up." His area of expertise is programming—for all Humongous games, they work in a proprietary language called SCUMM, which was developed by company cofounder Ron Gilbert. Some of the titles Moe has worked on as designer and programmer are, in chronological order, *Junior Field Trips: Let's Explore the Airport*, *Pajama Sam in There's No Need to Hide When It's Dark Outside*, *Backyard Baseball*, and most recently *Putt-Putt Enters the Race*.

NEWELL, GABE—VALVE SOFTWARE

Gabe Newell is the managing director at Kirkland, Washington's Valve Software. Their debut product, *Half-Life*, has won numerous print and online "Game of the Year" awards, as well as "Best PC Game" at the 1998 E3 from UGO.

NICHOLS, MIKE—SURREAL SOFTWARE

Mike Nichols is a VP, creative director, and founder at Surreal Software. He started in this industry about 10 years ago. One of his first projects was *NY Warriors* in 1989 for the Amiga, coin-op, and PC (back when it was CGA and EGA only). Since then, he has worked for several companies as an artist and designer, having put out some 20 or more products. Nichols' last employer was Boss Game Studios, where he was the lead designer for *Spider* on the PlayStation.

Nichols' responsibilities at Surreal include managing the art teams and contributing to shape the future of Surreal and the type of products they want to create—not to mention creating art for the products themselves. Surreal is first and foremost a games developer. They don't carry egos or the notion of becoming the biggest game company in the industry. Their aspirations are simple: "Work hard at creating what we love—games."

NOMURA, TETSUYA—SQUARESOFT

Tetsuya Nomura is a director and character designer at Squaresoft.

A longtime fan of Yoshitaka Amano's work, Tetsuya Nomura joined the Square graphics team in 1991, where he worked as a monster designer for *Final Fantasy V*.

Tetsuya Nomura continues to be an integral part of the *Final Fantasy* design team. In *Final Fantasy VII*, he created such memorable characters as Cloud and Aeris, which ignited his career as one of the premier character designers in the world. The title has sold 8 million copies to date worldwide.

After *Final Fantasy VII*, Tetsuya Nomura went on to design characters for *Parasite Eve* and the main characters in *Final Fantasy VIII*. He also directed a number of the famous CG sequences of *Final Fantasy VIII*, including the opening movie, the battles, and the forever memorable ballroom dance scene. He is a highly versatile artist who has become involved in all phases of game production at Square, and who will act as the director and character designer for a recently announced Disney/Square project, scheduled for release in late 2001.

Tetsuya Nomura was born in 1970 in Kochi pref., Japan.

O'CONNOR, PAUL—ODDWORLD INHABITANTS

As lead game designer at the Oddworld Inhabitants development studio, Paul O'Connor headed up *Oddworld: Abe's Oddysee* and *Oddworld: Abe's Exoddus* for the Sony PlayStation and PC. He has been a game designer in either a freelance or staff capacity more or less continuously since 1981, designing computer games, video games, board games, and role-playing games. He has also worked as a freelance writer, primarily writing comic books for Malibu and Marvel Comics.

O'DONNELL, MARTIN—TOTALAUDIO

Marty O'Donnell and TotalAudio were responsible for sound design, live action video foley, and final mix for *Riven: The Sequel to Myst*, and all original music, sound design, and voices for *Myth: The Fallen Lords*, *Myth II: Soulblighter*, and *Septerra Core: Legacy of the Creator*. Currently, they're working on *Oni* and *Halo* for Bungie Software. Marty O'Donnell received a Master of Music degree in composition at USC, a David Faith Memorial Award for Composition, and an Outstanding Graduate Award.

With his partner, Mike Salvatori, O'Donnell has produced hundreds of tracks for commercials on TV and radio (such as "We are Flintstones kids, 10 million strong and growing…"), won multiple awards, and scored many films and multimedia projects before getting the job to work on *Riven*, which was the recipient of numerous industry awards. They won the "Outstanding Use of Sound" award for *Myth*, which also won several "Game of the Year" awards. Their music, which featured members of the Chicago Symphony Orchestra, played for the unveiling of *Halo* at MacWorld New York during Steve Jobs' keynote address.

OSTERGARD, GENEVIEVE—SIERRA STUDIOS

Genevieve Ostergard, a senior PR manager at Sierra Studios, has been in the computer games business for five years and in PR for seven. She started at Interplay as an assistant communications manager doing PR for MacPlay and the console divisions. Six months later, she was promoted to communications manager and proceeded to spearhead PC and console games PR for Interplay. After Interplay, she was a senior account executive for the Shandwick PR agency, handling the Microsoft Games account.

Prior to her game PR experience, she did PR for Ziff-Davis Press, the former book publishing division of the most successful computer magazine publisher in the world.

PARDO, ROB—BLIZZARD ENTERTAINMENT

Rob Pardo is a producer/designer at Blizzard Entertainment. His credits include *Starcraft* and *Starcraft: Brood War*, and at Interplay he was a producer on the titles *Whiplash*, *Casper*, and *Tempest X*. His primary goal is to continue to produce and design AAA-quality games with Blizzard Entertainment.

PATMORE, ALAN—SURREAL SOFTWARE

Alan Patmore is the president and design director at Surreal Software. He is also the lead designer on *Drakan*. He has been an avid game player/designer since he was eight.

PERRY, DAVID—SHINY ENTERTAINMENT

David Perry is behind some of our industry's most beloved games, such as the *Earthworm Jim* series, *MDK*, and *Messiah*. He invites all who are interested to read his extensive bio at www.shiny.com.

PFEIFER, KURT— HUMONGOUS ENTERTAINMENT

Kurt Pfiefer worked on *Total Annihilation* while at the recently defunct Cavedog Entertainment, plus older titles *Duke Nukem* (Saturn port), *Microsoft Soccer*, *Powerslave*, *DinoPark Tycoon*, and *Magic School Bus Across the Solar System*.

"I think my bowling team won first place when I was twelve. Does that count as an accolade?"

PRINCE, BOBBY—BOBBY PRINCE MUSIC

Bobby Prince is a composer/sound designer for bobby prince Music (his logo has the *b* and the *p* as half notes).

Past products include *Commander Keen*, *Wolfenstein 3D*, *Duke Nukem II* and *3D*, *Doom* and *Doom 2*, *Zorro*, *Axis & Allies*, plus many early shareware games and other retail products. Back in 1991, Prince was fairly active on the MIDI/Computer Music section of Prodigy. This was before the Internet was the common mode of communications. One Saturday in April, a fellow by the name of Scott Miller posted a note asking to hear from people who were interested in writing music for computer games. A couple of weeks before that, he had downloaded the original *Commander Keen* and was extremely impressed with it. He didn't know at the time that Scott's new company, Apogee Software, had distributed *Commander Keen*, and Scott didn't mention that in his note. He figured that he was a wannabe but responded anyway. The next day, Scott called him up and when he mentioned *Commander Keen*, Prince knew that he'd like to work with him. He hired him, "music unheard." Several months later, he received a call from John Romero of id Software and began working on the music for the second *Commander Keen* series. As they say, the rest is history. Future aspirations are "to continue to have fun the rest of [his] life."

PRITCHARD, MATT—ENSEMBLE STUDIOS

Matt Pritchard has been a graphics programmer for a number of gaming titles (in chronological order): *Dragon Quest Pi*, *Overload*, *Age of Empires*, *Age of Empires: Rise of Rome*, and *Age of Empires II: Age of Kings*.

RESNICK, JOSH—PANDEMIC STUDIOS

Josh Resnick is the president of Pandemic Studios, but prior to starting his own development studio he produced *Mechwarrior 2*, directed *Dark Reign*, and oversaw the production of *Battlezone*. He has been in the industry for nearly five years, after starting at Activision as an associate producer.

REYNOLDS, BRIAN—BIG HUGE GAMES

Brian Reynolds began his career in computer gaming at Microprose Software, collaborating closely with Sid Meier on the design of *Sid Meier's Colonization*. He went on to design *Civilization II*, which topped the charts with sales of over one million copies worldwide. A founding partner of Firaxis, one of Reynolds' particular specialties is artificial intelligence. Addicted to strategy games himself, Brian is on a never-ending quest to "make the computer play as well as I do." Brian brings a rich and varied background as a summa cum laude graduate in the fields of history and philosophy from the University of the South, Sewanee, Tennessee. His computer wizardry is self-taught. He recently left Firaxis to start a new development company, Big Huge Games.

RIPPY, CHRIS—ENSEMBLE STUDIOS

Chris Rippy is the sound director at Ensemble Studios. Thus far at Ensemble he has helped develop two games: *Age of Empires* and *Age of Empires: The Rise of Rome* expansion pack. As a musician, Rippy says he "kind of stumbled" into the gaming world. Games had always been a hobby, but he never thought that he could combine two things that he enjoyed—sound and games—and make a good living at it. His brother, David Rippy, has worked with Ensemble Studios' President Tony Goodman for a number of years, and eventually word got out that Tony would be starting a game company. Well, David would be doing the music, and they asked Chris Rippy to join in and do the sound effects. With a background in radio and a history in recording studios, it was a natural fit (and a lucky one). "That was in 1994," says Rippy, and he's "been humming along ever since."

ROBINSON, SETH A.— ROBINSON TECHNOLOGIES

This 25-year-old CEO of Robinson Technologies, Inc. is also co-owner of Nexgen Gaming, a retail network gaming facility located in Salem, Oregon. Products under Seth Robinson's belt include *Legend of the Red Dragon 1* and *2*, *Planets: The Exploration of Space*, and most recently *Dink Smallwood*.

Robinson Technologies, Inc. has been selling shareware for over 10 years. At the time of this interview they had been subcontracted by ManMachine (published by Macmillan Digital Publishing) for work on a couple of new games. *Dink Smallwood* has been written about in many game magazines, including *PC Gamer* and *PC Games*, and is considered to be one of the highest-quality freeware RPGs in cyberspace.

ROPER, BILL—BLIZZARD ENTERTAINMENT

Bill Roper is the senior director of developer relations at the internationally renowned Blizzard Entertainment, a division of Havas Interactive. Past projects include *Warcraft: Orcs and Humans*, *Warcraft II: Tides of Darkness*, *Warcraft II: Beyond the Dark Portal*, *Diablo*, *Starcraft*, *Starcraft: Brood War*, and most recently *Diablo II*.

Says Roper: "I have had the good fortune of working on some fantastically talented teams to create some great titles and I look forward to making even more memorable games in the future."

SAKAGUCHI, HIRONOBU—SQUARESOFT

Born November 1962, Hironobu Sakaguchi became director of planning and development in September 1986 with the establishment of Square Co., Ltd. At that time, he managed the development department, responsible for all research and development aspects of the company. In April 1991, Sakaguchi became the executive vice president of Square Co., Ltd. (where he remains today), as well as president of SQUARE USA, INC.

His most famous work, with the *Final Fantasy* series, has proven popular among the public, with total worldwide sales surpassing 26,000,000 copies. Presently, he's working on the development of a full-CGI movie at the SQUARE USA Honolulu studios. The film is slated to be released in the summer of 2001. As a director, he hopes to create photorealistic CGI that rivals the facial expressions and motions of a movie utilizing real actors and backgrounds. In addition to this, he will oversee the recently announced online service project "Play Online" as director. "Play Online" will become available in 2001.

SALADINO, MICHAEL—PRESTO STUDIOS

Michael Saladino is a lead programmer for Presto Studios, but has been in the game industry for the last five years. The first two were spent with a small startup company named Mobeus Designs, where he was responsible for creating the 3D graphics engine. He then found himself at Volition, the creators of *Descent*, where he worked as one of two graphic-engine developers at the company. He was later promoted to lead programmer on a racing game, and eventually moved on to Presto Studios, where he now works as one of their engine programmers and lead on a new project that's still in the design phase. In five short years, he has had the luck to work on many different projects in many different capacities.

SANGER, GEORGE (THE FAT MAN)—FATMAN MUSIC

The Fat Man, or George Alistair Sanger, has been composing music for games since 1983. Along with Team Fat, his legendary team of three other cowboy composers, he is internationally recognized for having created music for over 130 games, including such sound-barrier-breaking greats as *Loom*, *Wing Commander I* and *II*, *The 7th Guest I* and *II*, *NASCAR Racing*, *Putt-Putt Saves the Zoo*, and *ATF*. He wrote the first general MIDI soundtrack for a game, the first direct-to-MIDI live recording of musicians, the first Redbook soundtrack included with the game as a separate disk, the first music for a game that was considered a "work of art," and the first soundtrack that was considered a selling point for the game.

Team Fat is the original out-of-house source for music for games. More than once they have set trends and raised the bar for what is expected musically from games, significantly increasing sales of hardware and software. On a 380-acre ranch on the Guadalupe River, The Fat Man hosts the annual Texas Interactive Music Conference and BBQ (Project BBQ), the computer/music industry's most prestigious and influential conference.

SAWYER, CHRIS—FREELANCE

The one and only Chris Sawyer is a self-employed game developer, designer, and programmer, working from his home studio in England. His past products include *Transport Tycoon* and *RollerCoaster Tycoon*, plus many PC conversions of Amiga games including *Frontier Elite 2*, *Xenomorph*, *Conqueror*, *Campaign*, *Virus*, *Goal*, and *Birds of Prey*.

As for future aspirations, Sawyer says he doesn't look further ahead than his current project, but plans to continue "creating original constructional/simulation style games."

SCHILDER, KEVIN—RAVEN SOFTWARE

Kevin Schilder is the manager of the audio department at Raven Software in Madison, Wisconsin. He is one of two people on staff who handle all the duties of sound design, music composition, and audio production for their games.

With 30+ years of experience in the music field and degrees in music performance and education, Schilder's background includes a wide variety of musical styles. Before working at Raven, he worked in the retail music industry and taught music in public schools for six years. He has been associated with Raven Software since its inception, but formally employed with the company since 1994. Projects include *Black Crypt* on the Amiga (all music), *Cyclones* (some sound effects), and all music and sound effects on *Heretic*, *Hexen*, *Necrodome*, *Hexen II*, *Portal of Praevus*, *Mageslayer*, *Take No Prisoners*, and *Heretic II*. He was also creative director on *Take No Prisoners*.

He became involved in doing game music by association with Brian and Steve Raffel, the founders of Raven Software. As a friend, he offered to work on some music for their first game attempt, *Black Crypt*. Schilder's broad music background, interest in computers, love of fantasy/science fiction movies and computer games, as well as a desire to compose, keep him interested in the field.

SCHNURR, CARL—RED STORM ENTERTAINMENT

"My mom claims I started playing games in the womb…if only I could remember the rules." Carl Schnurr has brought counter-terrorism to harrowing 3D life by overseeing the production of *Tom Clancy's Rainbow Six* and *Rogue Spear*. Carl is a stickler for research; in preparing the realistic movements of the characters, he led the rest of his production team to a real-life shooting range, where they learned the nuances of combat.

Before joining the company, Schnurr was vice president of game development for Fringe Multimedia, Inc., a Chapel Hill, North Carolina-based software and Web site development startup. While there, Carl oversaw the production of games and educational titles, as well as the development of TheBlip.com, an award-winning Web site. His gaming experience also includes having written numerous role-playing game supplements for White Wolf's popular *Ars Magica* game.

Outside of the gaming world, Schnurr's background is just as unique: he has written manuals for shuttle astronauts and holds a Ph.D. and master's degree in physics from Duke University and a B.S. in physics from the University of Texas at Austin. He is now so experienced in counter-terrorist activities, President Clinton might want to take notice. "But I'd hesitate to mention to him the singing telegrams and the ren-fest gigs that I used to do." Then again, maybe not.

SHELLEY, BRUCE C.—ENSEMBLE STUDIOS

Bruce Shelley is a senior game designer at Ensemble Studios; his impressive past computer game co-design credits include *Railroad Tycoon*, *Covert Action*, *Civilization*, *Age of Empires*, *Age of Empires II: Age of Kings*, and a new RTS game yet to be named.

SIMPSON, TOBY—CYBERLIFE TECHNOLOGIES

Toby Simpson is the creative director for *Creatures* products at CyberLife Technology Ltd., based in Cambridge, England. He was producer of *Creatures 1*, *Creatures 2*, and now *Creatures 3*, and has written two published white papers and several books—two of which are all about the *Creatures* products and cover the science behind it all. Simpson feels he is part of something very exciting, and that this approach of biologically inspired bottom-up modeling systems is the one most likely to yield the technologies necessary for massive shared-space virtual worlds of the future.

SMITH, BRANDON—HUMONGOUS ENTERTAINMENT

Brandon Smith is a communications manager at Humongous Entertainment and was involved in the success of *Total Annihilation* (and all the expansion packs) and *Total Annihilation: Kingdoms*. "In a past life," he worked on *Gex: Enter the Gecko*, *Blood Omen: Legacy of Kain*, *MDK*, *X-COM: Apocalypse*, *Worms 2*, and many more.

SMITH, RANDY—LOOKING GLASS STUDIOS

Randy Smith has been working at Looking Glass since 1997, mostly doing design, mission-building, and scripting for *Thief* and *Thief 2*. (He also pestered the *System Shock 2* people a bunch.) As a Looking Glass designer, he is a proponent of formal, abstract design tools, and he uses them frequently to build effective experiences and help solve design problems. Randy has a Bachelor of Science in computer science from Rensselaer Polytechnic Institute, and he abandoned a graduate school career in artificial intelligence to do something even more fun.

SPECTOR, WARREN—ION STORM

Warren Spector, a native of New York City, received his B.S. in speech from Northwestern University in Evanston, Illinois, and went on to earn an M.A. in radio-TV-film from the University of Texas in Austin, Texas, before leaving UT "just a dissertation short" of completing his Ph.D. After far too many years as a professional student and semi-professional professor, Spector left academia for what he had no idea would turn out to be a career in gaming.

He started at Steve Jackson Games, a small board game company, as a minimum-wage associate editor. There he worked on *Space Gamer* magazine, developed the award-winning *TOON* role-playing game, and edited, developed, or designed several other board games and role-playing games.

After rising to editor-in-chief at SJG, he moved on to a position as a game developer for TSR, Inc., best-known for the *Dungeons & Dragons* role-playing games. At TSR, he collaborated on the development, writing, and editing of the *Top Secret/S.I.* role-playing game, the *Bullwinkle & Rocky Party Roleplaying Game*, a board game or two, some of the *Advanced Dungeons & Dragons* rulebooks, as well as several role-playing adventures and supplements. While at TSR, he saw the publication of his first (and, to date, only) novel—a spy story entitled *The Hollow Earth Affair*.

Warren rose through the ranks to the position of supervisor of creative services (TSR's game division) but after five years in the paper game business, made the leap to computer gaming, taking a position as associate producer for ORIGIN Systems, Inc. There, he co-produced such hit games as *Ultima VI* (with Richard Garriott) and *Wing Commander* (with Chris Roberts). Warren was the producer of the award-winning *Ultima Underworld* series of fantasy role-playing games (with project director Doug Church); *Ultima VII, Part 2: Serpent Isle*; *System Shock*, an immersive 3D cyberpunk adventure (again with Doug Church); *Wings of Glory*, a World War I flight sim, and many more.

During his time at ORIGIN, Warren helped the company grow from 25 people to 300, watched it move from independence to wholly-owned subsidiary of Electronic Arts, and rose to the position of executive producer. However, after nearly eight years with ORIGIN, Warren joined Looking Glass Technologies, developers of the *Underworld* series and *System Shock*, to produce a line of role-playing games and to create a satellite production office in Austin, Texas.

Warren left Looking Glass in the fall of 1997 to create and lead the Austin production office of ION Storm, a computer game developer based in Dallas, Texas. In November of 1999, Warren accepted a partnership position and seat on the board of directors of ION Storm. He and his team are currently working on an action/role-playing game entitled *Deus Ex*, scheduled for release in 2000.

Warren is married to Caroline Spector, author of several fantasy and computer game novels. He writes semi-regularly on the subject of game design and development for a variety of magazines and websites, drives his BMW M3 way too fast, owns way too many books, lives for basketball (Go Knicks!), plays rhythm guitar in the band Wasted Youth, and has a menagerie of three or four cats at any given point in time, and at least one Bernese Mountain Dog (currently Rufus, aka "Goofball").

STELLMACH, TIMOTHY J.—LOOKING GLASS STUDIOS

Tim Stellmach is a senior game designer at Looking Glass Studios. His role on *Thief: The Dark Project* was lead designer, for which he was responsible for training and managing junior designers and overseeing the design of gameplay systems and missions. Previous products include *Ultima Underworld*, *Ultima Underworld II*, *System Shock*, and *Terra Nova*. His main aspiration right now is to transform *Thief* from a successful project into a successful series, "thus securing Looking Glass the well-deserved adulation of the masses."

STREET, GREG—ENSEMBLE STUDIOS

Dr. Greg T. Street is a game designer at Ensemble Studios. He worked on the *Age of Empires: Rise of Rome* expansion pack and has last applied his *savoir faire* to *Age of Empires II: The Age of Kings*. His responsibilities include designing campaigns and random map types, and he also helps contribute to unit and civilization balance, as well as providing historical background when needed.

He got the job by answering the help wanted section of Ensemble Studios' Web page. Before working at Ensemble, he was a marine biologist at the University of South Carolina. He had no professional game industry experience—"See, it IS possible," he says—but his education, writing talent, historical breadth, and extensive gameplay experience got him the job.

SUAREZ, GONZO—PYRO STUDIOS

Gonzo Suarez started in the video games industry around 1984–85, programming *Goody* for the Sinclair Spectrum, Amstrad CPC, MSX, Atari ST, and Commodore Amiga, at the company Opera Soft. It was distributed abroad by Alligata Soft. After that first title came *Sol Negro*, *Mot*, *Crazy Billiards*, and *Arantxa Super-Tennis*. Around 1989–90, the Spanish video game industry collapsed, and he moved to other types of software, such as graphic design applications. In 1996, together with a group of colleagues (most of whom are now part of the *Commandos* team), he built the company Arvirago Entertainment and created the design for the video game *HeadHunter*, for which Javier Arévalo programmed a technology prototype. They pitched the project to companies like SCI, with no luck. In January 1997, with Ignacio Pérez, they created Pyro Studios; thus *Commandos: Behind Enemy Lines* was born. In an alpha state, the game was sold to Eidos.

SWEENY, TIM—EPIC GAMES

Sweeny's bio is short and sweet: Tim Sweeny founded Epic Games and wrote *ZZT*, *Jill of the Jungle*, and the *Unreal* engine.

TALLARICO, TOMMY—TOMMY TALLARICO STUDIOS

Tommy Tallarico is the president of Tommy Tallarico Studios, Inc., the largest multimedia post-production audio company on the planet. He also hosts the "Electric Playground" weekly TV show. In total, Tallarico has worked on 140 games, yielding a total of $25 million in sales. Past products include *Tomorrow Never Dies*, *Prince of Persia*, *Global Gladiators*, *The Terminator*, *Cool Spot*, *Aladdin*, *Robocop vs. Terminator*, *Earthworm Jim 1* and *2*, *Skeleton Warriors*, *MDK*, *Treasures of the Deep*, *Wild 9*, and *Test Drive 4* and *5*, to name just a few. Current projects are *Messiah* and *Pac-Man 3D*. He has been in the industry for nine years and has won over two dozen awards.

Tallarico explains how he got started in the business:

> I'm originally from Springfield, Massachusetts. When I was a kid I always wanted to move to southern California to be a musician (doesn't everybody!). Anyway, when I turned 21 I left Massachusetts and drove across country to Southern Cal. The only thing I really knew out here was Hollywood, so I drove to Hollywood. I didn't have a place to stay, didn't know anybody, didn't have a job, and oh yeah, I didn't have any money!!! So I showed up in Hollywood, took a look around, and said, "What the h--- is this!!!" Those of you who have been to Hollywood, you know what I'm talking about. Hollywood isn't exactly the way they portray it on TV; it's pretty much a dump. I said to myself, "Self, there's no way I'm living here!!" The only other thing I knew in California was Disneyland, so I stopped some bum on the street and asked him where Mickey Mouse lived. He pointed me about 45 minutes south to Orange County. When I got to Orange County, I said, "Now this is more like it!"

So I picked up a newspaper and got a job the very next day selling keyboards at Guitar Center. (I was sleeping either in my car or on Huntington Beach at this point, so I was looking for anything I could find—I knew about music and keyboards, so what the h---.) The next day I started work and believe it or not, the very first person I waited on happened to be a producer for a new software company starting up called Virgin Mastertronic. I've loved music my whole life; I've been playing piano since I was three years old. My second love has always been video games. Never in my whole life did I ever think of putting my two loves together, until that day. I became the first tester at Virgin the next day. (A tester was somebody they paid to play games and find bugs in the programs.) There were only about 15 people at Virgin at the time, so they didn't need a full-time musician. When the first opportunity arose for music (*Prince of Persia* on the Game Boy), I jumped on it. I would sit down with the programmers and technicians every chance I got to learn about the machines. I know nothing about programming or any of that kind of stuff. I just know music. I think that has become a plus in my career—I mean, think about it, how do you program the blues or rock 'n' roll, that's just something you feel! Anyway, I worked on *Prince of Persia* for free on the weekends and after work, and the VP of the company was so impressed he made me the music guy!

TAYLOR, CHRIS—GAS POWERED GAMES

Chris Taylor is the president of Gas Powered Games. He started in the video games business 12 years ago; his first game was called *Hardball II*, a sequel to the very successful game by Bob Whitehead. The company that he worked for, Distinctive Software, was very well known for the game *Test Drive*. Taylor worked on *Test Drive II* for a month or so to help out when it fell behind schedule. As Taylor recalls, "Those were what we lovingly refer to now as the 'good old days.'" When he shipped *Hardball II*, it was "like giving birth—anyhow, the first one is always the toughest." The game went on to sell in the neighborhood of a hundred thousand units and won an SPA award for the "Best Sports Product of the Year." "Back in those days there wasn't much in the way of awards, so we made a big deal out of it," says Taylor.

After *Hardball II*, he went straight to work on a game called *4D Boxing* with Jay MacDonald. Taylor reminisces: "He was the one who really understood what motion-captured data could bring to a game. I learned a lot from working with him and we had a great time working on that game." The next significant title was *Triple Play*, even though he was often heard saying he would never do another baseball game again. "It was actually a much better experience than I would ever let on." He then did a port of *Virtua Stadium Baseball*, and shortly afterwards hooked up with Ron Gilbert and began work on *Total Annihilation*. "This was the game that I hoped would change a lot of things...including my will to live and continue in this business," remembers Taylor.

Taylor then left Cavedog/Humongous to start his own company, Gas Powered Games, which has recently signed a publishing deal with Microsoft. Its first release will be *Dungeon Siege*, a fantasy role-playing game due out in 2001.

THOMAS, CHANCE—HUGESOUND NETWORK

Chance Thomas is a multiple-award-winning composer (Emmy, Telly, Addy, Aurora) and music producer with a background in the advertising industry. His credits include such household names as McDonald's, Nissan, Tupperware, Rexall, the Salvation Army, the N.B.A. (Utah Jazz), and many others. His music has been broadcast throughout every television market in America, and across five continents.

His interactive credits include creating and producing Sierra's first live orchestral score, their first rock single, and their first game soundtrack album. He was among the first to design a highly interactive music system based on digital audio streams, as opposed to MIDI. His games include *Quest for Glory V*, *SWAT 2*, *The Realm*, *JRR Tolkien's Middle-Earth*, and *Navy SEALs*.

Chance is involved in a proactive effort to raise awareness for the quality and profile of music in games. He successfully lobbied the Academy of Interactive Arts and Sciences (AIAS) to provide greater opportunity and recognition for composers and musicians. As of March, 2000, video game music is now eligible for competing for a Grammy Award in the New Media division, thanks to Thomas' efforts. He writes articles and speaks out in the press on the virtue of high fidelity sound coupled with highly interactive music design.

Chance is a former entertainer, and has toured extensively as a lead singer and keyboardist. He has also performed as a solo pianist, entertaining such well-known personalities as Tom Cruise, John Travolta, Bruce Willis, and Sarah Vaughn. He is a cum laude Baccalaureate of Brigham Young University's School of Music, and a scholastic All-American.

THOMAS, GREG—SEGA OF AMERICA

As vice president of product development, Greg Thomas brings more than 12 years of experience to Sega of America. The mastermind behind the award-winning Sega Dreamcast title *Sega Sports NFL 2K*, Thomas has headed up more than 20 game development projects, including *Sega Sports NBA 2K*, *Clay Fighter*, *Madden '94*, *One*, *Weaponlord*, and *Tazmania*. He oversees all U.S. development and U.S. localization of Japanese and European product, and proactively seeks new content for Sega Dreamcast via game developers.

Prior to joining Sega, Thomas worked closely with Sega in developing sports titles for Sega Dreamcast, along with his team at Visual Concepts—a company in which Sega held a minority share at the time. The Visual Concepts team created *Sega Sports NFL 2K* and *Sega Sports NBA 2K*—two titles for Sega Dreamcast that boasted an incredible level of realism and gameplay, setting new standards in what sports video game developers strive for.

Thomas started Visual Concepts in 1988 in the hopes of pulling together the most passionate programmers and development staff for video games to create stellar video game content for many platforms. In Visual Concept's early days, Thomas' development teams created games for the Apple IIGS, NES, Game Boy, PC, SNES, Genesis, PSX, and Sega Saturn.

Currently, Thomas is working on expanding his knowledge of the Sega Dreamcast Network and developing online multiplayer games. He's developing original titles at Visual Concepts, including follow-up games for *Sega Sports NFL 2K* and *Sega Sports NBA 2K*. He's continually seeking new talent to create hit games for Sega Dreamcast as well as helping to localize Sega of Japan titles for the U.S. market.

THRON, DANIEL—LOOKING GLASS STUDIOS

Daniel Thron has been with Looking Glass since 1995. He has worked extensively on creating *Thief* and *Thief 2*'s visual style, and is responsible for those games' cutscenes as well as their logos and box design. He is currently the creative director of LG's next action/sneaker. Before joining Looking Glass, he was a traditional freelance illustrator.

VOGEL, JEFF—SPIDERWEB SOFTWARE, INC.

Jeff Vogel is the president of Spiderweb Software, Inc., a two-person (plus many freelancers) software company in Seattle that produces and sells shareware fantasy games for the Macintosh and Windows platforms. They've been designing games for six years now, and their annual sales are well into six figures at this point. They developed the *Exile* trilogy, *Blades of Exile*, and *Nethergate* in-house, and they also distribute *Ocean Bound*, a small, clever game for the Macintosh. Their games have been reviewed by practically every major gaming magazine, and *Exile III* won "Shareware Game of the Year" from *Computer Gaming World*. And, of course, as Vogel says, "We often get the most flattering award, which is $25–35 of people's hard-earned money."

WALLS, DAVID—HASBRO INTERACTIVE

David Walls is the creative director at Hasbro Interactive and has been for the last two years. He designs and directs design for most of Hasbro Interactive's games. Recent products are *Frogger*, *Centipede*, *Game of Life*, *Jeopardy*, *Wheel of Fortune*, *Clue*, and the *Tonka* series, to name a few. Future aspirations are to continue making top-quality games for Hasbro Interactive, and along the way, add some original games to the mix.

WILLITS, TIM—ID SOFTWARE

Tim Willits is the lead level designer for id Software, where he has been employed for the last three years. His early experiences with id and their products was *Doom*. When he first played *Doom*, he knew it was something special, something different. Later, when he discovered that he could create his own *Doom* levels, he knew creating virtual worlds was something that he wanted to do. He worked on a series of maps called the Raven series. These were *Doom II* singles as well as Deathmatch maps built to be played together.

At that time, luckily, id was looking for some contract maps for a product called the *Doom II Masters Levels*. They contracted Willits and he quickly started working for them. Also at that time, Rogue Entertainment needed a full-time map designer to work on a game called *Strife*, for which they hired Willits. He came to Texas and started his career a few doors down from id working full time for Rogue. As chance would have it, id soon needed another full-time level designer, so he left Rogue and went to work for id directly. He worked on the *Ultimate Doom* title and helped them finish *Quake*. He then became the lead designer on *Quake II*, and most recently *Quake III: Arena*.

WILSON, JAY—MONOLITH PRODUCTIONS

Jay Wilson is a game designer at Monolith Productions. The products he worked on are as follows: *Blood* (lead level designer), *Blood: Plasma Pak* (lead level designer), *Blood 2: The Chosen* (project lead), and *Blood 2 Add-on* (project lead).

WRIGHT, WILL—MAXIS SOFTWARE

Will Wright is Maxis' chief designer; he cofounded Maxis with Jeff Braun in 1987. Wright began working on what would become *SimCity—The City Simulator* in 1985. Using a complex technique, he found a way to bring realistic simulations to desktop PCs. Previously simulations of this sort were only available to the military, scientists, and academicians. But now, using an easy-to-use graphic interface, the world of simulations opened up to consumers.

Wright has had a lifelong fascination with simulations. His interest in plastic models of ships and airplanes during his childhood in Georgia eventually led to his designing computer models of cities, ecosystems, and ant colonies.

SimCity was released in 1989, and within a few months became a hit. The game has since won 24 domestic and international awards. With Fred Haslem, Wright co-designed *SimEarth—The Living Planet* in 1990, a simulation of a planet based on the Gaia theory of James Lovelock. In 1991, Wright and Justin McCormick designed *SimAnt—The Electronic Ant Colony*, a scientifically-accurate simulation of an ant colony. *SimCity 2000* and *SimCopter*, a helicopter flight game, are Wright's most recent releases. Taking computer entertainment to its most personal level yet, Wright's next game, *The Sims*, puts players in charge of the lives of a neighborhood of simulated people. This highly anticipated title, which Wright has been working on for seven years, is due for release in early 2000.

Wright has become one of the most successful designers of interactive entertainment in the world. In 1999 alone, Electronic Arts, which owns the Maxis studio, has sold well over a million copies of *SimCity 3000*, the latest incarnation of *SimCity*. In 1999 Wright was included in *Entertainment Weekly*'s "It List" of "the 100 most creative people in entertainment" as well as *Time Digital*'s "Digital 50," a listing of "the most important people shaping technology today." However, his interests are not limited to computer games. Each year Wright (along with his daughter) takes part in the annual Robot Wars contest in San Francisco. His past robots, which do battle with robots designed by other contestants, have taken top honors. Interestingly, it was Wright's interest in robots that eventually led him into computer programming.

ZUK, JON—RAVEN SOFTWARE

Jon Zuk is a designer (and more recently, lead designer, on Heretic II) at Raven Software. Past products include Take No Prisoners (designer), Hexen II: Portal of Praevus (lead designer), and Heretic II (lead designer). He is very happy working at Raven and can see himself there for a long time.

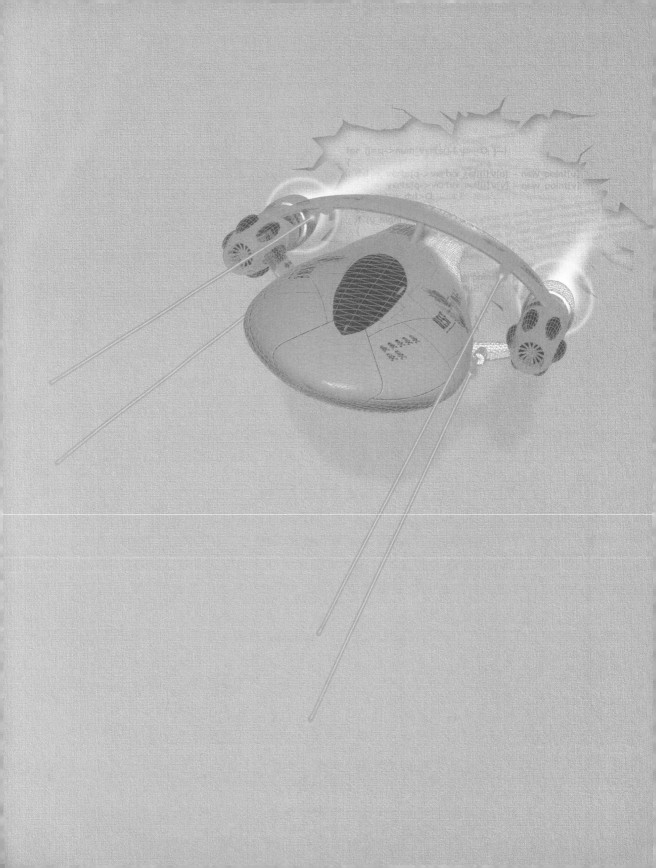

INDEX

C

D

H

I

J

K

L

N

O

P

S

T

X–Y–Z